Mystic Isles of the S

Frederick O'Brien (1869–1932).

Alpha Editions

This edition published in 2024

ISBN : 9789361477706

Design and Setting By
Alpha Editions
www.alphaedis.com
Email - info@alphaedis.com

As per information held with us this book is in Public Domain.
This book is a reproduction of an important historical work. Alpha Editions uses the best technology to reproduce historical work in the same manner it was first published to preserve its original nature. Any marks or number seen are left intentionally to preserve its true form.

Contents

Chapter I .... - 1 -
Chapter II .... - 10 -
Chapter III .... - 20 -
Chapter IV .... - 29 -
Chapter V .... - 44 -
Chapter VI .... - 51 -
Chapter VII .... - 67 -
Chapter VIII .... - 79 -
Chapter IX .... - 87 -
Chapter X .... - 100 -
Chapter XI .... - 119 -
Chapter XII .... - 135 -
Chapter XIII .... - 150 -
Chapter XIV .... - 167 -
Chapter XV .... - 183 -
Chapter XVI .... - 202 -
Chapter XVII .... - 212 -
Chapter XVIII .... - 229 -
Chapter XIX .... - 244 -
Chapter XX .... - 256 -
Chapter XXI .... - 274 -
Chapter XXII .... - 283 -
Chapter XXIII .... - 293 -
Chapter XXIV .... - 300 -
Chapter XXV .... - 310 -

Chapter XXVI ....- 321 -
IONEI OE! ....- 331 -

Chapter I

Departure from San Francisco—Nature man left behind—Fellow-passengers on the Noa-Noa—Tragedy of the Chinese pundit—Strange stories of the South Seas—The Tahitian Hula.

The warning gong had sent all but crew and passengers ashore, though our ship did not leave the dock. Her great bulk still lay along the piling, though the gangway was withdrawn. The small groups on the pier waited tensely for the last words with those departing. These passengers were inwardly bored with the prolonged farewells, and wanted to be free to observe their fellow-voyagers and the movement of the ship. They conversed in shouts with those ashore, but most of the meanings were lost in the noise of the shuffling of baggage and freight, the whistling of ferries, and the usual turmoil of the San Francisco waterfront. I was glad that none had come to see me off, for I was curious about my unknown companions upon the long traverse to the South Seas, and I had wilfully put behind me all that America and Europe held to adventure in the vasts of ocean below the equator.

But the whistle I awaited to sound our leaving was silent. Officers of the ship rushed about as if bent on relieving her of some pressing danger, and I caught fragments of orders and replies which indicated that until a search was completed she could not stir on her journey. Then I heard cries of anger and protest, and caught a glimpse of a man whose appearance provoked confusing emotions of astonishment, admiration, and laughter. He was dressed in a Roman toga of rough monk's-cloth, and had on sandals. He was being hustled bodily over the restored gangway, and was resisting valiantly the second officer, purser, and steward, who were hardly able to move him, so powerfully was he made. One of his sandals suddenly fell into the bay. He had seized hold of the rail of the gangway, and the leather sandal dropped into the water with a slight splash. His grasp of the rail being broken, he was gradually being pushed, limping, to the dock. His one bare foot and his half-exposed and shapely body caused a gale of laughter from the docks and the wharf.

The gangway was quickly withdrawn, and our ship began to move from the shore. The ejected one stood watching us with sorrow shadowing his large eyes. He was of middle size; with the form of a David of Michelangelo, though lithe, and he wore no hat, but had a long, brown beard, which, with his brown hair, parted in the middle and falling over his shoulders, and his archaic garb, gave me a singular shock. It was as if a boyhood vision, or something seen in a painting, was made real. His eyes were the deepest blue, limpid and appealing, and I felt like shouting out that if it was a matter of money, I would aid the man in the toga.

"Christ!" yelled the frantic dock superintendent. "Get that line cast off and let her go! Are you ceemented to that hooker?"

Instantly before me came Munkácsy's picture of the Master before Pilate, evoked by the profanity of the wharf boss, but explaining the vision of a moment ago. The *Noa-Noa* emitted a cry from her iron throat. The engines started, and the distance between our deck and the pier grew as our bow swung toward the Golden Gate. The strange man who had been put ashore, with his one sandal in his hand, and holding his torn toga about him, hastened to the nearest stringer of the wharf and waved good-by to us. It was as if a prophet, or even Saul of Tarsus, blessed us in our quest. He stood on a tall group of piles, and called out something indistinguishable.

The passengers hurried below, to return in coats and caps to meet the wind that blows from China, and the second officer and the surgeon came by, talking animatedly.

"Oh, yus," said the seaman, chuckling, "'e wuz 'auled out finally. The beggar 'ad 'id 'imself good and proper this time. 'E wuz in the linen-closet, and 'ad disguised 'imself as a bundle o' bloomin' barth-towels. 'E wuz a reg'lar grand Turk, 'e wuz. Blow me, if you'd 'a' knowed 'im from a bale of 'em, 'e wuz so wrapped up in 'em. 'E almost 'ad us 'ull down this time. The blighter made a bit of a row, and said as 'ow he just could n't 'elp stowin' aw'y every boat for T'iti."

"He's a bally nut," said the surgeon. "I say, though, he did take me back to Sunday school."

I recalled a man who walked the streets of San Francisco carrying a small sign in his upraised hand, "Christ has come!" He looked neither to the right nor the left, but bore his curious announcement among the crowds downtown, which smiled jestingly at him, or looked frightened at the message. If many had believed him, the panic would have been illimitable. He was dressed in a brown cassock, and looked like the blue-eyed man who had been refused passage to my destination. Probably, that American in the toga and sandals, exiled from the island he loved so well, had a message for the Tahitians or others of the Polynesian tribes of the South Seas; Essenism, maybe, or something to do with virginal beards and long hair, or sandals and the simple life. I wished he were with us.

We were in the Golden Gate now, that magnificent opening in the California shores, riven in the eternal conflict of land and water, and the rending of which made the bay of San Francisco the mightiest harbor of America. Before our bows lay the immense expanse of the mysterious Pacific.

The second officer was directing sailors who were snugging down the decks.

"What did the queer fellow want to go to Tahiti for?" I asked him.

He regarded me a moment in the stolid way of seamen.

"The blighter likes to live on bananas and breadfruit and that kind of truck," he replied. "The French won't let 'im st'y there. 'E's too bloomin' nyked. 'E's a nyture man. They chysed 'im out, and every steamer 'e tries to stow 'imself aw'y. 'E's a bleedin' trial to these ships."

That was puzzling. Did not these natives of Tahiti themselves wear little clothing? Who were they to object to a white man doffing the superfluities of dress in a climate where breadfruit and bananas grow? Or the French, the governors of Tahiti? Were they, in that isle so distant from Paris, their capital, practising a puritanism unknown at home? Was nature so fearful? The figure of the barefooted man often arose as I watched the Farallones disappear, the last of land we would see until we arrived at Tahiti, nearly two weeks later.

The days fell away from the calendar; they obliterated themselves as quietly as our ship's wake to the north, as we planed over the smooth waters toward the equator. Gradually the passengers took on character, and out of the first welter of contacts came those definite impressions which are almost always right and which, though we modify them or reverse them by acquaintance, we return to finally.

There was a Chinese, the strangest figure of an Asiatic, with a thin mustache, and wearing always a black frock-coat and trousers, elastic gaiters, and a stiff, black hat. His face was long and oval and the color of old ivory. He had tried to gain admission to Australia and New Zealand, and then the United States, and had been excluded under some harsh laws. He was plainly a scholar, but had brought with him from China a store of curios, probably to enable him to earn money in the land of the white. Australia had refused him; he had been shut out of San Francisco, and the very steamship that brought him was compelled to take him away. He had failed to bring a necessary certificate, or something of the sort, and the inexorable laws of three Christian countries had sent him wandering, so that it was inevitable he must return to China by the route he had come. He was the most mournful of sights, sitting most of the day in a retired spot, brooding, apparently over his fate. He never smiled, though I who have been much in China, tried to stir him from his sadness by exclamations and gestures. His race has a very keen sense of humor. They see a thousand funny things about them, and laugh inwardly; but they never see anything amusing in themselves. The individual man conceives himself a dignified figure in a world of burlesque.

This man's face was rid of any self-pity. I think he was stunned by the horror of the thing, that he, a man of Chinese letters, who had departed from the centuried custom of his pundit caste of remaining in their own country, who had left his family or clan to increase his store of lesser knowledge, should be denied the door by these inferior nations of the West. He might have recalled Chien Lung, a Manchu emperor, who, when apologized to in writing by a Dutch governor of Batavia who had murdered almost all the Chinese there, replied that China had no interest in wretches who had left their native land. A thousand years ago the Chinese put the soldier lowest in the scale and the scholar highest, with the man of business as of no importance. And yet these commercial peoples barred their gates to him! For a number of days he took his place in the shade of a davited boat, and now and again he read from a quaint book the Analects of Confucius.

We sailed on Wednesday, and on Sunday made the first tropic, nearly twenty-three and a half degrees above the line. No rough weather or unkindly wind had disturbed us from the hour we had left the "too nyked" man upon the wharf, and Sunday, when I went to take my bath before breakfast, I felt the soft fingers of the South caress my body, and looking out upon the purple ocean, whose expanse was barely dimpled by gleams of silver, I saw flying-fish skimming the crests of the swinging waves. The officers and stewards appeared in white; the passengers, too, put off their temperate-zone clothes, and the decks were gay with color. We all seemed to feel that we must be in consonance with the loving nature that had made the sky so blue and the sea so still.

The Chinese—he was Leung Kai Chu on the list—did not change his melancholy black. The deck sports were organized, ship tennis, quoits, and golf, and the disks rattled about his feet; but though he often moved his chair to aid those seeking a lost quoit or ring, and bowed ceremoniously to those who begged his pardon for bothering him, he kept his position. I felt a somber sense of gathering tragedy. In his face was a growing detachment from everything about him; he hardly knew that we were there, that he ate and slept, and took his seat by the boat. All of us felt this, but with many it meant merely remarking that "the Chink is getting off his head," and a wish that he would not obtrude his grief when we were filled with the joy of sunny skies and a merry company.

The tragedy came sooner than expected by me. I had cast a thought to my understanding that the philosophy of Confucius did not contemplate self-destruction, and had been divided between relief and wonder that it was so.

It was dusk of Monday. The sun had sunk behind the glowing rim of the western horizon, and the air was suffused with a trembling rose color, when Leung Kai Chu tapped at my cabin-door, which gave on the boat-deck. I opened it, and he bowed, and handed me an image. It was of porcelain, precious, and I was at a loss to know whether he had felt the need of a little money and had brought it to sell, or had been impelled to give it to me because of my feeble efforts to cheer him. I made a gesture which might have meant payment, but he raised his hand deprecatingly, and for the first time I saw him smile, and I was afraid. He bowed, and in the mandarin language invoked good fortune upon me. He had the aspect of one beyond good and evil, who had settled life's problem. When he left me I stood wondering, holding in my hands the majestic god seated upon the tiger, the symbol of the conquest of the flesh.

I heard a shout, and dropping the image, I rushed aft. Leung Kai Chu had thrown himself over the rail just by the purser's office. A steward had seen him fling himself into the white foam. I tore a gas-buoy from its rack and tossed it toward the screw, in which direction he must have been swept. A sailor ran to the bridge, the whistle blew, and the ship shook as the engines ceased revolving, and then reversed in stopping her. Orders were flung about fast. A man climbed to the lookout as the first officer began to put a boat into the water. The crew of it and the second officer were already at the oars and the tiller as the ropes slid in the blocks. The passengers came crowding from their cabins, where they were dressing for dinner, and there were many expressions of surprise and slight terror. Death aboard ship is terrible in its imminence to all. The buoy, with its flaming torch, had drifted far to leeward, and the lookout could do no more than follow its fainting light as the dark of the tropics closed in. An hour the *Noa-Noa* lay gently heaving upon the mysterious waters in which the despairing pundit had sought Nirvana, until the boat returned with a report that it had picked up the buoy, but had seen no sign of the man. Doubtless he had been swept into the propellers, but if not quickly given release in their cyclopean strokes, he may have watched for a few minutes our vain attempt to negative his fate. If so, I imagine he smiled again, as when he gave me the god upon the tiger.

As they hoisted the boat to its davits, I found in the lantern light his ancient volume, the "Analects of Confucius," and claimed it for my own. It was the very boat he had been accustomed to sit under, and he must have laid down the ancient philosopher to procure the gift for me, his grim determination already made. I had caught a glimpse of him Sunday morning listening to the Christian services conducted by the captain in the social hall, and when I told the brooding captain that, he was struck by the idea that perhaps some word of his preachment might have come to Leung Kai Chu's mind in his agony in the waters, and that at the last moment he might have repented and been saved.

"One aspiration, and he might be washed as white as snow. 'This day thou shalt be with Me in Paradise,'" said the commander, who was known as the parson skipper, dour, but ever on the watch for the first sign of repentance.

On the other hand, Hallman more nearly stated the general feeling:

"By God, he spoiled sport, that black ghost on deck. He was like a *tupapau*, a Polynesian demon."

Hallman was in his early forties, with twenty years of South-Seas trading, a tall, strong, well-featured, but hard-faced, European, with thin lips over nearly perfect teeth, and cold, small, pale-blue eyes. He talked little to men, but isolated young women whenever possible, and bent over them in attempted gay, but earnest, converse. He was one of those cold sensualists whose passion is as that of some animals, insistent, prowling, fierce, but impersonal. An English South-Sea trader aboard gave me an astonishing light upon him:

"Some dozen years ago," he said, "I made a visit of a few weeks to the Marquesas Islands. Hallman had kept a store there then for more than ten years, and had a good part of the business of buying and shipping copra and selling supplies to the natives and a few whites. He lived in a shack back of his little store, with his native woman and four or five half-naked children. They told me queer stories about his madness for women. They said he would go out of his house and into the jungle near the trails and would lie in wait. If a woman he coveted passed, he would seize her, and even if her husband or consort was ahead of her, in the custom of these people, he would grab her feet, and make her call out that she was delaying a minute, that her companion was to go along, and she would catch up in a minute. He had some funny power over those women. Anyhow, that's the story they told me in those cannibal islands. And yet, you know, there's something different in him, because he sent two of his sons to school, and afterward to a university in Europe. To make it queerer yet, one of them is here on this ship, in the second class, and wouldn't dare to speak to his father without being asked. Of course he's a half-Marquesan—the son—and looks it. I know them all, and only yesterday I heard Hallman call his son on the main-deck, away from where any one could see him, and threaten him with 'putting him back in the jungle, where he came from,' if he appeared again near the first-class space. I tell you, I'd hate to be in his hands if I was in his way."

Fictionists who take the South Seas for their scenery too often paint their characters in one tone—black, brown, or yellow, or even white. Their bad men are super-villains, and yet there are no men all bad. I know there are no supermen at all, bad or good, but only that some men do super acts now and then; none has the grand gesture at all times. Napoleon had a disgraceful affliction at Waterloo, which rid him of strength, mental and physical; the thief on the cross became wistful for an unknown delight.

Hallman had said to me in the smoking-room that he never drank alcohol or smoked tobacco, because "it took the edge off the game." Now, a poet might say that, or even a moralist, but he was neither.

That night I walked through the waist of the ship and on to the promenade-deck of the third-class passengers, where a huddle of stores, coiled ropes, and riff-raff prevented these poor from taking any pleasurable exercise. I stood at the taffrail and peered down at the welter of white water, the foam of the buffets of the whirling screws, and then at the wide wake, which in imagination went on and on in a luminous path to the place we had departed from, to the dock where we had left the debarred lover of nature. The deep was lit with the play of phosphorescent animalculae whom our passage awoke in their homes beneath the surface and sent questing with lights for the cause. A sheet of pale, green-gold brilliancy marked the route of the *Noa-Noa* on the brine, and perhaps far back the corpse of the celestial philosopher floated in radiancy, with his face toward those skies, so brazen to his desires.

A Swiss with a letter of introduction to me presented it when seven days out. It was from the manager of a restaurant in San Francisco, and asked me to guide him in any way I could. The Swiss was middle-aged, and talked only of a raw diet. He was to go to the Marquesas to eat raw food. One would have thought a crude diet to be in itself an end in life. He spoke of it proudly and earnestly, as if cooking one's edibles were a crime or a vile thing. He told me for hours his dictums—no alcohol, no tobacco, no meat, no fish; merely raw fruit, nuts, and vegetables. He was a convinced rebel against any fire for food, making known to any one who would listen that man had erred sadly, thousands of years ago, in bringing fire into his cave for cooking, and that the only cure for civilization's evils was in abolishing the kitchen. He would live in the Marquesas as he said the aborigines do. Alas! I did not tell him they ate only their fish raw.

Ben Fuller, the Australian theatrical manager, frowned on him. Fuller was as round as a barrel, and he also was certain of the remedies for a sick world.

"How you 're goin' a get any bloody fun with no roast beef, no mutton, no puddin', and let alone a drop of ale and a pipe?"

The Swiss smiled beatifically.

"You can get rid of all those desires," he said.

"My Gawd! I don't want to get rid o' them, I don't. I'm bringing up my kiddies right, and I'm a proper family man, but I want my meat and my bread and my puddin'. The world needs proper entertainment; that's what'll cure the troubles."

The Swiss was also ardent in attention to the women aboard, and I wondered if there was a new school of self-denial. The old celibate monks eschewed women, but had Gargantuan appetites, which they satisfied with meat pasties, tubs of ale, and vats of wine.

There were two Tahitians aboard, both females. One was an oldish woman, ugly and waspish. She counted her beads and spoke to me in French of the consolations of the Catholic religion. She had been to America for an operation, but despaired of ever being well, and so was melancholy and devout. I talked to her about Tahiti, that island which the young Darwin wrote, "must forever remain classical to the voyager in the South Seas," and which, since I had read "Rarahu" as a boy, had fascinated me and drawn me to it. She warned me.

"*Prenez-garde vous, monsieur!*" she said. "There are evils there, but I am ashamed of my people."

The other was about twenty-two years old, slender, kohl-eyed, and black-tressed. She was dressed in the gayest colors of bourgeois fashion in San Francisco, with jade ear-rings and diamond ornaments. Her face was of a lemon-cream hue, with dark shadows under her long-lashed eyes. Her form was singularly svelt, curving, suggestive of the rounded stalk of a young cocoa-palm, her bosom molded in a voluptuous reserve. Her father, a clergyman, had cornered the vanilla-bean market in Tahiti, and she was bringing an automobile and a phonograph to her home, a village in the middle of Tahiti.

One night when a Hawaiian *hula* was played on the phonograph, she danced alone for us. It was a graceful, insinuating step, with movements of the arms and hands, a rotating of the torso upon the hips, and with a tinge of the savage in it that excited the Swiss, the raw-food advocate. Hallman was also in the social hall, and, after waltzing with her several times, had persuaded her to dance the *hula*. He clapped his hands loudly and called out:

"*Maitai!*"

That is Tahitian for bravo, and I saw a look in Hallman's face that recalled the story by the Englishman of the jungle trail. He was always intent on his pursuit.

Was I hypercritical? There was Leung Kai Chu with the sharks, and the nature man left behind! The one had lost his dream of returning to Tahiti, in which the Chinese might freely have lived, and the other had thrown away life because he could not enter the America that the other wanted so madly to leave. The lack of a piece of paper had killed him. Was it that happiness was a delusion never to be realized? If the pundit had bribed the immigration authorities, as I had known many to do, he might now have been studying the strange religion and ethics which had caused the whites to steal so much of China, to force opium upon it at the cannon's mouth, to kill tens of thousands of yellow men, and to raise to dignities the soldiers and financiers whom he despised, as had Confucius and Buddha. And if that white of the sandals had kept his shirt on in Tahiti, he might be lying under his favorite palm and eating breadfruit and bananas.

People have come to be afraid to say or even to think they are happy for a bare hour. We fear that the very saying of it will rob us of happiness. We have incantations to ward off listening devils—knocking on wood, throwing salt over our left shoulders, and saying "God willing."

What was I to find in Tahiti? Certainly not what Loti had with Rarahu, for that was forty years ago, when the world was young at heart, and romance was a god who might be worshiped with uncensored tongue. But was not romance a spiritual emanation, a state of mind, and not people or scenes? I knew it was, for all over the earth I had pursued it, and found it in the wild flowers of the Sausalito hills in California more than among the gayeties of Paris, the gorges of the Yangtse-Kiang, or in the skull dance of the wild Dyak of Borneo.

Chapter II

The Discovery of Tahiti—Marvelous isles and people—Hailed by a windjammer—Middle of the voyage—Tahiti on the horizon—Ashore in Papeete.

What did Tahiti hold for me? I thought vaguely of its history. The world first knew its existence only about the time that the American colonies were trying to separate themselves from Great Britain. An English naval captain happened on the island, and thought himself the first white man there, though the Spanish claim its discovery. The Englishman called it King George Island, after the noted Tory monarch of his day; but a Frenchman, a captain and poet, the very next spring named it the New Cytherea, esteeming its fascinations like the fabled island of ancient Greek lore. It remained for Captain James Cook, who, before steam had killed the wonder of distance and the telegraph made daily bread of adventure and discovery, was the hero of many a fireside tale, to bring Tahiti vividly before the mind of the English world. That hardy mariner's entrancing diary fixed Tahiti firmly in the thoughts of the British and Americans. Bougainville painted such an ecstatic picture that all France would emigrate. Cook set down that Otaheite was the most beautiful of all spots on the surface of the globe. He praised the people as the handsomest and most lovable of humans, and said they wept when he sailed. That was to him of inestimable value in appraising them.

About the beginning of the nineteenth century the first English missionaries in the South Seas thanked God for a safe passage from their homes to Tahiti, and for a virgin soil and an affrightingly wicked people to labor with. The English, however, did not seize the island, but left it for the French to do that, who first declared it a protectorate, and made it a colony of France, in the unjust way of the mighty, before the last king died. They had come ten thousand miles to do a wretched act that never profited them, but had killed a people.

All this discovery and suzerainty did not interest me much, but what the great captains, and Loti, Melville, Becke, and Stoddard, had written had been for years my intense delight. Now I was to realize the dream of childhood. I could hardly live during the days of the voyage.

I remembered that Europe had been set afire emotionally by the first reports, the logs of the first captains of England and France who visited Tahiti. In that eighteenth century, for decades the return to nature had been the rallying cry of those who attacked the artificial and degraded state of society.

The published and oral statements of the adventurers in Tahiti, their descriptions of the unrivaled beauty of the verdure, of reefs and palm, of the majestic stature of the men and the passionate charm of the women, the boundless health and simple happiness in which they dwelt, the climate, the limpid streams, the diving, swimming, games, and rarest food—all these had stirred the depressed Europe of the last days of the eighteenth and the first of the nineteenth centuries beyond the understanding by us cynical and more material people. The world still had its vision of perfection.

Tahiti was the living Utopia of More, the *belle île* of Rousseau, the Eden with no serpent or hurtful apple, the garden of the Hesperides, in harmony with nature, in freedom from the galling bonds of government and church, of convention and clothing. The reports of the English missionaries of the nakedness and ungodliness of the Tahitians created intense interest and swelled the chorus of applause for their utter difference from the weary Europeans. Had there been ships to take them, thousands would have fled to Tahiti to be relieved of the chains and tedium of their existence, though they could not know that Victorianism and machines were to fetter and vulgarize them even more.

Afterward, when sailors mutinied and abandoned their ships or killed their officers to be able to remain in Tahiti and its sister islands, there grew up in England a literature of wanderers, runagates, and beach-combers, of darkish women who knew no reserve or modesty, of treasure-trove, of wrecks and desperate deeds, piracy and blackbirding, which made flame the imagination of the youth of seventy years ago. Tahiti had ever been pictured as a refuge from a world of suffering, from cold, hunger, and the necessity of labor, and most of all from the morals of pseudo-Christianity, and the hypocrisies and buffets attending their constant secret infringement.

One morning when we were near the middle of our voyage I went on deck to see the sun rise. We were that day eighteen hundred miles from Tahiti and the same distance from San Francisco, while north and west twelve hundred miles lay Hawaii. Not nearer than there, four hundred leagues away, was succor if our vessel failed. It was the dead center of the sea. I glanced at the chart and noted the spot: Latitude 10° N.; Longitude 137° W. The great god Ra of the Polynesians had climbed above the dizzy edge of the whirling earth, and was making his gorgeous course into the higher heavens. The ocean was a glittering blue, an intense, brilliant azure, level save for the slight swaying of the surface, which every little space showed a flag of white. The evaporation caused by the blazing sun of these tropics made the water a deeper blue than in cooler latitudes, as in the Arctic and Antarctic oceans the greens are almost as vivid as the blues about the line.

I watched the thousand flying-fishes' fast leaps through the air, and caught gleams of the swift bonitos whose pursuit made birds of their little brothers. Then, a few miles off, I saw the first vessel that had come to our eyes since we had sunk the headlands of California more than a week before. She was a great sailing ship, under a cloud of snowy canvas, one of the caste of clippers that fast fades under the pall of smoke, and, from her route, bound for the Pacific Coast from Australia. The captain of the Noa-Noa came and stood beside me as we made her out more plainly, and fetching the glasses, he glanced at her, started, and said in some surprise:

"She's signaling us she wants to send a boat to us. That's the first time in thirty years in this line I have ever had such a request from a wind-jammer. She left her slant to cross our path."

Half a mile away a beautiful, living creature, all quivering with the restraint, she came up into the eye of the wind, and backed her fore-yard. A boat put off from her, and we awaited it with indefinable alarm. It was soon at the gangway we had hastily lowered, unknowing whether woman or child might not be our visitor. It was a young Russian sailor whose hand had been crushed under a block a fortnight before, and who, without aid for his injury other than the simple remedies that make up the pharmacopoeia of sailing vessels, was like to die from blood-poisoning. Had our ship not been met, he would undoubtedly have perished, for no other steamer came to these points upon the chart, and, as we were to learn, his own ship did not reach her port for many weeks. He was a mere boy, his face was drawn with continued pain, but, with the strong repression of emotion characteristic of the sailor, he uttered no sound. The passengers, relieved from silent fears of any catastrophe aboard the sailing ship, and perhaps salving their souls for fancied failure toward the drowned Leung Kai Chu, crowded to fill the boat with books, fruit, and candy, and to help the unfortunate boy. When he had been made comfortable by the surgeon, he was overwhelmed with presents.

My vis-à-vis at table, Herr Gluck, a piano manufacturer of Munich, was a follower of Horace Fletcher, the American munching missionary. Unlike the Swiss, who craved raw food, Herr Gluck ate everything, but each mouthful only after thorough maceration, salivation, and slow deglutition. At breakfast he absorbed a glass of milk and a piece of toast, but took longer than I did to bolt melon, bacon and eggs, toast, coffee, and marmalade. He sold the pianos his family had made for a hundred years, and munched all about the world. He professed rugged health, and never tired of dancing; but he looked drawn and melancholy, and had naught of the rugged masculinity of the bolters. Once or twice he drank in my company a cocktail, and he munched each sip as if it were mutton. He would occupy the entire dinner-time with one baked potato. I was endeared to him because I had known his master, Fletcher, and with him, too, had chewed a glass of wine in the patio of the

Army and Navy Club in Manila. I longed to pit the Swiss and Herr Gluck in argument, but in sober thought had to give the laurel to the latter, because, in case of stress, one might, with his system, live on a trifle, while raw, nourishing food might be difficult to get in quantity.

Most of the passengers were Australians and New-Zealanders returning home, and only a few were bound for Tahiti—the Tahitian women, the Swiss, Hallman and his son, and M. Leboucher, a young merchant, born there, of a Spanish mother. William McBirney of County Antrim, but long in Raratonga, an island two days' steaming from Tahiti, was going back to his adopted home.

"Sure," he said, "I'm never happy away from the sound of the surf on the reef and the swish of the cocoanuts. I was fourteen years in the British army in England when I made up my mind to quit civilization. I put it to the missus, a London woman, and she was for it. I've had nearly ten years now in the Cook group. D'ye know, I've learned one thing—that money means very little in life. Why, in Aitutaki you can't sell fish. The law forbids it, but do you suppose people don't fish on that account? Why, a man goes out in his canoe and fishes like mad. He brings in his canoe, and as he approaches the beach he's blowing his *pu*, the conch-shell, to let people know he has fish. Fish to sell or to barter? Not at all. He wants the honor of giving them away. Now, if he makes a big catch, do you see, he has renown. People say, 'There's Taiere, who caught all those fish yesterday.' That's worth more to him than money. But if he could sell those fish, if there was competition, only the small-minded, the business souls, would fish. I'm not a socialist, but Aitutaki shows that, released from the gain, man will serve his fellows for their plaudits. And, mind you, no person took more fish than he needed. There was no greed."

"That's rot!" broke in Hallman, who entered the smoking-room. "The natives are frauds. You've got to kick 'em around or bribe 'em to do any work. Haven't I lived with 'em twenty years? They're swine."

"It depends on what you bring them and what you seek," said McBirney. "Ah, well, it's getting too civilized in Raratonga. There's an automobile threatening to come there, though you could drive around the island in half an hour. And they're teaching the Maoris English. I must get away to the west'ard soon. It's a fact there are two laws for every inhabitant."

Would I, too, "go native"? Become enamored of those simple, primitive places and ways, and want to keep going westward? Would I, too, fish to be honored for my string? Would I go to the Dangerous Archipelago, those mystic atolls that sent to the Empress Eugénie that magnificent necklace of pearls she wore at the great ball at the Tuileries when the foolish Napoleon made up his mind to emulate his great namesake and make war? Would I there see those divers who are said to surpass all the mermen of legend in the depths they go in their coral-studded lagoons in search of the jewels that hide in gold-lipped shells? Was it for me to wander among those fabulous coral isles flung for a thousand miles upon the sapphire sea, like wreaths of lilies upon a magic lake?

The doldrums brought rain before the southeast wind came to urge us faster on our course and to clear the skies. Now we were in the deep tropics, five or six hundred miles farther south than Honolulu, and plunging toward the imaginary circle which is the magic ring of the men who steer ships in all oceans. Our breeze was that they pray for when the wind alone must drive the towering trees of canvas toward Australia from America.

The breeze held on while games of the formal tournaments progressed, and prizes were won by the young and the spry.

One night I came on deck when the moon had risen an hour, and saw as strange and beautiful a sight as ever made me sigh for the lack of numbers in my soul. A huge, long, black cloud hung pendent from midway in the sky, with its lower part resting on the sea. It was for all the world of marvels like a great dragon, shaped rudely to a semblance of the beast of the Apocalypse, and with its head lifted into the ether, so that it was framed against the heavens. The moon was in its mouth; the moon shaped like an eye, a brilliant, glowing, wondrous orb, more intensely golden for its contrast with the ominous blackness of the serpentine cloud. I felt that I had found the origin of the Oriental fable. Some minutes the illusion held, and then the cloud lowered, and the moon, alone against a pale-blue background, the horizon a mass of scudding draperies of pearly hue, lit the ocean between the ship and the edge of the world in a tremulous and mellow gilded path.

There was dancing on the boat-deck, the Lydian measures of the Hawaiian love-songs, those passionate melodies in which Polynesian pearls have been strung on European filaments, filling the balmy air with quivering notes of desire, and causing dancers to hold closer their partners. The Occident seemed very far away; even older people felt the charm of clime that had come upon them, and laughter rang as stories ran about the group in the reclining-chairs.

The captain, though grim from a gripping religion that had squeezed all joy from his scripture-haunted soul, added an anecdote to the entertainment.

"Passing from Fiji to Samoa," he said, "I had to leave the mail at Niuafou, in the Tongan Islands. It is a tiny isle, three miles long by as wide, an old crater in which is a lagoon, hot springs, and every sign of the devastation of many eruptions. The mail for Niuafou was often only a single letter and a few newspapers. We sealed them in a tin can, and when we met the postmaster at sea, we threw it over. He would be three miles out, swimming, with a small log under arm for support, and often he might be in company with thirty or forty of his tribe, who, with only the same slight aids to keeping afloat, would be fishing leisurely. They carried their tackle and their catch upon their shoulders, and appeared quite at ease, with no concern for their long swim to shore or for the sharks, which were plentiful. They might even nap a little during the middle afternoon."

"When our people wanted to sleep at sea," said McBirney, "if there were two of them, though we never bothered to take along logs, one rested on the other's shoulder."

One listened and marveled, and smiled to think that, had one stayed at home, one might never know these things. Forgotten was the wraith of Leung Kai Chu, the jungle trail of Hallman, and even the trepidation with which we had awaited the sailing ship's boat. I was soon to be in those enchanted archipelagoes, and to see for myself those mighty swimmers and those sleepers upon the sea. I might even get a letter through that floating postmaster.

There was a Continental duchess aboard, whom I pitied. She was oldish and homely, and couldn't forget her rank. She had a woman companion, an honorable lady, a maid, and a courier, but she sat all day knitting or reading poor novels. She had nothing to do with the other passengers, eating with her companion at an aloof table, and sitting before her own cabin, apart from others. The courier and I talked several times, and once he said that her Highness was much interested in a statement I had made about the origin of the Maori race, but she did not invite me to tell her my opinion directly. Poor wretch! as Pepys used to say, she was entangled in her own regal web, and sterilized by her Continental caste.

For days and nights we moved through the calm sea, with hardly more than the sparkling crests of the myriad swelling waves to distinguish from a bounded lake these mighty waters that wash the newest and oldest of lands. It seemed as if all the world was only water and us. The ship was as steady in her element as a plane in those upper strata of the ether where the winds and clouds no longer have domain. The company in a week had found themselves, and divided into groups in which each sought protection from boredom, ease of familiar manners, and opportunity to talk or to listen.

Often when all had left the deck I sat alone in the passage before the surgeon's cabin to drink in the coolness of the dark, and to wonder at the problem of life. If a man had not his dream, what could life give him? In his heart he might know by experience that it never could come true, but without it, false as it might be, he was without consolation.

One night, the equator behind, I saw the Southern Cross for the first time on the voyage, its glittering crux, with the alpha and beta Centaur stars, signaling to me that I was beyond the dispensation of the cold and constant north star, and in the realm of warmth and everchanging beauty.

Tahiti, the second Sunday out, was a day off. I arose Monday with a feeling of buoyancy and expectancy that grew with the morning. I was as one who looks to find soon in reality the ideal on earth his fancy has created. The day became older, and the noontide passed. I had gone forward upon the forecastle head to seize the first sign of land, and was leaning over the cathead, watching the flying-fish leaping in advance of the bow, and the great, shining albacore throwing themselves into the rush of our advance, to be carried along by the mere drive of our bows.

I drew a deep breath of the salt air when there came to me a new and delicious odor. It seemed to steal from a secret garden under the sea, and I thought of mermaids plucking the blossoms of their coral arbors for the perfuming and adornment of their golden hair. But sweeter and heavier it floated upon the slight breeze, and I knew it for the famed zephyr that carries to the voyager to Tahiti the scents of the flowers of that idyllic land. It was the life vapor of the *hinano*, the *tiare* and the frangipani exhaled by those flowers of Tahiti, to be wafted to the sailor before he sights the scene itself, the breath of Lorelei that spelled the sense of the voyager. No shipwrecked mariner could have felt more poignancy in his search for a hospitable strand than I on the plunging prow of the *Noa-Noa* in my quest through the bright sunshine of that afternoon for the haven of desire. I strained my eyes to see it, to realize the gossamer dream I had spun since boyhood from the leaves of beloved poets.

It was shortly after three o'clock that the vision came in reality, more marvelous, more exquisite, more unimaginable than the conception of all my reveries—a dim shadow in the far offing, a dark speck in the lofty clouds, a mass of towering green upon the blue water, the fast unfoldment of emerald, pale hills and glittering reef. Nearer as sailed our ship, the panorama was lovelier. It was the culmination of enchantment, the fulfilment of the wildest fantasy of wondrous color, strange form, and lavish adornment.

The island rose in changing shape from the soft Pacific sea, here sheer and challenging, there sloping gently from mountain height to ocean sheen; different all about, altering with hiding sun or shifting view its magic mold, with moods as varied as the wind, but ever lovely, alluring, new.

I marked the volcanic make of it, cast up from the low bed of Neptune an eon ago, its loftiest peaks peering from the long cloud-streamers a mile and a half above my eyes, and its valleys embracing caverns of shadow. It was a stupendous precipice suspended from the vault of heaven, and in its massive folds secreted the wonders I had come so far to see. Every minute the bewildering contours were transmuted by the play of sun and cloud and our swift progression toward the land.

Red spots appeared rare against the field of verdure where the mountain-side had been stripped naked by erosion, and the volcanic cinnabar of ages contrasted oddly with the many greens of frond and palm and hillside grove. Curious, fantastic, the hanging peaks and cloud-capped scarps, black against the fleecy drift, were tauntingly reminiscent of the evening skies of the last few days, as if the divine artist had sketched lightly upon the azure of the heavens the entrancing picture to be drawn firmly and grandly in beetling crag and sublime steep.

Most of all, as the island swam closer, the embracing fringe of cocoanut-trees drew my eyes. They were like a girdle upon the beautiful body of the land, whose lower half was in the ocean. They seemed the freewaving banners of romance, whispering always of nude peoples, of savage whites, of ruthless passion, of rum and missionaries, cannibals and heathen altars, of the fierce struggle of the artificial and the primitive. I loved these palms, brothers of my soul, and for me they have never lost their romantic significance.

From the sea, the village of Papeete, the capital and port, was all but hidden in the wood of many kinds of trees that lies between the beach and the hills. Red and gray roofs appeared among the mass of growing things at almost the same height, for the capital rested on only a narrow shelf of rising land, and the mountains descended from the sky to the very water's-edge. Greener than the Barbadoes, like malachite upon the dazzling Spanish Main, Tahiti gleamed as a promise of Elysium.

A lighthouse, tall minister of warning, lifted upon a headland, and suddenly there was disclosed intimately the brilliant, shimmering surf breaking on the tortuous coral reef that banded the island a mile away. It was like a circlet of quicksilver in the sun, a quivering, shining, waving wreath. Soon we heard the eternal diapason of these shores, the constant and immortal music of the breakers on the white stone barrier, a low, deep, resonant note that lulls the soul to sleep by day as it does the body by night.

Guardian sound of the South Seas it is, the hushed, echoic roar of a Jovian organ that chants of the dangers of the sea without, and the peace of the lagoon within, the reef.

A stretch of houses showed—the warehouses and shops of the merchants along the beach, the spire of a church, a line of wharf, a hundred tiny homes all but hidden in the foliage of the ferns. These gradually came into view as the ship, after skirting along the reef, steered through a break in the foam, a pass in the treacherous coral, and glided through opalescent and glassy shallows to a quay where all Papeete waited to greet us.

The quay was filled with women and men and children and dogs. Carriages and automobiles by the score attended just outside. Conspicuous above all were the Tahitian and part-Tahitian girls. In their long, graceful, waistless tunics of brilliant hues, their woven bamboo or pandanus hats, decorated with fresh flowers, their feet bare or thrust into French slippers, their brown eyes shining with yearning, they were so many Circes to us from the sea. They smiled and looked with longing at these strangers, who felt curious thrills at this unknown openness of promise.

Louis de Bougainville wrote in his diary at his first coming to Tahiti a hundred and fifty years ago:

The boats were now crowded with women, whose beauty of face was equal to that of the ladies of Europe, and the symmetry of their forms much superior.

Leboucher called to his mother. *"Madre mia! Como estas tu?"*

Cries rang out in French, in Tahitian and in English. Islanders, returning, demanded information as to health, business ventures, happenings. Merry laughter echoed from the roof of the great shed, and I felt my heart suddenly become joyous.

The girls and women absorbed the attention of passengers not of Tahiti. The New-Zealanders of the crew called excitedly to various ones. Most of the men passengers, tarrying only with the vessel, planned to see a *hula*, and they wondered if any of those on the wharf were the dancers.

A white flower over the ear seemed a favorite adornment, some wearing it on one side and some on the other. What struck one immediately was the erect carriage of the women. They were tall and as straight as sunflower-stalks, walking with a swimming gait. They were graceful even when old. Those dark women and men seemed to fit in perfectly with the marvelous background of the cocoas, the bananas and the brilliant foliage. The whites appeared sickly, uncouth, beside the natives, and the white women, especially, faded and artificial.

The *Noa-Noa* was warped to the wharf, and I was within a few feet now of the welcoming crowd and could discern every detail.

Those young women were well called *les belles Tahitiennes*. Their skins were like pale-brown satin, but exceeding all their other charms were their lustrous eyes. They were very large, liquid, melting, and indescribably feminine—

feminine in a way lost to Occidental women save only the Andalusians and the Neapolitans. They were framed in the longest, blackest, curly lashes, the lashes of dark Caucasian children. They were the eyes of children of the sun, eyes that had stirred disciplined seamen to desertion, eyes that had burned ships, and created the mystery of the *Bounty*, eyes of enchantresses of the days of Helen.

"*Prenez-garde vous!*" said Madame Aubert, the invalid, in my ear.

Mixed now with the perfumes of the flowers was the odor of cocoanuts, coming from the piles of copra on the dock, a sweetish, oily smell, rich, powerful, and never in foreign lands to be inhaled without its bringing vividly before one scenes of the tropics.

The gangway was let down. I was, after years of anticipation, in Tahiti.

Chapter III

Description of Tahiti—A volcanic rock and coral reef—Beauty of the Scenery—Papeete the center of the South Seas—Appearance of the Tahitians.

Tahiti was a molten rock, fused in a subterranean furnace, and cast in some frightful throe of the cooling sphere, high up above the surface of the sea, the seething mass forming into mountains and valleys, the valleys hemmed in except at their mouths by lofty barriers that stretch from thundering central ridges to the slanting shelf of alluvial soil which extends to the sand of the beach. It is a mass of volcanic matter to which the air, the rain, and the passage of a million years have given an all-covering verdure except upon the loftiest peaks, have cut into strangely shaped cliffs, sloping hills, spacious vales, and shadowy glens and dingles, and have poured down the rich detritus and humus to cover the coral beaches and afford sustenance for man and beast. About the island countless trillions of tiny animals have reared the shimmering reef which bears the brunt of the breaking seas, and spares their impact upon the precious land. These minute beings in the unfathomable scheme of the Will had worked and perished for unguessed ages to leave behind this monument of their existence, their charnel-house. Man had often told himself that a god had inspired them thus to build havens for his vessels and abodes of marine life where man might kill lesser beings for his food and sport.

Always, in the approach to the island in steamship, schooner, or canoe, one is amazed and transported by the varying aspect of it. A few miles away one would never know that man had touched it. His inappreciable structures are erased by the flood of green color, which, from the edge of the lagoon to the spires of La Diadème, nearly eight thousand feet above the water, makes all other hues insignificant. In all its hundred miles or so of circumference nature is the dominant note—a nature so mysterious, so powerful, and yet so soft-handed, so beauty-loving and so laughing in its indulgences, that one can hardly believe it the same that rules the Northern climes and forces man to labor in pain all his days or to die.

The scene from a little distance is as primeval as when the first humans climbed in their frail canoes through the unknown and terrible stretches of ocean, and saw Tahiti shining in the sunlight. A mile or two from the lagoon the fertile land extends as a slowly-ascending gamut of greens as luxuriant as a jungle, and forming a most pleasing foreground to the startling amphitheater of the mountains, darker, and, in storm, black and forbidding.

Those mountains are the most wonderful examples of volcanic rock on the globe. Formed of rough and crystalline products of the basic fire of earth, they hold high up in their recesses coral beds once under the sea, and lava in many shapes, tokens of the island's rise from the slime, and of mammoth craters now almost entirely obliterated by denudation—the denudation which made the level land as fertile as any on earth, and the suitable habitation of the most leisurely and magnificent human animals of history.

A thousand rills that drink from the clouds ever encircling the crags, and in which they are often lost from view, leap from the heights, appearing as ribbons of white on a clear day, and not seldom disappearing in vapor as they fall sheer hundreds of feet, or thousands, in successive drops. When heavy rains come, torrents suddenly spring into being and dash madly down the precipitous cliffs to swell the brooks and little rivers and rush headlong to the sea.

Tahiti has an unexcelled climate for the tropics, the temperature for the year averaging seventy-seven degrees and varying from sixty-nine to eighty-four degrees. June, July, and August are the coolest and driest months, and December to March the rainiest and hottest. It is often humid, enervating, but the south-east, the trade-wind, which blows regularly on the east side of the islands, where are Papeete and most of the settlements, purifies the atmosphere, and there are no epidemics except when disease is brought directly from the cities of America or Australasia. A delicious breeze comes up every morning at nine o'clock and fans the dweller in this real Arcadia until past four, when it languishes and ceases in preparation for the vesper drama of the sun's retirement from the stage of earth.

Typhoons or cyclones are rare about Tahiti, but squalls are frequent and tidal waves recurrent. The rain falls more than a hundred days a year, but usually so lightly that one thinks of it as liquid sunshine. In the wet quarter from December until March there are almost daily deluges, when the air seems turned to water, the land and sea are hidden by the screen of driving rain, and the thunder shakes the flimsy houses, and echoes menacingly in the upper valleys.

Papeete, the seat of government and trade capital of all the French possessions in these parts of the world, is a sprawling village stretching lazily from the river of Fautaua on the east to the cemetery on the west, and from the sea on the north to half a mile inland. It is the gradual increment of garden and house upon an aboriginal village, the slow response of a century to the demand of official and trading white, of religious group and ambitious Tahitian, of sailor and tourist. Here flow all the channels of business and finance, of plotting and robbery, of pleasure and profit, of literature and art and good living, in the eastern Pacific. Papeete is the London and Paris of this part of the peaceful ocean, dispensing the styles and comforts, the inventions and luxuries, of civilization, making the laws and enforcing or compromising them, giving justice and injustice to litigants, despatching all the concomitants of modernity to littler islands. Papeete is the entrepot of all the archipelagoes in these seas.

The French, who have domination in these waters of a hundred islands and atolls between 8° and 27° south latitude, and between 137° and 154° west longitude, a stretch of about twelve hundred miles each way, make them all tributary to Papeete; and thus it is the metropolis of a province of salt water, over which come its couriers and its freighters, its governors and its soldiers, its pleasure-seekers and its idlers. From it an age ago went the Maoris to people Hawaii and New Zealand.

Papeete has a central position in the Pacific. The capitals of Hawaii, Australia, New Zealand, and California are from two and a half to three and a half thousand miles away. No other such group of whites, or place approaching its urbanity, is to be found in a vast extent of latitude or longitude. It is without peer or competitor in endless leagues of waves.

Yet Papeete is a little place, a mile or so in length and less in width, a curious imposition of European houses and manners upon a Tahitian hamlet, hybrid, a mixture of loveliness and ugliness, of nature savage and tamed. The settlement, as with all ports, began at the waterfront, and the harbor of Papeete is a lake within the milky reef, the gentle waters of which touch a strip of green that runs along the shore, broken here and there by a wall and by the quay at which I landed. Coral blocks have been quarried from the reef and fitted to make an embankment for half a mile, which juts out just far enough to be usable as a mole. It is alongside this that sailing vessels lie, the wharf being the only land mooring with a roof for the housing of products. A dozen schooners, small and large, point their noses out to the sea, their backs against the coral quay, and their hawsers made fast to old cannon, brought here to war against the natives, and now binding the messengers of the nations and of commerce to this shore. Where there are no embankments, the water comes up to the roots of the trees, and a carpet of grass, moss, and tropical vegetation grows from the salt tide to the roadway.

Following the contour of the beach, runs a fairly broad road, and facing this original thoroughfare and the sea are the principal shops of the traders and a few residences. French are some of these merchants, but most are Australasian, German, American and Chinese. France is ten thousand miles away, and the French unequal in the struggle for gain. Some of the stores occupy blocks, and in them one will find a limited assortment of tobacco, anchors, needles, music-boxes, candles, bicycles, rum, novels, and silks or calicos. Here in this spot was the first settlement of the preachers of the gospel, of the conquering forces of France, and of the roaring blades who brought the culture of the world to a powerful and spellbound people. Here swarmed the crews of fifty whalers in the days when "There she blows!" was heard from crows'-nests all over the broad Pacific. These rough adventurers, fighters, revelers, passionate bachelors, stamped Tahiti with its first strong imprint of the white man's modes and vices, contending with the missionaries for supremacy of ideal. They brought gin and a new lecherousness and deadly ills and novel superstitions, and found a people ready for their wares. An old American woman has told me she has seen a thousand whalemen at one time ashore off ships in the harbor make night and day a Saturnalia of Occidental pleasure, a hundred fights in twenty-four hours.

As more of Europe and America came and brought lumber to build houses, or used the hard woods of the mountains, the settlement pushed back from the beach. Trails that later widened into streets were cut through the brush to reach these homes of whites, and the thatched huts of the aborigines were replaced by the ugly, but more convenient, cottages of the new-comers. The French, when once they had seized the island, made roads, gradually and not too well, but far surpassing those of most outlying possessions, and contrasting advantageously with the neglect of the Spanish, who in three hundred years in the Philippines left all undone the most important step in civilization. One can drive almost completely around Tahiti on ninety miles of a highway passable at most times of the year, and bridging a hundred times the streams which rush and purl and wind from the heights to the ocean.

The streets of Papeete have no plan. They go where they list and in curves and angles, and only once in a mile in short, straight stretches. They twist and stray north and south and nor'nor'west and eastsou'east, as if each new-comer had cleft a walk of his own, caring naught for any one else, and further dwellers had smoothed it on for themselves.

I lost myself in a maze of streets, looked about for a familiar landmark, strolled a hundred paces, and found myself somewhere I thought a kilometer distant. Everywhere there are shops kept by Chinese, restaurants and coffee-houses. The streets all have names, but change them as they progress, honoring some French hero or statesman for a block or two, recalling some event, or plainly stating the reason for their being. All names are in French, of course, and many are quaint and sonorous.

As the sea-wall grew according to the demands of defense or commerce the sections were rechristened. The quai des Subsistences tells its purpose as does the quai de l'Uranie. The rue de l'Ecole and the rue de la Mission, with the rue des Remparts, speak the early building of school and Catholic church and fortifications.

Rue Cook, rue de Bougainville and many others record the giant figures of history who took Tahiti from the mist of the half-known, and wrote it on the charts and in the archives. Other streets hark back to that beloved France to which these French exiles gaze with tearful eyes, but linger all their years ten thousand miles away. They saunter along the rue de Rivoli in Papeete, and see again the magnificence of the Tuileries, and hear the dear noises of la belle Paris. They are sentimental, these French, patriots all here, and overcome at times by the flood of memories of la France, their birthplaces, and their ancestral graves. Some born here have never been away, and some have spent a few short months in visits to the homeland. Some have brown mothers, half-islanders; yet if they learn the tripping tongue of their French progenitor and European manners, they think of France as their ultimate goal, of Paris their playground, and the "Marseillaise" their *himene* par excellence.

One might conjure up a vision of a tiny Paris with such names in one's ears, and these French, who have been in possession here nearly four-score years, have tried to make a French town of Papeete.

They have only spoiled the scene as far as unfit architecture can, but the riot of tropical nature has mocked their labors. For all over the flimsy wooden houses, the wretched palings, the galvanized iron roofing, the ugly verandas, hang gorgeous draperies of the giant acacias, the brilliant flamboyantes, the bountiful, yellow allamanda, the generous breadfruit, and the uplifting glory of the cocoanut-trees, while magnificent vines and creepers cover the tawdry paint of the façades and embower the homes in green and flower. If one leaves the few principal streets or roads in Papeete, one walks only on well-worn trails through the thick growth of lantana, guavas, pandanus, wild coffee, and a dozen other trees and bushes. The paths are lined with hedges of false coffee, where thrifty people live, and again there are open spaces with vistas of little houses in groves, rows of tiny cabins close together. Everywhere are picturesque disorder, dirt, rubbish, and the accrued wallow of years of *laissez-aller*; but the mighty trade-winds and the constant rains sweep away all bad odors, and there is no resultant disease.

"My word," said Stevens, a London stockbroker, here to rehabilitate a broken corporation, "if we English had this place, wouldn't there be a cleaning up! We'd build it solid and sanitary, and have proper rules to make the bally natives stand around."

The practical British would that. They have done so in a dozen of their far-flung colonies I hare been in, from Singapore to Barbadoes, though they have failed utterly in Jamaica. Yet, I am at first sight, of the mind that only the Spanish would have kept, after decades of administration, as much of the simple beauty of Papeete as have the Gauls. True, the streets are a litter, the Government almost unseen as to modern uplift, the natives are indolent and life moves without bustle or goal. The republic is content to keep the peace, to sell its wares, to teach its tongue, and to let the gentle Tahitian hold to his island ways, now that his race dies rapidly in the spiritual atmosphere so murderous to natural, non-immunized souls and bodies.

Many streets and roads are shaded by spreading mango-trees, a fruit brought in the sixties from Brazil, and perfected in size and flavor here by the patient efforts of French gardeners and priests. The trees along the town ways are splendid, umbrageous masses of dark foliage whose golden crops fall upon the roadways, and which have been so chosen that though they are seasonal, the round mango is succeeded by the golden egg, and that by a small purple sort, while the large, long variety continues most of the year. Monseigneur Jaussen, the Catholic bishop who wrote the accepted grammar and dictionary of the Tahitian language, evolved a delicious, large mango, with a long, thin stone very different from the usual seed, which occupies most of the circumference of this slightly acidulous, most luscious of tropical fruits. Often the pave is a spatter of the fallen mangos, its slippery condition of no import to the barefooted Tahitian, but to the shod a cause of sudden, strange gyrations and gestures, and of irreverence toward the Deity.

Scores of varieties of fruits and flowers, shade-trees, and ornamental plants were brought to Tahiti by ship commanders, missionaries, officials, and traders, in the last hundred years, while many of the indigenous growths have been transplanted to other islands and continents by those whose interests were in them. The Mutiny of the *Bounty*, perhaps the most romantic incident of these South Seas, was the result of an effort to transport breadfruit-tree shoots from Tahiti to the West Indies. It is a beautiful trait in humankind, which, maybe, designing nature has endowed us with to spread her manifold creations, that even the most selfish of men delight in planting in new environments exotic seeds and plants, and in enriching the fauna of faraway islands with strange animals and insects. The pepper- and the gum-tree that make southern California's desert a bower, the oranges and lemons there which send a million golden trophies to less-favored peoples, are the flora of distant climes. Since the days of the white discoverers, adventurers and priests, fighting men and puritans, have added to the earth's treasury in Tahiti and all these islands.

Walking one morning along the waterfront, I met two very dark negresses. They had on pink and black dresses, with red cotton shawls, and they wore flaming yellow handkerchiefs about their woolly heads. They were as African as the Congo, and as strange in this setting as Eskimos on Broadway. They felt their importance, for they were of the few good cooks of French dishes here. They spoke a French patois, and guffawed loudly when one dropped her basket of supplies from her head. They were servants of the *procureur de la République*, who had brought them from the French colony of Martinique.

Many races have mingled here. One saw their pigments and their lines in the castes; here a *soupçon* of the French and there a touch of the Dane; the Chileño, himself a mestizo, had left his print in delicacy of feature, and the Irish his freckles and pug, which with tawny skin, pearly teeth, and the superb form of the pure Tahitian, left little to be desired in fetching and saucy allurement. Thousands of sailors and merchants and preachers had sowed their seed here, as did Captain Cook's men a century and a half ago, and the harvest showed in numerous shadings of colors and variety of mixtures. Tahiti had, since ship of Europe sighted Orofena, been a pasture for the wild asses of the *Wanderlust*, a paradise into which they had brought their snakes and left them to plague the natives.

There were phonographs shrieking at one from a score of verandas. The automobile had become a menace to life and limb. There were two-score motor-cars in Tahiti; but as the island is small, and most of them were in the capital, one met them all the day, and might have thought there were hundreds. Motor-buses, or "rubberneck-wagons," ran about the city, carrying the natives for a franc on a brief tour, and, for more, to country districts where good cheer and dances sped the night. A dozen five- and seven-passenger cars with drivers were for hire. Most nights until eleven or later the rented machines dashed about the narrow streets, hooting and hissing, while their care-free occupants played accordions or mouth-organs and sang songs of love. Louis de Bougainville, once a French lawyer, and afterward soldier, sailor, and discoverer and a lord under Bonaparte, had a monument in a tiny green park hard by the strand and the road that, beginning there, bands the island. He is best known the world about because his name is given to the "four-o'clock" shrub in warm countries, as in Tahiti, which sends huge masses of magenta or crimson blossoms climbing on trellises and roofs. I walked to this monument from the Tiare along the mossy bank of a little rivulet which ran to the beach. It was early morning. The humble natives and whites were about their daily tasks. Smoke rose from the iron pipes above the houses, coffee scented the air, men and women were returning from the market-place with bunches of cocoanuts, bananas, and breadfruit, strings of fish and cuts of meat in papers. Many of them had their heads wreathed in flowers or wore a *tiare* blossom over an ear.

The way in which one wears a flower supposedly signifies many things. If one wore it over the left ear, one sought a sweetheart; if over the right, it signified contentment, and though it was as common as the wearing of hats, there were always jokes passing about these flowers, exclamations of surprise or wishes of joy.

"What, you have left Terii?"

"*Aita.* No."

"*Aue!* I must change it at once."

Now, really there was no such idea in the native mind. It was invention for tourists. The Tahitian wears flowers anywhere, always, if he can have them, and they do express his mood. If he is sad, he will not put them on; but if going to a dance, to a picnic, or to promenade, if he has money in his pocket, or gaiety in his heart, he must bloom. Over one ear, or both, in the hair, on the head, around the neck, both sexes were passionately fond of this age-old sign of kinship with nature. The *lei* in Hawaii around the hat or the neck spells the same meaning, but the flood of outsiders has lost Hawaii all but the merest remnant of its ancient ways, while here still persisted customs which a century of European difference and indifference has not crushed out. Here, as there, more lasting wreaths for the hat were woven of shells or beads in various colors.

As I strolled past the houses, every one greeted me pleasantly.

"*Ia ora na*," they said, or "Bonjour!" I replied in kind. I had not been a day in Tahiti before I felt kindled in me an affection for its dark people which I had never known for any other race. It was an admixture of friendship, admiration, and pity—of affection for their beautiful natures, of appreciation of the magnificence of their physical equipment, and of sympathy for them in their decline and inevitable passing under the changed conditions of environment made by the sudden smothering of their instinctive needs in the sepia of commercial civilization. I saw that those natives remaining, laughing and full of the desire for pleasure as they were, must perish because unfit to survive in the morass of modernism in which they were sinking, victims of a system of life in which material profits were the sole goal and standard of the rulers.

The Tahitians are tall, vigorous, and superbly rounded. The men, often more than six feet or even six and a half feet in height, have a mien of natural majesty and bodily grace. They convey an impression of giant strength, reserve power, and unconscious poise beyond that made by any other race. American Indians I have known had much of this quality when resident far from towns, but they lacked the curving, padded muscles, the ease of movement, and, most of all, the smiling faces, the ingratiating manner, of these children of the sun.

The Tahitians' noses are fairly flat and large; the nostrils dilated; their lips full and sensual; their teeth perfectly shaped and very white and sound; their chins strong, though round; and their eyes black and large, not brilliant, but liquid. Their feet and hands are mighty—hands that lift burdens of great weight, that swing paddles of canoes for hours; feet that tread the roads or mountain trails for league on league.

The women are of middle size, with lines of harmony that give them a unique seal of beauty, with an undulating movement of their bodies, a coordination of every muscle and nerve, a richness of aspect in color and form, that is more sensuous, more attractive, than any feminine graces I have ever gazed on. They have the forwardness of boys, the boldness of huntresses, yet the softness and magnetism of the most virginal of their white sisters. One thinks of them as of old in soft draperies of beautiful cream-colored native cloth wound around their bodies, passed under one arm and knotted on the other shoulder, revealing the shapely neck and arm, and one breast, with garlands upon their hair, and a fragrant flower passed through one ear, and in the other two or three large pearls fastened with braided human hair.

The men never wore beards, though mustaches, copying the French custom, are common on chiefs, preachers, and those who sacrifice beauty and natural desires to ambition. The hair on the face is removed as it appears, and it is scanty. They abhor beards, and their ghosts, the *tupapau*, have faces fringed with hair. The usual movements of both men and women are slow, dignified, and full of pride.

Chapter IV

The Tiare Hotel—Lovaina the hostess, the best-known woman in the South Seas—Her strange ménage—The Dummy—A one-sided tryst—An old-fashioned cocktail—The Argentine training ship.

The Tiare Hotel was the center of English-speaking life in Papeete. Almost all tourists stayed there, and most of the white residents other than the French took meals there. The usual traveler spent most of his time in and about the hotel, and from it made his trips to the country districts or to other islands. Except for two small restaurants kept by Europeans, the Tiare was the only eating-place in the capital of Tahiti unless one counted a score of dismal coffee-shops kept by Chinese, and frequented by natives, sailors, and beach-combers. They were dark, disagreeable recesses, with grimy tables and forbidding utensils, in which wretchedly made coffee was served with a roll for a few sous; one of them also offered meats of a questionable kind.

The Tiare Hotel was five minutes' walk from the quay, at the junction of the rue de Rivoli and the rue de Petit Pologne, close by Pont du Remparts. It was a one-storied cottage, with broad verandas, half hidden in a luxuriant garden at the point where two streets come together at a little stone bridge crossing a brook—a tiny bungalow built for a home, and stretched and pieced out to make a guest-house.

I was at home there after a few days as if I had known no other dwelling. That is a distinctive and compelling charm of Tahiti, the quick possession of the new-comer by his environment, and his unconscious yielding to the demands of his novel surroundings, opposite as they might be to his previous habitat.

Very soon I was filled with the languor of these isles. I hardly stirred from my living-place. The bustle of the monthly steamship-day died with the going of the *Noa-Noa*, the through passengers departing in angry mood because their anticipated *hula* dance had been a disappointment—wickedness shining feebly through cotton gowns when they had expected nudity in a *pas seul* of abandonment. There was a violent condemnation by the duped men of "unwarranted interference by the French Government with natural and national expression."

Hogg, an American business traveler, said "The Barbary Coast in Frisco had Tahiti skinned a mile for the real thing," and Stevens, a London broker, that the dance was "bally tame for four bob."

Papeete, with the passing throng gone, was a quiet little town, contrasting with the hours when the streets swarmed with people from here and the suburbs, the band playing, the bars crowded, and all efforts for gaiety and coquetry and the selling of souvenirs and intoxicants. What exotic life there was beyond the clubs, the waterfront, and the Asiatic quarter revolved around the Tiare, and entirely so because of its proprietress, Lovaina. She was the best-known and best-liked woman in all these South Seas, remembered from Australia to the Paumotus, from London to China, wherever were people who had visited Tahiti, as "dear old Lovaina."

She was very large. She was huge in every sense, weighing much more than three hundred pounds, and yet there was a singular grace in her form and her movements. Her limbs were of the girth of breadfruit-trees, and her bosom was as broad and deep as that of the great Juno of Rome, but her hands were beautiful, like a plump baby's, with fascinating creases at the wrists, and long, tapering fingers. Her large eyes were hazel, and they were very brilliant when she was merry or excited. Her expansive face had no lines in it, and her mouth was a perfection of curves, the teeth white and even. Her hair was red-brown, curling in rich profusion, scented with the hinano-flower, adorning her charmingly poised head in careless grace.

When she said, "I glad see you," there was a glow of amiability, an alluring light in her countenance, that drew one irresistibly to her, and her immense, shapely hand enveloped one's own with a pressure and a warmth that were overpowering in their convincement of her good heart and illimitable generosity.

Lovaina was only one fourth Tahitian, all the remainder of her racial inheritance being American; but she was all Tahitian in her traits, her simplicity, her devotion to her friends, her catching folly as it flew, and her pride in a new possession.

One morning I got up at five o'clock and went to the bath beside the kitchen. It was a shower, and the water from the far Fautaua valley the softest, most delicious to the body, cool and balmy in the heat of the tropic. Coming and going to baths here, whites throw off easily the fear of being thought immodest, and women and men alike go to and fro in loin-cloths, pajamas, or towels. I wore the *pareu*, the red strip of calico, bearing designs by William Morris, which the native buys instead of his original one of *tapa*, the beaten cloth made from tree bark or pith.

I met Lovaina coming out of the shower, a sheet about her which could not cover half of her immense and regal body. She hesitated—I was almost a stranger,—and in a vain effort to do better, trod on the sheet, and pulled it to her feet. I picked it up for her.

"I shamed for you see me like this!" she said.

I was blushing all over, though why I don't know, but I faltered:

"Like a great American Beauty rose."

"Faded rose too big," exclaimed Lovaina, with the faintest air of coquetry as I hastily shut the door.

A little while later, when I came to the dining-room for the first breakfast, I met Lovaina in a blue-figured *aahu* of muslin and lace, a close-fitting, sweeping nightgown, the single garment that Tahitians wear all day and take off at night, a tunic, or Mother Hubbard, which reveals their figures without disguise, unstayed, unpetticoated. Lovaina was, as always, barefooted, and she took me into her garden, one of the few cultivated in Tahiti, where nature makes man almost superfluous in the decoration of the earth.

"This house my father give me when marry," said Lovaina. "My God! you just should seen that *arearea!* Las' all day, mos' night. We jus' move in. Ban's playin' from war-ship, all merry drinkin', dancin'. Never such good time. I tell you nobody could walk barefoot one week, so much broken glass in garden an' street."

Her goodly flesh shook with her laughter, her darkening eyes suffused with happy tears at the memory, and she put her broad hand between my shoulders for a moment as if to draw me into the rejoicing of her wedding feast. She led me about the garden to show me how she had from year to year planted the many trees, herbs, and bushes it contained. It had set out to be formal, but, like most efforts at taming the fierce fecundity of nature in these seas, had become a tangle of verdure, for though now and then combed into some regularity, the breezes, the dogs, the chickens, and the invading people ruffled it, the falling leaves covered the grass, and the dead branches sighed for burial. Down the narrow path she went ponderously, showing me the cannas, jasmine and rose, picking a lime or a tamarind, a bouquet of mock-orange flowers, smoothing the tuberoses, the hibiscus of many colors, the oleanders, *maile ilima*, Star of Bethlehem, frangipani, and, her greatest love, the *tiare* Tahiti. There were snakeplants, East-India cherries, coffee-bushes, custard-apples, and the hinano, the sweetness of which and of the *tiare* made heavy the air.

I said that we had no flower in America as wonderful in perfume as these.

Lovaina stopped her slow, heavy steps. She raised her beautiful, big hand, and arresting my attention, she exclaimed:

"You know that ol' *hinano*! Ol' time we use that Tahiti cologne. Girl put that on *pareu* an' on dress, by an' by make whole body jus' like flower. That set man crazee; make all man want kiss an' hug."

Doubtless, our foremothers when they sought to win the hunters of their tribes, took the musk, the civet, and the castor from the prey laid at their feet, and made maddening their smoke- and wind-tanned bodies to the cave-dwellers. When they became more housed and more clothed, they captured the juices of the flowers in nutshells, and later in stone bottles, until now science disdains animals and flowers, but takes chemicals and waste products to make a hundred essences and unguents and sachets for toilet and boudoir. These odors of the *hinano* and *tiare* were philters worthy of the beautiful Tahitian girls, with their sinuous, golden bodies so sensualized, so passionate, and so free.

The ordinary life of the Tiare Hotel was all upon the broad verandas which surrounded it, their high lattices covered with the climbing bougainvillea and stephanotis vines, which formed a maze for the filtering of the sunlight and the dimming of the activities of the streets. On these verandas were the tables for eating, and in the main bungalow a few bedrooms, with others in detached cottages within the inclosure.

There was a parlor, and it was like the parlors of all ambitious Europeans or Americans in all islands—a piano with an injured tone, chairs blue and scarlet with plush covers that perspiring sitters of years had made dark brown, a phonograph, and signed photographs of friends and visitors who had said farewell to Tahiti. There were paintings of flowers by Lovaina, showing not a little talent and much feeling. All these were the pride of her birthright—"Murricaine" fashion, as the hostess said pensively.

I have said that the life of the hotel was upon the veranda, and so it was at meal-time and for the casual tourist staying a day with a steamship to or from New Zealand or the United States; but to the resident of Tahiti, the American, Britisher, or non-Latin European, the place of interest in Papeete other than the clubs was a small porch approached from the street by a few steps.

On this tiny porch was a large table, and behind it a couch. The table was the only desk for letter-writing, the serving-stand for meals, the board for salad and cake-making, and the drink-bar. A few feet removed from this table, and against the wall, was a camphorwood chest on which two might sit in comfort and three might squeeze at angles. In the chest was kept all the bed and table linen, so that one might often be disturbed by the quest of sheets or napkins.

Upon this little porch the kitchen, bath, and toilets opened, a few feet from the table. It was the sleeping and amusement quarters of five dogs, the loafing place for the girls, the office of the hotel, the entry for guests to the dining-room or to the other conveniences. Through it streamed all who came to eat or drink or for any other purpose. The hotel having grown slowly from a home, hardly any changes of plumbing had been made, and men and women in dressing-gowns, in pajamas, or in other undress came and went, under the interested gaze of idlers and drinkers, and they had often to endure intimate questions or badinage. All were on a footing as to the arrangements, and I saw the haughty duchess of the *Noa-Noa* follow Lovaina's American negro chauffeur, while a former ambassador waited on the chest. There was no distinction of rank, since Tahiti, excepting for an occasional French official, was the purest democracy of manners in the world, a philosophy the whites had learned from the natives, who think all foreigners equally distinguished.

Those not of the South Seas, and unused to the primitive publicity of the natural functions there, suffered intensely at first from embarrassment, but in time forgot their squeamishness, and perhaps learned to carry on conversations with those who drank or chatted outside.

The Tahitian cook slept all day between meals on a chair, with his head hanging out a window. He was ill often from a rush of blood to his head. Lovaina had offered him a mat to lie on the floor, but he pleaded his habit. All the refuse of the kitchen was thrown into the garden under this window, and with the horses, chickens, dogs, and cats it was first come, first served.

On the couch back of the table Lovaina sat for many hours every day. Her great weight made her disinclined to walk, and from her cushions she ruled her domain, chaffing with those who dropped in for drinks, advising and joking, making cakes and salads, bargaining with the butcher and vegetable-dealer, despatching the food toward the tables, feeding many dogs, posting her accounts, receiving payments, and regulating the complex affairs of her ménage. She would shake a cocktail, make a gin-fizz or a Doctor Funk, chop ice or do any menial service, yet withal was your entertainer and your friend. She had the striking, yet almost inexplicable, dignity of the Maori—the facing of life serenely and without reserve or fear for the morrow.

Underneath the table dogs tumbled, or raced about the porch, barking and leaping on laps, cats scurried past, and a cloud of tobacco smoke filled the close air. Lovaina, in one of her sixty bright gowns, a white chemise beneath, her feet bare, sat enthroned. On the chest were the captain of a liner or a schooner, a tourist, a trader, a girl, an old native woman, or a beach-comber with money for the moment. It was the carpet of state on which all took their places who would have a hearing before the throne or loaf in the audience-chamber.

In her low, delightfully broken English, in vivid French, or sibilant Tahitian, Lovaina issued her orders to the girls, shouted maledictions at the cook, or talked with all who came. Through that porch flowed all the scandal of the South Seas—tales of hurricanes and waterspouts, of shipwrecks, of accidents, of lucky deals in pearls or shells, of copra, of new fashions and old inhabitants, of liaisons of white and brown, of the flirtations of tourists, of the Government's issuing an ultimatum on the price of fish, of how the consuls quarreled at a club dinner, and of how one threw three ribs of roasted beef at the other, who retorted with a whole sucking pig just from the native oven, of Thomas' wife leaving him for Europe after a month's honeymoon; and all the flotsam and jetsam of report and rumor, of joke and detraction, which in an island with only one mail a month are the topics of interest.

The porch was the clearing-house and the casual, oral record of the spreading South Seas. It was the strangest salon of any capital, and Lovaina the most fascinating of hostesses. Stories that would be frowned down in many a man's club were laughed at lightly over the table, but not when tourists, new-comers, were present. Then the dignified Lovaina, repressing the oaths of potvaliant skippers, putting her finger to her lips when a bald assertion was imminent, said impressively:

"That swears don't go! What you think? To give bad name my good house?"

Only when old-timers were gathered, between steamships, when the schooners came in a drove from the Paumotu atolls, and gold and silver rang on the table at all hours, there was little restraint.

With only one mail a month to disturb the monotony, and but trifling interest in anything north of the equator except prices of their commodities, these unrepressed rebels against the conventions and even the laws of the Occident must have their fling. On that camphor-wood chest had sat many a church-going woman and dignified man of Europe or America, resident for a month or longer in Tahiti, and shuddered at what they heard—shuddered and listened, eager to hear those curious incidents and astonishing opinions about life and affairs, and to mark the difference between this and their own countries. It was without even comment that people who at home or among the conventions would be shocked at the subjects or their treatment, in these islands listened thrilled or chucklingly to stories as naked as the children. *Double entendre* is caviar to the average man and woman of Tahiti, who call the unshrouded spade by its aboriginal name. The Tahitians were ever thus, and the French have not sought to correct their ways. I heard Atupu, one of the girls of the hotel, in a Rabelaisian passage of wit the while she opened Seattle beer for thirsty Britishers, old residents, traders, and planters. One could not publish the phrases if one could translate them.

Lovaina, in her bed just off the porch, was laughing at the retorts of Atupu, who by her native knowledge of the tongue was discomfiting the roisterers, who spoke it haltingly. I heard an apt interjection on the part of the proprietress which set them all roaring, and so lowered their self-esteem that they left summarily.

One day when I was hurrying off to swim in the lagoon, I asked Lovaina to guard a considerable sum of money in bank-notes. She assented readily, but when several days later I mentioned the money she struck her head in alarm. She thought and thought, but could not remember in what safe place she had hidden the paper francs.

"My God! Brien," she said in desperation, "all time I jus' like that crazee way. One time one engineer big steamship come here, he ask me keep two thousan' dollar for him. I busy jus' like always, an' I throw behin' that couch I sit on. My God! he come back I fore-get where I put. One day we look hard. I suffer turribil, but the nex' day I move couch and find money. Was n't that funny?"

I suggested we try the couch again, but though we turned up a number of lost odds and ends, it was not the cache of my funds. By way of cheering her, I ordered a rum punch, and when she went to crack the ice, a gleam of remembrance came to her, and, lo! my money was found in the reserve butter supply in the refrigerator, where she had artfully placed it out of harm's way. It was quite greasy, but intact.

The first breakfast at the Tiare began at 6:30, but lingered for several hours. It was of fruit and coffee and bread; *papayas*, bananas, oranges, pineapples, and alligator-pears, which latter the French call *avocats*, the Mexicans *ahuacatl*, and were brought here from the West Indies. To this breakfast male guests dropped in from the bath in pajamas, but the *déjeuner à la fourchette*, or second breakfast at eleven, was more formal, and of four courses, fish, bacon and eggs, curry and rice, tongues and sounds, beefsteak and potatoes, *feis*, roast beef or mutton, sucking pig, and cabbage or sauer-kraut. For dessert there was sponge- or cocoanut-cake. All business in Papeete opened at seven o'clock and closed at eleven, to reopen from one until five. Dinner at half-past six o'clock was a repetition of the late breakfast except that a vegetable or cabbage soup was also served.

Two Chinese youths, To Sen and Hon Son, were the regular waiters, but were supplemented by Atupu, Iromea, Pepe, Akura, Tetua, Maru, and Juillet, all Tahitian girls or young women who had a mixed status of domestics, friends, kinfolk, visitors, and *hetairae*, the latter largely in the sense of entertainers. I doubt if they were paid more than a trifle, and they were from the country districts or near-by islands, moths drawn by the flame of the town to soar in its feverish heat, to singe their wings, and to grow old before their time, or to grasp the opportunity to satiate their thirst for foreign luxuries by semi-permanent alliances with whites.

Lovaina's girls! How their memory must survive with the guests of the Tiare Hotel! One read of them in every book of travel encompassing Tahiti. One heard of them from every man who had dropped upon this beach. Once in Mukden, Manchuria, I sat up half the night while the American consul and a globe-trotter painted for me the portraits of Lovaina's girls.

I was atop a disorderly camel named Mark Twain nosing about the Sphinx when my companion remarked that that stony-faced lady looked a good deal like Temanu of Lovaina's. Then I had to have the whole story of Lovaina and her household. I have heard it away from Tahiti a dozen times and always different.

Doubtless, in the dozen years the gentle Lovaina ministered to the needs of travelers and residents, many girls came and went in her house. Some have married, and some have gone away without a ring, but all have been made much of by those they served, and have lived gayly and by the way.

Lovaina, herself, said to me:

"You know those girl', they go ruin. That girl you see here few minutes ago I bring her up just like Christian; be good, be true, do her prayers, make her soul all right. Then I go San Francisco. What you think? When I come back she ruin. 'Most break my heart. That man he come to me, he say: 'Lovaina, I take good care that girl. I love her.' That girl with him now. She happy, got plenty dress, plenty best to eat, and nice buggy. I tell you, I give up trying save those girl'. I think they like ruin best. I turn my back—they ruin."

Iromea was the sturdy veteran of the corps. Tall, handsome, straight, mother of four children, obliging, wise in the way of the white, herself all native.

"And the babies?" I inquired.

"They all scatter. Some in country; some different place," answered Iromea, who ran from English to French to Tahitian, but of course not with the ease of Lovaina, for that great heart knew many of the cities of her father's land, was educated in needlework style, and with a little dab of Yankee culture, now fast disappearing as she grew older. One marked that tendency to reversion to the native type and ways among many islanders who had been superficially coated with civilization, but whom environment and heredity claim inexorably.

Iromea was thirty years old. She had been loved by many white men, men of distinction here; sea-rovers, merchants, and lotus-eaters, writers, painters, and wastrels.

Juillet, whose native name was Tiurai, helped old Madame Rose to care for the rooms at the Tiare. She was thirteen years old, willowy, with a beautiful, smiling face, and two long, black plaits. Though innocent, almost artless, in appearance, she was an arch coquette, and flirted with old and young. One day a turkey that shared the back yard with two automobiles, a horse, three carriages, several dogs, ten cats, and forty chickens, disappeared. Juillet was sent to find the turkey. She was gone four days, and came back with a brilliant new gown. She brought with her the turkey, which she said she had been trying to drive back all the four days.

Juillet was named for the month of July. Her mother was the cook of a governor when she was born on the fourteenth of July, the anniversary of the fall of the Bastile, and the governor named her for the month. She was also named Nohorae, and *noho* means to be naked and *rae* forehead. Juillet had a high forehead.

Lovaina pointed out to me the man who had taken away her favorite helper. He was about forty years old, tall, angular, sharp-nosed, with gold eyeglasses. I would have expected to meet him in the vestry of a church or to have been asked by him at a mission if I were saved, but in Tahiti he had gone the way of all flesh. His voice had the timbre of the preacher. He had come to the hotel in an expensive, new automobile to fetch cooked food for himself and Ruiné.

"Seven or eight leper that man support," said Lovaina to me. "They die for him, he so good to them. He help everybodee. He give them leper the Bible, and sometime he go read them."

It would be the Song of Solomon he would read to Ruiné. She had red hair, red black or black red, a not unusual color in Tahiti, and her eyes had a glint of red in their brown. She was exquisite in her silken peignoir, a wreath of scarlet hibiscus-flowers on her head, and a string of gorgeous baroque pearls about her rounded neck.

My room at the Tiare was in the upper story of an old house that sat alone in the back garden, among the domestics, automobiles, carriages, horses, pigs, and fowls. The house had wide verandas all about it, and the stairway outside. A few nights after I had arrived in Tahiti I was writing letters on the piazza, the length of the room away from the stairs. I had a lamp on my table, and the noise of my type-writer hushed the sounds of any one entering the apartment. It was about ten o'clock, and between sentences I looked at the night. The stars were in coruscating masses, the riches of the heavens disclosed as only at such a cloudless hour in this southern hemisphere, the Milky Way showing ten thousand gleaming members of the galaxy that are hidden in our skies. I thought of those happy mariners who first sailed their small, wooden ships into these mysterious seas, and first of our race, saw this strangely brilliant macrocosm, and appreciated it for its marvels and its differences from their own bleaker, Western vault.

There were no doors in the openings into my room from the verandas, but hangings of gorgeous scarlet calico, pareus, kept out the blazing sun, and lent a little privacy at night. All the furniture was a chair, a dressing-table, and two large beds, canopied with mosquito-nets, evidently provided for a double lodging if needed.

As I finished my letters twenty feet away, a Tahitian girl parted the farther curtain nearest the stairway, and slipped into the room with the silence of the accustomed barefooted. Imagine her in her gayest gown of rose color, a garland of *hinano*-flowers on her glossy head, her tawny hair in two plaits to her unconfined waist, and her eyes shining with the spirit of her quest!

She looked through the room to where I sat in the semi-obscurity, and then knelt down by the first bed, and waited. I gazed again at the starry heavens, and, stepping over the threshold, entered the chamber, lamp in hand. I undressed leisurely, and putting about me the *pareu* Lovaina had given me, I threw the light upon the two beds to make my nightly choice. I surveyed them both critically, but the one nearest to me having the netting arranged for entrance, I selected it, and setting the lamp upon the dresser, extinguished it, groped to the bed in darkness, and lay down upon the coverless sheet. A few minutes I stayed awake going over the happenings of the day, and fell asleep in joyful mood that I was in the island I had sought so long in desire and dream. I knew nothing of my visitor, for she had made no audible sound, and the shadows had hidden her.

At breakfast the next morning I was waited on by Atupu, the beauty. Her face was tear-stained, and a deep weariness was upon her. She regarded me with a glance of mixed anger and hurt.

"*Vous etes faché avec moi?*" she inquired accusingly.

"I angry with you?" I repeated. "Why what have I done to show it?"

And then she told me of her visit and vigil. Seeing me alone in Tahiti, and kind-hearted, she said, she had thought to tell me of the Tahitian heart and the old ways of the land. She had robed, perfumed, and adorned herself, and entered my sleeping-place, as she said was the wont of Tahitian girls. I had certainly heard her enter, and seen her kneel to await my greeting, and if not then, I had seen her plainly when I lifted the lamp, for the light had streamed full upon her. She had remained there upon the floor half an hour until my audible breathing had compelled her to believe against her will that I was asleep. Then she had fled and wept the night in humiliation. Never in her young life had such a horror afflicted her.

I was stunned, and could only reiterate that I had not known of her presence, and with a trinket from my pocket I dried her tears.

Rupert Brooke in a letter to a friend in England drew a little etching of our lodging:

I am in a hovel at the back of my hotel, and contemplate the yard. The extraordinary life of the place flows round and near my room—for here no one, man or woman, scruples to come through one's room at any moment, if it happens to be a shortcut. By day nothing much happens in the yard—except when a horse tried to eat a hen, the other afternoon. But by night, after ten, it is filled with flitting figures of girls, with wreaths of white flowers, keeping assignations.... It is all—all Papeete—like a Renaissance Italy with the venom taken out, No, simpler, light-come and light-go, passionate and forgetful, like children, and all the time South Pacific, that is to say unmalicious and good-tempered.

When a steamship was in port the Tiare was a hurly-burly. Perhaps forty or even a hundred extra patrons came for meals or drinks. It was amusing to hear their uncomprehending anger at their failure to obtain quick service or even a smile by their accustomed manner toward dark peoples. The British, who were the majority of the travelers, have a cold, autocratic attitude toward all who wait upon them, but especially toward those of the colored races. In Tahiti they suffered utter dismay, because Tahitians know no servitude and pay no attention to sharp words.

I saw a red-faced woman giving an order for apéritifs to To Sen, the Chinese waiter.

"Two old-fashioned gin cocktails," she iterated. "You savee, gin and bitters? Be sure it's Angostura, and lemon and soda, and two Manhattans with rye whisky. Hurry along now! Old-fashioned, remember!"

In ten minutes Temanu came for the order. To Sen knew no English, and Temanu only, "Yais, ma darleeng," and "Whatnahell?"

"Spik Furanche?" she begged.

"Oui, oui!" said the red-faced lady. "Dooze cocktail! Vous savez cocktail, à la mode des ancients? Gin, oon dash bittair, lem' et soda!"

"Mais, madame, douze cocktail!" and the half-caste Chinese girl held up all her fingers and added two more. *"Vous n'êtes que quatre ici! Quatre cocktails, n'est-ce pas?"*

"Dooze gin, dooze Manhattan? My heavens! They ought to understand my French in this out-of-the-way place when they do in Paris. Listen! *Dooze* is two in French," and she held up two pudgy fingers. But Temanu was gone and returned with four cocktails made after her own liking.

All the girls, Atupu, Iromea, Pepe, Maru, Tetua, and Mme. Rose and Mama-Maru, helped in the service, some beginning with shoes and stockings, but soon slipping them off as the crowd grew and their feet became weary. Lovaina herself moved happily about the *salle-à-manger* telling her friends that she was a grandmother. A letter had given the information that her daughter had a child. She was a doting parent, and we all must toast the newborn. Two grave professors of the University of California, ichthyologists or entomologists, sat entranced at the unconventionality of the scene, drinking *vin ordinaire* and gazing at the Tahitian girls, or eating breadfruit, raw fish, and *taro,* as if they were on Mars and did not know how they got there.

I saw an entry in Lovaina's day-book on the table:

"Germani to Fany   3 feathers."

This was a charge made by Atupu against a Dane for three cocktails. He took his meals at Mme. Klopfer's restaurant. Her first name is Fanny, and Atupu thinks all men not English, French, or Americans, are Germans; so she identified the Dane as the German who went to Fanny's for his meals.

Lovaina said to me:

"I hear you look one house that maybe you rent. You don't get wise if you rent from that French woman. I don't say nothing about her, but you know her tongue? So sharp jus' like knife. All time she have trouble. Can't rent her house so sharp. Some artist he rent; she take box, peep over see what he do jus' because he have some girl. Nobody talk her down. No, I take back. Jus' one French woman who know to swear turribil. This swear woman she call her turribil name and say, 'Everybody don't know you was convict in Noumea for killing one man for money.' That turribil talk, and she jus' fell down. Good for her, I think."

Lovaina seldom rode in her automobile, which she kept primarily for renting to guests for country tours. She had had for years a carriage, a surrey, drawn by one horse, which had grown old and rickety with the vehicle. The driver was a mute, Vava, his name meaning dumb in Tahitian, and the English and Americans called him the Dummy. He was attached to Lovaina as a child to his mother—a wayward, jealous, cloudy-minded child, who almost daily broke into fits of anger over incidents misunderstood by his groping mentality, and because of his incommunicable feelings. The hotel was in a fearsome uproar when Vava fell into a tantrum, women patrons afraid of his possible actions and men threatening to club him into a mild frame of mind. I doubt if any one there could have subdued him physically, for he was a thick-bodied man in his thirties, with a stamina and a strength incredibly developed. I had seen him once lift over a fence a barrel of flour, two hundred pounds in weight, and without full effort. His skin was very dark, his facial expression one of ire and frustration, but of conscious superiority to all about him. He had had no aids to overcome his natal infirmity of deafness and consequent dumbness, none of the educational assistance modern science lends these unfortunates, no finger alphabet, or even another inarticulate for sympathy. He was like the mutes of history, of courts and romances, condemned to suffer in silence the humor and contempt of all about him, though he felt himself better than they in body and in the understanding of things, which he could not make them know. This repression made him often like a wild beast, though mostly he was half-clown and half-infant in his conduct. He had a gift of mimicry incomparably finer than any professional's I knew of. This, with his gestures, stood him instead of speech. A certain haughty English woman whose elaborate hats in an island where women were hatless, or wore simple, native weaves, were noted atrocities, and whose chin was almost nil, kept the carriage and me waiting for breakfast while she primped in her lodging. The Dummy uttered one of his abortive sounds, much like that of an angry puma, contorted his face, and put his hand above his head, so that I had a very vivid suggestion of the lady, her sloping chin and her hat, at which all Papeete laughed. Vava's gesticulations and grimaces were unerring cartoons without paper or ink. If one could have seen him draw one-self, one's pride would have tumbled. He saw the most ridiculous aspect of one. His indication of Lovaina's figure made one shriek, and the governor would have sentenced him for lese-majesty had he seen himself taken off. The sounds he made in which he greeted any one he liked, or in anger, were terrible, dismaying. They; must have been those made by our ancestors, the first primates, when they began the struggle toward intelligent language. Vava's sounds were as the muttering of an ape, deep in his throat, or, when he was roused, high and shrill, like the cry of a rabbit when the hound seizes it. He could make Lovaina know anything he wanted to, and she could direct him to do anything she wished. In that house of mirth, brightness, and laughter, he was as a cunning and, at times, hateful jester, feared by the Tahitians, and, indeed, to whites a shadowy skeleton at the feast, a thing of indescribable possibilities. I knew him, he liked me, and I drew from him by motions and expressions some measure of his feelings and sufferings. But I, too, occasionally, shuddered at the animal cries and frightful grimaces wrung from him in beating down his soul bent on murder.

Lovaina was a spendthrift, giving money liberally to relatives, lending it to improvident borrowers, and dispensing it with open hands when she had it, though always herself in debt. Yet she liked to make money, and to have her hotel filled with tourists who patronized her little bar or drank at meals other wines than the excellent Bordeaux, white or red, which was free with food. Most she loved the appearance of prosperity, the crowding of casual voyagers on steamer-days, the visit of war-ships, the sound of music in her parlor, the rustling of dancers, and the laughter and excitement when the maids were busied carrying champagne and cheaper drinks to the verandas.

I saw her at her best when *El Presidente Sarmiento,* an Argentine training-ship, came to port with a hundred cadets. A madness then possessed the girls of Tahiti.

Forsaking their old loves or those of the moment, they threw themselves into the arms of the visitors, determined on conquest. The quays where the launches of the *Sarmiento* landed their passengers, and the streets about the saloons, restaurants, and theaters, were thronged with the fairest and gayest girls of the island. They poured in from the country to share in the lovemaking. The cafés were filled with dancing and singing crowds, the volatile Argentineans matching the Tahitians in abandon and ardor.

Accordions, violins, guitars, and mandolins were played everywhere. The scores of public automobiles were engaged by joyous parties who sallied to the rural resorts, each Juan with his *vahine.* Mostly unable to exchange a word, they were kissing and embracing in their seats. The ship had been there a year before, and many of the men were hunting former sweethearts. They found that very difficult, as they had not accurate descriptions.

"A beauty named Atupu," or "A black-eyed girl?" They had no aid among the girls they interrogated.

"Why bother with some one who may be dead when we are here?" they asked. And Juan listened to the sirens and rested content.

At Lovaina's there were seventy to dinner. Captain and officers were cheek by jowl with gunners and plain sailors. The veranda was jammed with tables, corks hitting the ceiling, glasses clinking, and Spanish, French, English, and Tahitian confused in the chatter and the shouts of To Sen, Hon Son, the maids, and a dozen friends of the hostess who always came at such times to share the glory of the service.

Lovaina was at the serving-table with volunteers cutting cakes and taking the money. The parlor, with its red and blue plush chairs, was filled with Argentineans playing the piano and singing songs of their country. Suddenly Lovaina discovered that some one had stolen the album of portraits from the piano-top. These were of her family, and of notable visitors who had written grateful notes after their return home, and sent their pictures to her. Professor Hart, teacher of English aboard the *Sarmiento,* was asked to find the thief, and he promised that he would have the ship searched.

Lovaina lamented her loss, but counted her sovereigns. The Argentineans had English gold, and Lovaina passed the shining, new pieces from one hand to the other, enjoying their glitter and sound. She liked to play with coins, and often amused herself as did the king in the blackbird-pie melody.

"My God!" said Lovaina, as she pulled me down to her bench and rubbed my back, "that Argentina is good country! Forty dollars lime squash by himself." She opened her purse, and poured out more gold. With it fell a cloth medallion, red letters on white flannel, "The Apostleship of Prayer in League with the Sacred Heart of Jesus."

"I find that on the floor two day' 'go," said Lovaina, "and I put it in purse to see if good luck. What you think? Argentinas come in nex' day. I don' know, but that thing is good to me. See those bottle' champagne goin' in?"

Perhaps I shall carry longer than any other memory of Tahiti that of the endearing nature, the honest heart, and the laughing, starry eyes of Lovaina, with a *tiarè*-blossom over her ear, or a chaplet of those flowers upon her head, as she sat on her throne behind the serving-table, and I on the camphor-wood chest.

Chapter V

The Parc de Bougainville—Ivan Stroganoff—He tells me the history of Tahiti—He berates the Tahitians—Wants me to start a newspaper.

In the parc de Bougainville I sat down on a bench on which was an old European. He was reading a tattered number of "Simplicissimus," and held the paper close to his watery eyes. I said, "Good morning" and he replied in fluent though accented English.

His appearance was eccentric. He was stout, and with a rough, white beard all over his face and neck, and even on his chest. He wore a frock coat and a large cow-boy hat of white felt. His sockless feet were in old base-ball shoes of "eelskin," which were of the exact color of his coat, a dull green, like moldy, dried peas. Apparently the coat was his only garment; but it was capacious, and came almost to his knobby knees. Missing buttons down its front were replaced by bits of cord or rope. The pockets were stuffed with papers, mangos, and a hunk of bread. A stump of lead-pencil was behind his ear. His hair, a dusty white, met the frayed collar of the coat, and through the temporary gaps which he made in its length to cool his body, I saw it like a gnarled and mossy tree. His hands were grimy and his nails black-edged, but there was intellect in his eye, and a broken force in his huddled, loosed attitude. He was not decrepit, or with a trace of humility, but had the ease of the philosopher and also his detachment. It was plain he did the best he could with his garb, and was entirely undisturbed, and perhaps even unmindful, of its ludicrousness. He was as serene as Diogenes must have been when he crawled naked from his tub into the sun.

We talked first of the horses in the lagoon a dozen yards from us, their grooms or their owners submerging them, and squatting on the ground to chat as the horses wallowed willingly in five feet of salt water. We agreed that the Tahitians were as bad drivers as the Chinese, and that they were, wittingly or unwittingly, cruel to their beasts of burden. This led to a discussion of native traits, and he was caustic in his castigation of the Tahitians. He asked me my name and what brought me to Tahiti; and when, wanting to be as honest-spoken as he, I said, "Romance, adventure," he burst out that I was crazy.

"I have been here seventeen years," he said bitterly—"me, Ivan Stroganoff, who was once happy as secretary to the governor of Irkutsk! I was better off when I was on the *Merrimac* fighting the *Monitor*, or with Mosby, the guerilla, than I am in this accursed island. I think a man is mad who can leave Tahiti and stays here. I wish I could go away. I would like to die elsewhere. I am eighty years old, I starve here, and I sleep in a chicken-coop in the suburbs."

"You are lodged exactly as was Charlie Stoddard, who wrote 'South Sea Idylls,'" I interposed.

"They have lied always, those writers about Tahiti," said Ivan Stroganoff. "Melville, Loti, Moerenhout, Pallander, your Stevenson,—I don't know that Stoddard,—all are meretricious, with their pomp of words and no truth. I have comparisons to make with other nations. I am more than sixty years a traveler, and I am here seventeen years without cessation, in hell all the time."

"You Russians always like the French. How about their achievements here?" I questioned, hoping to lift his shade of melancholy.

"The French?" he repeated. "They are brigands and weak governors. They have been in Tahiti four generations. Do you want to know how they got hold here? A monarchy, a foolish Louis, sent a marine savant and soldier named Dumont D'Urville to the South Seas with the casual orders:

" '*D'apprivoiser les hommes, et de rendre les femmes un peu plus sauvages*;' to tame the men and make the women a little more savage. The French did both, and took all of this part of the world they could find unseized by Europe, and tamable, at not too great a shedding of French blood. They said that it was their duty to restore Temoana his kingdom in the Marquesas Islands, eight hundred miles from here, northward, Temoana had been a singer of psalms at the Protestant mission in his valley of Tai-o-hae, in the island of Nukahiva, a victim of shanghaiers, a cook on a whaler, a tattooed man in English penny shows, a repatriate, a protege of the Catholic archbishop of the Marquesans, and finally, through the influence of the Roman church, a king. He worked damned hard for the French flag and the church, and the generous colonial bureau of France paid his widow a pension of ten dollars a month until she died of melancholy among the nuns. I knew her and I knew men who knew him. He was given a gorgeous uniform of gold lace by his promoters, which I think killed him, though when he sweated, he would strip to his handsomely marked skin and sit naked in the breeze. The queen never wore more than a diaper or a gown.

"With the Marquesas Islands taken, the French warships came to Tahiti. French Catholic priests had been deported from here because the Protestants were already in possession, and objected to competition, saying that the priests were children of Beelzebub, and taught false doctrines and morals. The Queen of Tahiti, whose dynasty the Protestant missionaries had created, advised the pope's men to seek a heathen people not already worshiping the true God. The zealous priests who had come with explicit commands to found a mission in Tahiti, launched the curse of Rome upon the king, the Protestant ministers, and especially upon Mr. Pritchard, the British consul and the queen's physician and spiritual adviser.

"Pritchard had the interests of England and the Lord at heart, and his whispers in the queen's ear sent the earnest priests aboard a ship bound for a distant port. They complained, and the French admiral then arrived and pointed his guns at the palace and the Protestant mission, and demanded thirty thousand dollars for the insult to the French flag; and for the jibe at the pope, the matching of every Protestant church in the islands, by a Catholic edifice. The queen had a panic and fled to Moorea in a canoe. The admiral then put Consul Pritchard in jail for ten days, and after chastening his mood, put him on an English ship at sea homeward bound. France and England were showing their teeth at each other over more important differences, which ended in a revolution in Paris and a change of kings, so that the admiral had his way. The queen came back, the priests established their mission and their churches, and the Tahitians with any blood in them went to war again. The French built forts about the island, and killed off with their guns all the natives they could get sight of. Then they took all the other islands around here that England didn't have, declared Tahiti had to be a protectorate in 1843, and in 1880 gave King Pomaré Fifth twelve thousand dollars a year to let them annex his kingdom. You see, after all, his crown was made by the British puritans, and taken from him by the French or Romish Church."

The aged Russian laughed in his huge whiskers. He fished in the rear of his frock and produced the stump of a cigar, for which I yielded a match.

"I found that on the steps of the Roman Catholic bishop's carriage, which was standing near here an hour ago," he said. "They'll tell you that you will burn in hell; but they smoke here, and good Havana tobacco."

"I think it's a pity the Tahitians weren't left alone," I asserted.

He gave me a look such as Diogenes might have given the man who stood in his sunlight. He lit his cigar-end, puffed it diligently for a minute, and then said arbitrarily:

"The Tahitian is, first, a coward, afraid to fight the white; but if he can, in a group or by secret, kill or hurt you, he will. He is treacherous, and the more he pretends to be your friend, the more he connives to cheat you. I should have said first of all that he is lazy, but that is not to be disputed. He was corrupt to begin with, and religion accentuates every evil passion in him. He is a profound hypocrite, and yet a puritan for observance of the ceremonies and interdictions of his faith. He has more guile than a Japanese guide, and in land deals can skin a Moscow Jew. He will sell you land and get the money, and later prove that his father or brother is the real owner, and that relation will do the same, and you will pay several times for the same land. In the Paumotus, where the missionaries are like a swarm of gnats, this deception is threefold as bad."

"But the Tahitians are at least generous," I broke in.

Stroganoff combed his whiskers with a twig of the flamboyant tree under which we sat. He glared at me.

"Generous! If you have money they will overwhelm you with presents, looking for a double return; but if you are poor, they will treat you as dirt under their feet. I know, for I am poor, and I live among them. They are like those mina birds here, which will steal the button off your coat if you do not guard it."

"Does not Christianity improve them?"

"No. The combats between Protestants, Catholics, and Mormons ended all hope of that. They are never sincere except when they become fanatics, and even then they never lose their native superstitions. Beliefs in the ghosts of Tahiti, the *tupapau*, *ihoiho*, and *varua ino*, are common to all of them."

"My dear Mr. Stroganoff," I expostulated, "your czars believed in icons. My grandmother believed in werewolves and banshees, and we burned blessed candles and sprinkled holy water in our houses on All Souls' night to keep away demons. I have seen a clergyman, educated in Paris and Louvain, exorcising devils with bell, book, and candle in Maryland, in one of the oldest and proudest cities of the United States. I have seen the American Governor-General of the Philippines carrying a candle in a procession in honor of a mannikin from a shrine at Antipolo, near Manila. Why, I could tell you—"

"Please, please, let me talk," Ivan Stroganoff interrupted. "What I say is true, nevertheless. The Tahitian has not one good quality. He is not to be compared with the American negro for any desirable trait."

"Do you know the negro?" I asked.

The old man grunted. He relit his cigar, now only an inch long, and said:

"I was on the *Merrimac* when she fought the *Monitor* in two engagements. I was a sailor on other Confederate men-of-war. I was one of Colonel Mosby's guerillas, and was wounded with them. I have lived thirteen years in the United States. I know the coon well. I fought to keep him a slave."

"You are not an American?"

"I am a Russian, an anarchist once, and now I am for Root and Lodge, the stand-pats. I lived in Russia in its darkest days, under several czars, when your life was the forfeit of a wink. I was a lawyer there, a politician, an intrigant. I knew Bebel and Jaurès and the men before them. I lived in Germany many years, in France, in England, anywhere, everywhere. I first came to New York from Siberia. I was broke. The Civil War was on. There were agents of Lee and Jeff Davis in New York seeking sailors. They offered lots of money,—thousands,—and I went along, smuggled into the South by an underground road."

Stroganoff threw away the shreds of tobacco, now a mere fiery wafer that threatened his mouth's seine of silver strands. He put his hand in his Prince Albert and scratched his stomach.

"Mr. Stroganoff," I queried, with a moral tide rising, "how could you join in a life-and-death issue like that of the Civil War, and kill men without hatred of their cause in your heart?"

He patted my shoulder.

"My dear young American," he replied, "you join anything, even a sheriff's posse, into which you are dragged, and have a bullet from the other side slit your ear, or a round shot bang against your deck, and you'll soon convince yourself that you are in the right, or, anyway, that your adversary is a scoundrel. I handled a gun on the *Merrimac* in Hampton Roads when that cheese-box of a *Monitor* rattled her solid shot on our slippery sides. I was two years in that damned un-Civil War, and as I started on the Southern side, I stayed on it. I left the navy to go with John Mosby and burn houses. When the war was over, and I recovered from my wound, I went to 'Frisco and crossed to Siberia, and thus back to Moscow. No, I never was an exile in Siberia or in a Russian prison. I knew and worked for the leaders of the old Nihilists. I was with them till I knew them, and then I saw they were selfish and fakers. I knew the socialist chiefs in France and Germany, the fathers of the present movement there. I was red-hot for the cause until I knew them, and I quit."

He sat meditatively for a few moments.

"I'm all but eighty years old," the raider of the '60's continued sorrowfully. "I work now for Chinese, preparing their mail, their custom-house papers, and orders. I scrape along like a watch-dog in a sausage factory, getting sufficient to eat, but fearful all the time that the job will kill me. Most of the time I live a few kilometers from Papeete, toward Fa'a, and come in to town about steamer-time. I sleep in the chicken-coop or anywhere. I make about forty francs a month." He stamped upon the grass. "I take it you are a journalist, and, do you know, what is needed here most is publicity. Graft permeates the whole scheme. Mind you, there are no secrets. You could not whisper anything to a cocoanut-tree but that the entire island would know it to-morrow. But there is no open publicity. Start a newspaper!"

"In what language?" I demanded, interested.

"Huh? That's it. If in French, only the French would read it; and if in Tahitian, the French won't touch it; and English is known only by the Chinese and the few British and Americans here. I hate that Tahitian. I don't know a word of it after seventeen years. Say what you will, Roosevelt made them stand around. I liked him for many things; but, after all, the old order must stand, and Root is the boy for me. This fellow Wilson is a regular pedagogue."

"But they have newspapers here?" I asked.

"Newspapers? They call them that."

He stood up and searched in the pockets of his voluminous coat, which he opened. I saw that the lining was of silk, but now worn and torn. He brought out a roll of papers.

"Here is 'La Tribune de Tahiti,'" he said. "It is edited by Jean Delpit, the lawyer whose offices are next to the Bellevue Restaurant. It's a monthly, published in San Francisco, and has a brief summary of world events, besides articles on the administrative affairs of Tahiti. It's against the Government. Then there's 'Le Liberal,' a socialist journal, with Eugène Brunschwig editor, which pours hot shot into the Government. Look at his announcement! Do you understand that? He is fierce. He is an anarchist and wants to be bought up. Of course he is attacking from outside Tahiti.

"There is no newspaper printed here except the 'Journal Officiel' which, of course, is not a newspaper, but a gazette of governmental notices, etc. The Government has its own printing-office, but if these other, the 'Tribune' and the 'Liberal,' had establishments here, they would be raided and closed, for they would hardly be allowed to criticize the Government as harshly as they do. The 'Tribune' is in French and Tahitian, the 'Liberal' and the 'Journal Officiel' in French. One time it was recommended that the official paper might be more popular if it had some fiction for the natives, so they printed a translation of 'Ali Baba and the Forty Thieves,' but everybody laughed, so it was dropped.

"The Mormons have the best paper here. It is a monthly, too. There is plenty need here for a fearless newspaper. The faults, weaknesses, and venality of the Government call for publicity, but I'm afraid the journalist might soon find himself in prison. You can do nothing. The fault is in this damned climate—*la fièvre du corail*. Paul Deschanel, senator of France, who wrote a book on this island without ever leaving his chair in Paris, says:

"In presence of the apparent facts one is forced to ask himself if there is not in the climate of this enchanted Tahiti, in the soft air that one breathes, a force sweet but invincible which at length penetrates the soul, enervates the will and enfeebles all sense of usefulness or right, or the least energy necessary to make them triumph.

"It is this spirit, without any harmony, bereft of all real cordiality between neighbors, of family and family, which one must find in the ambient air and which is called the coral fever."

"It torments these French, former sailors or petty officials gone into trade or speculation, with delusions and ambitions of grandeur. There is no remedy. The King of Apamama said it all when he divided the whites into three classes, 'First, him cheat a litty; second, him cheat plenty; and third, him cheat too much.' "

Stroganoff got on his feet, rubbed his knees to limber them, and began to move off slowly toward Fa'a, his place of abode.

"But, Mr. Stroganoff," I called to him, "you said all that about the Tahitians, also."

The Russian octogenarian drew an over-ripe mango from his skirt, and bit into it, with dire results to his whiskers and coat,—it should be eaten only in a bathtub,—and replied wearily:

"I except nobody here."

Chapter VI

The Cercle Bougainville—Officialdom in Tahiti—My first visit to the Bougainville—Skippers and merchants—A song and a drink—The flavor of the South Seas—Rumors of war.

In Papeete there were two social clubs, the Cercle Bougainville and the Cercle Militaire. Even in Papeete, which has not half as many people as work in a certain building in New York, there is a bureaucracy, and the Cercle Militaire, in a park near the executive mansion on the rue de Rivoli, is its arcanum. Only members of the Government may belong, and a few others whose proposals must be stamped by the political powers. There is a garden, with a small library, but not many read in this climate, and the atmosphere of the Cercle Militaire was tedious. The governor himself and the black *procureur de la Republique*, born in Martinique, the secretary-general, naval officers, and the file of the upper office-holders frequent the shade of the mangos and the palms, but themselves confessed it deadly dull there. Bureaucracy is ever mediocre, ever jealous, and in Papeete the feuds among the whites were as bitter as in a monastery or convent. Every man crouched to leap over his fellow, if not by position, at least by acclaim. None dared to discuss political affairs openly, but nothing else was talked of. It was a round of whispered charges and recriminations and audible compliments. A few jolly chaps, doctors or naval lieutenants, passed the bottle and laughed at the others.

Every now and then a new governor supplanted the incumbent, who returned to France, and a few of the chiefer officials were changed; but the most of them were Tahitian French by birth or long residence. Republics are wretched managers of colonies, and monarchies brutal exploiters of subject peoples. Politics controlled in the South Seas, as in the Philippines, India, and Egypt. Precedence at public gatherings often caused hatreds. The *procureur* was second in rank here, the governor, of course, first, the secretary-general third, and the attorney-general fourth. When the secretary-general was not at functions, the wife of the governor must be handed in to dinner and dances by the negro *procureur*. This angered the British and American consuls and merchants, and the French inferior to him in social status, although the Martinique statesman was better educated and more cultivated in manners than they.

The indolence of mind and body that few escape in this soft, delicious air, the autocracy of the governing at such a distance from France, and the calls of Paris for the humble taxes of the Tahitians, robbed the island of any but the most pressing melioration. The business of government in these archipelagoes was bizarre comedy-drama, with *Tartarins* at the front of the stage, and a cursing or slumbrous audience.

Count Polonsky, a Russian-born Frenchman, appeared in court to answer to the charge of letting his automobile engine run when no one was in the car. He was fined a franc, which he would take from his pocket then and there, but must wait many days to pay, until circumlocution had its round, six weeks after the engine had been at fault. I was assessed two sous duty on a tooth-brush. I reached for the coins.

"*Mais, non*" said the *préposé de le douane*, "*pas maintenant.* No hurry. We will inform you by post."

These officials had pleasing manners, as do almost all Frenchmen, and though they uttered many *sacrés* against the home Government and that of these islands, they were fiercely chauvinistic toward foreigners, as are all nationals abroad where jingoism partakes of self-aggrandizement. The American consul, a new appointee, addressed the customs clerk in his only tongue, Iowan, and received no response. I spoke to him in French, and the *préposé* replied in mixed French and English, out of compliment to me. The consul was enraged, considering himself and the American eagle affronted. I interposed, but the customs-man answered coldly in English:

"This is a French possession, and French is the language, or Tahitian. I speak both. Why don't you? You are supposedly an educated man."

The Stars and Stripes were unfolded in a breeze of hot words that betrayed the consul's belief in the *préposé*'s sinister ancestry and in eternal punishment. No entente cordiale could ever be cemented after that lingual blast.

The consuls all had honorary memberships in the Cercle Militaire, and none of them entered the Cercle Bougainville, it not being *de rigueur*. I had a *carte d'invite personelle* to that club, and there I went with roused curiosity to hear the other sides of questions already settled for me by the amiable officials and officers on the rue de Rivoli. I had been warned against the Cercle Bougainville by staid pensioners as being the resort of commoners and worse, of British and American ruffians, of French vulgarians, and of Chinese smugglers. This advice made a seductive advertisement of the club to me, anxious to know everything real and unveiled about the life here, and to find a contrast to the ennui of the official temple.

A consul said to me: "Look out for some of those gamblers in that Bougainville joint! They'll skin you alive. They drink like conger-eels."

M. Leboucher, my fellow-passenger on the *Noa-Noa*, sent me the card to the Jacobin resort, and I got in the habit of going there just before the meat breakfast and before dinner. I found that the warning of the aristocratic bureaucrats was of a piece with their philosophy and manners, hollow, hypocritical, and calculated to deny me the only real human companionship I could endure. From about eleven to one o'clock and from five until seven, and in the evenings, the Cercle Bougainville held more interesting and merry white skins than the remainder of Tahiti. Merchants and managers of enterprises and shops, skippers of the schooners that comb the Dangerous Archipelago and the dark Marquesas for pearl and shell and copra, vanilla- and pearl-buyers, planters, and lesser bureaucrats, idlers or retired adventurers living in Tahiti, and tourists made the club for a few hours a day a polyglot exchange of current topics between man and man, a place of initiation and of judgment of business deals, a precious refuge against smug bores and a sanctuary for refreshment of body and soul with cooling drinks. Naturally, every one played cards, dominoes, or dice for the honor of signing the *chits*, and it goes without saying that one might roar out an oath against the Government and go unscathed. Even in the Bougainville lines were drawn; only heads of commercial affairs were admitted. It was bourgeois absolutely, but bosses could not imbibe and play freely in the presence of their employees whom they might have to reprimand severely for bad habits, nor scold them for inattention to trade when their employers spent precious hours at écarté or razzle-dazzle.

The club was within fifty feet of the lagoon, close to the steamship quay, its broad verandas overlooking the fulgent reef and the quiet waters within it. In odd hours one might find Joseph, the steward, angling on the coral wall for the black and gold fish, and a shout from the balcony would bring him to the swift succor of a thirsty member. During the four hours before the late *déjeuner* and dinner, he had incessant work to answer the continuous calls.

When Joseph became overwhelmed with orders he summoned his family from secret quarters in the rear, and father, mother, and children squeezed, shook, and poured for the impatient crowd.

When the monthly mail between America and Australasia was in, few packs of cards were sold, for every one was busied with letters and orders for goods. But only three or four days a month were so disturbed, and for nearly four weeks of the month Papeete lolled at ease, with endless time for games and stimulants. Leisure, the most valuable coin of humanity in the tropics, was spent by white or brown in pleasure or idleness with a prodigality that would have made Samuel Smiles weep.

The entrance to the Cercle Bougainville was very plain, with no name-plate, as had the Militaire,—a mere hole in the front wall of Leboucher's large furniture shop. One could be going along the street in full view of important and respectable people, and suddenly disappear. A few steep stairs, a quick turn, and one was on the broad balcony, with easy-chairs and firm tables, and bells to hand for Joseph's ear.

In a room off the balcony there was a billiard-table, the cloth patched or missing in many spots, and with cues whose tips had long since succumbed to perpetual moisture. A few old French books were on a shelf, and a naughty review or two of Paris on a dusty table. Undoubtedly, this club had begun as a mariner's association, and there was yet a decided flavor of the sea about it. Indeed, all Tahiti was of the sea, and all but the mass of natives who stayed in their little homes were at times sailors, and all whites passengers on long voyages. Everything paid tribute to the vast ocean, and all these men had an air of ships and the dangers of the waves.

Nautical almanacs, charts, and a barometer were conspicuous, and often were laid beside the social glasses for proof in hot arguments. Occasionally an old Chinese or two, financiers, pearl-dealers, labor bosses, or merchants, drained a glass of *eau de vie* and smoked a cigarette there. One sensed an atmosphere of mystery, of secret arrangements between traders, or hard endeavors for circumvention of competitors in the business of the dispersed islands of French Oceania.

A delightful incident enlivened my first visit, and gave me an acquaintance with a group of habitués, When I reached the balcony I saw a group of Frenchmen at a table who were singing at the top of their voices. I sat down at the farthest table and ordered a Dr. Funk.

I did not look at them, for I felt *de trop;* but suddenly I heard them humming the air of "John Brown's Body," and singing fugitive words.

"Grory, grory, harreruah!" came to my ears, and later, "Wayd' 'un S'ut' in le land de cottin."

They were making fun of me I thought, and turned my head away. It would not do to get angry with half a dozen jovial Frenchmen.

"All Coons Look alike to Me," I recognized, though they sang but fragments of the text.

Through a corner of my eye I saw them all anxiously staring at me; then one of the merrymakers came over to me. I had a fleeting thought of a row before he bowed low and said in English:

"If you please, we make good time, we sing your songs, and must be happy to drink with you."

He announced himself as M. Edmond Brault, chief clerk of the office of the secretary-general, fresh-faced, glowing and with a soul for music and for joy.

He was so smiling, so ingenuous, that to refuse him would have been rank discourtesy. I joined the group.

"I am twenty-eight times married this day," said M. Brault, "and my friends and I make very happy."

The good husband was rejoicing on his wedding anniversary, and I could but accept the champagne he ordered. "I am great satisfaction to drink you," he said. "My friends drink my wife and me."

We toasted his admirable wife, we toasted the two republics; Lafayette, Rochambeau, and Chateaubriand.

"*Ah, le biftek!*" said M. Leboucher.

We toasted Thomas Jefferson and Benjamin Franklin, and then we sang for an hour. M. Brault was the leading composer of Tahiti. He was the creator of Tahitian melodies, as *Kappelmeister* Berger was of Hawaiian. For our delectation Brault sang ten of his songs between toasts. I liked best "*Le Bon Roi Pomare*," the words of one of the many stanzas being:

Il était un excellent roi
Dont on ne dit rien dans l'histoire,
Qui ne connaissait qu'une Loi:
Celle de chanter, rire, et boire.
Fervent disciple de Bacchus
Il glorifiait sa puissance,
Puis, sacrifiait à Venus
Les loisirs de son existence.
REFRAIN:

Toujours joyeux, d'humeur gauloise,
Et parfois même un peu grivoise
Le généreux Roi Pomarè
Par son peuple est fort regretté.
S'il avait eu de l'eloquence
Il aurait gouverné la France!
Mais nos regrets sont superflus;
Puisqu'il est mort, n'en parlons plus!

"Ah, he was a chic type, that last King of Tahiti," said M. Brault, who had written so many praiseful, merry verses about him. "He would have a *hula* about him all the time. He loved the national dance. He would sit or lie and drink all day and night. He loved to see young people drink and enjoy themselves. Ah, those were gay times! Dancing the nights away. Every one crowned with flowers, and rum and champagne like the falls of Fautaua. The good king Pomaré would keep up the *upaupa*, the *hula* dance, for a a week at a time, until they were nearly all dead from drink and fatigue. *Mon dieu! La vie est triste maintenant.*"

Before we parted we sang the "Marseillaise" and the "Star-Spangled Banner." Nobody knew the words, I least of any; so we la-la-la'd through it, and when we parted for luncheon, we went down the crooked stairway arm in arm, still giving forth snatches of "Le Bon Roi Pomaré" in honor of our host:

Mais, s'il aimait tant les plaisirs,
Les chants joyeux, la vie en rose,
Le plus ardent de ses désirs,
Pour lui la plus heureuse chose,
Fut toujours que l'humanité
Regnât au sein de son Royaume;
De même que l'Egalité
Sous son modeste toit de chaume.

Hallman, with whom I journeyed on the *Noa-Noa*, dropped into the Cercle Bougainville occasionally, but he was ordinarily too much occupied with his schemes of trade. Besides, he had only one absorbing vice other than business, and with merely wine and song to be found at the club, Hallman went there but seldom, and only to talk about pearl-shell, copra, and the profits of schooner voyages. However, through him I met another group who spoke English, and who were not of Latin blood. They were Llewellyn, an islander—Welsh and Tahitian; Landers, a New Zealander; Pincher, an Englishman; David, McHenry, and Brown, Americans; Count Polonsky, the Russo-Frenchman who was fined a franc; and several captains of vessels who sailed between Tahiti and the Pacific coast of the United States or in these latitudes.

The *Noa-Noa* was overdue from New Zealand, by way of Raratonga, and her tardiness was the chief subject of conversation at our first meeting. A hundred times a day was the semaphore on the hill spied at for the signal of the *Noa-Noa's* sighting. High up on the expansive green slope which rises a few hundred feet behind the Tiare Hotel is a white pole, and on this are hung various objects which tell the people of Papeete that a vessel is within view of the ancient sentinel of the mount. An elaborate code in the houses of all persons of importance, and in all stores and clubs, interprets these symbols. The merchants depended to a considerable extent upon this monthly liner between San Francisco and Wellington and way ports, and all were interested in the mail and food supplies expected by the *Noa-Noa*. Cablegrams sent from any part of the world to New Zealand or San Francisco were forwarded by mail on these steamships. Tahiti was entirely cut off from the great continents except by vessel. There was no cable, and no wireless, on this island, nor even at the British island of Raratonga, two days' steaming from Papeete. The steamships had wireless systems, and kept in communication with San Francisco or with New Zealand ports for a few days after departure.

There were many guesses at the cause of the delay.

"Nothing but war!" said the French post-office clerk who sat at another table, with his glass of Pernoud. "Germany and England have come to blows. Now that accursed nation of beer-swillers will get their lesson."

The subject was seriously discussed, the armaments of the two powers quoted, and the certainty of Germany's defeat predicted, the Frenchman asserting vehemently that France would aid England if necessary, or to get back Alsace-Lorraine. There were gatherings all over Papeete, the war rumor having been made an alleged certainty by some inexplicable communication to an unnamed merchant.

The natives hoped fervently that the war was between France and Germany, and that France would be defeated. After generations of rule by France, the vanquished still felt an aversion to their conquerors here, as in the Holy Land when Herod ruled.

"I hope France get his," said a chief, aside, to me.

The mail's delay upset all business. Letters closed on the day the liner was expected were reopened. For three days the girls at Lovaina's had worn their best peignoirs, and several times donned shoes and stockings to go to the quay. Passengers for San Francisco who had packed their trunks had unpacked them. The air of expectancy which Papeete wore for a day or two before steamer-day had been so heated by postponement that nerves came to the surface.

Tahiti was a place of no exact knowledge. Few residents knew the names of the streets. Some of the larger business houses had no signs to indicate the firms' names or what they sold. Hardly any one knew the names of the trees or the flowers or fishes or shells.

A story once told, even facts thoroughly well known, changed with each repetition. A month after an occurrence one might search in vain for the actuality. It was more difficult to learn truthful details than anywhere I had been. The French are niggardly of publications concerning Tahiti. An almanac once a year contained a few figures and facts of interest, but with no newspapers within thousands of miles, every person was his own journal, and prejudices and interest dictated all oral records.

McHenry hushed war reports to talk about Brown, an American merchant who had left the club a moment before, after a Bourbon straight alone at the bar. McHenry was a trader, mariner, adventurer, gambler, and boaster. Rough and ready, witty, profane, and obscene, he bubbled over with tales of reef and sea, of women and men he had met, of lawless tricks on natives, of storm and starvation, and of his claimed illicit loves. Loud-mouthed, bullet-headed, beady-eyed, a chunk of rank flesh shaped by a hundred sordid deeds, he must get the center of attention by any hazard.

"Brown's purty stuck up now," he said acridly. "I remember the time when he didn't have a pot to cook in. He had thirty Chile dollars a month wages. We come on the beach the same day in the same ship. His shoes were busted out, and he was crazy to get money for a new girl he had. There was a Chink had eighteen tins of vanilla-beans worth about two hundred American dollars each. He got the Chink to believe he could handle the vanilla for him, and got hold of it, and then out by the vegetable garden Brown hit the poor devil of a Chink over the nut with a club."

McHenry got up from the table, and with Llewellyn's walking-stick showed exactly how the blow was struck. He brought down the cane so viciously against the edge of the table that he spilled our rum punches.

"Mac," exclaimed Llewellyn, testily, as he shot him a hot glance from the melancholy eyes under his black thatch of brows, "behave yourself! You know you're lying."

McHenry laughed sourly, and went on:

"I was chums with Brown then, and when I caught up to him,—I was walkin' behind them,—he asked me to see if the Chink was dead. I went back to where he had tumbled him. He was layin' on his back in a kind o' ditch, and he was white instead o' yeller. He was white as Lyin' Bill's schooner. How would you 'a' done? Well, to protect that dirty pup Brown, I covered him over with leaves from head to foot—big bread-fruit and cocoanut-leaves. He never showed up again, and Brown had the vanilla. That's how he got his start, and, so help me God! I never got a franc from the business."

There was venom in McHenry's tone, and he looked at me, the newcomer, to see what impression he had made. The others said not a word of comment, and it may have been an often-told tale by him. He had emptied his glass of the potent Martinique rum four or five times.

"Was the Chinaman sure dead when you put the leaves over him?" I asked, influenced by his staring eyes.

McHenry grinned foully.

"Aye, man, you want too much," he replied. "I say his face was white, and he was on his back in the marsh. If he was alive, the leaves didn't finish him, and if he was croaked, it didn't matter. I was obligin' a friend. You'd have done as much." He took up his glass and muttered dramatically, "A few leaves for a friend."

I shuddered, but Landers leaned over the table and said to me, *sotto voce*:

"McHenry's tellin' his usual bloody lie. Brown got the vanilla all right, but what he did was to have the bloomin' Chink consign it to him proper', and not give him a receipt. Then he denied all knowledge of it, and it bein' all the bleedin' Chinaman had, he died of a broken heart—with maybe too many pipes of opium to help him on a bit. McHenry and Pincher are terrible liars. They call Pincher 'Lyin' Bill,' though I 'd take his word in trade or about schooners any day."

I had been introduced to a Doctor Funk by Count Polonsky, who told me it was made of a portion of absinthe, a dash of grenadine,—a syrup of the pomegranate fruit,—the juice of two limes, and half a pint of siphon water. Dr. Funk of Samoa, who had been a physician to Robert Louis Stevenson, had left the receipt for the concoction when he was a guest of the club. One paid half a franc for it, and it would restore self-respect and interest in one's surroundings when even Tahiti rum failed.

"Zat was ze drink I mix for Paul Gauguin, ze *peintre sauvage*, here before he go to die in *les îsles Marquises*," remarked Levy, the millionaire pearl-buyer, as he stood by the table to be introduced to me.

"Absinthe *seul* he general' take," said Joseph, the steward.

"I bid fifty thousand francs for one of Gauguin's paintings in Paris last year," Count Polonsky said as he claimed his game of écarté against Tati, the chief of Papara district. "I failed to get it, too. I bought many here for a few thousand francs each before that."

"Blow me!" cried Pincher, the skipper of the *Morning Star*. "'E was a bleedin' ijit. I fetched 'im absinthe many a time in Atuona. 'E said Dr. Funk was a bloomin' ass for inventin' a drink that spoiled good Pernoud with water. 'E was a rare un. 'E was like Stevenson 'at wrote 'Treasure Island.' Comes into my pub in Taiohae in the Marquesas Islands did Stevenson off'n his little *Casco*, and says he, "Ave ye any whisky,' 'e says, 'at 'asn't been watered? These South Seas appear to 'ave flooded every bloomin' gallon,' 'e says. This painter Gauguin wasn't such good company as Stevenson, because 'e parleyvoud, but 'e was a bloody worker with 'is brushes at Atuona. 'E was cuttin' wood or paintin' all the time."

"He was a damn' fool," said Hallman, who had come in to the Cercle to take away Captain Pincher. "I lived close to him at Atuona all the time he was there till he died. He was bughouse. I don't know much about painting, but if you call that crazy stuff of Gauguin's proper painting, then I'm a furbelowed clam."

"*Eh bien*," Count Polonsky said, with a smile of the man of superior knowledge, "he is the greatest painter of this period, and his pictures are bringing high prices now, and will bring the highest pretty soon. I have bought every one I could to hold for a raise."

Polonsky was a study in sheeny hues. He was twenty-seven, his black and naturally curled hair was very thin, there were eight or nine teeth that answered no call from his meat, and he wore in his right eyesocket a round glass, with no rim or string, held by a puckering of cheek and brow, giving him a quizzical, stage-like stare, and twisting his nose into a ripple of tiny wrinkles. He weighed, say, one hundred pounds or less, was bent, but with a fresh complexion and active step. I saw him rise naked from his cot one morning, and the first thing he put on was the rimless monocle. The natives, who name every one, called him *"Matatitiahoe,"* "the one-windowed man." He had journeyed about the world, poked into some queer places, and in Japan had himself tattooed. On his narrow chest he had a terrible legendary god of Nippon, and on his arms a cock and a skeleton, the latter with a fan and a lantern. On his belly was limned a nude woman. He had certain other decorations the fame of which had been bruited wide so that a keen curiosity existed to see them, and they were discussed in whispers by white femininity and with many *"Aues!"* of astonishment by the brown. They were Pompeiian friezes in their unconventionality of subject and treatment.

Llewellyn, McHenry, David, and I accompanied the count to his residence on the outskirts of Papeete to taste a vintage of Burgundy he had sent him from Beaune. Like most modern houses in Tahiti, his was solely utilitarian, and was built by a former American consul. It exactly ministered to the comforts of a demanding European exquisite. The house was framed in wide verandas, and was in a magnificent grove of cocoanut-trees affording beauty and shade, with extensive fields of sugar-cane on the other side of the road, and a glimpse of the beach and lagoon a little distance away. A singing brook ran past the door. The bedrooms were large and open to every breeze, and the tables for dining and amusement mostly set upon the verandas.

Polonsky's toilet-table was covered with gold boxes and bottles and brushes; scents and powders and pastes. If he moved out, Gaby de Lys might have moved in and lacked nothing. He was a *boulevardier*, his clothes from Paris, conforming not at all to the sartorial customs of Tahiti, and his varnished boots and alpine hat, with his saffron automobile, marked him as a person.

In that he resembled Higby, an Englishman in Papeete, who wore the evening dress of London whenever a steamship came in, though it might be noon, and on the king's birthday and other British feasts put it on when he awoke. He was the only man who went to dinner at the Tiare in the funeral garb of society. He said he was setting up a proper standard in Tahiti. It was suspected really that he was short of clothes, with perhaps only one or two cotton suits, and that when those were soiled he had to resort to full dress during the laundering.

Little sister guards her flock

About to plunge in

Photo by Bopp

While David and I inspected the house and grounds, McHenry and Llewellyn sat at the wine. Polonsky had a curious and wisely chosen household. His butler was a Javanese, his chef a Quan-tung Chinese, his valet a Japanese, his chambermaid a Martinique negress, and his chauffeur an American expert. These had nothing in common and could not ally themselves to cheat him, he said.

The haven of Papetoai, in Moorea

As I came back to the front veranda McHenry and Llewellyn were talking excitedly.

"I've had my old lady nineteen years," said McHenry, boastfully, "and she wouldn't speak to me if she met me on the streets of Papeete. She wouldn't dare to in public until I gave her the high sign. You're a bloody fool makin' equals of the natives, and throwin' away money on those cinema girls the way you do."

This incensed Llewellyn, who was of chiefly Tahitian blood, and who claimed kings of Wales as his ancestors. Although extremely aristocratic in his attitude toward strangers, his native strain made him resent McHenry's rascally arrogance as a reflection upon his mother's race.

"Shut up, Mac!" he half shouted. "You talk too much. If it hadn't been for that same old lady of yours, you'd have died of delirium-tremens or fallen into the sea long ago."

"Aye," said the trader, meditatively, "that *vahine* has saved my life, but I'm not goin' to sacrifice my dignity as a white man. If ye let go everything, the damn' natives'll walk over ye, and ye'll make nothin' out o' them."

Lovaina had occasionally called me Dixey, and had explained that I was the "perfec' im'ge" of a man of that name, and that he owned a little cutter which traded to Raiaroa, on which atoll he lived. I walked like him, was of the same size, and had the "same kin' funny face."

She piqued my curiosity, and so when I found him at the round table of the Polonsky-Llewellyn group at the Cercle Bougainville, I looked him over narrowly. His name was Dixon,—Lovaina never got a name right,—an Englishman, a wanderer, with an Eton schooling, short, solidly built, with a bluff jaw and a keen, blue eye. He was not good-looking. He had learned the nickname given me, and was in such a happy frame of mind that he ordered drinks for the club.

"I'm lucky to be here at all," he said seriously. "I have a seven-ton cutter, and left the Paumotus four days ago for Papeete. We had eight tons of copra in the hold, filling it up within a foot of the hatch. Eight miles off Point Venus the night before last, at eleven o'clock, we hoped for a bit of wind to reach port by morning. It was calm, and we were all asleep but the man at the wheel, when a waterspout came right out of the clear sky,—so the steersman said,—and struck us hard. We were swamped in a minute. The water fell on us like your Niagara. Christ! We gave up for gone, all of us, the other five all kanakas. We heeled over until the deck was under water,—of course we've got no freeboard at all,—and suddenly a gale sprung up. We pulled in the canvas, but to no purpose. Under a bare pole we seemed every minute to be going under completely. We have no cabin, and all we could do was to lay flat on the deck in the water, and hold on to anything we could grab. The natives prayed, by God! They're Catholics, and they remembered it then. The mate wanted to throw the copra overboard. I was willing, but I said, 'What for? We're dead men, and it'll do no good. She can't stand up even empty.' We stayed swamped that way all night, expecting to be drowned any minute, and I myself said to the Lord—I was a chorister once—that if I had done anything wrong in my life, I was sorry—"

"But you knew you had?" I interposed.

"Of course I did, but I wasn't going to rub it in on myself in that fix. I knew He knew all about me. My father was a curate in Devon. Well, we pulled through all right, because here I am, and the copra's on the dock. What do you think—the wind died away completely, and we had to sweep in to Papeete."

I touched his glass with mine. He was very ingenuous, a four-square man.

"Did the prayers have anything to do with your pulling through and saving the copra?" I questioned, curious.

"I don't know. I didn't make any fixed promises. I was bloody well scared, and I meant what I said about being sorry. But that's all gone. Let's drink this up and have another. Joseph!"

Hélas! the waterspout did not harm my twin half so much as the rum-spout, which soon had him three sheets in the wind and his rudder unmanageable.

When I went down the rue de Rivoli that night to the Cercle Militaire, he had drifted into the Cocoanut House, and was sitting on a fallen tree telling of the storm to a woman in a scarlet gown with a hibiscus-blossom in her hair. I got him by the arm, and with an expressed desire to know more of the details of the escape, steered him to the Annexe, where he had a room.

A good sort was Dixon. He had in the Paumotus a little store, a dark mother-girl of Raiaroa who waited for him, and a new baby. He had been only a year in the group. He referred to "my family" with honest pride.

The captains of the *Lurline* and the *O. M. Kellogg* were at the club. The *Lurline* was twenty-seven years old, and the *Kellogg*, too, high up in her teens, if not twenties. Their skippers were Americans, the *Kellogg's* master as dark as a negro, burned by thirty years of tropical sun.

"I used to live in Hawaii in the eighties," he said. "I used to pass the pipe there in those days. There'd be only one pipe among a dozen kanakas, and each had a draw or so in turn. They have that custom in the Marquesas, too, and so had the American Indians."

I walked with the *Kellogg's* skipper to his vessel, moored close to the quay in front of the club. He gave an order to the mate, who told him to go to sheol. The mate had been ashore.

"Come aboard," cried the mate, "and I will knock your block off."

The whole waterfront heard the challenge. Stores were deserted to witness the imminent fight.

The dark-faced captain ascended the gang-plank, and walked to the forecastle head, where the mate was directing the making taut a line.

"Now," said the skipper, a foot from the mate, "knock!"

The mate hesitated. That would be a crime; he would go to jail and the captain would be delighted.

The master taunted him:

"Knock my block off! Touch my block, and I'll whip you so your mother wouldn't know you, you dirty, drunken, son of a sea-cook!"

The mate looked at him angrily, but uncertainly. He heard the laughter and the cheers of the bystanders on the quay and in the embowered street. He looked down at the deck, and he caught sight of a capstan-bar, which he gazed at longingly. Any blow would send him to prison, but why not for a sheep instead of a lamb?

He hesitated, and lifted his eyes to the black brow of the skipper, lowering within touch.

"Make fast your line about that cannon!" said the master, sharply.

The sailors waited joyfully for the fray, and the Raratonga stevedores on other vessels stopped their work. But nothing happened.

"Aye, aye, sir," said the mate, and shouted the order to the men ashore. The captain regarded him balefully, muttered a few words, and returned to the club for a Dr. Funk. That medical man ranked here above Colonel Rickey, who invented the gin-rickey in America.

Herr Funk was better known in the Cercle Bougainville than Charcot or Lister or Darwin. The doctor part of the drink's name made it seem almost like a prescription, and often, when amateurs sought to evade a second or third, the old-timers laughed at their fears of ill results, and said:

"That old Doctor Funk knew what he was about. Why, he kept people alive on that mixture. It's like mother's milk."

Chapter VII

The *Noa-Noa* comes to port—Papeete *en fête*—Rare scene at the Tiare Hotel—The New Year celebrated—Excitement at the wharf—Battle of the Limes and Coal.

The *Noa-Noa* came in after many days of suspense, during which rumors and reports of war grew into circumstantial statements of engagements at sea and battles on land. A mysterious vessel was said to have slipped in at night with despatches for the governor. All was sensation and canard, *on dit* and *oui dire*, and all was proved false when the liner came through the passage in the reef. Nothing had happened to disturb the peace of nations, but a dock strike in Auckland had tied up the ship. The relief of mind of the people of Papeete caused a wave of joy to pass over them. Business men and officials, tourists who expected to leave for America and the outside world on the *Noa-Noa*, overflowed with evidence of their delight. The consuls of the powers met at the Cercle Militaire the governor, and laughed hectically at the absurd balloon of tittle-tattle which had been pricked by the *Noa-Noa's* facts. There had been absolutely nothing to the rumors but the fears or the antipathies of nationals in Tahiti.

It was the holiday season, the New Year at hand, and, moreover, there was added cause for rejoicing in the safety of the *Saint Michel*, a French-owned inter-island steamship which had been missing six weeks. She had left one of the Paumotu atolls and failed to reach her next port, thirty miles away. Rumor had sent her to the bottom. She was a crank vessel, with a perpetual list, and a roll of twenty-five degrees in the quietest sea; the dread of all compelled by affairs to take passage on her.

"She's sunk; rolled over too much, and turned turtle," was the verdict at the Cercle Bougainville. Her agents had sent the *Cholita*, a small power schooner, to go over the *Saint Michel's* course, and find trace of her, if possible. Imagine the excitement along the waterfront when, almost coincident with the sighting of the *Noa-Noa*, the *Saint Michel* appeared, pulled by the *Cholita*. Familiar faces of passengers appeared on her deck as she made fast to the quay, holding cigarettes as if they had waked up after a night in their own beds. The *Cholita* had found the *Saint Michel* at the Marquesas Islands, whither she had drifted after losing her rudder on a rock. After a month lying inert at the Marquesas, the *Cholita* had taken hold and dragged the crippled *Saint* back to Papeete.

The joy and surprise of the families and friends of the passengers and the crew must have the vent usual here, and what with the *Noa-Noa's* crew of amateur sailors, firemen, and yachtsman, and six licensed captains, taking the places of the strikers, the town was filled with pleasure-seekers. A high mass of thanksgiving at the cathedral was followed by a day of explanations, anathemas upon the owners of the *Saint Michel*, and the striking labor-unions, and of music, dancing, and toasts.

New Year's eve, two picture shows, hulas, and the festivities of the wedding of Cowan, the prize-fighter, brought in a throng from the districts to add to the Papeete population and the voyagers.

The streets were a blaze of colored gowns and flower-crowned girls and women. The quays were lined with singing and playing country folk. Small boats and canoes were arriving every few minutes during the afternoon with natives who preferred the water route to the Broom Road. Cowan was a favorite boxer, and shortly to face the noted Christchurch Kid, of Christchurch, New Zealand, whose fist was described on the bill-boards as "a rock thrown by a mighty slinger." Cowan, a half-Polynesian, was beloved for his island blood, and was marrying into a Tahitian family of note and means. The nuptials at the church were preceded by a triumphal procession of the bride and groom in an automobile, with a score of other cars following, the entire party gorgeously adorned with wreaths,—*hei* in Tahitian,—and the vehicles lavishly decorated with sugar-cane and bamboo tassels. The band of the cinema led the *entourage*, and played a free choice of appropriate music, "Lohengrin" before the governor's palace, and "There'll be a Hot Time in the Old Town To-night" as they passed Lovaina's. The company sang lustily, and toasts to the embracing couple were drunk generously from spouting champagne-bottles as the cortege circled the principal streets.

There was rare life at Lovaina's, for besides all the diners in ordinary and extraordinary in the *salle-à-manger*, Stevens, the London stockbroker, had a retired table set for the American, British, and German consuls, and their wives. The highest two officials of France in this group, Messieurs, l'Inspecteurs des Colonies, were there, eating solemnly alone, as demanded by their exalted rank, and their mission of criticism. They glanced down often at their broad bosoms to see that their many orders were on straight, to note the admiration of lesser officialdom, and to make eyes at the women. Their long and profuse black beards were hidden by their napkins, which all Frenchmen of parts hereabouts tuck in their collars, and draw up to their mouths, a precaution which, when omitted, is seen to have been founded on an etiquette utilitarian and esthetic.

The company was complex. At a table opposite me sat the *juge inférieur* and the daughter of the Chinese cook at the Hotel Central, a smart, slender woman with burning eyes, and with them, in full uniform, were two French civil officials, who wore, as customary, clothes like soldiers. One unfamiliar with their regalia might mistake, as I did, a pharmacist for an admiral. Mary, the cook's half-Tahitian daughter, was in elaborate European dress, with a gilded barret of baroque pearls in her copious, ebon tresses, and with red kid shoes buckled in silver and blister pearls.

The son of Prince Hinoe, who would have been the King of Tahiti had the dynasty continued to reign, had a dozen chums at a table, oafs from seventeen to twenty, and with the fish course they began to chant. The captain of the *Saint Michel* was with Woronick, the pearl-buyer, who had made the fearful trip to the Marquesas with him. There was Heezonorweelee, as the natives call the Honorable Walter Williams, the most famous dentist within five thousand miles, and the most distinguished white man of Tahiti; Landers; Polonsky; David; McHenry; Schlyter, the Swedish tailor; Jones and Mrs. Jones, the husband, head of a book company in Los Angeles; a Barbary Coast singer and her man; a demirep of Chicago and her loved one; three Tahitian youths with wreaths; the post-office manager, and with him the surgeon of the hospital; a notary's clerk, the governor's private secretary; the administrateur of the Marquesas Islands, Margaret, Lurline and Mathilde, Lena, and Lucy, lovely part-Tahitian girls who clerked in stores; the Otoman, chauffeur for Polonsky; English tourists; Nance, the California capitalist; and others.

Curses upon *Saint Michel,* threats of damage suits for fright and delay, laughable stories of the mistakes of the volunteer crew of the *Noa-Noa;* discussions of the price of copra, mingled with the chants of the native feasters and ribald tales. The Tiare girls, all color and sparkle, exchanged quips with the male diners, patted their shoulders, and gigglingly fought when they tried to take them into their laps.

In the open porch, Lovaina, gaily adorned, her feet bare, but a wreath of ferns on her head, sped the dishes and the wine. She kept the desserts before her and cut portions to suit the quality of her liking for each patron.

"Taporo e taata au ahu" said Atupu.

"The lime and the tailor," that means, and identified Landers and Schlyter. Landers was the "lime" because a former partner of his establishment exported limes, and Landers succeeded to his nickname. Landers and Schlyter were good customers, so they got larger slices of dried-apple pie.

Chappe-Hall, being bidden farewell on his leaving for Auckland, was apostrophizing Tahiti in verse, all the stanzas ending in "And the glory of her eyes over all." There were bumpers and more, and "Bottoms up," until a slat-like American woman bounced off the veranda with her sixth course uneaten to complain to Lovaina that her hotel was no place for a Christian or a lady. Lovaina almost wept with astonishment and grief, but kept the champagne moving toward the Chappe-Hall table as fast as it could be cooled, meanwhile assuring the scandalized guest that nothing undecorous ever happened in the Tiare Hotel, but that it were better it did than that young men should go to evil resorts for their outbursts.

"My place respectable," Lovaina said dignifiedly. "I don' 'low no monkey bizeness. Drinkin' wine custom of Tahiti. Make little fun, no harm. If they go that Cocoanut House, get in bad."

Lovaina told me all about it. She was quite hurt at the aspersions upon her home, and entered the dining-room in a breathing spell to sit at my table, a rather unusual honor I deeply felt. I pledged my love for her in Pol Roger, but she would have nothing but water.

"I no drink these times," she explained. "Maybe some day I do again. Make fat people too much bigger. That flat woman from 'Nited States, ain't she funny? I think missionary."

From the screened area in which the consuls dined with the broker one heard:

"Here's to the king, God bless him!" *"Hoch der Kaiser!" "Vive la Republique!"* "The Stars and Stripes!" as the glasses were emptied by the consuls and their wives and host.

Lovaina had taken up the rug in the parlor, and a graphophone ground out the music for dancing. Ragtime records brought out the Otoman, a San Franciscan, bald and coatless. He took the floor with Mathilde, a chic, petite, and graceful half-caste, and they danced the *maxixe*. David glided with Margaret, Landers led out Lucy, and soon the room was filled with whirling couples. A score looked on and sipped champagne, the serving girls trying to fill the orders and lose no moment from flirtation. On the camphor-wood chest four were seated in two's space.

When midnight tolled from the cathedral tower, there was an uncalled-for speech from a venerable traveler who apparently was not sure of the date or the exact nature of the fête:

"Fellow-exiles and natives bujus Teetee. We are gathered together this Fourth of July—"

Cries of *"Altaī"* *"Ce n'est-pas vrai!"* "Shove in your high! It's New Year!"

"—to cel'brate the annivers'ry of the death of that great man—"

Yells of "Sit down!" "Olalala!" *"Aita maitai!"* and the venerable orator took his seat. He was once a governor of a territory under President Harrison, and now lived off his pension, shaky, *sans* teeth, *sans* hair, but never *sans* speech.

The Englishmen and Americans clattered glasses and said "Happy New Year!" and the Tahitians: "*Rupe-rupe tatou iti*! *I teienei matahiti api*!" "Hurrah for all of us! Good cheer for the New Year!"

Monsieur Lontane, second in command of the police, arrived just in time to drink the *bonne année*. He executed a *pas seul*. He mimicked a great one of France. He drank champagne from a bottle, a clear four inches between its neck and his, and not a drop spilled.

Lovaina sat on her bench in the porch and marked down the debits:

Fat face............	3 Roederer..........
New Doctor..........	5 champag...........
Hair on nose........	2 champ.............
Willi...............	4 pol..............

The electric lights went out. There was a dreadful flutter among the girls. Some one went to the piano and began to play, "Should Auld Acquaintance be Forgot," and the Americans and English sang, the French humming the air. The wine flattened in the glasses and open bottles, but no one cared. They gathered in the garden, where the perfume of the tiare scented the night, and the stars were a million lamps sublime in the sky. Song followed song, English and French, and when the lazy current pulsated again, the ball was over.

We walked to the beach, Nance and I.

"It's hell how this place gets hold of you," said Nance, who had shot pythons in Paraguay and had a yacht in Los Angeles harbor. "I dunno, it must be the cocoanuts or the breadfruit."

Walking back alone through a by-path, I saw the old folks sitting on their verandas and the younger at dalliance in the many groves. Voices of girls called me:

"*Haere me ne!*" "Come to us!" "*Hoere mai u nei ite po ia u nei!*"

The *Himene tatou Arearea* of our Moorea expedition came from many windows, the accordions sweet and low, and the subdued chant in sympathy with the mellow hour. "The soft lasceevious stars leered from these velvet skies."

Lovaina had gone to bed, but, with the lights on again, patrons of the prize-fight had dropped in. The Christchurch Kid had beaten Teaea, a native, the match being a preliminary clearing of the ground before the signal encounter with the bridegroom.

The glass doors of the *salle-à-manger* were broken in a playful scuffle between the whiskered doctor of the hospital, and Afa, the majordomo of the Tiare. The medical man ordered five bottles of champagne, and, putting them in his immense pockets, returned to his table and opened them all at once. He had them spouting about him while their fizz lasted, and then drank most of their contents. He then threw all the crockery of his table to the roadway, and Afa wrestled him into a better state, during which process the doors were smashed. When the bombilation became too fearful, Lovaina called out from her bed:

"Make smaller noise! Nobody is asleep!"

At two in the morning the gendarmes advised the last revelers to retire, and the Tiare became quiet. But Atupu slept in a little alcove by the bar, and any one in her favor had but to enter her chamber and pull her shapely leg to be served in case of dire need.

The incidents of the departure of the *Noa-Noa* that day for San Francisco will live in the annals of Papeete. Its calamitous happenings are "in the archives." I have the word of the secretary-general of the Etablissments Français de l'Oceanie for that, and in the saloons and coffee-houses they talked loudly of the *"bataille entre les cochons Anglais et les héros les Français et les Tahitiens."*

It was a battle that would have rejoiced the heart of Don Quixote, and that redoubtable knight had his prototype here in the van of it, the second in command of the police of Papeete, M. Lontane, the mimic of the Tiare celebration.

The *Noa-Noa's* amateur crew of wretched beach-combers, farm laborers, and impossible firemen, stokers, and stewards, a pitiable set, were about the waterfront all day, dirty, dressed in hot woolen clothes, bedraggled and as drunk as their money would allow. The ship was down to leave at three-thirty o'clock, but it was four when the last bag of copra was aboard. There were few passengers, and those who booked here were dismayed at the condition of the passageways, the cabins, and the decks. The crowd of "scabs," untrained white sailors, and coal passers was supplemented by Raratonga natives, lounging about the gangway and sitting on the rails. On the wharf hundreds of people had gathered as usual to see the liner off. Lovaina was there in a pink lace dress, seated in her carriage, with Vava at the horse's head. Prince Hinoe had gathered about him a group of pretty girls, to whom he was promising a feast in the country. All the tourists, the loafers, the merchants, and the schooner crews were there, too, and the iron-roofed shed in which it is forbidden to smoke was filled with them. The *Noa-Noa* blew and blew her whistle, but still she did not go. The lines to the wharf were loosened, the captain was on the bridge, the last farewells were being called and waved, but there was delay. Word was spread that some of the crew were missing, and as at the best the vessel was short-handed, it had to tarry.

At last came three of the missing men. They, too, had welcomed the New Year, and their gait was as at sea when the ship rises and falls on the huge waves. They wheeled in a barrow a mate whose mispoise made self-locomotion impossible. The trio danced on the wharf, sang a chantey about "whisky being the life of man," and declared they would stay all their lives in Tahiti; that the "bloody hooker could bleedin' well" go without them. They were ordered on board by M. Lontane, with two strapping Tahitian gendarmes at his back.

If there are any foreigners the average British roustabout hates it is French gendarmes, and the ruffians were of a mind to "beat them up." They raised their fists in attitudes of combat, and suddenly what had been a joyous row became a troublesome incident.

Sacré bleu! those scoundrels of English to menace the uniformed patriots of the French republic! The second in command drew a revolver, and pointing at the hairy breast of the leader of the Noa-Noans, shouted: "*Au le vapeur! Diable*! What, you whisky-filled pigs, you will resist the law?"

He took off his helmet and handed it to one of the native policemen while he unlimbered the revolver more firmly in the direction of the seamen. The sailor shrank back in bewilderment. Guns were unknown in shore squabbles.

"I'll 'ave the British Gov'ment after ye," roared the leader. "I'll write to the Sydney papers. Ye've pulled a gun in me face."

Steadily and with some good nature the Tahitian officers pushed the trio toward the gangway and up it. Once aboard, the gangway was hoisted, the pilot clambered up the side, and it seemed as if the liner was away. But no; the three recalcitrants jumped on the bulwarks, and joined by a dozen others, yelled defiance at the authorities. As the *Noa-Noa* gradually drew out these cries became more definite, and the honor of France and of all Frenchmen was assailed in the most ancient English Billingsgate. Gestures of frightful significance added to the insults, and these not producing retorts in kind from the second in command and the populace, a shower of limes began to fall upon them.

Sacks of potatoes, lettuce-heads, yams, and even pineapples, deck cargo, were broken open by the infuriated crew to hurl at the police. The crowd on the wharf rushed for shelter behind posts and carriages, the horses pranced and snorted, and M. Lontane leaped to the fore. He advanced to the edge of the quay, and in desperate French, of which his adversaries understood not a word, threatened to have them dragged from their perches and sent to New Caledonia.

A well-aimed lime squashed on his cheek, and with a *"Sapristi!"* he fled behind a stack of boxes. The riot became general, the roustabouts heaving iron bars, pieces of wood, and anything they could find. No officer of the *Noa-Noa* said a word to stop them, evidently fearing a general strike of the crew, and when the missiles cut open the head of a native stevedore and fell even among the laughing girls, the courtesies began to be returned. Coal, iron nuts, stones, and other serious projectiles were thrown with a hearty good-will, and soon the crew and the passengers of the *Noa-Noa* were scuttling for safety.

The storm of French and Tahitian adjectives was now a cyclone, Tahitian girls, their gowns stained by the fruity and leguminous shot of the Australasians, seized lumps of coal or coral, and took the van of the shore legions. Atupu struck the leader of the *Noa-Noa* snipers in the nose with a rock, and her success brought a paean of praise from all of us.

The *entente cordiale* with Britain was sundered in a minute. The mêlée grew into a fierce battle, and only the increasing distance of the vessel from shore stopped the firing, the last shots falling into the lagoon.

The second in command had been reinforced by the first in command, and now, summoned by courier, appeared the secretary-general of the Etablissements Françaises de l'Oceanie, bearded and helmeted, white-faced and nervous, throwing his arms into the air and shrieking, *"Qu' est-que ce que ça?* Is this war? Are we human, or are these savages?"

Lovaina, in the rear of whose carriage I had taken refuge, exclaimed:

"They say Tahiti people is savage! Why this crazy people must be finished. Is this business go on?"

"Non, non!" replied the secretary-general, with patriotic anger, "We French are long suffering, but *c'est assez maintenant.*"

He spoke to the first in command, and an order was shouted to M. Wilms, the pilot, to leave the *Noa-Noa*. That official descended into his boat and returned to the quay, while the liner hovered a hundred yards away, the captain afraid to come nearer, fearful of leaving port without expert guidance, and more so that the crew might renew the combat.

The secretary-general conferred with the private secretary of the governor, the first and second in command, and several old residents. They would apply to the British consul for warrants for the arrest of the ruffianly marksmen, they would wrench them from the rails, and sentence them to long imprisonments.

So for an hour more the steamship puffed and exhausted her steam, while the high officials paced the wharf shaking their fists at the besotted stokers, who shook theirs back.

The stores, closing at five o'clock, sent their quota of clerks to swell the mob at the quay, and the "rubberneck wagon," alert to earn fares, took the news of the fray into the country, and hauled in scores of excited provincials, who had vague ideas that *la guerre* was on. The wedding party, only six motor-cars full on the second day, all in wreaths of tuberoses and wild-cherry rind, the bride still in her point-lace veil, and the groom and all the guests cheered with the champagne they had drunk, drove under the shed from the suburbs and honked their horns, to the horror of the secretary-general and the others.

The situation was now both disciplinary and diplomatic.

"C'est tres serieux," whispered the secretary to the governor's private secretary, a dapper little man whose flirting had made his wife a Niobe and alarmed the husbands and fathers of many French *dames et filles*.

"Serious, monsieur?" said the private secretary, twisting his black wisp of a mustache, "it is more than serious now; it is no longer the French Establishments of Oceania. It is between Great Britain and France."

A peremptory order was given to drive every one off the quay, and though the crowd chaffed the police, the sweep of wharf was left free for the marchings and counter-marchings of the big men.

"What would be the result? Would the entire British population of the ship resist the taking away of any of the crew? Oh, if the paltry French administration at Paris had not removed the companies of soldiers who until recently had been the pride of Papeete! And crown of misfortune, the gunboat, sole guardian of French honor in these seas, was in Australia for repairs. *Eh bien, n'importe*! Every Frenchman was a soldier. Did not Napoleon say that? *Nom de pipe*!"

Wilfrid Baillon, a cow-boy from British Columbia, was standing near me with his arms folded on his breast and a look of stern determination on his sunburned face.

"We must look sharp," he said to me. "We may all have to stand together, we whites, against these French frog-eaters."

The tension was extreme. The warrants had not come from the British consul, and there seemed no disposition on the *Noa-Noa* to save the face of *la belle republique*, for the blackened and blackguardly stokers still dangled their legs over the rail and made motions which caused the officials to shudder and the ladies to shut their eyes.

The agent of the vessel in Papeete, an American, appeared. He talked long and earnestly with the secretary-general and the first and second, and to lend even a darker color to the scene, the *procureur-général*, the Martinique black, tall, protuberant, mopping his bald head, took the center of the conclave. Noses were lowered and brought together, feet were stamped, hands were wiggled behind backs, and right along the American, the agent, talked and talked.

They demurred, they spat on the boards, they lifted their hands aloft—and then they ordered the pilot to return to the *Noa-Noa*, and that vessel, whistling long and relievedly, pointed her nose toward the opening in the reef.

Mon Dieu! the suspense was over. The people melted toward their homes and the restaurants, for it was nearly seven o'clock. I drifted into the knot about the officials.

"It is in the archives," said the secretary-general. "It will go down in history. That is enough."

The delightful M. Lontane, in khaki riding breeches,—he, as all police, ride bicycles—his khaki helmet tipped rakishly over his cigarette, blew a ringlet.

"*C'est comme ça.* We would not press our victory," he said gallantly. "We French are generous. We have hearts."

The secretary-general, the *procureur-général*, the first in command and the private secretary, sighted the carriage of the governor, who had not appeared until the *Noa-Noa* was out of the lagoon, and they went to tell him of the great affair.

The agent of the line, grim and unsmiling, climbed to the wide veranda of the Cercle Bougainville, and ordered a Scotch and siphon.

"There she goes," he said to me, and pointed to the steamer streaking through the reef gate. "There she goes, and I'm bloody well satisfied."

At tea the next afternoon the British consul cast a new light on the international incident. He was playing bridge with the governor and others when the demand for the warrants was brought.

"The blighters interrupted our rubber," said the consul, "and the governor was exceedingly put out. I told them the *Noa-Noa* couldn't proceed without the stokers, and as it carries the French mail, they patched it up to arrest them when they return. We quite lost track of the game for a few minutes."

But the cruel war would not down. There was not a good feeling between the English and French in Tahiti. A slight opposition cropped out often in criticism expressed to Americans or to Tahitians, or to each other's own people. New Zealand governs the Cook group, of which Raratonga is the principal island. Comparisons of sanitation, order, neatness, and businesslike management of these islands, with the happy-go-lucky administration of the Society, Paumotus, Marquesas, and Austral archipelagoes, owned by the French, were frequent by the English. The French shrugged their shoulders.

"The Tahitians are happy, and we send millions of francs to aid France," they said. "The English talk always of neatness and golf links and cricket-grounds. *Eh bien*! There are other and better things. And as for drink, *oh, la, la*! Our sour wines could not fight one round of the English *boxe* with whisky and gin and that awful ale."

The French residents protested at the missiles of the crew and the *laissez-faire* of the *Noa-Noa* officers, and the British consul received a letter from the governor in which the affair of the riot was revived in an absurd manner.

One might understand M. Lontane, second in command of the police forces,—six men and himself,—magnifying the row between the tipsy stokers and his battalions, but to have the governor, who was a first-rate hand at bridge, and even knew the difference between a straight and a flush, putting down in black and white, sealed with the seal of the *Republique Française*, and signed with his own hand, that "France had been insulted by the actions of the savages of the *Noa-Noa*," was worthy only of the knight of La Mancha.

So thought the consul, but he was a diplomat, his adroitness gained not only in the consular ranks, but also in Persia as a secretary of legation, and in many a fever-stricken and robber-ridden port of the Near and Far East. He pinned upon his most obstreperous uniform the medal won by merit, straddled a dangling sword, helmeted his head, and with an interpreter, that the interview might lack nothing of formality, called upon the governor at his palace.

He told him that the letter of complaint had roused his wonderment, for, said his British Majesty's representative, "There can be no serious result, diplomatically or locally, of this Donnybrook Fair incident. In a hundred ports of the world where war-ships and merchant ships go, their crews for scores of years have fought with the police. Besides, I am informed that Monsieur Lontane put a revolver against the stomach of one of the stokers, and that provoked the nastiness. Until then it had been uncouth mirth caused by the vile liquor sold by the saloons licensed by the Government, and against the Papeete regulations that no more intoxicants shall be sold to a man already drunk. But when this British citizen, scum of Sydney or Glasgow as he might be, saw the deadly weapon, he felt aggrieved. This revolver practice is all too common on the part of Monsieur Lontane. Six such complaints I have had in as many months. As to that part of your letter that the crew of the *Noa-Noa* not be allowed to land here on its return to Papeete, I agree with you, but it will be for you to enforce this prohibition."

It was agreed that on the day the *Noa-Noa* arrived on her return trip, all gendarmes and available guard be summoned from the country to preserve order, and that, as asked in the letter, the consul demand that the captain of the steamship punish the rioters.

And all this being done through an interpreter, and the consul having unlimbered his falchion and removed his helmet, he and the governor had an absinthe frappé and made a date for a bridge game.

"Te tamai i te taporo i te arahu i te umaru," the natives termed the skirmish. "The conflict of the limes, the coal, and the potatoes." A new *himene* was improvised about it, and I heard the girls of the *Maison des Cocotiers* chanting it as I went to Lovaina's to dinner.

It was something like this in English:

"Oh, the British men they drank all day
And threw the limes and iron.
The French in fear they ran away.
The brave Tahitians alone stood firm."

And there were many more verses.

Chapter VIII

Gossip in Papeete—Moorea, a near-by island—A two-days' excursion there—Magnificent scenery from the sea—Island of fairy folk—Landing and preparation for the feast—The First Christian mission—A canoe on the lagoon—Beauties of the sea-garden.

My acquaintances of the Cercle Bougainville, Landers, Polonsky, McHenry, Llewellyn, David, and Lying Bill, were at this season bent on pleasure. Landers, the head of a considerable business in Australasia, with a Papeete branch, had time heavy on his hands. Lying Bill and McHenry were seamen-traders ashore until their schooner sailed for another swing about the French groups of islands. Llewellyn and David were associates in planting, curing, and shipping vanilla-beans, but were roisterers at heart, and ever ready to desert their office and warehouse for feasting or gaming. Polonsky was a speculator in exchange and an investor in lands, and was reputed to be very rich. He, too, would leave his strong box unlocked in his hurry if cards or wassail called. These same white men were sib to all their fellows in the South Seas except a few sour men whom avarice, satiety, or a broken constitution made fearful of the future and thus heedful of the decalogue.

These merry men attended to business affairs for a few hours of mornings, unless the night before had been devoted too arduously to Bacchus, and the remainder of the day they surrendered to clinking glasses, converse, Rabelasian tales, and flirting with the gay Tahitian women in the cinemas or at dances. There was a tolerance, almost a standard, of such actions among the men of Tahiti, though of course consuls, high officials, a banker or two of the Banque de l'Indo-Chine, and a few lawyers or speculators sacrificed their flesh to their ambitions or hid their peccadillos.

A chorus of wives and widows—there were no old maids in Tahiti—condemned scathingly the conduct of the voluptuaries, and the preachers of the gospel lashed them in conversation or sermon now and then. But on the whole there was not in Tahiti any of the spirit of American towns and villages, which wrote scarlet letters, ostracized offenders against moral codes, and made Philistinism a creed. Gossip was constant, and while sometimes caustic, more often it partook of curiosity and mere trading of information or salacious prattle.

Tahitian women concealed nothing. If they won the favors of a white man, they announced it proudly, and held nothing sacred of the details. One's peculiarities, weaknesses, idiosyncrasies, physical or spiritual blemishes, all became delectable morsels in the mouths of one's intimates and their acquaintances. One's passions, actions, and whisperings were as naked to the world as the horns on a cow. Every one knew the import of Polonsky's dorsal tattooings, that Pastor —— had a case of gin in his house, and that the governor, after a bottle or two of champagne, had squeezed so tightly the waist of an English lady with whom he waltzed that she had cried out in pain. Though bavardage accounted for much of the general knowledge of every one's affairs, there was an uncanny mystery in the speed at which a particular secret spread. One spoke of the bamboo telegraph.

It was proposed at the Cercle Bougainville that we have a series of jaunts to points some distance away. I promised that I would see fully the way my acquaintances enjoyed themselves in the open. Llewellyn was given charge of the first excursion. It was to Moorea, an island a dozen miles or so to the northwest from Papeete, and which, with Tetiaria and Mehetia and Tahiti, constitute *les îles de Vent*, or Windward Islands of the Society archipelago.

In clear weather one cannot look out to sea from Papeete, to the north or west, without Moorea's weird grandeur confronting one. The island of fairy-folk with golden hair, it was called in ancient days by the people of other islands. A third of the size of Tahiti, it was, until the white man came, the abode of a romantic and gallant clan. Eimeo, it was called by the first whites, but the name of Moorea clings to it now. Over it and behind it sets the sun of Papeete, and it is associated with the tribal conflicts, the religion, and the journeys of the Tahitians. Now it is tributary to this island in every way, and small boats run to and from with passengers and freight almost daily.

We met at seven o'clock of a Saturday morning at the point on the coral embankment where the *Potii Moorea* was made fast, the gasolene-propelled cargo-boat which we had rented for the voyage. A hundred were gathered about a band of musicians in full swing when I appeared at the rendezvous on the prick of the hour. The bandsmen, all natives but one, wore garlands of *purau*, the scarlet hibiscus, and there was an atmosphere of abandonment to pleasure about them and the party.

A schooner swung at her moorings near by, under a glowing, flamboyant tree, and her crew was aboard in expectation of sailing at any hour. Another small craft, a sloop, was preparing to sail for Moorea, also. She was crowded with passengers and cargo, and all about the rail hung huge bunches of *feis*, the mountain bananas. Most of the people aboard had come from the market-place with fruit and fish and vegetables to cook when they arrived at home. A strange habit of the Tahitians under their changed condition is to take the line of least resistance in food, eating in Chinese stores, or buying bits in the market, whereas, when they governed themselves, they had an exact and elaborate formula of food preparation, and a certain ceremoniousness in despatching it. Only feasts bring a resumption nowadays of the ancient ways.

The crews of the schooner and of the other Moorea boat besides our own had a swarm of friends awaiting the casting off. Even a journey of a few hours meant a farewell ceremony of many minutes. They embrace one another and are often moved to tears at a separation of a few days. When one of them goes aboard a steamship for America or Australasia, the family and friends enact harrowing scenes at the quay. They are sincerely moved at the thought of their loved ones putting a long distance between them, and I saw a score of young and old sobbing bitterly when the *Noa-Noa* left for San Francisco though they stormed the stokers lustily when aroused. Their life is so simple in these beloved islands that the dangers of the mainland are exaggerated in their minds, and to the old the civilization of a big city appears as a specter of horrible mien. The electric cars, the crowds, the murders they read of and are told of, the bandits in the picture-shows, the fearful stranglers of Paris, the lynchers, the police, who in the films are always beating the poor, as in real life, the pickpockets, and the hospitals where willy-nilly they render one unconscious and remove one's vermiform appendix—all these are nightmares to the aborigines whose relations are departing.

When heads were counted, Landers's was missing, and jumping into Llewellyn's carriage, an old-fashioned phaëton, I drove to Lovaina's, where he occupied the room next to mine in the detached house in the animal-yard. He was sound asleep, having played poker and drunk until an hour before; but when I awoke him I could not but admire the serenity of the man. His body was in the posture in which he had lain down, and his breathing was as a child's.

"Landers, get up!" I shouted from the doorway. He opened his eyes, regarded me intently, and without a word went to the shower-bath by the camphor-wood chest, returned quickly, and dressed himself. I fancied him a man who would have answered his summons before a firing-squad as calmly. He had a perfection of ease in his movements; not fast, for he was very big, but with never an unnecessary gesture nor word. He was one of the finest animals I had ever seen, and fascinating to men and women of all kinds.

The *Potii Morea* had taken on her passengers when we returned, and we put off from the sea-wall at once, with two barrels of bottled beer, and half a dozen demi-johns of wine prominent on the small deck. Often the sea between Tahiti and Moorea is rough in the daytime, and passage is made at night to avoid accident, but we were given a smooth way, and could enjoy the music. We sat or lay on the after-deck while the bandsmen on the low rail or hatch maintained a continuous concert.

During the several days between our first planning the trip and the going, a song had been written in honor of the junketing, and this they played scores of times before we set foot again in Papeete. It was entitled: *"Himene Tatou Arearea,"* which meant, "Our Festal Song."

One easily guessed the meaning of the word *himene*. The Polynesians' first singing was the hymns of the missionaries, and these they termed *himenes*; so that any song is a *himene*, and there is no other word for vocal music in common use. The words of the first stanza of the *"Himene Tatou Arearea"* and the refrain were:

I teie nei mahana
Te tere no oe e Hati
Na te moana
Ohipa paahiahia
No te au
Tei tupi i Moorea
tamau a
Tera te au
Ei no te au
Tamua a—aue

Ei reo no oe tau here
I te pii raa mai
Aue oe Tamarii Tahiti te aroha e
A inu i te pia arote faarari

Faararirari ta oe Tamarii Tahiti
La, Li.

Llewellyn put the words into approximate meaning in English, saying it was as difficult to translate these intimate and slang phrases as it would be to put "Yankee Doodle" into French or German. His translation, as he wrote it on a scrap of paper, was:

Let us sing joyful to-day
The journey over the sea!
It is a wonderful and agreeable thing to happen in Moorea,
Hold on to it! That is just it;
And because it is just it,
Why hold on to it!

Your voice, O, Love, calls to us.
O Tahitian children,
Love to you!
Let us all drink beer,
And wet our throats!
And wet them again
To you, Tahitian Children!

The bandsmen were probably all related to Llewellyn, or at least they were of his mother's clan. His own son and nephew by unmarried mothers were among them; so that they were of our party, and yet on a different footing. They were our guests, we paying them nothing, but they not paying their scot. They did not mingle with us intimately, although probably all the whites except myself knew them well, and at times were guests at their houses outside Papeete.

The air to which the *himene* was sung eluded me for long. It was, "Oh, You Beautiful Doll!" They had changed the tune, so that I had not recognized it. The Tahitians have curious variations of European and American airs, of which they adapt many, carrying the thread of them, but differentiating enough to cause the hearer curiously mixed emotions. It was as if one heard a familiar voice, and, advancing to grasp a friendly hand, found oneself facing a stranger.

None of these island peoples originally had any music save monotones. In fact, in Hawaii, after the missionaries, *Kappelmeister* Berger, who came fifty years ago from Germany to Honolulu, was largely the maker of the songs we know now as distinctively Hawaiian. He fitted German airs to Hawaiian words, composed music on native themes, and spontaneously and by adaptation he, with others, gave a trend to the music of Hawaii nei that, though European in the main, is yet charmingly expressive of the soft, sweet nature of the Hawaiians and of the contrasts of their delightful gaiety and innate melancholy. These native tongues of the South Seas, with their many vowels and short words, seem to be made for singing.

The voyage from Tahiti to Moorea was a two-hours' panorama of magnificence and anomalism in the architecture of nature. Facing my goal was Moorea, and behind me Tahiti, scenes of contrary beauty as the vessel changed the distance from me to them. Tahiti, as I left it, was under the rays of the already high sun, a shimmering beryl, blue and yellow hues in the overpowering green mass, and from the loftiest crags floating a long streamer-cloud, the cloud-banner of Tyndal.

Moorea was the most astonishing sight upon the ocean that my eyes had ever gazed on. It was as if a mountain of black rock had been carved by the sons of Uranus, the mighty Titans of old, into gigantic fortresses, which the lightnings, temblors, and whirlwinds of the eons had rent into ruins. Its heights were not green like Tahiti's, but bare and black, true children of the abysmal cataclysm which in the time of the making of these oases of the sea thrust them up from the fires of the deep.

Far up near the peak of Afareaitu, nearly a mile above the wave, in one of the colossal splinters of the basalt rocks, was an eye, an immense round hole through which the sky shone. One saw it plainly from Tahiti. It was made by the giant Pai of Tautira when he threw his spear a dozen miles and pierced a window in the solid granite that all might know his prowess. One felt like a fool to rehearse to a Tahitian, telling one the tale, the statement of scientists that the embrasure had been worn by water when Afareaitu was under the ocean during its million-year process of rising from the mud. It would be like asking Flammarion, the wisest of French astronomers, to cease believing in the mystery of transubstantiation. He would smile as would the autochthon.

There was one picture in murky monochrome which never could be forgotten—a long sierra of broken pinnacles and crags which had all the semblance of a weathered and dismantled castle. It stood out against the tender blue of the morning sky like the ancient stronghold of some grisly robber-baron of medieval days; towers of dark sublimity, battlements whence invaders might have been hurled a thousand feet to death, slender minarets, escarpments and rugged casements through which fleecy clouds peeped from the high horizon. I once saw along the Mediterranean in Italy or France the fastness of a line of nobles, set away up on a lonely hill, glowering, gloomy, and unpeopled, the refuge, mayhap, of the mountain goat, the abiding-place of bats and other creatures of the night. Moorea's fortress conjured up the vision of it, its wondrous ramparts and unscalable precipices strangely the counterpart of the Latin castle.

But if one dropped one's eyes from the hills, gone was the recollection of aught of Europe. There was a scene which only the lavish colors of the tropics could furnish. The artist had spilled all his shades of green upon the palette, and so delicately blended them that they melted into one another in a very enchantment of green. The valleys were but darker variants of the emerald scheme.

The confused mass of lofty ridges resolved into chasms and combes, dark, sunless ravines, moist with the spray of many waterfalls, which nearer became velvet valleys of pale green, masses of foliage and light and shadow. The mountains of Moorea were only half the height of Tahiti's, but so artfully had they been piled in their fantastic arrangement that they seemed as high, though they were entirely different in their impress upon the beholder. Tahiti from the sea was like a living being, so vivid, so palpitating was its contour and its color, but Moorea, when far away, was cold and black, a beautiful, ravishing sight, but like the avatars of a race of giants that had passed, a sepulcher or monument of their achievements and their end.

As about Tahiti, a silver belt of reef took the rough caresses of the lazy rollers, and let the glistening surf break gently on the beach. Along this wall of coral, hidden, but charted by its crown of foam, we ran for miles until we found the gateway—the blue buckle of the belt, it appeared at a distance.

Within the lagoon the guise of the island was more intimate. Little bays and inlets bounded themselves, and villages and houses sprang up from the tropic groves. The band, which so far as I knew had not been silent a moment to awaken me from my adoration of the sculpture and painting of nature, now poured out the *"Himene Tatou Arearea"* in token of our approaching landing, which was at Faatoai, the center of population. All its hundred or two inhabitants were at the tiny dock to greet us, except the Chinese, who stayed in their stores.

Headed by the pipe and accordion, the brass and wood, now playing "Onward, Christian Soldier,"—which, if one forgot the words, was an especially carnal melody,—we tramped, singing a parody, through the street of Faatoai, and into a glorious cocoanut grove, where breakfast was spread.

A pavilion had been erected for our feasting. It was of bamboo and pandanus, the interior lined with tree ferns and great bunches of scarlet oleander, and decorated with a deep fringe woven of hibiscus fiber. The roof was a thatch of pandanus and breadfruit leaves, the whole structure, light, flimsy, but a gamut of golds and browns in color and cool and beautiful.

A table fifty feet or longer was made of bamboo, the top of twenty half sections of the rounded tubes, polished by nature, but slippery for bottles and glasses. A bench ran on both sides, and underfoot was the deep-green vegetation that covers every foot of ground in Moorea except where repeated footfalls, wheels, or labor kills it, and which is the rich stamp of tropic fertility.

The barrels of beer were unheaded, the demi-johns from Bordeaux were uncorked, and from the opened bottles the sugary odor of Tahiti rum permeated the hot air. The captain of the *Potii Moorea* and the hired steward began to set the table for the *déjeuner* and to prepare the food, some of which was being cooked a few feet away by the steward's kin. The guests disposed themselves at ease to wait for the call to meat, the bandsmen lit cigarettes and tuned their instruments or talked over their program, while they wetted their throats with the rum, as admonished by the *"Himene Tatou Arearea."*

I strolled down the road along the shore of the lagoon. Here was erected the first Christian church in this archipelago. British Protestant missionaries, who had led a precarious life in Tahiti, and fled from it to Australia in fear of their lives, were induced to come here and establish a mission. The King of Tahiti, Pomaré, had fled to Moorea after a desperate struggle with opposing clans, and he welcomed the preachers as additions to his strength. The high priest of the district, Patii, collected all the gods under his care, and they were burned, with a Bible in sight, to the exceeding fear of the native heathen, and the holy anger of the other native clergy, who felt as Moses did when he saw his disciples worshiping a golden calf. On the very spot I stood had been the *marae*, or Tahitian temple, in which the images were housed, now a rude heap of stones. A hundred years ago exactly this exchange of deities had been made. Alas! it could not have been the true Christ who was brought to them, for they had flourished mightily under Oro, and they began almost at once to die. Not peace, but a sword, a sword of horrors, of frightful ills, was brought them.

There was a little canoe under a noble cocoanut-tree on the shell-strewn and crab-haunted coral beach, the roots of the palm partly covered by the salt water, and partly by a tangle of lilac marine convolvulus. I pushed the tiny craft into the brine, and paddled off on the still water of the shining lagoon.

No faintest agitation of the surface withheld a clear view of the marvelous growths upon the bottom. I peered into a garden of white and vari-colored flowers of stone, of fans and vases and grotesque shapes, huge sponges and waving bushes and stunted trees. Fish of a score of shapes and of all colors of the spectrum wove in and out the branches and caverns of this wondrous parterre.

Past the creamy reef the purple ocean glittered in the nooning sun, while the motionless waters of the lagoon were turquoise and bice near by and virescent in the distance. Looking toward the shore, the edge of milky coral sand met the green matting of moss and grass, and then the eye marked the fields of sugar-cane, the forests of false coffee on which grew the vanilla-vines, the groves of cocoanuts, and then the fast-climbing ridges and the glorious ravines, the misty heights and the grim crags.

Chapter IX

The Arearea in the pavilion—Raw fish and baked feis—Llewellyn, the Master of the Revel; Kelly, the I.V.W., and His Himene—The Upaupahura—Landers and Mamoe prove experts—The return to Papeete.

The company was assembled in the pavilion when I walked through the streets of Faatoai again, and the food was on the bamboo table. One might have thought the feast would have been spread on soft mats on the sward, as is the Tahitian custom, but these whites are perverse and proud, and their legs unbending to such a position.

We had raw fish cut up, with bowls of cocoanut sauce. It was delicious in taste, but raw fish is tough and at first hard to chew until one becomes accustomed to the texture. Whites learn to crave it.

This fish was cut in small pieces thicker and bigger than a domino, and steeped in fresh lime-juice for half a day. The sauce was made by pouring a cup of seawater over grated cocoanuts and after several hours' straining through the fiber of young cocoanut shoots. It was thick, like rich cream.

We had excellent raw oysters and raw clams on the shell, crabs stewed with a wine sauce that was delicious, fish, boiled chicken, and baked pig. I had not tasted more appetizing food. It was all cooked in the native fashion on hot stones above or under ground. We saw the pig's disinterment. On the brink of the stream which flowed past the bower the oven had been made. The cooks, Moorea men, removed a layer of earth that had been laid on cocoa-palm leaves. This was the cover of the oven. Immediately below the leaves were yams and *feis* and under them a layer of banana leaves. The pig came next. It had been cut into pieces as big as mutton-chops and had cooked two and a half hours. It was on stones, coral, under which the fire of wood had been thoroughly ignited, the stones heated, and then the different layers placed above. The pig was tender, succulent, and the yams and *feis* finely flavored.

The two native men, in *pareus*, and with crowns of scarlet hibiscus, waited on us, while the son of Llewellyn uncorked the bottles. As usual, the beverages were lavishly dispensed, beginning with Scotch whisky as an appetizer, and following with claret, sauterne, vintage Burgundy, and a champagne that would have pleased Paris. These more expensive beverages were for us hosts only.

We were an odd company: Llewellyn, a Welsh-Tahitian; Landers, a British New-Zealander; McHenry, Scotch-American; Polonsky, Polish-French;

Schlyter, the Swedish tailor; David, an American vanilla-grower; "Lying Bill," English; and I, American. There was little talk at breakfast. They were trenchermen beyond compare, and the dishes were emptied as fast as filled. These men have no gifts of conversation in groups. Though we had only one half-white of the party, Llewellyn, he to a large degree set the pace of words and drink. In him the European blood, of the best in the British Isles, arrested the abandon of the aborigine, and created a hesitant blend of dignity and awkwardness. He was a striking-looking man, very tall, slender, about fifty years old, swarthy, with hair as black as night, and eyebrows like small mustaches, the eyes themselves in caverns, usually dull and dour, but when he talked, spots of light. I thought of that *Master of Ballantrae* of Stevenson's, though for all I remember he was blond. Yet the characters of the two blended in my mind, and I tried to match them the more I saw of him. He was born here, and after an education abroad and a sowing of wild oats over years of life in Europe, had lived here the last twenty-five years. He was in trade, like almost every one here, but I saw no business instincts or habits about him. One found him most of the time at the Cercle Bougainville, drinking sauterne and siphon water, shaking for the drinks, or playing écarté for five francs a game.

Below the salt sat his son and his nephew, men of twenty-five years, but sons of Tahitian mothers, and without the culture or European education of their fathers. With them two chauffeurs were seated. One of these, an American, the driver for Polonsky, had tarried here on a trip about the world, and was persuaded to take employment with Polonsky. The other was a half-caste, a handsome man of fifty, whose employer treated him like a friend.

Breakfast lasted two hours for us. For the band it kept on until dinner, for they did not leave the table from noon, when we sat down, until dark. When they did not eat, they drank. Occasionally one of us slipped down and took his place with them. I sat with them half an hour, while they honored me with "Johnny Burrown," "The Good, Old Summertime," and "Everybody Doin' It."

The heavy leads of the band were carried by an American with a two-horsepower accordion. He told me his name was Kelly. He was under thirty, a resolute, but gleesome chap, red-headed, freckled, and unrestrained by anybody or anything. He had no respect for us, as had the others, and had come, he said, for practice on his instrument. He had a song-book of the Industrial Workers of the World, a syndicalistic group of American laborers and intellectuals, and in it were scores of popular airs accompanied by words of dire import to capitalists and employers. One, to the tune of "Marching through Georgia," threatened destruction to civilization in the present concept.

"I'm an I. W. W.," said Kelly to me, with a shell of rum in his hand. "I came here because I got tired o' bein' pinched. Every town I went to in the United States I denounced the police and the rotten government, and they throwed me in the calaboose. I never could get even unlousy. I came here six weeks ago. It's a little bit of all right."

When Kelly played American or English airs and the Tahitians sang their native words, he gave the I. W. W. version in English. Some of these songs were transpositions or parodies of Christian hymns, and one in particular was his favorite. Apparently he had made it very popular with the natives of the band, for it vied with the *"Himene Tatou Arearea"* in repetition. It was a crude travesty of a hymn much sung in religious camp-meetings and revivals, of which the proper chorus as often heard by me in Harry Monroe's mission in the Chicago slums, was:

Hallelujah! Thine the glory! Hallelujah! Amen!
Hallelujah! Thine the glory! revive us again!

Kelly's version was:

Hallelujah! I'm a bum! Hallelujah! Bum again!
Hallelujah! Give us a hand-out! To save us from sin.

He had the stanzas, burlesquing the sacred lines, one of which the natives especially liked:

Oh, why don't you work, as other men do?
How the hell can we work when there 's no work to do?

None of us had ever heard Kelly's songs, nor had any one but I ever heard of his industrial organization, and I only vaguely, having lived so many years out of America or Europe. But they all cheered enthusiastically except Llewellyn. He was an Anglican by faith or paternal inheritance, and though he knew nothing of the real hymns, they being for Dissenters, whom he contemned, he was religious at soul and objected to making light of religion. He called for the *"Himene Tatou Arearea."* He took his pencil and scribbled the translation I have given.

"This is the rough of it," he said. "To write poetry here is difficult. When I was at Heidelberg and Paris I often spent nights writing sonnets. That merely tells the sense of the *himene*, but cannot convey the joy or sorrow of it. Well, let's sink dull care fifty fathoms deep! Look at those band-boys! So long as they have plenty of rum or beer or wine and their instruments, they care little for food. Watch them. Now they are dry and inactive. Wait till the alcohol wets them, They will touch the sky."

Llewellyn's deep-set eyes under the beetling brows were lighting with new fires.

His idea of inactivity and drought was sublimated, for the musicians were never still a moment. They played mostly syncopated airs of the United States, popular at the time. All primitive people, or those less advanced in civilization or education, prefer the rag-time variants of the American negro or his imitators, to so-called good or classical music. It is like simple language, easily understood, and makes a direct appeal to their ears and their passions. It is the slang or argot of music, hot off the griddle for the average man's taste, without complexities or stir to musing and melancholy.

The musicians had drunk much wine and rum, and now wanted only beer. That was the order of their carouse. Beer was expensive at two francs a bottle, and so a conscientious native had been delegated to give it out slowly. He had the barrel containing the quartbottles between his legs while he sat at the table, and each was doled out only after earnest supplications and much music.

"Horoa mai te pia!" "More beer!" they implored.

"Himene" said the inexorable master of the brew.

Up came the brass and the accordion, and forth went the inebriated strains.

Between their draughts of beer—they drank always from the bottles—the Tahitians often recurred to the song of Kelly. Having no *g, l*, or *s* among the thirteen letters of their missionary-made alphabet, they pronounced the refrain as follows:

Hahrayrooyah! I'm a boom! Hahrayrooyah! Boomagay!
Hahrayrooyah! Hizzandow! To tave ut fruh tin!

Landers being very big physically, they admired him greatly, and his company having been two generations in Tahiti, they knew his history. They now and again called him by his name among Tahitians, "Taporo-Tane," ("The Lime-Man"), and sang:

E aue Tau tiare ate e!
Ua parari te afata e!
I te Pahi no Taporo-Toue e!

Alas! my dear, some one let slip

A box of limes on the lime-man's ship,
And busted it so the juice did drip.

The song was a quarter of a century old and recorded an accident of loading a schooner. Landers's father's partner was first named Taporo-Tane because he exported limes in large quantities from Tahiti to New Zealand. The stevedores and roustabouts of the waterfront made ballads of happenings as their forefathers had chants of the fierce adventures of their constant warfare. They were like the negroes, who from their first transplantation from Africa to America had put their plaints and mystification in strange and affecting threnodies and runes.

All through the incessant *himenes* a crowd of natives kept moving about a hundred feet away, dancing or listening with delight. They would not obtrude on the feast, but must hear the music intimately.

The others of our party, having breakfasted until well after two, sought a house where Llewellyn was known. McHenry and I followed the road which circles the island by the lagoon and sea-beach. In that twelve leagues there are a succession of dales, ravines, falls precipices, and brooks, as picturesque as the landscape of a dream. We walked only as far as Urufara, a mile or two, and stopped there at the camp of a Scotsman who offered accommodation of board and lodging.

His sketchy hotel and outhouses were dilapidated, but they were in the most beautiful surrounding conceivable, a sheltered cove of the lagoon where the swaying palms dipped their boles in the ultramarine, and bulky banana-plants and splendid breadfruit-trees formed a temple of shadow and coolth whence one might look straight up the lowering mountain-side to the ghostly domes, or across the radiant water to the white thread of reef.

We met McTavish, the host of the hotel, an aging planter, who kept his public house as an adjunct of his farm, and more for sociability than gain. He was in a depressed and angry mood, for one of his eyes was closed, and the other battered about the rim and beginning to turn black and blue.

He knew McHenry, for both had been in these seas half their lives.

"In all my sixty years," he said, "I have not been assaulted quite so viciously. I asked him for what he owed me, and the next I knew he was shutting out the light with his fists. I will go to the gendarme for a contravention against that villain. And right now I will fix him in my book."

"Why, who hit you, and what did you do?" asked McHenry.

"That damned Londoner, Hobson," said McTavish. "He was my guest here several years ago, and ate and drank well for a month or two when he hadn't a *sou marquis*. I needed a little money to-day, and meeting him up the road, I demanded my account. He is thirty years younger than me, and I would have kept my eyes, but he leaped at me like a wild dog, and knocked me down and pounded me in the dirt."

I sympathized with McTavish, though McHenry snickered. The Scot went into an inner room and brought back a dirty book, a tattered register of his guests. He turned a number of pages—there were only a few guests to a twelvemonth—and, finding his assailant's name, wrote in capital letters against it, "THIEF."

"There," he said with a magnificent gesture. "Let the whole world read and know the truth!"

He set out a bottle of rum and several glasses, and we toasted him while I looked over the register. Hardly any one had neglected to write beside his name tributes to the charm of the place and the kind heart of McTavish.

Charmian and Jack London's signatures were there, with a hearty word for the host, and "This is the most beautiful spot in the universe," for Moorea and Urufara.

There were scores of poems, one in Latin and many in French. Americans seem to have been contented to quote Kipling, the "Lotus Eaters," or Omar, but Englishmen had written their own. English university men are generous poetasters. I have read their verses in inns and outhouses of many countries. Usually they season with a sprig from Horace or Vergil.

"I'm goin' to the west'ard," said McTavish. "There are too many low whites comin' here. When Moorea had only sail from Tahiti, the blackguards did not come, but now the dirty gasolene boat brings them. I must be off to the west'ard, to Aitutaki or Penrhyn."

Poor Mac! he never made his westward until he went west in soldier parlance.

McHenry, on our way back to Faatoai, said:

"McTavish is a bloody fool. He gives credit to the bleedin' beach-combers. If I meet that dirty Hobson, I'll beat him to a pulp."

From under the thatched roof of our bower came the sounds of:

Faararirari
to oe Tamarii Tahiti
La Li.

The *himene* was in its hundredth encore. The other barrel of bottled beer had been securely locked against the needs of the morrow, and the bandsmen's inspiration was only claret or sauterne, well watered.

We sat down for dinner. The *déjeuner* was repeated, and eggs added for variety. We had risen from breakfast four hours before, yet there was no lack of appetite. The drink appeared only to make their gastric juices flow freely. I hid my surfeit. The harmonies had by now drawn the girls and young women from other districts, word having been carried by natives passing in carts that a parcel of *papaa* (non-Tahitians) were *faarearea* (making merry).

These new-comers had adorned themselves for the *taupiti*, the public fête, as they considered it, and as they came along the road had plucked ferns and flowers for wreaths. Without such sweet treasures upon them they have no festal spirit. There were a dozen of these Moorea girls and visitors from Tahiti, one or two from the Tiare Hotel, whose homes were perhaps on this island.

The dinner being finished, the bandsmen laid down their instruments and the girls were invited to drink. Tahitian females have no thirst for alcohol. They, as most of their men, prefer fruit juices or cool water except at times of feasting. They had no intoxicants when the whites came, not in all Polynesia. It was the humor of the explorers, the first adventurers, and all succeeding ones, to teach them to like alcohol, and to hold their liquor like Englishmen or Americans. Kings and queens, chiefs and chiefesses, priests and warriors, were sent ashore crapulous in many a jolly-boat, or paddled their own canoes, after *areareas* on war-ships and merchantmen. Some learned to like liquor, and French saloons in Papeete and throughout Tahiti and Moorea encouraged the taste. Profits, as ever under the business rule of the world overweighed morals or health.

These girls in our bower drank sparingly of wine, but needed no artificial spirits to spur their own. Music runs like fire through their veins.

The spirit of the *upaupa* veiled in cotton garments

Iromea of the Tiare Hotel—perhaps some of Lovaina's maidens knew our plans and came over on the packet—took the accordion from Kelly. She began to play, and two of the Moorea men joined her, one with a pair of tablespoons and the other with an empty gasolene-can. The holder of the spoons jingled them in perfect harmony with the accordion, and the can-operator tapped and thumped the tin, so that the three made a singular and tingling music. It had a timbre that got under one's skin and pulsated one's nerves, arousing dormant desires. I felt like leaping into the arena and showing them my mettle on alternate feet, but a Moorea beauty anticipated me.

Matalini seeks a cocoanut for me

She placed herself before the proud Llewellyn, half of her own blood, and began an *upaupahura*. She postured before him in an attitude of love, and commenced an improvisation in song about him. She praised his descent from his mother, his strength, his capacity for rum, and especially his power over women. He was own brother to the great ones of the Bible, Tolomoni and Nebutodontori, who had a thousand wives. He drew all women to him.

The dance was a gambol of passion. It was a free expression of uninhibited sex feeling. The Hawaiian *hula*, the nautch, and minstrelsy combined. So rapid was the movement, so fast the music, so strenuous the singing, and so actual the vision of the dancer, that she exhausted herself in a few minutes, and another took the turf.

A thousand years the Tahitians had had these *upaupahuras*. Their national ballads, the achievements of the warrior, the fisherman, the woodsman, the canoe-builder, and the artist, had been orally recorded and impressed in this manner in the conclaves of the Arioi. Dancing is for prose gesture what song is for the instinctive exclamation of feeling, and among primitive peoples they are usually separated; but those cultured Tahitians from time immemorial had these highly developed displays of both methods of manifesting acute sensations. The Kamchadales of the Arctic—curious the similarities of language and custom between these far Northerners and these far Southerners—danced like these Tahitians, so that every muscle quivered at every moment.

The dancing in the bower was at intervals, as the desire moved the performers and bodily force allowed. The *himene* went on continuously, varying with the inspiration of the dancer or the whim of the accordion-player. They snatched this instrument from one another's hands as the mood struck them, and among the natives, men and women alike had facility in its playing. Pepe of Papara, and Tehau of Papeari, their eyes flashing, their bosoms rising and falling tumultuously, and their voices and bodies alternating in their expressions of passion, were joined by Temanu of Lovaina's, the oblique-eyed girl whom they called a half-Chinese, but whose ancestral tree, she said, showed no celestial branch. Temanu was tall, slender, serpent-like, her body flexuous and undulatory, responding to every quaver of the music. Her uncorseted figure, with only a thin silken gown upon it, wreathed harmoniously in tortile oscillations, her long, black hair flying about her flushed face, and her soul afire with her thoughts and simulations.

Now entered the bower Mamoe of Moorea, a big girl of eighteen. She was of the ancient chiefess type, as large as a man, perfectly modeled, a tawny Juno. Her hair was in two plaits, wound with red peppers, and on her head a crown of tuberoses. She wore a single garment, which outlined her figure, and her feet were bare. She surveyed the company, and her glance fell on Landers.

She began to dance. Her face, distinctly Semitic, as is not seldom the case in Polynesia, was fixed a little sternly at first; but as she continued, it began to glow. She did not sing. Her dance was the *upaupa*, the national dance of Tahiti, the same movement generally as that of Temanu, but without voice and more skilled. One saw at once that she was the *première danseuse* of this isle, for all took their seats. Her rhythmical swaying and muscular movements were of a perfection unexcelled, and soon infected the bandsmen, now with all discipline unleashed. One sprang from the table and took his position before her. Together they danced, moving in unison, or the man answering the woman's motions when her agitation lulled. The spectators were absorbed in the *hula*. They clapped hands and played, and when the first man wearied, another took his place.

Mamoe stopped, and drank a goblet of rum. Her eyes wandered toward our end of the table, and she came to us. She put her hand on Landers. The big trader, who was dressed in white linen, accepted the challenge. He pushed back the bench and stood up.

Landers in looks was out of a novel. If Henry Dixey, the handsome actor, whose legs made his fame before he might attest his head's capacity, were expanded to the proportions of Muldoon, the wrestler, he might have been Landers. Apparently about thirtythree, really past forty, he was as big as the young "David" of the Buonarroti, of the most powerful and graceful physique, with curling brown hair, and almost perfect features; a giant of a man, as cool as an igloo, with a melodious Australasian voice pitched low, and a manner with men and women that was irresistible.

He faced Mamoe, and Temanu seized the accordion and broke into a mad *upaupa*. An arm's-length from Mamoe Landers simulated every pulsation of her quaking body. He was an expert, it was plain, and his handsome face, generally calm and unexpressive, was aglow with excitement. Mamoe recognized her gyratory equal in this giant, and often their bodies met in the ecstasy of their curveting. Landers, towering above her, and bigger in bone and muscle than she in sheer flesh, was like a figure from a Saturnalia. The call of the isles was ringing in his ears, and one had only to glance at him to hear Pan among the reeds, to be back in the glades where fauns and nymphs were at play.

I saw Landers a care-free animal for the moment, rejoicing in his strength and skill, answering the appeal of sex in the dance. When he sat down the animal was still in him, but care again had clouded his brow. I think our early ancestors must have been much like Landers in this dance, strong, and merry for the time, seeking the woman in pleasures, fiery in movement for the nonce, and relapsing into stolidity. I can see why Landers, who takes what he will of womankind in these islands, still dominates in the trading, and bends most people his way. The animal way is the way here. The way of the city, of mere subtlety, of avoidance of issues, of intellectual control, is not the way of Polynesia. Bulk and sinew and no fear of God or man are the rules of the game south of the line, as "north of 53."

With Landers dancing, so must the others. Hobson had dropped in, and he, David, McHenry, Schlyter, and Lying Bill, trod a measure, and I, though with only a Celtic urge and a couple of years in Hawaii to teach me, faced Temanu. The bandsmen could not remain still, and, with Kelly to play the accordion, the rout became general. McHenry did not molest Hobson, who remained.

When we retired from the scene late at night, the *upaupa* was still active. We went to the house of Pai, a handsome native woman, whose half-caste husband was Mr. Fuller. There were only three beds in the house, which

Landers, Lying Bill, and McHenry fell on before any one else could claim them. I contented myself with a mat on the veranda, and noticed that, besides the remainder of our party, Pai and her *tane* were also on that level.

At half past two in the morning we lay down. I could not sleep. From the bower the song and music rang out continuously, mingled with laughter and the sounds of shuffling feet.

I got up at five, and with a *pareu* about me, followed the stream until I found a delicious pool, where I bathed for an hour, while I read "The Ballad of Reading Gaol." The level land between the sea and the mountains was not more than a quarter mile broad, and the near hills rose rounded and dark green, with mysterious valleys folded in between them. All about were cocoanuts and bananas, their foliage wet with the rain that had fallen gently all night. The stream was edged with trees and ferns and was clear and rippling. At that early hour there was no sensation of chill for me, though the men of native blood balked at entering the water until the sun had warmed it. A Chinese vegetablegrower sat on the bank with his Chinese wife and cleaned heads of lettuce and bunches of carrots. She watched me apathetically, as if I were a little strange, but not interesting.

A dozen natives came by and by to bathe in the next pool. They observed me, and called to me, pleasantly, "*Ia ora na!*" which is the common greeting of the Tahitian, and is pronounced "yuranna." The white is always a matter of curiosity to the native. These simple people have not lost, though generations of whites have come and bred and died or gone, at least some of their original awe and enjoyment of their conquerors and rulers.

When we had coffee in the morning, our serious and distinguished native hosts stood while we ate and drank. We, guests in their own comfortable house, did not ask them to join us. Llewellyn, when I put the question, answered:

"No. I am both white and of too high native rank. You cannot afford to let the native become your social equal."

McHenry said:

"You're bloody well right. Keep him in his stall, and he's all right; but out of it, ye'll get no peace."

So the gentle Pai and her husband—they are religious people, and went to the Faatoai church three times this Sunday—stood while we lolled at ease. Courtesy here seems a native trait, though even a little native blood improves on the white as far as politeness is concerned. *En passant*, the average white here is not of the leisure class, in which manners are an occupation; the native, on the other hand, is of a leisure class by heredity, and it is only when tainted by a desire to make money quickly or much of it that he loses his urbanity.

We had breakfasted in the bower at ten o'clock, with the band in attendance. Not one of the musicians had slept except Kelly, who said he had forty winks. When the pastors and their flocks of the various competing churches passed on their way to services, the band was keyed up in G, and was parading the streets, so that the faith of the Tahitians was severely tried. Even the ministers tarried a minute, and had to hold tightly their scriptures to control their legs, which itched to dance.

Aboard the *Potii Moorea* the bandsmen came sober, a revelation in recuperation. Again we passed the idyllic shores of Moorea, glimpsed the grove of Daphne and McTavish's bungalow at Urufara, and saw the heights, the desolated castle, the marvels of light and shade upon the hills and valleys, left the silver circlet of the reef, and made the open sea.

The glory of the Diadem, a crown of mountain peaks, stood out above the mists that cover the mountains of Tahiti, and the green carpet of the hills fell from the clouds to the water's-edge, as if held above by Antæus and pinned down by the cocoanut-trees.

At landing I discovered that the bandsmen had stolen away the sleeping Mamoe, and had carried her aboard the *Potii Moorea*, and deposited her in the hold. She emerged fresh from her nap, and apparently ready for an *upaupa* that night. We marched to the Cercle Bougainville to recall the incidents of the excursion over a comforting Dr. Funk.

Chapter X

The storm on the lagoon; Making safe the schooners—A talk on missing ships—A singular coincidence—Arrival of three of crew of the shipwrecked *El Dorado*—The Dutchman's story—Easter Island.

It blew a gale all one day and night from the north, and at break of the second day, when I went down the rue de Rivoli from the Tiare Hotel to the quay, the lagoon was a wild scene. Squall after squall had dashed the rain upon my verandas during the night, and I could faintly hear the voices of the men on the schooners as they strove to fend their vessels from the coral embankment, or hauled at anchor-ropes to get more sea-room.

The sun did not rise, but a gray sky showed the flying scud tearing at the trees and riggings, and the boom of the surf on the reef was like the roaring of a great steelmill at full blast. The roadway was littered with branches and the crimson leaves of the flamboyants. The people were hurrying to and from market in vehicles and on foot, soaked and anxious-looking as they struggled against the wind and rain. I walked the length of the built-up waterfront. The little boats were being pulled out from the shore by the several launches, and were making fast to buoys or putting down two and three anchors a hundred fathoms away from the quays.

The storm increased all the morning, and at noon, when I looked at the barometer in the Cercle Bougainville it was 29.51, the lowest, the skippers said, in seven years. The *William Olsen*, a San Francisco barkentine, kedged out into the lagoon as fast as possible, and through the tearing sheets of rain I glimpsed other vessels reaching for a holding-ground. The *Fetia Taiao* had made an anchorage a thousand feet toward the reef. The waves were hammering against the quays, and the lagoon was white with fury.

In the club, after all had been made secure, the skippers and managers of trading houses gathered to discuss the weather. Tahiti is not so subject to disastrous storms as are the Paumotu Islands and the waters toward China and Japan, yet every decade or two a tidal-wave sweeps the lowlands and does great injury. Though this occurs but seldom, when the barometer falls low, the hearts of the owners of property and of the people who have experienced a disaster of this kind sink. The tides in this group of islands are different from anywhere else in the world I know of in that they ebb and flow with unchanging regularity, never varying in time from one year's end to another.

Full tide comes at noon and midnight, and ebb at six in the morning and six in the evening, and the sun rises and sets between half past five and half past six o'clock. There is hardly any twilight, because of the earth's fast rotation in the tropics. This is a fixity, observed by whites for more than a century, and told the first seamen here by the natives as a condition existing always. Another oddity of the tides is that they are almost inappreciable, the difference between high and low tide hardly ever exceeding two feet. But every six months or so a roaring tide rolls in from far at sea, and, sweeping with violence over the reef, breaks on the beach. Now was due such a wave, and its possibilities of height and destruction caused lively argument between the traders and the old salts. More than a dozen retired seamen, mostly Frenchmen, found their Snug Harbor in the Cercle Bougainville, where liberty, equality, and fraternity had their home, and where Joseph bounded when orders for the figurative splicing of the main-brace came from the tables.

George Goeltz, a sea-rover, who had cast his anchor in the club after fifty years of equatorial voyaging, was, on account of his seniority, knowledge of wind and reef, and, most of all, his never-failing bonhommie, keeper of barometer, thermometer, telescopes, charts, and records. When I had my jorum of the eminent physician's Samoan prescription before me, I barkened to the wisdom of the mariners.

Captain. William Pincher, who had at my first meeting informed me he was known as Lying Bill, explained to me that some ignorant landsmen stated that this tidal regularity was caused by the steady drift of the tradewinds at certain hours of the day.

"That don't go," said he, "for the tides are the same whether there's a gale o' wind or a calm. I've seen the tide 'ighest 'ere in Papeete when there wasn't wind to fill a jib, and right 'ere on the leeward side of the bloody island, sheltered from the breeze. How about it at night, too, when the trade quits? The bleedin' tide rises and falls just the same at just the same time. Those trades don't even push the tidal waves because they always come from the west'ard, and the trades are from the east."

"I can look out of the veranda of this Cercle Bougainville and tell you what time it is to a quarter of an hour any day in the year just by looking at the shore or the reef and seein' where the water is," said Goeltz. "You can't do that any place on the globe except in this group."

A beneficent nature has considered the white visitor in this concern, for he can go upon the reef to look for its treasures at low tide, at sun-up or sun-fall, when it is cool.

We fell to talking about missing ships, and Goeltz insisted on Lying Bill telling of his own masterful exploit in bringing back a schooner from South America after the captain had run away with it and a woman. Pincher was mate of the schooner, which traded from Tahiti, and the skipper was a handsome fellow who thought his job well lost for love. He became enamored of the wife of another captain. One night when by desperate scheming he had gotten her aboard, he suddenly gave orders to up anchor and away. The schooner was full of cargo, copra and pearl-shell and pearls, and was due to return to Papeete to discharge. But this amative mariner filled his jibs on another tack, and before his crew knew whither they were bound was well on his long traverse to Peru.

Lying Bill was the only other white man aboard, and he took orders, as he had to by law and by the might of the swashbuckler captain. The lady lived in the only cabin—a tiny corner of the cuddy walled off—and ate her meals with her lover while Pincher commanded on deck. At a port in Peru the pirate sold the cargo, and taking his mistress ashore, he disappeared for good and all from the ken of the mate and of the South Seas.

"Now," said Captain George Goeltz, "Bill here could 'a' followed suit and sold the vessel. Of course they had no papers except for the French group, but in South America twenty-five years ago a piaster was a piaster. Bill was square then, as he is now, and he borrows enough money to buy grub, and he steers right back to Papeete. *Gott im Himmel!* Were the owners glad to see that schooner again? They had given her up as gone for good when the husband told them his wife had run away with the captain. That's how Bill got his certificate to command vessels in this archipelago, which only Frenchmen can have."

Goeltz picked up the "Daily Commercial News" of San Francisco, and idly read out the list of missing ships. There was only one in the Pacific of recent date whose fate was utterly unknown. She was the schooner *El Dorado*, which had left Oregon months before for Chile, and had not been sighted in all that time. The shipping paper said:

What has become of the *El Dorado*, it is, of course, impossible to say with any degree of accuracy, but one thing is almost certain, and that is that the likelihood of her ever being heard of again is now practically without the range of possibility. Nevertheless she may still be afloat though in a waterlogged condition and drifting about in the trackless wastes of the South Pacific. Then again she may have struck one of the countless reefs that infest that portion of the globe, some entirely invisible and others just about awash. She is now one hundred and eighty-nine days out, and the voyage has rarely taken one hundred days. She was reported in lat. 35:40 N., long. 126:30 W., 174 days ago.

"There'll be no salvage on her," said Captain Pincher, "because if she's still afloat, she ain't likely to get in the track of any bloody steamer. I've heard of those derelic's wanderin' roun' a bloody lifetime, especially if they're loaded with lumber. They end up usually on some reef."

This casual conversation was the prelude to the strangest coincidence of my life. When I awoke the next morning, I found that the big sea had not come and that the sun was shining. My head full of the romance of wrecks and piracy, I climbed the hill behind the Tiare Hotel to the signal station. There I examined the semaphore, which showed a great white ball when the mail-steamships appeared, and other symbols for the arrivals of different kinds of craft, men-of-war, barks, and schooners. There was a cozy house for the lookout and his family, and, as everywhere in Tahiti, a garden of flowers and fruit-trees. I could see Point Venus to the right, with its lighthouse, and the bare tops of the masts of the ships at the quays. Gray and red roofs of houses peeped from the foliage below, and a red spire of a church stood up high.

The storms had ceased in the few hours since dawn, and the sun was high and brilliant. Moorea, four leagues away, loomed like a mammoth battle-ship, sable and grim, her turrets in the lowering clouds on the horizon, her anchors a thousand fathoms deep. The sun was drinking water through luminous pipes. The harbor was a gleaming surface, and the reef from this height was a rainbow of color. All hues were in the water, emerald and turquoise, palest blue and gold. I sat down and closed my eyes to recall old Walt's lines of beauty about the

—World below the brine.
Forests at the bottom of the sea, the branches and leaves.
Sea-lettuce, vast lichens, strange flowers and seed.
The thick tangle,... and pink turf.

When I looked again at the reef I espied a small boat, almost a speck outside the coral barrier. She was too small for an inter-island cutter, and smaller than those do not venture beyond the reef. She was downing her single sail, and the sun glinted on the wet canvas. I called to the guardian of the semaphore, and when he pointed his telescope at the object, he shouted out:

"*Mais, c'est curieux!* Et ees a schmall vessel, a sheep's boat!"

I waited for no more, but with all sorts of conjectures racing through my mind, I hurried down the hill. Under the club balcony I called up to Captain Goeltz, who already had his glass fixed. He answered:

"She's a ship's boat, with three men, a jury rig, and barrels and boxes. She's from a wreck, that's sure."

He came rolling down the narrow stairway, and together we stood at the quai du Commerce as the mysterious boat drew nearer. We saw that the oarsmen were rowing fairly strongly against the slight breeze, and our fears of the common concomitants of wrecks,—starvation and corpses—disappeared as we made out their faces through the glasses. They stood out bronzed and hearty. The boat came up along the embankment, one of the three steering, with as matter of fact an air as if they had returned from a trip within the lagoon. There was a heap of things in the boat, the sail, a tank, a barrel, cracker-boxes, blankets, and some clothing.

The men were bearded like the pard, and in tattered garments, their feet bare. The one at the helm was evidently an officer, for neither of the others made a move until he gave the order:

"Throw that line ashore!"

Goeltz seized it and made fast to a ring-bolt, and then only at another command did the two stand up. We seized their hands and pulled them up on the wall. They were as rugged as lions in the open, burned as brown as Moros, their hair and beards long and ragged, and their powerful, lean bodies showing through their rags.

"What ship are you from?" I inquired eagerly.

The steersman regarded me narrowly, his eyes squinting, and then said taciturnly, "Schooner *El Dorado*." He said it almost angrily, as if he were forced to confess a crime. Then I saw the name on the boat, "*El Dorado* S. F."

"Didn't I tell you so?" asked Lying Bill, who was in the crowd now gathered. "George, didn't I say the *El Dorado* would turn up?"

He glared at Goeltz for a sign of assent, but the retired salt sought kudos for himself.

"I saw her first," he replied. "I was having a Doctor Funk when I looked toward the pass, and saw at once that it was a queer one."

The shipwrecked trio shook themselves like dogs out of the water. They were stiff in the legs. The two rowers smiled, and when I handed each of them a cigar, they grinned, but one said:

"After we've e't. Our holds are empty. We've come thirty-six hundred miles in that dinghy."

"I'm captain N.P. Benson of the schooner *El Dorado*." vouchsafed the third. "Where's the American Counsul?"

I led them a few hundred feet to the office of Dentist Williams, who was acting as consul for the United States. He had a keen love of adventure, and twenty years in the tropics had not dimmed his interest in the marvelous sea. He left his patient and closeted himself with the trio, while I returned to their boat to inspect it more closely.

All the workers and loafers of the waterfront were about it, but Goeltz would let none enter it, he believing it might be needed untouched as evidence of some sort. There are no wharf thieves and no fences in Tahiti, so there was no danger of loss, and, really, there was nothing worth stealing but the boat itself.

Captain Benson and his companions hastened from the dentist's to Lovaina's, where they were given a table on the veranda alone. They remained an hour secluded after Iromea and Atupu had piled their table with dishes. They drank quarts of coffee, and ate a beefsteak each, dozens of eggs, and many slices of fried ham, with scores of hot biscuits. They never spoke during the meal. A customs-officer had accompanied them to the Tiare Hotel, for the French Government wisely made itself certain that they might not be an unknown kind of smugglers, pirates, or runaways. Their boat had been taken in charge by the customs bureau, and the men were free to do what they would.

When they came from their gorging to the garden, they picked flowers, smelled the many kinds of blossoms, and then the sailors lighted their cigars. This pair were Steve Drinkwater, a Dutchman; and Alex Simoneau, a French-Canadian of Attleboro, Massachusetts.

"Where's the *El Dorado*?" I asked of the captain.

Again he looked at me, suspiciously.

"She went down in thirty-one degrees: two minutes, south and one hundred twenty-one: thirty-seven west," he said curtly, and turned away. There was pride and sorrow in his Scandinavian voice, and a reticence not quite explicable. The three, as they stood a moment before they walked off, made a striking group. Their sturdy figures, in their worn and torn clothes, their hairy chests, their faces framed in bushes of hair, their bronzed skins, and their general air of fighters who had won a battle in which it was pitch and toss if they would survive, made me proud of the race of seamen the world over. They are to-day almost the only followers of a primeval calling, tainted little by the dirt of profit-seeking. They risk their lives daily in the hazards of the ocean, the victims of cold-blooded insurance gamblers and of niggardly owners, and rewarded with only a seat in the poorhouse or a niche in Davy Jones's Locker. I was once of their trade, and I longed to know the happenings of their fated voyage.

Next morning the three were quite ordinary-looking. They were shorn and shaved and scrubbed, and rigged out in Schlyter's white drill trousers and coats. They had rooms under mine in the animal-yard. They were to await the first steamship for the United States, to which country they would be sent as shipwrecked mariners by the American consulate. This vessel would not arrive for some weeks. The captain sat outside his door on the balcony, and expanded his log into a story of his experiences. He had determined to turn author, and to recoup his losses as much as possible by the sale of his manuscript. With a stumpy pencil in hand, he scratched his head, pursed his mouth, and wrote slowly. He would not confide in me. He said he had had sufferings enough to make money out of them, and would talk only to magazine editors.

"There's Easter Island," he told me. "Those curiosities there are worth writing about, too. I've put down a hundred sheets already. I'm sorry, but I can't talk to any one. I'm going to take the boat with me, and exhibit it in a museum and speak a piece."

He was serious about his silence, and as my inquisitiveness was now beyond restraint, I tried the sailors. They would have no log, but their memories might be good.

Alex Simoneau, being of French descent, and speaking the Gallic tongue, was not to be found at the Tiare. He was at the Paris, or other cafe, surrounded by gaping Frenchmen, who pressed upon him Pernoud, rum, and the delicate wines of France. So great was his absorption in his new friends, and so unbounded their hospitality, that M. Lontane laid him by the heels to rest him. Simoneau was wiry, talking the slang of the New York waterfront, swearing that he would "hike for Attleboro, and hoe potatoes until he died." I was forced to seek Steve Drinkwater. Short, pillow-like, as red-cheeked as a winter apple, and yellow-haired, he was a Dutchman, unafraid of anything, stolid, powerful, but not resourceful. I called Steve to my room above Captain Benson's, and set before him a bottle of schnapps, in a square-faced bottle, and a box of cigars.

"Steve," I said, "that squarehead of a skipper of yours won't tell me anything about the El Dorado's sinking and your great trip in the boat. He said he's going to write it up in the papers, and make speeches about it in a museum. He wants to make money out of it."

"Vere do ve gat oop on dat?" asked the Hollander, sorely. "Ve vas dere mit 'im, und vas ve in de museum, py damage? Dot shkvarehet be'n't de only wrider?"

I shuddered at the possible good fortune. I transfixed him with a sharp eye.

"Steve," I asked gentry, "did you keep a log? Pour yourself a considerable modicum of the Hollands and smoke another cigar."

"Vell," said the seaman, after obeying instructions, "I yoost had vun hell of a time, und he make a long rest in de land, I do py dammage! I keep a leedle book from off de day ve shtart ouid."

I heard the measured pace of the brave "shkvarehet" below as he racked his brains for words. I would have loved to aid him, to do all I could to make widely known his and his crew's achievements and gain him fortune. However, he would sow his ink and reap his gold harvest, and I must, by master or by man, hear and record for myself the wonderful incidents of the *El Dorado's* wreck. The insurance was doubtless long since paid on her, and masses said for the repose of the soul of Alex Simoneau. The world would not know of their being saved, or her owners of the manner of her sinking, until these three arrived in San Francisco, or until a few days before, when the steamship wireless might inform them.

Steve came back with a memorandum book in which he had kept day by day the history of the voyage. But it was in Dutch, and I could not read it. I made him comfortable in a deep-bottomed rocker, and I jotted down my understanding of the honest sailor's Rotterdam English as he himself translated his ample notes in his native tongue. I pieced these out with answers to my questions, for often Steve's English was more puzzling than pre-Chaucer poetry.

The *El Dorado* was a five-masted schooner, twelve years old, and left Astoria, Oregon, for Antofagasta, Chile, on a Friday, more than seven months before, with a crew of eleven all told: the captain, two mates, a Japanese cook, and seven men before the mast. She was a man-killer, as sailors term sailing ships poorly equipped and undermanned. The crew were of all sorts, the usual waterfront unemployed, wretchedly paid and badly treated. The niggardliness of owners of ships caused them to pick up their crews at haphazard by paying crimps to herd them from lodging-houses and saloons an hour or two before sailing to save a day's wages. Once aboard, they were virtual slaves, subject to the whims and brutality of the officers, and forfeiting liberty and even life if they refused to submit to all conditions imposed by these petty bosses.

Often the crimps brought aboard as sailors men who had never set foot on a vessel. On the *El Dorado* few were accustomed mariners, and the first few weeks were passed in adjusting crew and officers to one another, and to the routine of the overloaded schooner. When they were fifteen days out they spoke a vessel, which reported them, and after that they saw no other. The mate was a bucko, a slugger, according to Steve, and was hated by all, for most of them during the throes of seasickness had had a taste of his fists.

On the seventy-second day out the *El Dorado* was twenty-seven hundred miles off the coast of Chile, having run a swelling semicircle to get the benefit of the southeast trades, and being far south of Antofagasta. That was the way of the wind, which forced a ship from Oregon to Chile to swing far out from the coast, and make a deep southward dip before catching the south-west trades, which would likely stay by her to her port of discharge.

They had sailed on a Friday, and on Wednesday, the eleventh of the third month following, their real troubles began. Steve's diary, as interpreted by him, after the foregoing, was substantially as follows, the color being all his:

"From the day we sailed we were at the pumps for two weeks to bale the old tub out. Then she swelled, and the seams became tight. There was bad weather from the time we crossed the Astoria bar. The old man would carry on because he was in a hurry to make a good run. The mate used to beat us, and it's a wonder we didn't kill him. We used to lie awake in our watch below and think of what we'd do to him when we got him ashore. All the men were sore on him. He cursed us all the time, and the captain said nothing. You can't hit back, you know. He would strike us and kick us for fun. I felt sure he'd be murdered; but when we got into difficulty and could have tossed him over, we never made a motion.

"On the seventy-third day out, came the terror. The wind is from the southeast. There is little light. The sea is high, and everything is in a smother. We took down the topsails and furled the spanker. The wind was getting up, and the call came for all hands on deck. We had watch and watch until then. That's four hours off and four hours on. When the watch below left their bunks, that was the last of our sleep on the *El Dorado*. A gale was blowing by midnight. We were working all the time, taking in sail and making all snug. There was plenty of water on deck. Schooner was bumping hard on the waves and making water through her seams. We took the pumps for a spell.

"We had no sleep next day. In the morning we set all sails in a lull, but took them down again quickly, because the wind shifted to the northwest, and a big gale came on. Now began trouble with the cargo. We had the hold filled with lumber, planks and such, and on the deck we had a terrible load of big logs. These were to hold up the walls and roofs in the mines of Chile. Many of them were thirty-six feet long, and very big around. They were the trunks of very big trees. They were piled very high, and the whole of them was fastened by chains to keep them from rolling or being broken loose by seas. In moving about the ship we had to walk on this rough heap of logs, which lifted above the rails. They were hard to walk on in a perfectly smooth sea, and with the way the *El Dorado* rolled and pitched, we could hardly keep from being thrown into the ocean.

"This second day of the big storm, with the wind from the northeast, the *El Dorado* began to leak badly again. All hands took spells at the pumps. We were at work every minute. We left the ropes for the pumps and the pumps for the ropes. We double-reefed the mizzen, and in the wind this was a terrible job. It nearly killed us. At eight o'clock to-night we could not see five feet ahead of us. It was black as hell, and the schooner rolled fearfully. The deck-load then shifted eight inches to starboard. This made a list that frightened us. We were all soaking wet now for days. The after-house separated from the main-deck, and the water became six feet deep in the cabin.

"We had no sun at all during the day, and at midnight a hurricane came out of the dark. All night we were pulling and hauling, running along the great logs in danger always of being washed away. We had to lash the lumber, tightening the chains, and trying to stop the logs from smashing the ship to pieces. It did not seem that we could get through the night.

"This is Friday. When a little of daylight came, we saw that everything was awash. The sea was white as snow, all foam and spindrift. It did not seem that we could last much longer. The small boat that had been hanging over the stern was gone. It had been smashed by the combers. We should have had it inboard, and the mate was to blame. Now we took the other boat, the only one left, and lashed it upright to the spanker-stays. In this way it was above the logs and had a chance to remain unbroken.

"We sounded the well, and the captain ordered us again to the pumps. These were on deck between the logs, which were crashing about. We couldn't work the pumps, as there was seven feet of water in there on deck. The second mate spoke to the captain that it would be best to start the steam pump. The smokestack and the rest of the steam fittings were under the fo'c's'le head. It took a long time to get them out, and then the steam pump would not work. The water gained on us all the time now, and the captain ordered us to throw the deck-load overboard. We were nearly dead, we were so tired and sleepy and sore. This morning, the cook served coffee and bread when daylight came at six o'clock. That was the last bit of food or drink we had on the *El Dorado*.

"The taking off of the great chain was a murderous job. When we loosened it, the huge seas would sweep over the logs and us while we tried to get them overboard. It was touch and go. We had to use capstanbars to pry the big logs over and over. We tried to push them with the rolling of the ship. One wave would carry a mass of the logs away, and the next wave would bring them back, crashing into the vessel, catching in the rigging, and nearly pulling it down, and the masts with it. Dodging those big logs was awful work, and if you were hit by one, you were gone. They would come dancing over the side on the tops of the waves and be left on the very spot from which we had lifted them overboard. The old man should have thrown the deck-load over two days before. The water now grew deeper all the time, and the ship wallowed like a waterlogged raft. The fo'c's'le was full of water. The *El Dorado* was drowning with us aboard.

"We were all on deck because we had nowhere else to go. There was nothing in the cabin or the fo'c's'le but water. The sea was now like mountains, but it stopped breaking, so that there was a chance to get away. We were hanging on to stays and anything fixed.

"The captain now gave up hope, as we had long ago. He ordered all hands to make ready to lower the one boat we had left, and to desert the ship. We had a hard time to get this boat loose from the spanker-stay, and we lowered it with the spanker-tackle. Just while we were doing that, a tremendous wave swept the poop, with a battering-ram of logs that had returned. Luckily, the boat we were lowering escaped being smashed, or we had all been dead men now.

"We filled a tank with twenty-five gallons of water from the scuttle-butts and carried it to the boat. The old man ordered the cook and the boy to get some grub he had in a locker in his cabin, high up, where he had put it away from the flood. The cook and the boy were scared stiff, and when they went into the cabin, a sea came racing in, and all saved was twenty pounds of soda crackers, twelve one-pound tins of salt beef, three of tongue, thirty-two cans of milk, thirty-eight of soup, and four of jam.

"We went into the boat with nothing but what we wore, and that was little. Some of us had no coats, and some no hats, and others were without any shoes. We were in rags from the terrible fight with the logs and the sea. The old man went below to get his medicine-chest. He threw away the medicine, and put his log and the ship's papers in it. He took up his chronometer to bring it, when a wave like that which got the cook and the boy knocked the skipper over and lost the chronometer. All he got away with was his sextant and compass and his watch, which was as good as a chronometer.

"We got into the boat at four o'clock. The boat had been put into the water under the stern and made fast by a rope to the taffrail. We climbed out the spankerboom and slid down another rope. The seas were terrific, and it was a mercy that we did not fall in. We had to take a chance and jump when the boat came under us. Last came the old man, and took the tiller. He had the oars manned, and gave the order to let go. That was a terrible moment for all of us, to cast loose from the schooner, bad as she was. There we were all alone in the middle of the ocean, bruised from the struggle on deck, and almost dying from exhaustion and already hungry as wolves. In twenty-four hours we had had only a cup of coffee and a biscuit.

"It was very dark, and we had no light. We were, however, glad to leave the *El Dorado*, because our suffering on her for weeks had been as much as we could bear. The last I saw of the schooner she was just a huge, black lump on the black waters. We rose on a swell, and she sank into a valley out of sight.

"The captain spoke to us now: 'We have a good chance for life,' he said. 'I have looked over the chart, and it shows that Easter Island is about nine hundred miles northeast by east. If we are all together in trying, we may reach there.'

"None of us had ever been to Easter Island, and hardly any of us had ever heard of it. It looked like a long pull there. All night the captain and the mate took turns in steering, while we, in turn, pulled at the oars. We did not dare put a rag of canvas on her, for the wind was big still. The old man said that as we had both latitude and longitude to run, we would run out the latitude first, and then hope for a slant to the land. We were then, he said, in latitude 31° south, and longitude 121° west. That being so, we had about three hundred miles to go south and about six hundred east. He said that Pitcairn Island was but six hundred miles away, but that the prevailing winds would not let us sail there. We set the course, then, for Easter Island. We wondered whether Easter Island had a place to land, and whether there were any people on it. There might be savages and cannibals.

"It rained steady all night, and the sea spilled into the boat now and then. Two of us had to bale all the time to keep the boat afloat. We were soaked to the skin with fresh and salt water, weak from the days of exposure and hunger, and we were barely able to keep from being thrown out of the boat by its terrible rocking and pitching, and yet we all felt like singing a song. All but the Japanese cook. Iwata had almost gone mad, and was praying to his joss whenever anything new happened. During that night a wave knocked him over and crushed one of his feet against the tank of drinking water. The salt water got into the wound and swelled it, and he was soon unable to move.

"The second day in the small boat was the captain's forty-eighth birthday. The old man spoke of it in a hearty way, hoping that when he was forty-nine he would be on the deck of some good ship. There was no sign of the *El Dorado* that morning. But with wind and sea as they were, we could not have seen the ship very far, and we had made some distance under oarpower during the night. We put up our little sail at nine o'clock, though the wind was strong. The skipper said that we could not expect anything but rough weather, and that we had to make the best of every hour, considering what we had to eat and that we were eleven in the boat. The wind was now from the southwest, and we steered northeast. We had to steer without compass because it was dark, and we had no light.

"We had our first bite to eat about noon of this second day out. We had then been nearly three months at sea, or, to be exact, it was seventy-eight days since we had left port. It was thirty hours after the coffee and biscuit on the *El Dorado*, and God knows how much longer since we had had a whole meal, and now we didn't have much. The old man bossed it. He took a half-bucket of fresh water, and into this he put a can of soup. This he served, and gave each man two soda crackers and his share of a pound of corned beef. We dipped the crackers into the bucket. (I tell you it was better than the ham and eggs we had at the hotel when we landed.) We had this kind of a meal twice a day, and no more.

"The next day the wind was again very strong, with thunder and lightning, and we ran dead before the wind with no more sail than a handkerchief. The sea began to break over the boat, and our old man said that we could not live through it unless we could rig up a sea-anchor. We were sure we would drown. We made one by rolling four blankets together tightly and tying around them a long rope with which our boat was made fast to the ship when we embarked. This we let drag astern about ninety-feet. It held the boat fairly steady, and kept the boat's head to the seas. We fastened it to the ring in the stern. We used this sea-anchor many times throughout our voyage, and without it we would have gone down sure. Of course we took in a great deal of water, anyhow; but we could keep her baled out, and the sea-anchor prevented her from swamping.

"The nights were frightful, and many times all of us had terrible dreams, and sometimes thought we were on shore. Men would cry out about things they thought they saw, and other men would have to tell them they were not so. We were always up and down on top of the swells, and our bodies ached so terribly from the sitting-down position and from the joggling of the motion that we would cry with pain. The salt water got in all of our bruises and cracked our hands and feet, but there was no help for us, and we had to grin and bear it. A shark took hold of our sea-anchor and we were afraid that he would tear it to pieces.

"Every day the captain took an observation when he could, and told us where we were. We made about a hundred miles a day, but very often we steered out of our course because we had no matches or lantern.

"On the eighteenth we were in latitude 26° 53' South, and the captain said that Easter Island was in the 27th degree, so after all we had steered pretty well.

"On the night of the nineteenth, we had a fearful storm. It seemed worse than the hurricane we had on the *El Dorado*. All night long we thought that every minute would end us, and we lay huddled in misery, not caring much whether we went down or not. But the next morning, we set part of the sail again, and at noon that day the captain took a sight and found that we were in latitude 27° 8' south. Easter Island is 27° 10' south. And now we began to fear that we might run past Easter Island. If we did, we knew we could never get back with the wind. We had squall after squall now, but we felt sure that soon we must see land. Our soup was all gone, and we were living on the soda crackers mixed with water and milk. Each of us got a cupful of this stuff once a day.

"On the twenty-second, when we were nine days out, I saw the land at ten o'clock in the morning, thirty miles away. We felt pretty good over that, and had two cupfuls of the mixture, because we felt we were nearly safe. My God! what we felt when we saw the rise of that land! The captain said it was Easter Island for certain, but that it was not a place that any merchant ships ever went, as there was no trade there. Once we saw the land we could not get any nearer to it. We tried to row toward it, but the wind was against us. Two days we hung about the back of that island, just outside the line of breakers. We were afraid to risk a landing, for the coast was rocky. On the eleventh day we saw a spot where the rocks looked white, and we rowed in toward it with great pains and much fear. A big sea threw us right upon a smooth boulder, and we leaped from the boat and tried to run ashore. We were weak and fell down many times. Finally we got a hold and we carried everything out of the boat, and after hours hauled it up out of reach of the breakers.

"There was a cliff that went right up straight from the rocks, and we could not climb it, we were so weak from hunger and the cramped position we had had to keep in the boat. We laid down a while, and then it was decided that the first and second mates should have a good feed and try to get up the precipice. We were taking risks, because we had very little grub left. It was about a hundred feet up, and we watched them closely as they went slowly up. They did not come back, and we were much afraid of what they might find. We did not know but there might be savages there. During the day the other sailors also got up, leaving the old man and me to watch the boat.

"Help arrived for us. The mates had walked all night, and at daybreak they reached the house of the head man, employed by the owner of Easter Island. It was a sheep and horse island. The mates were fed, and then they went on to the house of the manager. Horses were gotten out, and bananas and *poi* sent to us. The water just came in time, because we were all out. They brought horses for all of us then, and after we had started the people of the island went ahead and came back with water and milk, which did us a world of good. At the house of the governor we had a mess of brown beans, and then we all fell asleep on the floor. God knows how long we slept, but when we waked up we were like wolves again. We then had beans with fresh killed mutton, and that made us all deathly sick because our stomachs were weak."

* * * * *

Underneath us, while the red-cheeked and golden-haired Steve uttered his puzzling sentences in English, I heard from time to time the heavy tread of Captain Benson. He was, doubtless, living over again the hours of terror and resolution on the *El Dorado* and in the boat, and seeking to find words to amplify his log by his memories. I heard him sit down and get up more than once; while opposite me in an easy-chair, with his glass of Schiedam schnapps beside him, was the virile Dutchman, hammering in his breast-swelling story of danger and courage, of starvation and storm. I sighed for a dictaphone in which the original Dutch-English might be recorded for the delight of others.

Alex Simoneau came back after a night of the hospitality of M. Lontane, and soon was joyous again, telling his wondrous epic of the main to the beach-combers in the parc de Bougainville or in the Paris saloon, where the brown and white toilers of land and sea make merry.

"A man that goes to sea is a fool," he said, with a bang of his fist on the table that made the schnapps dance in its heavy bottle. "My people in Massachusetts are all right, and like a crazy man I will go to sea when I could work in a mill or on a farm. They must think I'm dead by now."

Alex was corroborative of all that Steve said, but I could not pin him down to hours or days. He was too exalted by his present happy fate—penniless, jobless, family in mourning, but healthy, safe, and full-stomached, not to omit an ebullience of spirits incited by the continuing wonder of each new listener and the praise for his deeds and by the conviviality of his admirers.

Alex was sure of one point, and that was that the *El Dorado* was overloaded.

"Dose shkvarehet shkippers vould dake a cheese-box to sea mit a cargo of le't," commented Steve. "All dey care for is de havin' de yob. De owner he don't care if de vessel sink mit de insurance."

When Alex had shuffled out of the cottage, I gave the Dutchman the course of his narrative again.

"You were safe on Easter Island, and ill from stuffing yourself with fresh mutton," I prompted, "And now what?"

Steve spat over the rail.

"Ram, lam', sheep, und muddon for a hundred und fife days. Dere vas noding odder. Dot's a kveer place, dot Easter Island, mit shtone gotts lyin' round und det fulcanoes, und noding good to eat. Ve liffed in a house de English manager gif us. Dere's a Chile meat gompany owns de island, und grows sheep. Aboud a gouple of hundred kanakas chase de sheep. Ve vas dreaded vell mit de vimmen makin' luff und the kanakas glad mit it. Dere vas noding else to do. De manager he say no ship come for six months, und he vanted us to blant bodadoes, und ve had no tobacco. He say de bodadoes get ripe in eight months, und I dink if I shtay dere eight months I go grazy. Ve vas ragged, und efery day ve go und look for a vessel. Ve gould see dem a long vay ouid, und ve made signals und big fires, but no ship efer shtopped. De shkipper made a kvarrel mit de mates, und de old man he say he go away in de boat, und he bick Alex und me because ve was de bestest sailormen. Ve vas dere nearly four months ven ve shtart ouid. De oder men dey vas sore, but dey vanted de old man to bromise to gif dem big money, und ve go for noding. Ve fix oop de boat und ve kvit."

Steve went on to describe how they fixed up the boat for the voyage by making guards of canvas about the sides, and an awning which they could raise and lower. They took a ten-gallon steel oil-drum and made a stove out of it. They cut it in two at the middle and kept the bottom half. They then made a place for holding a pot, with pieces of scrap-iron fixed to the side of the drum, so that they could make a fire under the pot without setting fire to the boat. Then the captain set them to learning to make fire by rubbing sticks, and after many days they learned it. The manager had a steer killed, and they jerked the meat and loaded up their boat beside with sweet potatoes, taro, white potatoes, five dozen eggs, and twenty gallons of water in their tank, with twenty-five more in a barrel.

Then bidding good-by to everybody who gathered to see them off, they steered for Pitcairn Island. They soon found that the prevailing wind would not permit them to make that course, and so they laid for Mangareva in 23° south and 134° west, sixteen hundred miles distant. They had to go from 28° south and 110° west, 5° of latitude and 24° of longitude. Again they were at the mercy of the sea, but now they had only three men in the boat, and had enough food for many days, rough as it was. In the latitude of Pitcairn, the island so famous because to it fled the mutineers of the Bounty, they all but perished. For two days a severe storm nearly overwhelmed them. The boat was more buoyant, and with the sea-anchor trailing, they came through the trial without injury. Steve said the lightning was "yoost like a leedle bid of hell." It circled them about, hissed in the water, and finally struck their mast repeatedly, so that the wise captain took it down. The entire heavens were a mass of coruscating electricity, and they could feel the air alive with it. They were shocked by the very atmosphere, said Steve, and feared for their lives every moment. The sea piled up, the wind blew a gale, and death was close at hand. They wished they had not left Easter Island, and envied those who had remained there.

But they rode it out, with their pile of blankets a-trail, and with helm and oars alert to keep the boat afloat.

The gale amended after several days, and on the sixteenth day from their departure they reached Mangareva. That island is in the Gambier group, and a number of Europeans live there. The castaways were received generously, and were informed that a schooner was expected in a fortnight, which might carry them to some port on their way home. But the old man said they must push on. He had to report to his owners the loss of the *El Dorado*; he had to see his family. They had come twenty-six hundred miles since deserting the schooner, and the thousand miles more to Tahiti was not a serious undertaking. He persuaded Steve and Alex to his manner of thinking, and with the boat stocked with provisions they took the wave again, after a couple of days at Mangareva.

Now the bad weather was over. The sea was comparatively smooth, and the breeze favorable. But fate still had frowns for them, as if to keep them in terror. Sharks and swordfish, as though resenting the intrusion of their tiny craft in waters where boats were seldom seen, attacked them furiously. Five times a giant shark launched himself at their boat, head on, and drove them frantic with his menace of sinking them. They were so filled with this dread that they fastened a marlinespike in the spar, and despite probability of provoking the shark to more desperate onslaughts, maneuvered so that they were able to kill him with a blow.

The next day a swordfish of alarming size played about them, approaching and retreating, eying them and acting in such a manner that they felt sure he was challenging the boat as a strange fish whose might he disputed. One thrust of his bony weapon, and they might be robbed of their chance for life. They shouted and banged on the gunwales, and escaped.

Steve hurried through this part of his diary. So near to safety then, he had had not much thought for a record. There was little more to tell, for after the lightning, the sharks, and the swordfish, they had had no unusual experiences. They had made the voyage of nearly four thousand miles from the pit of water in which they had left the *El Dorado*, and were glad that they had not stayed behind on Easter Island. Steve had only good words for the skipper's skill as a seaman, but now that they were there, he would like to be assured of his wages. The captain said he did not know what the owners would do about paying Steve for the time since the *El Dorado* sank. He was sure she had gone down immediately, for, he said, he would not have left his ship had he not been certain she could not stay on the surface. He contrasted his arrival in Papeete with his coming years before in the brig *Lurline*, when he brought the first phonograph to the South Seas. Crowds had flocked to the quay to hear it, and it was taken in a carriage all about the island.

The superb courage of these men, their marvelous seamanship, and their survival of all the perils of their thousands of miles' voyage were not lessened in interest or admiration by their personality. But one realized daily, as one saw them chewing their quids, devouring rudely the courses served by Lovaina, or talking childishly of their future, that heroes are the creatures of opportunity. It is true Steve and Alex were picked of all the crew for their sea knowledge and experience, their nerve and willingness, by the sturdy captain, and that he, too, was a man big in the primitive qualities, a viking, a companion for a Columbus; but—they were peculiarly of their sept; types molded by the wind-swept spaces of the vasty deep, chiseled by the stress of storm and calm, of burning, glassy oceans, and the chilling, killing berg; men set apart from all the creeping children of the solid earth, and trained to seize the winds from heaven for their wings, to meet with grim contempt the embattled powers of sky and wave, and then, alas! on land to become the puny sport of merchant, crimp, and money-changer, and rum and trull.

Goeltz, Lying Bill, Llewellyn, and McHenry sat in the Cercle Bougainville with eager looks as I read them the diary of Steve Drinkwater. The seamen held opinions of the failure of Captain Benson's seamanship at certain points, and all knew the waters through which he had come.

"Many of the people of Mangareva came from Easter Island," said Lying Bill. "There was a French missionary brought a gang of them there. 'E was Père Roussel, and 'e ran away with 'em because Llewellyn's bloody crowd 'ere tried to steal 'em and sell 'em. They lived at Mangareva with 'im till he died a few years ago, and they never went back."

Llewellyn lifted his dour eyes. There was never such a dule countenance as his, dark naturally with his Welsh and Tahitian blood, and shaded by the gloom of his soul. He looked regretfully at Captain Pincher.

"You are only repeating the untruthful assertion of that clergyman," he said accusingly. "He put it in a pamphlet in French. My people have had to do with Easter Island for forty years. I lived there several years and, as you know, I made that island what it is now, a cattle and sheep ranch. It is the strangest place, with the strangest history in the world. If we knew who settled it originally and carved those stone gods the Dutch sailor spoke of, we would know more about the human race and its wanderings.

"The Peruvians murdered and stole the Easter Islanders. Just before we took hold there, a gang of blackbirders from Peru went there and killed and took away many hundreds of them. They sold them to the guano diggings in the

Chincha Islands. Only those escaped death or capture who hid in the dark caverns. Nearly all those taken away died soon. We then made contracts with some of those left, and took them to Tahiti to work. It is true they died, too, most of them, but some you can find where McHenry lives half a mile from here at Patutoa. We sold off the stock to Chileans, and that country owns the island now.

"I think the island had a superior race once. There are immense platforms of stone, like the *paepaes* of the Marquesas, only bigger, and the stones are all fitted together without cement. They built them on promontories facing the sea. Some are three hundred feet long, and the walls thirty feet high. On these platforms there were huge stone gods that have been thrown down; some were thirty-seven feet high, and they had redstone crowns, ten feet in diameter. There were stone houses one hundred feet long, with walls five feet thick. How they moved the stones no one knows, for, of course, these people there now were not the builders. Some race of whom they knew nothing was there before them.

"They are one of the greatest mysteries in the world. Easter is the queerest of all the Maori islands. They had nothing like the other Maoris had in any of these islands, but they had plenty of stone, their lances were tipped with obsidian, and they were terrible fighters among themselves. They had no trees, and so no canoes; and they depended on driftwood and the hibiscus for weapons. They are all done for now."

Captain Benson was still busied with his log when the steamship from New Zealand arrived to take the shipwrecked men away. The *El Dorado's* boat was stowed carefully on the deck of the liner. I saw the skipper watching it as the deck-hands put chocks under it and made it fast against the rolling of the ship. That boat deserved well of him, for its stanchness had stood between him and the maws of the sharks many days and nights.

I bade him and the two seamen good-by on the wharf. The old man was full of his plan to exhibit the boat in a museum and of selling his account of his adventures to a magazine.

The crew left on Easter Island were rescued sooner than they had expected. A British tramp, the *Knight of the Garter*, put into Easter Island for emergency repairs, having broken down. The castaways left with her for Sydney, Australia, and from there reached San Francisco by the steamship *Ventura*, ten months after they had sailed away on the *El Dorado*. That schooner was never sighted again.

Chapter XI

I move to the Annexe—Description of building—The baroness and her baby—Evoa and poia—The corals of the lagoon—The Chinese shrine—The Tahitian sky.

Lovaina suggested, since I liked to be about the lagoon, that I move to the Annexe, a rooming-house she owned and conducted as an adjunct to the Tiare. I moved there, and regretted that I had stayed so long in the animal-yard. And yet I should have missed knowing Lovaina intimately, the hour-to-hour incidents of her curious menage, the close contact with the girls and the guests, the *El Dorado* heroes, the Dummy, and others.

The Annexe fronted the lagoon. It was a two-story building, with broad verandas in front and rear, and stood back a few feet from the Broom Road. It had a very large garden behind, with tall cocoanut trees, and the finest rose-bushes in Tahiti. Vava, the Dummy, put all the sweepings from his stable on the flower beds, and Lovaina cut the roses for the tables at the Tiare Hotel and for presents to friends and prosperous tourists. Vava was often about the garden, and drove Lovaina to and fro in her old chaise.

When he brought me and my belongings from the Tiare, Lovaina came with us. She signed to him to go to the *glacerie*, the ice- and soda-water factory, to buy ice for the hotel. The Dummy was intensely jealous of new-comers whom Lovaina liked. He left on foot, but merely took a walk, and, returning, answered her question by opening his hands and shaking his head, conveying perfectly the statement that the *glacerie* had refused Lovaina credit because of her debt to it of two hundred francs, and that cash was demanded. He intimated that the proprietor had ridiculed her.

"That dam' lie," said Lovaina to him and to me,—she always supplemented her gestures to him with words,—and she made a sign that she had paid the bill. He uttered a choking sound of anger, accompanied by a dreadful grimace, and after a little while came back with a large piece of ice, which he placed in the carriage. Lovaina told him to break off a lump for my room. He became indignant, and in pantomime vividly described the suffering of guests at the Tiare with the ice exhausted, and Lovaina's plight if she could sell no more drinks.

Lovaina persisted, and when I went to take the ice myself, he struck me with his horsewhip. Temanu, who had come with Lovaina, rushed out shrieking, and the Dummy, seeing his advantage, began to threaten all who came at the noise. Afa, a half-white, who lives in a cottage in the garden, and who alone could control him, slapped his face. The wretched mute sat down and wept bitterly until Lovaina rubbed his back, and informed him that he was again in her good graces. I, too, smiled upon him, and he became a happy child for a moment.

The Annexe was decaying fast. In the great storm of 1906 it was partly blown down, and was poorly restored. It was the prey of rat and insect, dusty, neglected, but endearing. It had had a season of glory. It was built for the first modern administration office of the French Government, over sixty years before, and was painted white with blue trimmings. In its bare and dusty entrance-hall hung two steel engravings entitled, "The Beginning of the Civil War in the United States" and "The End of the Civil War in the United States." The former showed Freedom in the center; Justice with a sword and balance; the Stars and Stripes being torn from a liberty-tree, with a snake winding about it; an aged man labeled Buchanan asleep on a big book; and a gentleman named Floyd counting a bag of money; on the other side Abraham Lincoln exhorted a white-haired general who commanded a file of soldiers, and some rich-looking men were throwing money on the floor.

The other picture was indeed florid. It represented three ladies, Freedom, Justice, and Mercy, disputing the center, slaves being unshackled, the army of victory led by Grant claiming honors, Lee handing over a sword, an ugly fellow toting off a bag of gold (graft?) and a gang of conspirators egging on the madman Booth to slay Lincoln. In both these engravings there were scores of supposed likenesses, but I could not identify them. They were published by Kimmel & Forster in New York in 1865, and had probably decorated Papeete walls for half a century. There were large, ramshackle chambers on the first floor, and an exquisite winding staircase, with a rosewood balustrade, led to the second story, where I lived.

In this building all the pomp and circumstance of the Nations in Tahiti had been on parade, kings and queens of the island had pleaded and submitted, admirals and ensigns had whispered love to dusky *vahines*, and the petty wars of Oceanic had been planned between waltzes and wines. Here Loti put his arms about his first Tahitian sweetheart, and practised that vocabulary of love he used so well in "Rarahu," "Madame Chrysantheme," and his other studies of the exotic woman. A hundred noted men, soldiers, and sailors, scientists and dilettanti, governors and writers, had walked or worked in those tumbling rooms.

Lovaina had owned the building many years, buying it from the thrifty French Government.

My apartment was of two rooms, and my section of the balcony was cut off by a door, giving privacy unusual in Tahiti. The coloring of the wall was rich in hue.

Any color, so it's red, said a satirist, who might have been characterizing my rooms. Turkey-red muslin with a large, white diamond figure was pasted on the plaster walls and hung in the doorways.

"It very bes' the baroness could do in T'ytee," explained Lovaina. "She must be bright all about, and she buy and fix rooms. She have whole top floor Annexe, and spen' money like gentleman, two or three thousand dollar' every month. I wish you know her. She talk beautiful', and never one word smut. Hones', true. Johnny, my son, read 'Three Weeks' that time, and he speak the baroness, 'You jus' like that woman in the book.' She have baby here and take with her to Paris. She want that baby jus' like 'Three Weeks.' Oh, but she live high! She have her own servants, get everything in market, bring peacocks and pheasants and turkeys from America. How you think? Dead? No. She sen' man to bring on foot on boat. You go visit her, she give champagne jus' like Papenoo River. She beautiful? My God! I tell you she like angel. She speak French, English, Russian, German, Italian, anything the same. She good, but she don't care a dam' what people say. When she go 'way Europe she give frien's all her thing'. Now she back in her palace with her baby. She write once say she come back T'ytee some day by'n'by. She love T'ytee somethin' crazee."

At the Cercle Bougainville Captain William Pincher told me more of the baroness.

"Is the bloody meat-safe still on the back porch? The baroness made a voyage with me to the Paumotus just for the air. She sat on deck all the time, rain or shine. I'd put a' awnin' over 'er in fair weather or when it rained and there wasn't much wind. She was a bloody good sailor, too, and ate like us, only she never went below except at night. I give her my cabin. She'd spen' hours lookin' over the side in a calm—we had no engine—an' she'd listen to all the yarns."

Lying Bill burst out with one of his choicest oaths.

"She wasn't like some of those ladees I've 'ad aboard. She was a proper salt-water lass. She loved to 'ear my yarns of the sea. When she was big with child an' I ashore, I 'ad the 'abit o' droppin' in o' afternoons and 'avin' a slice of 'am or chicken out o' the safe. Afa ran 'er bloody show for 'er, an' it cost 'er a bloody fortune. I used to lie for 'er to 'ear 'er laugh. You know I'm called Lyin' Bill, but McHenry tells more real lies in a day than I do in a bloody year. She was the finest-looking girl of the delicate kind I ever saw, all pink and white an' with fringy clothes an' little feet. Oh! there was nothing between us but the sea, an' I know that subject."

Lying Bill sighed like a diver just up from the bottom of the lagoon.

"You know that big cocoanut tree in the garden of the Annexe? She would sit under that with me an' smoke her Cairo cigarettes an' talk about her bally kiddie. She wanted him to be strong an' to love the sea, and she thought by talking with me about 'im an' ships an' the ocean she could sort of train him that way, though he'd been got in Paris an' might be a girl. Is there anything in that bleedin' idea? She could quote books all right about it."

Ah, beautiful and brave baroness! I often thought of you during those months in the Annexe. You will come again, you say, to Tahiti, bathe again in its witching waters, and let the spell of its sweetness bind you again to its soil. Maybe, but baroness, you will never again be as you were, flinging all body and soul into the fire of passion, and yearning for motherhood! Such times can never be the same. We burn, even desire, and consume our dreams. Child of aristocracy, you found in this South Sea eyot the freedom your atavism, or shall I say, naturalness, craved, and you drank your cup to the lees and thought it good. I shall not be the one to point a finger at you, nor even to think too vivid the scarlet of my toilet set. That flamboyant outside my window, once yours, is as garish, and yet lacks no consonance with all about it.

The scene from my veranda was a changing picture of radiance and shadow. Directly below was the Broom Road. Umbrageous flamboyants—the royal poincianas, or flame-trees—sheltered the short stretch of sward to the water, and their blossoms made a red-gold litter upon the grass. A giant acacia whose flowers were reddish pink and looked like thistle blooms, protected two canoes, one my own and one Afa's. The Annexe was bounded by the Broom Road and the rue de Bougainville, and across that street was the restaurant of Mme. Fanny. It was built over a tiny stream, which emptied fifty feet away into the lagoon. A clump of banana-trees hid the patrons, but did not obscure their view from Fanny's balcony.

In the lagoon, a thousand yards from me, was Motu Uta, a tiny island ringed with golden sand, a mass of green trees half disclosing a gray house. Motu Uta was a gem incomparable in its beauty and its setting. It had been the place of revels of old kings and chiefs, and Pomaré the Fourth had made it his residence. Cut off by half a mile of water from Papeete, it had an isolation, yet propinquity, which would have persuaded me to make it my home were I a governor; but it was given over to quarantine purposes, with an old caretaker who came and went in a commonplace rowboat.

The Annexe housed many rats. I brought to my rooms a basket of bananas, and put it on a table by my bed, the canopied four-poster in which the son of the baroness was born. In the night I was awakened by a tremendous thump on the floor and a curious dragging noise. I listened breathlessly. But the rat must have heard me, for he ceased operations, only returning when he thought I was asleep. He leaped on the table, scratched a banana from the basket, threw it to the floor, and pulled it to his den near the wardrobe. The joists and floor boards were eaten away by the ants, and in one hole six or seven inches long this rat had entrance to his den between the floor and the ceiling of the room below. He had trading proclivities, and in exchange brought me old and valueless trifles. I once knew a miner in Arizona who found a rich gold-vein through a rat bringing him a piece of ore in exchange for a bit of bacon. He traced the rat to his nest and discovered the source of the ore. The rats had their ancient enemies to guard against, and the cats of Tahiti, not indigenous, slept by day and hunted by night. They cavorted through the Annexe in the smallest hours, and one often wakened to their shrieks and squeals of combat. The tom-cats had tails longer than their bodies, the climate, their habits and food developing them extraordinarily.

The roosters grew to a size unequaled, and those in the garden of the Annexe roused me almost at dawn. Their voices were horrific, and one that had fathered a quartet of ducks—an angry tourist had killed the drake because of his quacking—was a *vrai Chantecler*. When he waked me, the sun was coming over the hills from Hitiaa, brightened Papenoo and leaped the summits to Papeete, but it was long before the phantom of false morning died and the god of day rode his golden chariot to the sea. The Diadem was gilded first, and down the beach the long light tremulously disclosed the faint scarlet of the flamboyant-trees, their full, magnificent color yet to be revealed, and their elegant contours like those graceful, red-tiled pagodas on the journey to Canton in far Cathay.

Motu Uta crept from the obscurity of the night, and the battlements of Moorea were but dim silhouettes. The lagoon between the reef and the beach was turning from dark blue to azure pink. The miracle of the advent of the day was never more delicately painted before my eyes.

In my crimson *pareu* I descended the grand staircase, which had often echoed to the booted tread of admiral and sailor, of diplomat and bureaucrat, and outside the building I passed along the lower rear balcony to the bath. The Annexe, like the Tiare Hotel, made no pretense to elegance or convenience. The French never demand the latter at home, and the Tahitian is so much an outdoor man that water-pipes and what they signify are not of interest to him.

The bath of the Annexe was a large cement tank, primarily for washing clothes. Its floor was as slippery as ice. One held to the window-frame at the side, and turned the tap.

A shower fell a dozen feet like rose-leaves upon one. Ah, the waters of Tahiti! Never was such gentle, velvety rain, a benediction from the *tauupo o te moua*, the slopes of the mountains.

I deferred my pleasure a few minutes as the place under the shower was occupied by an entrancing pair, Evoa, the consort of Afa, and her four-months-old infant, Poia. Evoa was sixteen years old, tall, like most Tahitians, finely figured, slender, and with the superb carriage that is the despair of the corseted women who visit Tahiti. Her features were regular, but not soft. Her skin was ivory-white, with a glint of red in cheek and lip, and the unconfined hair that reached her hips was intensely black and fine, I could see no touch or tint of the Polynesian except in the slight harshness of the contours of her face, and that her legs were more like yellow satin than white. Her foot would have given Du Maurier inspiration for a brown *Trilby*. It was long, high-arched, perfect; the toes, never having known shoes, natural and capable of grasp, and the ankle delicate, yet strong. Her father she believed to have been a French official who had stayed only a brief period in Bora-Bora, her mother's island, and whose very name was forgotten by her. She had not seen her mother since her first year, having, as is the custom here, been adopted by others.

Poia had a head like a cocoanut, her eyes shiny, black buttons, her body roly-poly, and her pinkish-yellow feet and hands adorable. Evoa was dressing her for the market in a red muslin slip, a knitted shawl of white edged with blue, and, shades of Fahrenheit! a cap with pink ribbons, and socks of orange. Evoa herself would wear a simple tunic, which was most of the time pulled down over the shoulder to give Poia ingress to her white breast. Poia was like a flower, and I had never heard her cry, this good nature being accounted for perhaps by an absence of pins, as she was usually naked. She had two teeth barely peeping from below.

Evoa spoke only Tahitian, which is the same tongue as that spoken in Bora-Bora, and she was totally without education. Afa had found her, and brought her to his cabin in the garden. He did not claim to be the father of Poia, but was delighted, as are all Polynesians, to find a mate and, with her, certainty of a little one. They have not our selfishness of paternity, but find in the assumed relation of father all the pride and joy we take only with surety of our relationship.

Afa was a handsome half-caste, his mustache and light complexion, his insouciance and frivolity, his perfect physique, skill with canoe and fish-net and spear, his flirtations with many women, and his ability to provide amusement for the guests, making him a superior type of the white-brown blood. There was a black tragedy in this life which, with all his heedlessness, often and again imprisoned him in deep melancholy.

His father was a wealthy Italian who lived near the home of a Tahitian princess, and who won the girl's love against her father's commands. Afa was born, the princess was sent away, and the child brought up in a good family. When he was fourteen years old he was taken to the United States. His father became engaged in a quarrel with certain natives whom he forbade to cross his land to gather *feis* in the mountains. As they had always had this right, they resented his imposition, and plotted to kill him. He disappeared, and a long time afterward his body was found loosely covered with earth, the feet above the surface. In court the surgeons swore that he had been alive when buried. A number of men were tried for the crime and sentenced to life imprisonment in New Caledonia.

Afa returned from America to find that much of his father's property had been stolen or claimed by others, and he became a cook and servant. He had been many years with Lovaina, and though he owned valuable land, he preferred the hotel life, half domestic, half manager and confidant, to the quietude of the country. In Afa's single room were two brass bedsteads, many gaudy tidies, an engraving of the execution of Nathan Hale, and a toilet-table full of fancy notions. Evoa was always barefooted, but Afa, on steamer days and when going to the cinematograph, appeared in immaculate white and with canvas shoes. Otherwise he wore only a fold of cloth about the loins, the real garment of the Tahitian, and the right one for that climate.

Again on my balcony, I saw the sun had passed the crown of the Diadem and was slanting hotly toward Papeete. Moorea was emerging from darkness, its valleys a deep brown, and the tops of the serried mountains becoming green.

Along the reef, outside, a schooner, two-masted, was making for the harbor. She was very graceful, and as she entered the lagoon through the passage in the barrier I was struck by her lines, slender, swelling, and feminine. She passed within a few hundred feet of me, and I saw that she was the *Marara*, the *Flying-Fish*.

I did not know it then, but I was to go on that little vessel to the blazing atolls of the Dangerous Archipelago, and to see stranger and more fascinating sights than I had dreamed of on the *Noa-Noa* during my passage to Tahiti.

I dragged my canoe to the edge of the quai des Subsistances, so-called because of the naval depot. The craft was dubbed out of a breadfruit-tree trunk, and had an outrigger of *purau* wood, a natural crooked arm, with a small limb laced to it. The canoe was steady enough in such smooth water, and I paddled off to Motu Uta. That islet is a rock of coral upon which soil had been placed unknown years before, and which produced fruits and flowers in abundance under the hand of the caretaker. Motu Uta is about as large as a city building lot, and the coral hummock shelves sharply to a considerable depth. Under this declining reef were the rarest shapes and colors of fish. They swam up and down, and in and out of their blue and pink and ivory-colored homes, slowly and majestically, or darting hither and thither, angered at the intrusion of my canoe in their domain, courting and rubbing fins, repelling invaders. The little ones avoiding dexterously the appetites of their big friends, and these moving pompously, but warily, seeking what they might devour.

A collector of corals would find many sorts there. They are wonderful, these stony plants, graceful, strange, bizarre. The Tahitian, who has a score of names for the winds, and who classifies fish not only by their names, but changes these names according to size and age, makes only a few lumps of the coral. It is *to'a*, and when round is *to'a ati*, *to'a apu*; when branching, *uruhi*, *uruana*; when in a bank, *to'a aau*; when above the surface of the water, *to'a raa*. A submerged mass is *to'a faa ruru*, and the coral on which the waves break, *to'a auau*. However, the native knows well that one species of coral, the *ahifa*, is corrosive, irritating the skin when touched, and another, which is poisoned by the *hara* plants, is termed *to'a harahia*.

Coral makes good lime for whitening walls, and is cut into blocks for building. Many churches in Tahiti were built of coral blocks. The puny fortifications erected by the French in the war with the Tahitians decades ago were of coral stones, and are now black with age and weather.

I headed my canoe toward the barrier reef, and tied it to a knob of coral. Then I stepped out upon the reef itself, my tennis shoes keeping the sharp edges from cutting my feet. It was the low tide succeeding sunrise, and the water over the reef was a few inches deep, so that I could see the marine life of the wall, the many kinds of starfish, the sea-urchins, and the curious bivalves which hide with their shell-tips just even with the floor of the lagoon, and, keeping them barely even, wait for foolish prey.

The floor of the lagoon was most interesting; the prodigality of nature in the countless number of low forms of life, their great variety, their beauty, and their ugliness, and, appealing to me especially, the humor of nature in the tricks she played with color and shape, her score of clowns of the sea equaling her funny fellows ashore, the macaws, the mandrills, the dachshunds, and the burros.

The sunlight on the water at that hour was like silver spangles on a sapphire robe. I paddled near to the *Marara*, and watched her let go her anchor and send her boat ashore with a stern line. Fastened to a cannon and passed around a bitt on the schooner, the crew hauled her close to the embankment, and soon she was broadside to, and her gangway on the quay. Her captain, M. Moet, Woronick, a pearl merchant, a government physician, and the passengers from the Paumotus were soon ashore shaking hands with friends. I walked behind them to Lovaina's for coffee, and was introduced to them all.

Woronick took me to his house across the street from the Tiare Hotel, and there opened a massive safe and showed me drawer after drawer of pearls. They were of all sizes and shapes and tints, from a pear-shaped, brilliant, Orient pearl of great value, to the golden *pipi* of inconsiderable worth. Woronick spoke of a pearl he had bought some years ago in Takaroa, the creation of which, he said, had cost the lives of three men including a great savant.

"If you go to Takaroa," said Woronick, "be sure to see old Tepeva a Tepeva. He used to be one of the best divers in the Low Islands, but he's got the bends. He sold me the greatest pearl ever found in these fisheries in the last twenty years, and I made enough profit on it to buy a house in Paris and live a year. Get him to tell you his yarn. It beats Monte Cristo all hollow."

Which I made a note to do.

In the afternoon, with Charlie Eager, a guest at the Annexe, I went to the worship-place of the Chinese, on the Broom Road. Outwardly, it had not the flaunting distinction of the joss-houses of the Far East or those of New York or San Francisco. The Chinese usually builds his temples even in foreign lands in the same Oriental superfluity of color and curve and adornment that makes them exclusively the Middle Kingdom's own; but here he had been content to have a simple, whitewashed church which might be a meeting-house or school. It was set in the center of a great garden in which mango and cocoa and breadfruit abounded. We were struck by the superb breadth and immense height of a breadfruit-tree the shadows of which fell over a small brick pagoda. This tree was a hundred feet tall, and the always glorious leaves, as large as aprons, indented and a glossy, dark green, made it a temple in itself worthier of the ministrations of priests than the ugly brick or frame structure of our cities. The Druids in their groves were nearer to the real God than the pursy bishop in the steam-heated cathedral.

A native woman, aged and bent, said "Ia ora na!" to us, and we replied. With my few words of Tahitian I gained from her that the joss-house was open. We entered it, and found no one there. The center was wide to the sky, that the rain might fall and the stars shine within it. The altars were brilliant with memorial tablets, the green, red, and gold flower vases, and sandalwood taper-holders, so familiar to me, and all about were the written prayers of devotees, soliciting the favor of Heaven, asking success in business, or the averting of illness. They were evidently painted by the bonze of the fane, for his slab of India ink was on a table nearby, as also the brushes for the ideographs.

Sons expressed their filial duties in glittering excerpts from Confucius, carved and gilded on expansive boards, and the incense of the poor arose from the humble punksticks stuck in dishes of sand upon the floor.

No Levite sat within the shrine or watched to see if profane hand touched the sacred symbols, and were Charlie Eager sure of that before we left, he had secured a trophy. Not knowing but that from one of the numerous crannies or mayhap from the open roof the wrathful eye of a hierophant was upon him, he had to content himself with a prayer from the pagoda, which proved on close inspection to be a furnace for the burning of the paper slips on which the aspirations of the faithful were written. Whether the prayers had been granted, were out of date, or the time paid for hanging in the joss-house had expired, the crematory was four feet deep with the red and white rice-paper legends, awaiting an auspicious occasion for incineration. Eager of Inglewood, California, fished secretly, hidden by my body, until he found a particularly long and intricate set of hieroglyphics, and deposited it in his pocket. Then we fled.

More than two thousand Chinese in Tahiti, nearly all kin within a few degrees, found in this humble church a substitute for their family temples in China, where usually each clan has its own place of worship. The laboring class of this fecund people seldom extend their real devotion beyond their ancestors and the principle of fatherhood, their reasoning being that of the wise Jewish charge to honor one's father (and mother) that one's life may be long. Loving sons take care of old parents. It is the old Oriental patriarchy sublimated by the imposition of commerce upon agriculture.

The Chinese came to Tahiti during the American Civil War. They were brought by an English planter to grow cotton, then scarce on account of the blockade and desolation of the South. With the end of the war, and the looms of Manchester again supplied, the plantation languished, and the Chinese took other employment, became planters themselves, or set up little shops. They now had most of the retail business of the island, and all of it outside Papeete.

The secretary-general gave me figures about them.

"There are twenty-two hundred Chinese in Tahiti now," said he. "We are willing to receive all who come. They are needed to restore the population. Who would keep the stores or grow vegetables if we did not have the Chinese? We exact no entrance fee, but we number every man, and photograph him, to keep a record. There is no government agent in China to further this emigration, but those here write home, and induce their relatives to come. We hope for enough to make labor plentiful. All cannot keep stores."

"Have you no Japanese?"

"Only those who work for the phosphate company at the island of Makatea," replied the secretary-general. "They are well paid, their fare to Tahiti and return secured, and otherwise they are favored. The Government has agreed with a company to promote Chinese emigration to the Marquesas. There are thousands needed. In French Oceanie there are twelve thousand possible workers for nearly a million acres of land. This land could easily feed two hundred thousand people. The natives are dying fast, and we must replace them, or the land will become jungle."

"Couldn't you bring French Chinese from Indo-China?" I asked.

"We haven't any workers to spare there," he answered.

In Papeete the Chinese were, as in America, a mysterious, elusive race, the immigrants remaining homogeneous in habits, closely united in social and business activities, and with a solid front to the natives and the whites. They lived much as in China, though in more healthful surroundings. Every vice they had in China they brought to Tahiti; their virtues they left behind, except those strict ethics in commerce and finance which must be carried out successfully to "save face." Their community in this island, with a climate and people as different from their own as the land from the sea, was in their thoughts a part of Canton and the farms of Quan-tung. All the bareness, dirt, and squalid atmosphere of home they had sought to bring to the South Seas. They saw the other nationals here as objects of ridicule and spoilage. The amassing of a competence before old age or against a return to China, and the marrying there, or the resumption of marital relations with the wife he had left to make his fortune, was the fiercely sought goal of each.

Loti wrote nearly fifty years ago, a decade after their influx:

"The Chinese merchants of Papeete were objects of disgust and horror to the natives. There was no greater shame than for a young woman to be convicted of listening to the gallantries of one of them. But the Chinese were wicked and rich, and it was notorious that several of them, by means of presents and money, had obtained clandestine favors which made amends to them for public scorn."

Had Admiral Julien Viaud returned now to Tahiti, he would have found the Chinese stores thronged by the handsomest girls, their restaurants thriving on their charms, and the Chinese the possessors of the pick of the lower and middle classes of young women. Ah Sin is persistent; he has no sense of Christian shame, and as in the Philippines, he dresses his women gaily, and wins their favors despite his evil reputation, his ugliness, and his being despised.

At the Cercle Bougainville I saw more than one Chinese playing cards and drinking. These were Chinese who had made money, and who in the give and take of business have pushed themselves into the club of the other merchants, who feared and watched them.

Women were not allowed in barrooms in Papeete. The result was that they went to the Chinese restaurants and coffee-houses to drink beer and wine at tables, as legalized. A concomitant of this was that men went to these places to meet women, and further that women were retained or persuaded by the Chinese to frequent their places so as to stimulate the sale of intoxicants. The Chinese restaurants naturally became assignation houses.

Walking back, late in the afternoon, from the joss-house, we met Lovaina in her automobile, with the American negro chauffeur, William, and Temanu, Atupu, and Iromea. She invited me to accompany them to swim in the Papenoo River, a few miles towards Point Venus. Other guests of the Tiare Hotel came in hired cars, and twenty or thirty joined in the bath. The river was a small flood, rains having swelled it so that a current of five or six knots swept one off one's feet and down a hundred and fifty feet before one could seize the limb of an overhanging tree. We undressed in the bushes, and the men wore only *pareus*, while the girls had an extra gown. They were expert swimmers, climbing into the tops of the trees, and hurling themselves with screams into the water. They struck it in a sitting posture making great splashes and reverberations. Their muslin slips outlined their strong bodies, so that they were like veiled goddesses, their brownblack hair floating free, as they leaped or fought and tumbled with the tide. We stayed an hour at this sport, joined when school was dismissed by all the youth of Papenoo. Under twelve they bathed naked, but those older wore *pareus*.

It was hard to keep on a *pareu* in a swift-running stream unless one knew how to tie it. I lost mine several times, and had to grope shamefacedly in the race for it, until finally Lovaina made the proper knots and turned it into a diaper.

"I not go swim now," she said regretfully, "'cep' some night-time. Too big. Before I marry, eighteen seven'y-nine, and before my three children grow up, I swim plenty then."

"Lovaina," I said, "it was hardly eighteen seventynine you were married. You are only forty-three now. Was it not eighty-nine?"

"Mus' be," she replied thoughtfully. "I nineteen when marry. My father give me that house, now Tiare Hotel, for weddin' present. All furnish. You should see that marry! My God! there was bottle in yard all broken. Admiral

French fleet send band; come hisself with all his officer'. Five o'clock mornin'-time still dance and drink. Bigges' time T'ytee. You not walk barefoot long time 'count broken glass everywhere."

I had heard that delicious incident before, but it never lost savor.

After dinner and a prolonged session upon the camphor-wood chest to hear Lovaina's chatter, I came leisurely to the Annexe along the shore of the lagoon. It was after midnight, and the heavens sang with stars as the ripe moon dipped into the western sea.

The tropics only know the fullness of the firmament, the myriad of suns and planets, the brilliancy of the constellations, and the overpowering revelation of the infinite above. In less fervent latitudes one can never feel the bigness of the vault on high, nor sense the intimacy one had here with the worlds that spin in the measureless ether.

Two lofty-sparred ships but newly from the California coast swung at moorings within a dozen feet of the grass that borders the coral banks, and on their decks, under the light of lamps, American sailors lifted a shanty of the rolling Mississippi. I remembered when I had first heard it. I was a boy, and had stolen away on a bark, the *Julia Rollins*, bound for Rio, and as we hauled in the line let go by the tow-boat, a seaman raised the bowline song. To me, with "Two Years Before the Mast" and Clark Russell's galley yarns churning in my mind, it was sweeter far than ever siren voiced to lure her victims to their death, and rough and tarry as was the shanty-man, Caruso had never seemed to me such a glorious figure.

This fascination of the sea and of its border had never left me, though I had passed years on ships and nearly all my life within sound of the surf. It is as strong as ever, holding me thrall in the sight of its waters and its freights, and unhappy when denied them. Best of all literature I love the stories of old ocean, and glad am I

That such as have no pleasure
For to praise the Lord by measure,
They may enter into galleons and serve him on the sea.

In Tahiti the sea was very near and meant much. One felt toward it as must the mountaineer who lives in the shadow of the Matterhorn; it was always part of one's thoughts, for all men and things came and went by it, and the great world lay beyond it.

But dear or near as the sea might be to such a man as I, a mere traveler upon it to reach a goal, to the Tahitian it was life and road and romance, too. Legends of it filled the memories of those old ones who, though in tattered form, preserved yet awhile the deeds of daring of their fathers and the terrors of storm and sea monster, of long journeys in frail canoes, of discoveries and conquerings, of brides taken from other peoples, and of the gods and devils who were in turn masters of the deep.

Once a Tahitian stopped the sun as it sank beyond Moorea not to wage war, as Joshua, but to please his old mother. The sea and the heavens are brothers to the Tahitian. The sky had two great tales for him—guidance for his craft and prophecies for his soul; but he did not inhabit it with his gods or his dead, as do Christians and other religionists, for the mountains, the valleys, and the caves were the abiding-places of spirits, and the Tahitian had named only those stars which blazed forth most vividly or served him as compass on the sea. He did, however, mark the various phases of the sky, and in his musical tongue named them with particularity.

The firmament is *te ao*, *te rai*, and the atmosphere *te reva*, and when peaceful, *raiatea*. This is the name of one of the most beautiful islands of this Society group, "Raiatea la Sacrée," it is called, "Raiatea the Blessed," and its own serenity is betokened in its name.

E hau maru, e maru to oe rai
E topara, te Mahana
I Ra' i-atea nei!

So ran the rhyme of Raiatea:

Full of a sweet peace, serene thy sky;
Bright are all thy days
At Raiatea here.

Rai poia or *poiri*, they say for the gloomy heavens, and *rai maemae* when threatening, *parutu* when cloudy, *moere* if clear; if the clouds presage wind, *tutai vi*. The sunset is *tooa o te ra*, and the twilight *marumarupo*.

The night is *te po* or *te rui*, and the moment before the sun rises *marumaru ao*. A hundred other words and phrases differentiate the conditions of sky and air. I learned them from Afa and Evoa and others.

The moon is *te marama*, and the full moon *vaevae*. Mars is *fetia ura*, the red star; the Pleiades are *Matarii*, the little eyes; and the Southern Cross, *Tauha*, *Fetia ave* are the comets, the "stars with a tail," and the meteors *pao*, *opurei*, *patau*, and *pitau*.

The moon was gone, but the stars needed no help, for they shone as if the trump of doom were due at dawn, and they should be no more. Blue and gold, a cathedral ceiling with sanctuary lamps hung high, the dome of earth sparkled and glittered, and on the schooners by the Cercle Bougainville *himenes* of joy rang out on the soft air.

I passed them close, so close that a girl of Huahine who was dancing on the deck of the *Mihimana* seized me by the arm and embraced me.

"Come back, stranger!" she cried in Tahitian. "There is pleasure here, and the night is but just begun."

A dozen island schooners swayed in the gentle breeze, their stays humming softly, their broadsides separated from the quays by just a dozen or twenty feet, as if they feared to risk the seduction of the land, and felt themselves safer parted from the shore. On all the street-level verandas, the entrances to the shops and the restaurants, the hundreds of natives who had not wanted other lodging slept as children in cradles until they should rise for coffee before the market-bell.

From the Chinese shop at the corner the strains of a Canton actor's falsetto, with the squeak of the Celestial fiddles issued from a phonograph, but so real I fancied I was again on Shameen, listening over the Canton River to the noises of the night, the music, and the singsong girls of the silver combs.

I went on, and met the peanut-man. He sold me two small bags of roasted goobers for eight sous. He wore the brown, oilskin-like, two-piece suit of the Chinese of southern China, and he had no teeth and no hair, and his eyes would not stay open. He had to open them with his fingers, so that most of the time he was blind; but he counted money accurately, and he had a tidy bag of silver and coppers strapped to his stomach. He looked a hundred years old.

When I paid for the two bags, he raised his lids, believed that I was a speaker of English, and said, "Fine businee!"

As I went past the queen's palace, the two *mahus* were chanting low, as they sat on the curbing, and they glanced coquettishly at me, but asked only for cigarettes. I gave them a package of Marinas, made in the Faubourg Bab-el-oued, in Algiers, and they said "Maruru" and "Merci" in turn and in unison. Strange men these, one bearded and handsome, the other slender and in his twenties, their dual natures contrasting in their broad shoulders and their swaying hips, their men's *pareus* and shirts, and bits of lace lingerie. I met them half a dozen times a day, and as I was now known as a resident, not the idler of a month, they bowed in hope of recognition.

In the Annexe all was quiet, but in the great sailing canoe of Afa, on the grass by the water, there were two girls smoking and humming, and waiting for the cowboy and the prize-fighter who lived beside me, and who were dancing to-night at Fa'a. Like Indians, these Tahitians, especially the women, would sit and watch and wait for hours on hours, and make no complaint, if only their dear one—dear mayhap for only a night—came at last.

I was awakened from happy sleep by the cries of a frightened woman, confused with outlandish, savage sounds. I lit my lamp and leaned over the balcony. Under a flamboyant-tree was a girl defending herself from the attack of Vava. She was screaming in terror, and the Dummy, a giant in strength, was holding her and grunting his bestial laugh. I threw the rays full in his face, and he looked up, saw me, and ran away up the beach, yelping like a frustrated beast. In voice and action he resembled an animal more than any human I had ever seen. The guilelessness and cunning of child and fiend were in his dumb soul.

Chapter XII

The princess suggests a walk to the falls of Fautaua, where Loti went with *Rarahu*—We start in the morning—The suburbs of Papeete—The Pool of Loti—The birds, trees and plants—A swim in a pool—Arrival at the cascade—Luncheon and a siesta—We climb the height—The princess tells of Tahitian women—The Fashoda fright.

The falls of Fautaua, famed in Tahitian legend, are exquisite in beauty and surrounding, and so near Papeete that I walked to them and back in a day. Yet hardly any one goes there. For those who have visited them they remain a shrine of loveliness, wondrous in form and unsurpassed in color. Before the genius of Tahiti was smothered in the black and white of modernism, the falls and the valley in which they are, were the haunt of lovers who sought seclusion for their pledgings.

A princess accompanied me to them. She was not a daughter of a king or queen, but she was near to royalty, and herself as aristocratic in carriage and manner as was Oberea, who loved Captain Cook. I danced with her at a dinner given by a consul, and when I spoke to her of Loti's visit to Fautaua with *Rarahu*, she said in French:

"Why do you not go there yourself with a *Rarahu*! Loti is old and an admiral, and writes now of Egypt and Turkey and places soiled by crowds of people, but *Rarahu* is still here and young. Shall I find you her?"

I looked at her and boldly said:

"I am a stranger in your island, as was Loti when he met *Rarahu*. Will you not yourself show me Fautaua?"

She gave a shrill cry of delight, and in the frank, sweet way of the Tahitian girl replied:

"We will run away to-morrow morning. Wear little, for it will be warm, and bring no food!"

"I will obey you literally," I said, "and you must find manna or charm ravens to bring us sustenance."

I had coffee opposite the market place in the shop of Wing Luey, and chatted a few moments with Prince Hinoe, the son of the Princesse de Joinville, who would have been king had the French not ended the Kingdom of Tahiti. No matter what time Hinoe lay down at night, he was up at dawn for the market, for his early roll and coffee and his converse with the sellers and the buyers.

There once a day for an hour the native in Papeete touched the country folk and renewed the ancient custom of gossip in the cool of the morning.

The princess—in English her familiar Tahitian name, Noanoa Tiare, meant Fragrance of the Jasmine—was in the Parc de Bougainville, by the bust of the first French circumnavigator.

"Ia ora na!" she greeted me. "Are you ready for adventure?"

She handed me a small, soft package, with a caution to keep it safe and dry. I put it in my inside pocket.

The light of the sun hardly touched the lagoon, and Moorea was still shrouded in the shadows of the expiring night. As we walked down the beach, the day was opening with the "morning bank," the masses of white clouds that gather upon the horizon before the tradewind begins its diurnal sweep, to shift and mold them all the hours till sunset.

Fragrance of the Jasmine was in a long and clinging tunic of pale blue, with low, white shoes disclosing stockings also of blue, and wore a hat of pandanus weave. She carried nothing, nor had I anything in my hands, and we were to be gone all day. I regretted that I had not lingered longer with Prince Hinoe over the rolls and coffee.

We fared past the merchants' stores, the Cercle Bougainville, and the steamship wharf, and over the Pont de l'Est, or Eastern bridge, to Patutoa. The princess pointed out to me many wretched straw houses, crowded in a hopeless way. They were like a refugee camp after a disaster, impermanent, uncomfortable, barely holding on to the swampy earth. One knew the occupants to be far from their own Lares and Penates.

"Those are the habitations of people of other islands," she said. "The people of the Paumotus, the Australs, and of Easter Island settled there. They were brought here by odious labor contractors, and died of homesickness. Those men murdered hundreds of them to gain *un pen d'argent*, a handful of gold. *Eh b'en*, those who did it have suffered. They have faded away, and most of their evil money, too. *Aue!*"

Llewellyn's dark face as he protested against Lying Bill's sarcastic statement of guilt came before me.

To lighten the thought of the princess I told her the thread of "The Bottle Imp," and that the magic bottle had disappeared out of the story right there, by the old calaboose. She was glad that the white sailor who did not care for life had saved the Hawaiians.

Framed in the door of a rough cabin I saw McHenry. He was in pajamas, barefooted, and unshaven. I recalled that he had an "old woman" there.

Llewellyn had reproved him for speaking contemptuously of her as beneath him socially. I waved to McHenry, who nodded charily, and pulled down the curtain which was in lieu of a door. The shack looked bare and cheap, as if little money or effort had been spent upon it. Perhaps, I thought, McHenry could afford only the drinks and cards at the Cercle Bougainville and economized at home. He did not reappear, but a comely native woman drew back the curtain, and stood a moment to view us. She was large, and did not look browbeaten, as one would have supposed from McHenry's boast that he would not permit her even to walk with him except at a "respectful distance." Of course I knew him as a boaster.

The church of the curious Josephite religion was near by, and in the mission house attached to it I saw the American preachers of the sect.

"What do they preach?" I asked Noanoa Tiare.

"Those missionaries, the Tonito? Oh, they speak evil of the Mormons. I do not know how they speak of God." She laughed. "I am not interested in religions," she explained. "They are so difficult to understand. Our own old gods seem easier to know about."

We had arrived at the part of the beach into which the broad avenue of Fautaua debouched.

The road was beside the stream of Fautaua, and arching it were magnificent dark-green trees, like the locust-trees of Malta. This avenue was in the middle of the island, and looking through the climbing bow of branches I saw Maiauo, the lofty needles of rock which rise black-green from the mountain plateau and form a tiara, Le Diademe, of the French. A quarter of an hour's stroll brought us to a natural basin into which the stream fell. It was of it Louis Marie Julien Viaud, shortly after he had been christened Loti, wrote:

The pool had numerous visitors every day; beautiful young women of Papeete spent the warm tropical days here, chatting, singing and sleeping, or even diving and swimming like agile gold fish. They went here clad in their muslin tunics, and wore them moist upon their bodies while they slept, looking like the naiads of the past.

We were already warm from walking, and I, in my *pareu* and light coat of pongee silk, looked longingly at the water sparkling in the sun, but the princess took me by the hand and led me on.

"It were better to go directly up the valley and out of the heat," she advised. "We shall have many pools to bathe in."

It was at the next that I took from my pocket "Rarahu, ou le mariage de Loti," a thin, poorly printed book in pink paper covers that I had possessed since boyhood, and which I had read again on the ship coming to Tahiti. The princess, like all reading Tahiti, knew it better than I, for it was the first novel in French with its scenes in that island, and for more than forty years had been talked about there.

"Here at this pool," she said, with her finger on the page, "*Loti* surprised *Rarahu* one afternoon when for a red ribbon she let an old and hideous Chinese kiss her naked shoulder. *Mon dieu!* That French naval officer made a *bruit* about a poor little Tahitian girl! We will talk about her when we are at *déjeuner.*"

Déjeuner! My heart leaped. Whence would the luncheon come? Had this child of Tahiti arranged beforehand that she should be met by a jinn with sandwiches and cakes? I dared not ask.

We pushed on, and passed many residences of natives. They were almost all of European construction, board cottages, because the houses of native sort are forbidden within the municipal limits. Beyond them we saw no houses. The Tahitian families were cooking their breakfasts, brought from the market, on little fires outside their houses. They all smiled, and called to us to partake with them.

"*Ia ora na! Haere mai amu!*"

"Greeting! Come eat with us!"

They looked happy in the sunshine, the smoke curling about them in milky wreaths, the men naked except for *pareus*, and the children quite as born. Fragrance of the Jasmine answered all with pleasant badinage, and each must know whither we were bound. They thought it not at all odd, apparently, that a princess of their race should be going to the waterfalls with a foreigner, and they beamed on me to assure me of their interest and understanding.

The broad avenue lessened into a broken road, roofed by many kinds of trees. Though the sun ascended from the ocean on the other side of Tahiti above the fantastic peak of Maiauo, it had not shed a beam upon the ferns and mosses. The guava was a dense growth. Like the lantana of Hawaii and Ceylon, imported to Tahiti to fill a want, it had abused hospitality, and become a nuisance without apparent remedy. How often man works but in circles! Everywhere in the world plants and insects, birds and animals, had been pointed out to me that had been acquired for a beneficent purpose, and had become a curse.

The mina-bird was brought to Tahiti from the Moluccas to eat wasps which came from South America, and were called Jack Spaniards. The mina, perhaps, ate the insects, but he also ate everything else, including fruit. He stole bread and butter off tables, and his hoarse croak or defiant rattle was an oft-repeated warning to defend one's food. The minas were many in Tahiti, and, like the English sparrow in American cities and towns, had driven almost all other birds to flight or local extinction. The sparrow's urban doom might be read in the increasing number of automobiles, but the mina in Tahiti, as in Hawaii, had a sinecure.

Noanoa Tiare said that the guava had its merits. Horses and cattle ate its leaves and fruit, and the wood was a common fuel throughout Tahiti. The fruit was delicious, and in America or England would be all used for jelly, but only Lovaina preserved it. The passion-flowers of the granadilla vines, white and star-like, with purpling centers, were intermingled with the guavas, a brilliant and aromatic show, the fruit like miniature golden pumpkins. Their acid, sweetish pulp contained many seeds, each incased in white jelly. One ate the seeds only, though the pulp, when cooked, was palatable.

The road dwindled into a narrower path, and then a mere trail. The road had crossed the brook many times on frail bridges, some tottering and others only remnants. Habitations ceased, and we were in a dark, splendid gorge, narrow, and affording one no vision straight ahead except at intervals.

The princess named many of the growths we passed, and explained their qualities. The native is very close to the ground. The lantana, with its yellow and magenta flowerets, umbrella ferns, and *aihere*, the *herbe de vache*, and the bohenia, used by the Tahitians for an eye lotion, were all about. Palms, with cocoanuts of a half dozen stages of growth, and giant banana-plants lined the banks, and bushes with blue flowers like violets, and one with red buttons, intermingled with limes and oranges to form a thicket through which we could hardly force our way.

We were yet on the level of the rivulet, but now, the princess said, must take to the cliff. We had come to a pool which in symmetry and depth, in coolness and invitingness, outranked all before. I was very hot, the beads of perspiration like those in a steamroom.

"We will rest here a few minutes, and you may bathe," said my lovely guide. "I have not been to Fautaua *vaimato* for several years, but I never forget the way. I will make a basket, and here we will gather some fruit for our *déjeuner* for fear there might not be plenty at the waterfalls."

I took off my tennis-shoes, hung my silk coat on a limb, and plunged into the pool. Never but in the tropics does the human being fully enjoy the dash into cool water. There it is a tingling pleasure. I dived time and again, and then sat in the small glitter of sunlight to dry and to watch Noanoa Tiare make the basket. She said she had a wide choice there, as the leaves of the banana, cocoanut, bamboo, pandanus, or *aihere* would serve. She had selected the *aihere*, the common weed, and out of its leaves she deftly fashioned a basket a foot long and wide and deep.

Although she had been in Paris and London and in New York, knew how to play Beethoven and Grieg and Saint-Saëns, had had gowns made by Paquin, and her portrait in the salon, she was at home in this glade as a Tahitian girl a hundred years ago. The airs of the avenue de l'Opéra in Paris, and, too, of the rue de Rivoli in Papeete, were rarefied in this simple spot to the impulses and experiences of her childhood in the groves and on the beaches of her beloved island.

When I had on my coat, we gathered limes, bananas, oranges, and a wild pineapple that grew near by in a tangle of coffee and vanilla, and the graceful acalypha. The yellow *tecoma*, a choice exotic in America, shed its seeds upon the sow thistle, a salad, and the *ape* or wild *taro*. The great leaves of the *ape* are like our elephant's ear plant, and the roots, as big as war-clubs, are tubers that take the place of potatoes here. In Hawaii, crushed and fermented, and called *poi*, they were ever the main food. The juice of the leaf stings one's skin.

The princess removed her shoes and stockings, and I carried them over my shoulder. We deflected from the rivulet to the cliff above it, and there forced our way along the mountain-side, feeling almost by instinct the trail hidden by the mass of creepers and plants.

It was a real jungle. Man had once dwelt there when his numbers in this island were many times greater. Then every foot of ground from the precipices to the sea was cleared for the breadfruit, the *taro*, the cocoanut, and other life-giving growths, which sowed themselves and asked no cultivation. Now, except for the faint trail, I was on primeval ground, from all appearances.

The cañon grew narrower and darker. The undefined path lay inches deep in water, and the levels were shallow swamp. Nature was in vast luxuriance, in a revel of aloofness from human beings, casting its wealth of blazing colors and surprising shapes upon every side. We slid down the edge of the hill to the burn, where the massive boulders and shattered rocks were camouflaged by the painting of moss and lichen, the ginger, turmeric, caladium, and dracaena, and by the overhanging palms covered with the rich bird's-nest ferns.

We sat again in this wild garden of the tropic to invite our souls to drink the beauty and quietude, the absence of mankind and the nearness of nature. We became very still, and soon heard the sounds of bird and insect above the lower notes of the brawling stream.

The princess put her finger on her lips and whispered in my ear:

"Do you hear the warbling of the *omamao* and the *olatare?* They are our song-birds. They are in these high valleys only, for the mina has frightened them from below—the mina that came with the ugly Chinese."

"Noanoa Tiare," said I, "you Tahitians are the birds of paradise of the human family. You have been driven from the rich valleys of your old life to hills of bare existence by the minas of commerce and politics. I feel like apologizing for my civilization."

She pressed my hand.

"*Taisez-vous!*" she replied, smiling. "*Aita peapea.* I am always happy. Remember I still live in Tahiti, and this is my time. My foremothers' day is past. *Allons!* We will be soon at the *vaimato*, and there we will have the *déjeuner.*"

As we moved on I saw that the yellow flowers of the *purau*, dried red by the sun,—poultices for natives' bruises,—and candlenuts in heaps,—torches ready to hand,—littered the moss.

The mountain loomed in the distance, and the immense Pic du Français towered in shadow. Faintly I heard the boom of the waterfall, and knew we were nearing the goal.

The cañon grew yet narrower and darker, and the crash of water louder. We had again attained a considerable height over the stream, and the trail seemed lost. The princess took my hand, and cautiously feeling the creepers and plants under our feet, we slipped and crept down the hidden path. Suddenly, the light became brilliant, and I found myself in a huge broken bowl of lava rock, the walls almost vertical. From the summit of the precipice facing me fell a superb cascade into a deep and troubled tarn. The stream was spun silver in the sun, which now was warm and splendid. So far it fell that much of it never reached the pool as water, but, blown by the gentle breeze, a moiety in spume and spray wet the earth for an acre about. Like the veil of a bride, the spindrift spread in argent clouds, and a hundred yards away dropped like gentle rain upon us. Verdure covered everything below except where the river ran from the tarn and hurried to the lesser things of the town. The giant walls, as black as the interior of an old furnace, were festooned with magnificent tree ferns, the exquisite maidenhair, lianas, and golden-green mosses, all sparkling in the sun with the million drops of the *vaimato*.

We withdrew a few paces from the vapor, and found a place on the edge of the brook to have our fruit and, perhaps, a siesta. A carpet of moss and green leaves made a couch of Petronian ease, and we threw ourselves upon it with the weariness of six miles afoot uphill in the tropics. It was not hot like the summer heat of New York, for Tahiti has the most admirable climate I have found the world over, but at midday I had felt the warmth penetratingly. Noanoa Tiare made nothing of it, but suggested that we both leap into the tarn.

I knew a moment of squeamishness, echo of the immorality of my catechism and my race conventions. I felt almost aghast at finding myself alone with that magnificent creature in such a paradisiacal spot. I wondered what thoughts might come to me. I had danced with her, I had talked with her under the stars, but what might she expect me not to do? And what was an Occidental, a city man, before her? She retired behind a bird's-nest fern, on the long, lanceolate leaves of which were the shells of the mountain snail. At her feet was the bastard canna, the pungent root of which makes Chinese curry.

When she emerged, she was an amazing and enchanting personage. She had removed her gown, and wore a *pareu* of muslin, with huge scarlet leaves upon white. She was tall and voluptuously formed, but she had made the loin-cloth, two yards long and a yard wide, cover her in a manner that was modest, though revealing. It was the art of her ancestors, for this was the shape of their common garment of tapa, a native cloth. With a knot or two she arranged the *pareu* so that it was like a chemise, coming to a foot above her knees and covering her bosom.

Her black, glossy hair was loose and hung below her waist, and upon it she had placed a wreath she had quickly made of small ferns. That was their general custom, to adorn themselves when happy and at the bath. The eyes of Fragrance of the Jasmine were very large, deep brown, her skin a coppery-cinnamon, with a touch of red in the cheeks, and her nose and mouth were large and well formed. Her teeth were as the meat of the cocoanut, brilliant and strong. Her limbs were rounded, soft, the flesh glowing with health and power. She was of that line of Tahitian women who sent back the first European navigators, the English, to rave about an island of Junos, the French to call Tahiti La Nouvelle Cythère, the new isle of Venus.

I had but to tie up my own *pareu* of red calico with white leaves in the manner Lovaina had shown me to have an imitation of our usual swimming-trunks.

"*Allons!*" cried the princess, and running toward the waterfall, she climbed up the cliff to a height of a dozen feet, and threw herself, wreathed as she was, with a loud "*Aue!*" into the pool.

I followed her, and she dived and swam, brought up bottom, treaded water, and led me in a dozen exercises and tricks of the expert swimmer. The water was very cool, and ten minutes in it, with our sharpening hunger, were enough delight. Fragrance of the Jasmine, as she came dripping from water and lingered a few moments on the brink, was a rapturous object. With unconscious grace she flung back her head many times to shake the moisture from her thick hair, and ran her fingers through it until the strands were fairly separated. The *pareu* disclosed the rounded contour of her figure as if it were painted upon her. She was one of those ancient Greek statues, those semi-nudes on which the artists painted in vivid tints the blush of youth, the hue of hair, and a shadow of a garment. She entranced me, and I called out to her, "*Nehenehe!*" "Beautiful!"

She ran to her boudoir behind the bird's-nest fern, and soon returned in her tunic, still barefoot, and with her *pareu* in her hand for drying on a rock. She brought two wreaths now and put one upon me. We resumed our couches upon the green sward, and the princess laid the basket of fruit between us.

"*Maintenant pour le déjeuner!*" she said.

We ate the bananas first, and then the pineapple, which we cut with a sliver of basalt,—we were in the stone age, as her tribe was when the whites came,—and last the oranges. She made cups of leaves and filled them with water, and into them we squeezed the limes for a toast.

"*Inu i te ota no te!*" she said and lifted her cup. "A health to you! He who eats the *fei* passes under a spell; he must return again to the islands. Have you eaten the *fei?*"

"Not yet, Princess," I replied.

"There they are in abundance on the hillside," she said. "Look! If we had fire, I would roast one for you, but to-morrow will be another day."

The *fei*, the mountain banana, the staple of the Tahitian, was there aplenty. The plant or stalk was that of the banana, but very dark at the base, and the leaves thicker. The fruit was two or three times as large, and red, and a striking difference was that it was placed on the bunches erect, while bananas hang down from the stem.

I drank to her increasing charm, and I told her how much the beauty and natural grace of the Tahitians appealed to me; how I intended to leave Papeete and go to the end of the island to be among the natives only; that I had remained thus long in the city to learn first the ways of the white in the tropics, and then to gain the contrast by seeking the Tahitian as nearly as possible in his original habitat.

Noanoa Tiare took the orange-peel and rubbed it upon her hair.

"*Noanoa!*" she said. "*Mon ami américain*, I will give you a note to Aruoehau a Moeroa, the *tava*, or chief of Mataiea district, and you can stay with him. You will know him as Tetuanui. He will gladly receive you, and he is wise in our history and our old customs. Do not expect too much! We ate in the old day the simple things at hand, fish and breadfruit, *fei* and cocoanut milk, mangoes and bananas and oranges. Now we eat the dirty and prepared food of the Tinito, the Chinaman, and we depend on coffee and rum and beer for strength. The thin wheat bread has no nourishment compared with the breadfruit and the *fei*, the yam and the *taro*. And clothes! The fools taught us that the *pareu*, which left the body exposed to the air, clean and refreshed by the sun and the winds, was immodest. We exchanged it for undershirts and trousers and dresses and shoes and stockings and coats, and got disease and death and degeneration.

"You are late, my friend," the princess went on, with a note of pity in her soft voice. "My mother remembered the days Loti depicted in '*Rarahu.*' My grandmother knew little Tarahu of Bora-Bora of whom he wrote. Viaud was then a midshipman. We did not call him Loti, but Roti, our coined word for a rose, because he had rosy cheeks. But he could not call himself Roti in his novel, for in French, his language, that meant roasted, and one might think of *boeuf à la rôti*. We have no L in Tahitian. We also called him Mata Reva or the Deep-Eyed One. Tarahu was not born on Bora-Bora, but right here in Mataiea."

She lay at full length, her uptilted face in her hands, and her perfect feet raised now and then in unaware accentuation of her words.

"What Tahitian women there were then! Read the old French writers! None was a pigmy. When they stood under the waterfall the water ran off their skins as off a marble table. Not a drop stayed on. They were as smooth as glass."

Fragrance of the Jasmine sighed.

"*Aue! Hélas!*"

I had it in my mouth to say that she was as beautiful and as smooth-skinned as any of her forebears. She was as enticing as imaginable, her languorous eyes alight as she spoke, and her bare limbs moving in the vigor of her thoughts. But I could not think of anything in French or English not banal, and my Tahitian was yet too limited to permit me to *tutoyer* her. She was an islander, but she had seen the Midnight Follies and the Bal Bullier, the carnival in Nice, and once, New Year's Eve in San Francisco. An Italian and a Scandinavian prince had wooed her.

I spoke of Loti again, and of other writers' comments upon the attitude of women in Tahiti toward man.

The princess sat up and adjusted her *hei* of ferns. She studied a minute, and then she said:

"I have long wanted to talk with an intelligent American on that subject; with some one who knew Europe and his own country and these islands. There is a vast hypocrisy in the writing and the talking about it. Now, Maru (I already had been given my native name), the woman of Tahiti exercises the same sexual freedom as the average white man does in your country and in England or France. She pursues the man she wants, as he does the woman. Your women pursue, too, but they do it by cunning, by little lies, by coquetry, by displaying their persons, by flattery, and by feeding you.

"The Tahitian woman makes the first advances in friendship openly, if she chooses. She arranges time and place for amours as your women do. She does not take from the Tahitian man or from the foreigner his right to choose, but she chooses herself, too. I feel sure that often an American woman would give hours of pain to know well a certain man, but makes no honest effort to draw him toward her. They have told me so!"

I got up, and standing beside her, I quoted:

"Ships that pass in the night and speak each other in passing;
Only a signal shown and a distant voice in the darkness;
So on the ocean of life we pass and speak one another,
Only a look and a voice; then darkness again and silence."

"Mais, c'est vrai!" she said, musingly. "The Tahitian woman will not endure that. She is on a par with the man in seeking. Without fear and without shame, and, *attendez*, Maru, without any more monogamy than you men. I have told some of those suffrage ladies of London and of Washington that we are in advance of their most determined feminism. They will come to it. More women than men in Europe will bring it there."

Her long, black lashes touched her cheeks.

"We are a little sleepy, *n'est-ce pas?*" she asked. "*B'en*, we will have a *taoto*."

She made herself a pillow of leaves with her *pareu*, and arranging her hair in two braids, she stretched herself out, with her face toward the sky, and a cool banana-leaf laid over it. I copied her action, and lulled by the falling water, the rippling of the pool, and the drowsy rustling of the trees, I fell fast asleep, and dreamed of Eve and the lotus-eaters.

When I awoke, the princess was refreshing her face and hands in the water.

"*A hio!* Look!" she said eagerly. "*O tane* and *O vahine!*"

In the mist above the pool at the foot of the cascade a double rainbow gleamed brilliantly. *O tane* is *the* man, which the Tahitians call the real arch, and *O vahine*, the woman, the reflected bow. They appeared and disappeared with the movement of the tiny, fleecy clouds about the sun. The air, as dewy as early morn in the braes o' Maxwelton, was deliciously cool.

"If you have courage and strength left," the princess said excitedly, "we will go to the fort of Fautaua, and I will show you where the last of my people perished fighting to drive out the French invader, and where the French officials fled with the treasure-box when they feared war with England not very long ago."

She pointed up to the brim of the precipice, where the river launched itself into the air, to drop six hundred feet before it fed the stream below. Sheer and menacing the black walls of the crevasse loomed, as if forbidding approach, but through a network of vines and bushes, over a path seldom used, we climbed, and after half a mile more of steeps, reached the fort. Rugged was the way, and we aided each other more than once, but rejoiced at our effort when we surmounted the summit.

The view was indescribably grand. One felt upon the roof of the island, though the farther heights of the valley culminated in a gigantic crag-wall, a saddle only a yard across, and wooded to the apex, and above that even towered Orohena, nearly a mile and a half high, and never reached by man despite many efforts. Tropic birds, the bo's'ns of the sailor, their bodies whitish gray, with their two long tail-feathers, had their haunt there, and piped above the trees. The river was a fierce torrent, and leaped into a water-hewn lava basin, where it swirled and foamed before it rushed, singing, through a stone funnel to the border of the chasm, and sprang with a dull roar into the ether.

There was a chorus of sounds from the cataract, the river, the wind, the trees, and the birds, a mighty music of elements of the earth and of life, rising and falling rhythmically, and inspiring, but nerve-racking. Fragrance of the Jasmine seized my hand and held it.

"Let us go to a more peaceful spot, where I can tell you the story," she said in my ear. We passed the rough fort, broken-down and mossy, and moving carefully along the trail, clambering over rocks and tearing away twigs and broad leaves, we reached a dismantled and crumbling chalet.

We sat down upon its steps, and I removed my coat and was naked to my *pareu* in the afternoon zephyr.

"That fort," said the princess, "was built by the French in the forties, when they were stealing my country. From it they could command the gorge of Fautaua and that and other valleys. This place was the last stronghold of the Tahitian warriors before the enemy overcame them, and erected the ramparts and the fort. The last man to die fell by the river basin. The band of heroes would have held out longer, but were betrayed by a Tahitian. He led the French troops by night and by secret paths to a hill overlooking them, so that they were shot down from above. The traitor lived to wear the red ribbon of the Legion of Honor and to spend pleasantly the gold the French Government gave him. *C'est la vie.*"

We cast our eyes over the scene. There was a forest of wild ginger, ferns, and dracasna all about. Thousands of roses perfumed the air, and other flowers and strawberries, and feis, green or ripe-red, wondrous clusters of fruit, awaited man's culling. The stream purled about worn rocks, and we came to two gloomy pools, black from the reflection of their bowls, the water bubbling and surging from springs beneath. It was deliciously cold, and we drank it from leaf cups.

"How about the time the French came here with the treasure?" I inquired. "Have we time for that history?"

"Mais, oui!" said Noanoa Tiare. "That is too good for you not to know. You know that the French are excitable, *n'est-ce pas?* B'en, a French officer, Major Marchand, put up the tricolor in some place called Fashoda in Africa, and the English objected. There was some parleying between the two nations, and the information arrived in Tahiti that England was going to make war on France. The French papers or the American papers said so, and every one was alarmed.

" 'The treacherous *Anglais* might strike at any moment,' said the French, and they were afraid. Then one night some one rode in from near Point Venus and reported to the Governor that two British frigates had been sighted. *Mon dieu!* what to do? There was only a French transport at Papeete, worth nothing for defense. They tore the trimmings from that vessel and prepared to scuttle her. The guns were rushed to Faere Hill for a last, desperate stand against odds. They could die like Frenchmen! All lights were ordered extinguished, and even the beacon of Point Venus was dark. The enlisted natives were sent to watch on every headland, a cabinet meeting was held,— the apothecary, and the governor, and the secretaries, and the doctor,—and it was determined to save the money of the city and the archives of the Government. The valuables and the papers were put in strong boxes and the governor and all of them made a mad race for this fort."

The princess covered her mouth with her hand to still her laughter.

"Was it not funny? They arrived here at daybreak, and buried the boxes. They were still at it when an officer of marines came hurrying to notify them that the frigates were French schooners from the Paumotus. The whole population had hidden itself away in the meantime. Well, they had many jokes about it and many songs, but the governor built this house on the steps of which we sit as a permanent depository for archives in case of war, and here he used to come for picnics until a few years ago. There was a post-office, with a guard of sailors, here. They planted the garden, the flowers, and strawberries that now run wild. You know our chiefs were always being secretly warned that England, which owns most of the islands in these seas, wanted to seize our island."

Over the Diadem the dark shadows were lengthening. The daring pinnacles of Maiauo were thrust up like the mangled fingers of a black hand against the blue sky.

Noanoa Tiare pointed to them.

"The *ahiahi* comes. Night is not far off," she said warningly. "If we lingered here much longer, we might have to stay all the night."

"How memorable to me would be a sunrise from here," I replied. "I would never forget it."

She looked at me archly over her shoulder.

"I would like it myself. It would be magnificent, and I have never spent the night just here."

She considered a moment, and my mind took up the matter of arrangements. We could cook *feis*, and there was plenty of other fruit, with shelter in the house, if we needed that. We could start down early and be at Lovaina's for the first *déjeuner*. Zeus! to pass the night in such a solitude! To hear in the pitch darkness the mysterious voices of *po*, the *tenebræ* of the Tahitian gods; the boom of the cascade in the abyss; the deep bass of the river in the rocky chute; the sigh of the wind in the trees; the murmur of the stream near by; the fantasia and dirge of the lofty night in the tropics. What a setting for her telling some old legend or fairy-tale of Tahiti!

Fragrance of the Jasmine ended my reverie. She slapped her thigh.

"I dine and dance to-night at eight o'clock," she said. "*A rohi!* We must go! Besides, Maru, it would be too cold without blankets. The mercury here goes to sixty of your thermometer."

We descended by the route we had come, picking up her shoes and stockings and our hats by our couch, and with the princess leading, hurrying along the obscuring trail. We passed a Tahitian youth who had been gathering *feis*, probably near the tarn, and who was bringing them to the market of the next morning. He was burdened with more than a hundred pounds of fruit, which he carried balanced on a pole over his shoulder, and with this he was to go seven or eight miles from their place of growth. He was a pillar of strength, handsome, glowing with effort, clad in a gorgeous *pareu* of red, and as we went by him, he smiled and said, "*Ia ora na! I hea! Vaimato?*" Greeting! Where have you been? The waterfall?"

"E, *hitahita*. Yes, we are hurrying back," the princess called vivaciously.

"Those are our real men, not the Papeete dolts," she said. "If we had time, we would catch shrimp in the river. I love to do that."

When we came to where the habitations began and the road became passable for vehicles, Noanoa Tiare sat down on a stone. She put on her pale-blue silk stockings and her shoes, and asked me for the package she had given me at starting. She unfolded it, and it was an *aahu*, a gown, for which she exchanged, behind a banana-plant, her soiled and drenched tunic. The new one was of the finest silk, diaphanous, and thus to be worn only at night. The sun was down, and the lagoon a purple lake when we were again at the bust of Bougainville.

I thanked her at parting.

"Noanoa Tiare," I said, "this day has a heavenly blue page in my record. It has made Tahiti a different island for me."

"Maru, *mon ami*, you are sympathetic to my race. We shall be dear friends. I will send you the note to Tetuanui, the chief of Mataiea, to-morrow. *Au revoir* and happy dreams."

Chapter XIII

The beach-combers of Papeete—The consuls tell their troubles—A bogus lord—The American boot-blacks—The cowboy in the hospital—Ormsby, the supercargo—The death of Tahia—The Christchurch Kid—The Nature men—Ivan Stroganoff's desire for a new gland.

I played badminton some afternoons at the British consulate. The old wooden bungalow, with broad verandas, stood in a small garden a dozen yards from the lagoon, where the Broom Road narrowed as it left the business portion of Papeete and began its round of the island. There was just room enough on the salt grass for the shuttlecock to fall out of bounds, and for the battledores to swing free of the branches of the trees. The consul, though he wore a monocle, was without the pretense of officialdom except to other officials and, of course, at receptions, dinners, and formal gatherings. After the games, with tea on the veranda, I heard many stories of island life, of official amenities, and the compound of nationalities in our little world.

Half a dozen intimates of the consul dropped in about four, Willi, the rich dentist and acting American consul; Stevens, the London broker; Hobson, who closed an eye for the Moorean, McTavish; and others. All were British except me, but our home tongue and customs drew us closer together than to Frenchmen, and we could speak with some freedom on local affairs. If no woman was present other than the cosmopolitan wife of the consul, born in Persia, we were quite at ease.

Both consuls were usually worried because of the refusals of crews of vessels flying their flags to leave Tahiti, complaints of the police of the misconduct of their nationals, or appeals for assistance from impecunious or spendthrift tourists. It was an every-week happening for sailors of American vessels and of the New Zealand steamships to flee to the distant districts or to Moorea, to live in a breadfruit grove with dryads who asked no vows, or to escape the grind of work and discipline at sea.

They must be pursued by the French gendarmes, under the warrant of their own flag, caught, and sent in irons aboard their ships, with fees paid by their furious captains. Many times the chase was futile, so well did the dryads secrete them, and the natives of the district abet the offense. To a Tahitian an amorous adventure, either as principal or aid, is half of life, and he would risk his liberty and property to thwart, in his opinion, hard and stupid officials who wanted to separate loving hearts.

We talked about the kinds of men, other than these sailors, who made Tahiti their playground, to the annoyance of their consuls. Crime among the Tahitians was almost unknown. A petty theft rarely happened. They were never paupers, for their own people cared for them, and unless absolutely mat-ridden, they could find food on the trees about them. The whites—and not the French whites either—caused the trouble, and but for them M. Lontane might have left off his revolver and club.

"There is a type of Britisher," said the consul, "who thinks Tahiti is his oyster, to be opened with false pretenses, and a pearl found. This type has two varieties, impecunious, but well-educated, youths, younger sons, maybe; and valets and varlets. These scoundrels afflict me dreadfully, because they all ultimately claim the protection of the British flag or are reported by the police for skullduggery. There is a fellow now on my hands who is threatenin' suicide. I wish to Gog and Magog that he would take to the reef or find a stick of dynamite. Monsieur Lontane, that busy French gendarme, found him tryin' to borrow a revolver or a stiletto, and thought he was going to kill a Frenchman. He put him in the calaboose and brought his effects to me. They consisted of a book of poems and a letter, but not a ha'penny."

"What does the bounder look like?" asked Stevens.

"He looks like a beadle in a dissentin' church, with a long, skinny neck, a pasty face, and a cockney accent. I went to see him, and he talked like an underdone curate who had had a bad night. When he got off the ship, where he owed everybody, includin' the smokin'-room, he came to see me with some crazy papers for me to sign. He said then he had not a shillin', and I advised him to go to work. He said there wasn't any work; so knowin' Llewellyn was badly in need of people, I sent him to his vanilla plantation out Mataiea way. You know here they haven't the bees or whatever it is that transfers the pollen from the stigma to the anther or what-d 'ye-call-it, and so they do it by hand with a piece of bamboo or a stem of grass. The girls do it mostly, but I thought this jackpuddin' could make an honest pound or two. He came tearin' back to me sayin' I'd insulted him with the work, askin' him, a nobleman, to pander in the vegetable kingdom."

"I know him. He was at Lovaina's," I interposed. "He was at the bar all the time, quoting Pope and Dryden and himself. He said he was going around the globe on a wager of a fortune. He was a poisonous bore, and always popped up for a drink. By the way, he wears a monocle."

"You've named him," went on the consul. "That's more of the cockney's pretense. Here's the poem he wrote in the calaboose. He did it on his shirt-front because the economical French gave him no paper. Lontane thought it might be his will or a plot, and brought the shirt here, and I copied the accursed thing for my record, as I am compelled to by the rules of the august devils of Downing Street."

THE HOME-LAND CALL

Why wilt thou torture me with unripe call,

Bringing these visions of the dear old land?

Dost think 't is sweet to let thy mock'ry fall?

For me to hear forgotten noises in the Strand?

Insidious voice that will not grant my plea,

The mem'ry of thy pleasures dost remain:

Oxonian-Cantabs club; blue-lit Gaiety!'

"What he needs is a permanent permit to patronize the opium den the Government runs here for the Chinese," said Hobson. "He's off his dope."

"Just a minute," continued the consul. "He claims to be a lord and a millionaire. Here's the letter. He needs no opium to have nightmares:

Tuesday.

Of course, I will be called coward now, but the same people who call me this are those who have caused me to seek death, for they branded me liar and wastrel, simply on an untrue report appearing in an American newspaper. Chief among these people are that most despicable cad Hallman, and secondly, the British Consul. Even had I been guilty of all that has been said, why were they not manly and generous enough to give or find me congenial employment? They are not blind and could see how anxious and willing I was to obtain this. No, they only gloated over my starving and pitiable condition. Well, they spring from the proletariat class and not much else could be expected.

God only knows how much I want to live and how I dread having to take my own life, but only for the sake of my people. If I could only see them again it would be easier. How did I ever fall so low! God help me! Is there nothing else for me but this ignominious death? But I must save my people from knowing. I am not using my correct name here, so it will be useless for any one to make inquiries. A volume of poems will be found in my pocket. I wonder if the Bishop would kindly post these to Miss B. Wilmer, Broken Hill, West Australia, but only telling her I died here, without particulars, and saying I have written these since leaving home. Oh, why did I ever leave there, where love and all that is good and pure was lavished on me?

If it is possible, could I be buried in the sea? Just placed in a coffin and dropped into the peaceful ocean, peace that I have not known for four years. Please have this done for me.

I do not think I am committing suicide, rather I am being murdered by men who have none of the nobler feelings, ungenerous, unsympathetic and cruelly unkind. The fact of my death will not affect one of those who ruined my reputation here, who deprived me of obtaining food, and a room to sleep in. They have no more conscience so cannot feel remorse. I will not sign my true name but only part of it. Gordon Innes.

"He's off his onion," Stevens commented. "The bally fool needs hard labor and raw *feis*."

The consul grinned.

"Wait till you hear me read the document with the suicide note. It's as good as Marie Corelli."

"All right, old thing," answered Stevens. "Fire the whole broadside!"

"No, no; I'm goin' to spare you the whole official document. It pretends to be a formal instruction to this beef-headed flunky, from his guardian, of a test to prove his mettle and gain experience to fit him for the highest posts of the diplomatic service by going round the bally world and doin' other people in for their tin. It is a yard long, and was undoubtedly written by the same dish-washer who wrote that doggerel on his shirt. It promises him half a million sterling when he comes back to London after visiting Australasia, China, India, and other countries, and pickin' up his tucker free as he goes. Also, the shark is permitted to send back for coin at this date, and he must get married to a Tahitian. He probably fixes it different in every country. It's signed, 'Your affectionate guardian, James Kitson, Baron Airedale of Gledhow.'"

"Whew!" spluttered Hobson, "the blighter has no limits. Do you mean to tell me he gets away with that folderol?"

"For months he has lived at Lovaina's, Fanny's, and even on the Chinese. He has borrowed thousands of francs, and spent it for drink and often for champagne. He did old Lovaina up for money as well as board. She believes in him yet, and calls him Lord Innes or Sir Gordon, but says she has no more to risk. He promised to build her a big hotel where the Annexe is. He's got many of the Tahitian girls and their mothers mad over his style and his prospects. Finally, he was warned by me to leave the island, and the result was his tryin' to borrow the lethal weapon, the poem and the letter. The Baron Airedale document he showed me when he first landed, to try to get my indorsement. There's no Burke in the South Seas, and there probably is no such bloomin' baron. Sounds more like a dog." The consul chuckled.

"Those lairds are as plentiful as brands of Scotch whisky made in England," Stevens said derisively. "What will you do to uphold the honor of the British crown? Is the Scotch bastard to go on with his fairy-tale and do brown the colonials?"

"I am going to have the diplomat repair the roads of Tahiti for two months, and then ship him third-class to New Zealand, where he has to go to carry out his blasted fate," the consul declared, and ordered all glasses filled.

We discussed the sudden and abnormal appearance of boot-blacks. One had set up an ornate stand on the rue de Rivoli. He was an American, Tom Wilkins, and the first ever known to practise his profession in the South Seas. He had come like a non-periodic comet, and suddenly flashed his brass-tagged platform and arm-chair upon the gaping natives. Most of them being barefooted, one would have thought his customers not many; but the novelty of a white man doing anything for them was irresistible to all who had shoes. He did not lower himself in their estimation. It is noteworthy that the Tahitian does not distinguish between what we call menial labor and other work. Nor did we until recently. The kings and nobles of Europe were actually served by the lords of the bedchamber and the maids in waiting. The American boot-black was really a boot-white, as all wore white canvas shoes except preachers and sailors.

The boot-white called out, "Shine!" and the word, unpronounceable by the native, entered a *himene* as *tina*. Within a week he had his Tahitian consort doing the shining most of the time while he loafed in the Paris saloon. He lived at the Annexe, and told me that he was not really a boot-cleaner, but was going around the world on a wager of twenty thousand dollars, "without a cent." He, too, had a credulous circle, who paid him often five francs for a shine to help him win his bet by arriving at the New York City Hall on a fixed date with a certain sum of money earned by his hands. He raised the

American flag over his stand, and referred to Uncle Sam as if he were a blood relation to whom he could appeal for anything at any time.

All the foregoing was brought out in our conversation at the British consul's. Willi, temporarily conducting American affairs in French Oceanie, gave a denouement.

"The shine isn't a bad fellow," he said, "but he's serious about the twenty thousand dollars. His statement was doubted to-day by an English sailor, who called him 'a blarsted Hamerican liar,' and the shine took off his own rubber leg, and knocked the sailor down. He could move faster on his one leg than the other on two, and Monsieur Lontane had to summon two assistants to take him to the calaboose. He wouldn't resume his rubber leg. I saw him being led and pulled by my office, calling out, 'Tell the 'Merican consul a good American is in the grip of the frogs.'"

Within a month of the rubber-legged shiner's début, there were two other boot-blacks on the streets. A madness possessed the people, Tahitians and French, who all their lives had cleaned their own shoes, to sit on the throne-like chairs, and women and girls waited their turns. John Conroy and a negro from Mississippi were the additions to the profession, and during the incarceration of the premier artist, his sweetheart, a former *hula danseuse*, remained faithful to his brushes. When a shoeless man or woman regarded the new-fangled importations interestedly, the proprietors offered to beautify their naked feet, and, ridiculous as it may seem, attempted it.

Although I heard odd tales at the consulate, it was at the parc de Bougainville that I met the gentleman of the beach intimately.

There I often sat and talked with whomever loafed. Natives frequented the *parc* hardly ever, but beach-combers, tourists, and sailors, or casual residents in from the districts, awaited there the opening of the stores or the post-office, or idled. The little park, or wooded strip of green, named after the admiral, and containing his monument, skirted the quay, and was between the establishment of Emile Levy, the pearl-trader, and the artificial pool of fresh water where the native women and sailors off the ships washed their clothes. From one's bench one had a view of all the harbor and of the passers-by on the Broom Road.

In the morning the pool was thronged with the laundresses, and one heard their paddles chunking as they beat the clothes. The French warship, the *Zélée*, was moored close by, and often the linen of its crew hung upon lines in the *parc*, and the French sailors came and went upon their duties, or sat on the coral wall and smoked and sang *chansons*. In the afternoon horses were brought down to bathe, and guests of the Annexe swam in the lagoon. People afoot, driving carts or carriages, on bicycles and in automobiles, went by on the thoroughfare about the island, the Frenchmen always talking as if excited over cosmic affairs, and the natives laughing or calling to one another.

If there happened to be a shoal of fish near the quays, I was sure to see Joseph, to whom the wise Dr. Funk had confided his precious concoction. He would desert the Cercle Bougainville, but still within hail of a stentorious skipper whose coppers were dry, and with a dozen other native men and women, boys and girls, lure the fish with hooks baited with bits of salted shrimp. Joseph was as skilful with his rod as with a shaker, and he would catch twenty *ature*, four or five inches long, in half an hour.

The water, about fifteen feet deep near the made embankment, was alive with the tiny fish, squirming in a mass as they were pursued by larger fish. The son of Prince Hinoe, a round-shouldered lout, very tall, awkward, and merry, held a bamboo pole. His white suit was soiled and ragged, and he whistled "All Coons Look alike to Me!" The peanut-vender had brought a rod, and was fishing with difficulty and mostly by feel. He could keep one eye open only, as one hand was occupied, but he pulled in many *ature*.

The *parc* was the occasional assembling-place for the drifting whites made thoughtful by trolling the jolly, brown bowl, and by those to whom lack of francs denied the trolling. It was there I first met Ivan Stroganoff, the aged Russian philosopher, and it was from there I took Wilfrid Baillon to the hospital. Baillon was a very handsome cow-boy from British Columbia, and was housed in Papeete with a giant Scandinavian who owned a cattle ranch in South America. He was generally called the Great Dane, and was the person meant in the charge for three cocktails at Lovaina's: "Germani to Fany, 3 feathers."

The cow-boy became ill. I prescribed castor-oil, and Mme. Fanny, half a tumbler of Martinique rum, with the juice of a lime in it. She was famous for this remedy for all internal troubles, and I took one with the cowboy as a prophylactic, as I might have been exposed to the same germs. He did not improve, though he followed Fanny's regimen exactly. He was sitting dejectedly in the *parc*, looking pale and thin, when I broached the subject.

"As the Fanny physic fails to straighten you out," I said to him, "why not try the hospital?"

He recoiled.

"Have you ever lamped it?" he asked. "It looks like a calaboose."

"It ain't so bad," said Kelly, the I.W.W., who was proselyting as usual among the flotsam and jetsam of the waterfront. "I 've been in worse joints in the United States."

The cow-boy yielding, I escorted him to the institution, carrying his bag, as what with his disease and his antidote he was weak. The hospital was a block away from the lagoon. It was surrounded by a high stone wall, and as it was built by the military, it was ugly and had the ridiculous effrontery of the army and all its lack of common sense. The iron gate was shut, and a sign said, "*Sonnez s'il vous plait!*" A toothless French *portière* of thirty years let us in. All the doctors of Tahiti had left the island for a few days on an excursion, and the gay scientist who opened the champagne in his pockets at the Tiare Hotel New Year's eve was in command. He sat in an arm-chair in a littered office and was smoking a pipe. His beard had a diameter of a foot, and obviated any need of collar or shirt-band, for it grew from his shoulder-blades up, so that his forehead, eyes, nose, and lips were white islands in a black sea, and even his nose was not bare, for he had been debited by Lovaina for his champagne as "Hair on nose."

He was reading a novel, and asked gruffly what we were there for. I told him, and Baillon was assigned a room at twelve francs a day, and was required to pay for ten days in advance.

The next morning I visited him. He could speak no French, so I questioned Blackbeard in his office, where we had an aperitif. He was voluble.

"He has amoeban dysentery," said he. "It is contagious and infectious, specifically, and it is fortunate your friend is attended by me. I have had that disease and know what's what."

I, too, had had it in the Philippine Islands, and I was amazed that it was infectious. How could he have got it?

"*Alors,*" replied the physician, "where has he taken meals?"

"Lovaina's, Fanny's, and some with the Chinese."

The Frenchman threw his arms around the door in mock horror. He gagged and spat, exciting the cowboy into a fever.

"*Oh! la! la!*" he shouted. "*Les Chinois! Certainement*, he is ill. He has eaten dog. Amoeban dysentery! *Mais*, monsieur, it is a dispensation of the *bon dieu* that he has not hydrophobia or the leprosy. *Les Chinois! Sacré nom de chien!*"

Lovaina had often accused her rivals, the Chinese *restaurateurs*, of serving dog meat for beef or lamb. Perhaps it was so, for in China more than five millions of dogs are sold for food in the market every year, and in Tahiti I knew that the Chinese ate the larvae of wasps, and M. Martin had mountain rats caught for his table.

The cow-boy's room was bare and cheerless, but two Tahitian girls of fourteen or fifteen years of age were in it. One was sitting on his bed, holding his hand, and the other was in a rocking-chair. They were very pretty and were dressed in their fête gowns. The girl on the bed was almost white, but her sister fairly brown. Probably they had different fathers. They told me that they had seen Baillon on the streets, had fallen in love with him, and though they had never spoken to him, wanted to comfort him now that he was sick. Jealousy did not rankle in their hearts, apparently. That absence often shocked non-Polynesians. Brothers shared wives, and sisters shared husbands all over old Polynesia.

This pair of love-lorn maidens had never exchanged a word with Baillon, for he spoke only English. The whiter girl wore a delicate satin gown, a red ribbon, and fine pearls in her hair. The cow-boy lay quietly, while she sat with her bare feet curled under her on the counterpane, looking actually unutterable passion.

"Shucks!" said he to me, safe in their ignorance of his tongue, "this is getting serious. They mean business, and I was foolin'. I got a little girl in the good ol' United States that would skin her alive if she saw her sittin' like that on my sheets. A man's takin' chances here that bats his eye at one o' these T'itian fairies. Do you know, their mother came here with them this morning?"

"They mean to have you in their family," I said. "That mother may have had a white husband or lover, and aids in the pursuit of you for auld lang syne."

Wilfrid Baillon was out of the hospital in just ten days. His release, as cured by the doctor, coincided curiously with his payment in advance. I saw him off for New Zealand by the steamship leaving the next day.

"Those people were awful good to me," he said in farewell. "It hurts me to treat those girls this way, but I'm scairt o' them. They're too strong in their feelings."

He ran away from a mess of love pottage that many men would have gone across seas to gain.

Ormsby, an Englishman in his early twenties, good-looking and courteous, with an air of accustomedness to luxury, but of being roughened by his environment, was sitting on a bench one morning with a girl. He called me over to meet her.

"You are an old-timer here now," he began, "and I've got to go away on the schooner to the Paumotus to-morrow. Drop in at Tahia's shack once in a while and cheer her up. She lives back of the Catholic mission, and she's pretty sick."

Tahia was desperately ill, I thought. She was thin, the color of the yellow wax candles of the high altar, and her straight nose, with expanded nostrils, and hard, almost savage mouth, features carved as with the stone chisel of her ancient tribe, conjured up the profile of Nenehofra, an Egyptian princess whose mummy I had seen. She was stern, silent, resigned to her fate, as are these races who know the inexorable will of the gods.

"Is she your girl?" I asked Ormsby.

He colored slightly.

"I suppose so, and the baby will be mine if it's ever born. At any rate, I'm going to stick to her while she's in this fix. I'll tell you on the square, I'm not gone on her; but she had a lover, an Australian I knew, and he was good to her, but he got the consumption and couldn't work. Maybe he came here with it. They hadn't a shilling, and Tahia built a hut in the hills up there near where the nature men live, and put him in it, and she fed and cared for him. She went to the mountains for *feis* she came down here to the reef to fish, and she found eggs and breadfruit in other people's gardens. She kept him alive, the Lord knows how, until he could secure money from Sydney to go home and die. Now, she's got the con from him, I suppose, and it would be a shabby trick to leave her when she's dying and will be a mother in two months, according to Doctor Cassiou!"

He made a wry face and lit his pipe. The girl could not understand a word and sat immovable.

"She's Marquesan," he went on. "Her mother has written through a trader in Atuona, on Hiva-Oa, to send her to her own valley, but she's quit. She sits and broods all day. I'd like to go back to my own home in Warwickshire. I know I'm changing for the bad here. I live like a dam' beach-comber. I only get a screw of three hundred francs a month, and that all goes for us two, with medicines and doctors. She'd go to Atuona if I'd go; but I can't make a living there, and I'm rotten enough now without living off her people in the cannibal group. She's skin and bones and coughs all night."

Ormsby puffed his pipe as Tahia put her hand in his. Her action was that of a small dog who puts his paw on his master's sleeve, hesitating, hopeful, but uncertain. She regarded me with slightly veiled hostility. I was a white who might be taking him away to foreign things.

"She's heard us talking about Atuona and Hiva-Oa, and she thinks maybe I've concluded to go. I can't do it, O'Brien. If I go there, I'll go native forever. I've got a streak of some dam' savage in me. Listen! I've got to go on the *Etoile* to Kaukura tojmorrow. Now, the natives are always kind to any one, but sickness they are not interested in. You go and see her, won't you? She's about all in, and it won't hurt you."

Ormsby went to the Dangerous Isles on the *Etoile*, and did not return for three weeks. He did not find Tahia in her shack on the hill. She was in the cemetery,—in the plot reserved for the natives of other islands,—and her babe unborn. She had died alone. I think she made up her mind to relieve the Englishman of her care, and willed to die at once. Dr. Cassiou, with whom I visited her, said:

"She ought to have lasted several months. *Mais, c'est curieux.* I have treated these Polynesians for many years, and I never found one I could keep alive when he wanted to die. She had already sent away her spirit, the *âme*, or *essence vitale*, or whatever it is, and then the body simply grows cold."

Ormsby and I talked it all over in the *parc*. He was deeply affected, and he uncovered his own soul, as men seldom do.

"I 'm dam' glad she's dead," he said, with intense feeling. "I might have failed, and she died before I did fail. I'm going back to Warwick now at first chance, and whatever I do or don't do, I've got that exception to my credit. It's one, too, to the credit of the whites that have cursed these poor islanders."

He had chalked it down on a record he thought quite black, but which I believe was better than our average. He and I went to the cemetery and had a wooden slab put up:

Tahia a Atuona
Tamau te maitai.

Tahia of Atuona
She held fast.

The Christchurch Kid and I were friendly, and he allowed me once a day during his training periods to put on the gloves with him for a mild four rounds. He was an open-hearted fellow, with a cauliflower ear and a nose a trifle awry from "a couple of years with the pork-and-beaners in California," as he explained, but with a magnificent body. He also lived at the Annexe, and did his training in the garden under Afa's clever hands. The Dummy must have admired him, for he would watch him exercising and boxing for hours, and make farcical sounds and grotesque gestures to indicate his understanding of the motions and blows.

The Kid asked me if I knew Ernest Darling, "the nature man," and identified the too naked wearer of toga and sandals on the San Francisco wharf as Darling.

"'E looked like Christ," said the boxer. "'E was a queer un. How'd you like to chyse up there to his roost in the 'ills?"

The next morning at five—it was not daybreak until six—we met at Wing Luey's for coffee and bread, which cost four cents. Prince Hinoe was there as usual, and asked us whither away. He laughed when we told him, and said the nature men were *maamaa*, crazy. The Kid was of the same mind.

We went up the rue de Sainte Amelie to the end of the road, and continued on up the valley. We could see far above us a small structure, which was the Eden that Darling had made for the Adamic colony he had established.

The climb was a stiff one on a mere wild pig-trail.

"The nyture man would 'ike up 'ere several times a day, after the frogs closed his road," said the New Zealander. "There was less brush than now, though, because 'e cut it aw'y to carry lum'ber and things up and to bring back the things 'e grew for market. 'E and 'is gang believed in nykedness, vegetables, socialism, no religion, and no drugs. The nytives think they're bug-'ouse, like Prince Hinoe, and I don't think they 're all there, but you couldn't cheat him. 'E'd myke a Glasgow peddler look sharp in buyin' or sellin'."

The Christchurch Kid was himself strictly conventional, and had been genuinely shocked by Darling's practices, and especially by his striking resemblance to the Master as portrayed by the early painters, and by Munkácsy in Christ Before Pilate.

"'E was all right," he explained to me as we climbed, "but 'e ought to been careful of 'is looks. I was 'ard up 'ere in Papeete once, and was sleepin' in an ole ware'ouse along with others. Darling slept on a window-sill, and 'e used to talk about enjoyin' the full sweep o' the tradewind. We doubted that, an' so one night we crept upstairs and surprised him. 'E was stretched out on a couple o' sacks, and a reg'ler gale was blowin' on him. 'E bathed a couple o' times a day in the lagoon or in fresh water, but 'e believed in rubbin' oil on his skin, and when a bloke is all greasy and nyked, 'e looks dirty. 'Is whiskers were too flossy in the tropics."

It took all my wind to reach the Eden, a couple of miles from our starting-point, and we were on all fours part of the way.

"'E could run up here like an animal," declared the fighter. "Once when a crowd of us went to visit 'im, 'e ran up this tr'il a'ead of us, and when we arrived all winded, blow me up a bloomin' gum-tree if 'e 'ad n't a mess of *feis* and breadfruit cooked for us."

We came to a sign on the trail. "Tapu," it said, which means taboo, or keep away; and farther on a notice in French that the owner forbade any one to enter upon his land.

"'E's a cryzy Frenchman with long whiskers," said the Kid. "'E 'as a grudge against any one who speaks English and also against the world. They s'y that 'is American wife ran aw'y from 'im, or an American took 'is nytive wife aw'y. 'E packs a revolver."

Everywhere the mountain-side was terraced, and planted in cocoanuts, breadfruits, bananas, flowers, and other plants, more than two thousand growths. Darling's toil had been great, and my heart bled at the memory of his standing on the piling as we steamed away. He had intended to have a colony, with bare nature-worshipers from all over the world. He had written articles in magazines, and tourists and authors had celebrated him in their stories. A score of needy health-seekers had arrived in Papeete and joined him, but could not survive his rigid diet and work. He had talked much of Eves, white, in the Eden, but none had offered.

On a platform fifteen hundred feet above the sea Darling had built a frame of beams, boards, and branches, with bunks and seats, much like a woodcutter's temporary shelter in the mountains, a mere lean-to. The view was stupendous, with the sea, the harbor, Moorea, and Papeete hardly seen in the foliage. He had thought his work in life to be peopling these hills with big families of nature children and the spread of socialism and reformed spelling.

His dream was transient. He had been treated with contempt, and had been driven from his garden, as had his first father, and without an Eve or a serpent. The whiskered Frenchman had bought Eden for a song, and had made it taboo to all.

We shouted in vain for the Frenchman, so we searched the premises. The boxer was afraid that after we left he might roll a rock down our trail because of our breaking his taboo. We found the spring from which he drank, and a pool dug by Darling for bathing, now only a mass of vegetation. Evidently the present tenant was not an ablutionist.

"There's a beastly German down on that next level," remarked the Christchurch Kid. "'E 'ates this Frenchman. Now they don't speak, but they sent warnin' to each other o' trouble. The frog carries the revolver for the sauer-kraut. Some day they'll kill each other right 'ere. They're both 'ermits, and 'ermits are terrible when they get excited."

It was almost a straight drop to the German's, a small promontory, with an acre of land, a platform raised eight feet on poles for a roof, and under it a berth. A chest held his belongings. He lived on the fruit he raised and the fish he caught in the sea, to which he went every day. He tried to keep chickens, but the mountain rats, of which Darling had trapped more than five thousand, ate most of them. The German, too, was away from his simple home. Both these men sought in life only peace and plain living, yet were consumed with hate. One day the upper dweller had accidentally caused a small stone to roll down upon the other's roof. The German had shouted something to the Frenchman, hot words had passed, and now they carried revolvers to intimidate or shoot each other. Their days and nights were spent on plans to insult or injure. And because of their feud they hated the whole world.

Once again in Papeete, we met the Swiss of the Noa-Noa who had intended to eat raw foods in the Marquesas. He was to return to America on the next steamer.

"De wegetables in Tahiti have no wim in dem," he said. "In California I ead nudds und raisins mit shtrent' in dem. I go back."

The fighter pointed out the "cryzy" Frenchman of Eden. He was the customs employee who had provoked the American consul by refusing to understand English.

I asked M. Lontane, the second in command of the police, why Darling had gone.

The hero of the battle of the limes, coal, and potatoes, looked at me fiercely.

"Is the French republic to permit here in its colony the whites who enjoy its hospitality to shame the nation before the Tahitians by their nakedness? That *sacrée bête* wore a *pareu* in town because the law compelled him to, but, monsieur, on the road, in his aerial resort, he and all his disciples were as naked as—"

"I have seen artistes at the music-halls of Paris," I finished.

"*Exactement*," he spluttered. "Are we to let Tahiti rival Paris?"

Ivan Stroganoff I met two or three times a month. He stayed in his chicken-coop except when the opportunities came for gaining a few francs, at steamer-time, and when sheer boredom drove him to Papeete for converse. With his dislike for the natives and his disdainful attitude toward the French, he had to seek other nationals in town, for there were none at Fa'a except a Chinese storekeeper. Stroganoff at eighty was as keen for interesting things as a young man, but his philosophy was fatal to his enjoyment. He saw the flaw in the diamond the sunbeam made of the drop of water on the leaf. He had lived too long and was too wise in disappointments. He was generous in his poverty, for he brought me a tin of guava-jelly he had made and a box of dried bananas. These had had their skins removed, and were black and not desirable-looking, but they were delicious and rare. In turn, not wishing to exaggerate the difference between our means, I gave him a box of cigars I had brought from America. I visited him at Fa'a, and found his coop had been a poultry shelter, and was humble, indeed; but I had slept a hundred nights in many countries in worse. He had a box for a table for eating and writing, and a rude cot. A few dishes and implements, and a roost of books and reviews in Russian, English, French, German, and other languages, completed his equipment.

He had several times reiterated his earnest wish to leave Tahiti, and his longing rested heavily on my heart. Upon lying down at night I had felt my own illiberality in not making it possible for him to realize his desire. A hundred dollars would send him there, with enough left over for a fortnight's keep. But my apology for not buying him a ticket was the real fear of his unhappiness. What could a friendless man of eighty do to exist in the United States other than become the inmate of a poorhouse? The best he could hope for would be to be taken in by the Little Sisters of the Poor, who house a few old men. They were, doubtless, kind, but probably insistent on neatness and religiosity.

The cold, the brutal policemen and guards, the venial justice, the crystallized charity in the name of a statistical Christ, arrested my hand. I had known it all at first hand, asking no favor. I believed that he would be worse off than in his chicken-coop. He could wear anything or nearly nothing in Tahiti, and his old Prince Albert comforted him; but he would have to conform to dress rules in a stricter civilization. Nature was a loving mother here and a shrewish hag there, at least toward the poor. And yet I was uneasy at my own argument.

For a month or two he had led the talk between us and any others in the *parc* to new discoveries in medicine. From his Fa'a seclusion he followed these very closely through European publications, for which his slender funds went. He had a curiously opposed nature, quoting with enthusiasm the idealistic philosophers, and descending into such abject materialism as haunting the bishop's palace for the cigar-stubs.

He would say that the purest joy in life is that which lifts us out of our daily existence and transforms us into disinterested spectators of it.

"This divine release from the common ways of men can be found only through art," Stroganoff would apostrophize. "The final and only true solution of life is to be found in the life of the saint. True morality passes through virtue, which is rooted in sympathy into asceticism. Renunciation only offers a complete release from the evils and terrors of existence."

Kelly was on the bench one day when the Russian uttered this rule of the cenobite school. They were good friends, but differed. They agreed that the world was sick and needed a radical medicine. Kelly was for a complete cure by ending private business through the workers seizing it when the time was ripe, which he believed would be soon. Stroganoff was for an empery of wise men, of scientists, philosophers, and artists, who would kick out the statesmen and politicians, and manage things by enlightened pragmatism. For the individual man who sought happiness his formula was as above—retirement to an aery.

When Kelly was gone to practise on his accordion,—he had opened a dancing academy at Fa'a,—the octogenarian asked me if I had read of the recent achievements of the scientists who were making the old young. He elaborated on the discoveries and experiments of Professor Leonard Huxley in England with thyroid gland injections, of Voronoff in France with the grafting of interstitial glands of monkeys, and of Eugen Steinach in Austria and Roux in Germany, with germ glands and X-rays. Steinach, especially, he discoursed on, and drew a magazine picture of him from his Prince Albert. The Vienna savant had a cordon of whiskers that made him resemble Stroganoff, and his eyes in the photograph peered through all one's disguises.

"That is what grates me," said Stroganoff. "I am far from all these worth-while things, these men of brain. I knew Ilya Ilich Metchnikoff before he became director of the Pasteur Institute. Here I am a rotting hulk. In the Caucasus I had *kephir*, and I used to carry *kephir* grains, and in America I, at least, could have kumiss or Ilya Ilich's *lait caille*. Look! I came here as Ponce de León to Florida to find youth, or to keep from growing older; in a word to escape *anno Domini*."

I turned and looked at him. He was a venerable figure, but there was no sign of eighty years in him. Rid of that white, hirsute mask, so associated with age, Stroganoff might have been twenty years younger. I said so, but it did not allay his yearning.

"I am well enough," he said, "because I have not dissipated for thirty years. I turned a leaf, as did Leo Nikolaievitch, after 'War and Peace.' Now I feel myself slipping into the grave."

He gazed ruminantly away from the lagoon to the pool of Psyche, where the Tahitian women squatted on their shapely haunches and thumped their clothes.

"See," he said earnestly. "I am old and useless. Why should not Steinach or the others make the grand experiment on me? If they succeed, very good; if they fail, there is no loss. They say those glands make a man over, no matter what his age. I offer myself freely. I am not afraid of death. Me, I am a philosopher."

He spoke excitedly. His eyes were fixed on distance, and I followed them.

Auro, the Golden One, as her name meant, had been washing her muslin slips in the pool of Psyche, and now stood in the entrance to it. She was for a fleeting second in her *pareu* only, her tunic raised above her head to pull on, and her enravishing form disclosed from her waist to her piquant face, over which tumbled her opulent locks.

It flashed on me that, wise and old as he was, the spectrum of the philosopher's soul had all the colors of the ignorant and the young. I looked from the nymphs of the pool to his darkening eyes, and I had a revelation of the persistence of common humanity in the most learned and the most philosophical. My castigation of myself for not buying his steamship ticket ceased in a moment, though not the less did I continue to enjoy his fount of learning and experience.

Chapter XIV

The market in Papeete—Coffee at Shin Bung Lung's with a prince—Fish the chief item—Description of them—The vegetables and fruits—The fish strike—Rumors of an uprising—Kelly and the I. W. W.—The mysterious session at Fa'a—Hallelujah! I'm a Bum!—The strike is broken.

The market in Papeete, the only one in Tahiti, has an air all its own. It is different in its amateur atmosphere and roseate color, in its isothermal romance and sheer good humor, from all others I have seen—Port of Spain, Peking, Kandy, or Jolo. It is more fascinating in its sensuous, tropical setting, its strange foods, and its laughing, lazy crowds of handsome people, than any other public mart I know. There is no financial exchange in Tahiti. Stocks and bonds take the shape of cocoanuts, vanilla-beans, fish, and other comforts. The brokers are merry women. The market is spot, and buyers must take delivery immediately, as usually not a single security is left at the end of the day's trading.

One must be at the market before five o'clock to see it all. Sunday is the choicest day of all the week, because Sunday is a day of feasting, and the *marché* then has a more than gala air. The English missionaries had once made even cooking a fish on Sunday a crime, severely punished; but the French priests changed all that, and the French Sabbath, the New York Sabbath, was *en règle*.

All the east is purple and red, gorgeous, flaring, when I awake. There are no windows in my connecting rooms in the Annexe. The sun rises through their wallless front, and sets through their opening to the balcony. What more liberal dispensation of nature? I am under the shower in two minutes, long enough to go down the curved staircase, with its admirable rosewood balustrade, and through the rear veranda to the room in which the large cement basin serves for bath and laundry and to lend a minute to the Christchurch Kid, the prize-fighter, to inform me that he is to open a school of the manly art, with diplomas for finished scholars and rewards for excellence. The recitals are to be public, a fee charged, and all ambitious pupils are to be guaranteed open examination in pairs and a just decision. The Kid and Cowan are to be *hors de combat*.

A daughter of a French governor of the Low Archipelago is in the basin, the door ajar, and the spray blinding her to my presence. She is seventeen, *café au lait—beaucoup de lait*, kohl-eyed, meter-tressed, and slim-bodied. She sings the *himene* of the battle of the limes and coal and potatoes, with a new stanza concerning the return of the *Noa-Noa*, and the vengeance of the Tahitian braves upon the pigs of Peretania, Britain.

"*Ia or a na! Bonjour*, Goo' night!" she says impartially, and modestly slips her *pareu* about her.

"*Ia ora na oe*!" I reply. "All goes well?"

"By cripe' yais; dam' goo'!" she answers, and goes humming on her way to her shanty in the yard. She is the maid of my chamber, gentle, willing, but never to be found for service. She learns English from the Kid, the rubber-legged boot-black, and other gentleman adventurers and tars of America and Europe, and she pours out bad words—I cannot mention them—in innocent faith in their propriety. In French or Tahitian she speaks correctly.

Outside the bath I hear the vehicles hurrying to market, and dressing quickly in white drill, and wearing on my Paumotu hat a brilliant scarlet *pugaree*, once the badge of subjugation to the Mohammedan conquerors of India, I join the procession.

Bon dieu! what a morning! The reds and purples are dying in the orient, and the hills are swathed in the half-white light of day. The lagoon is now a glistening pearly gray. Moorea, the isle of the fairy folk, is jagged and rough, as if a new throe of earth had torn its heights and made new steeps and obelisks. Moorea is never the same. Every hour of the day and every smile and frown of the sun creates valleys and spires, and alters the outlines of this most capricious of islets.

Past the bust of Bougainville, past the offices of Emile Levy, the pearler whom, to Levy's intense anger, Jack London slew in "The House of Mapuhi"; past the naval depot, the American consulate with the red, white, and blue flung in the breeze; the *Commissariat de Police*, the pool of Psyche, and all the rows of schooners that line the quays, with their milken sails drying on their masts, and I am by the stores of the merchants. The dawn is slipping through the curtain of night, but lamps are still burning. The traffic has roused the sleepers, and they are dressing. They have brought, tied in *pareus*, their Sunday clothes. Women are changing gowns, and men struggle with shirts and trousers, awkward inflictions upon their ordinarily free bodies.

All the night people who have journeyed from Papara, from Papenoo, or nearer districts slumber upon the sidewalks. This sleeping about anywhere is characteristic of the Tahitian. On the quays, in the doorways of the large and small stores, in carriages, and on the decks of the vessels, men and women and children lie or crouch, sleeping peacefully, with their possessions near them.

In the *fare tamaaraa*, the coffee-houses of the *Tinitos*, the Chinese, the venders of provender and the marketers alike are slipping their *taofe tau*, their four-sous' worth of coffee, with a tiny pewter mug of canned milk, sugar, and a half-loaf of French bread with butter.

My vis-á-vis at Shin Bung Lung's is Prince Hinoe, the heir to the broken throne, a very large, smiling brown gentleman, who sits with the French secretary of the governor, the two, alack! patting the shoulders, pinching the cheeks, and fondling the long, ebon plaits of the bevy of beauties who are up thus early to flirt and make merry. Tahiti is the most joyous land upon the globe. Who takes life seriously here is a fool or a liver-ridden penitent. The shop is full of peals of laughter and stolen kisses. Those sons of Belial who taught the daughter of the governor of the Dangerous Isles her unspeakable vocabulary are here. They have been to the Paris, the premier saloon of Papeete, for their morning's morning, an absinthe, or a hair of the dog that bit them yester eve.

What jokes they have! Stories of what happened last night in the tap-room of the cinematograph, how David opened a dozen bottles of Roederer, and there was no ice, so all alike, barefooted and silk-stockinged, drank the wine of Champagne warm, and out of beer glasses; of Captain Minne's statement that he would kill a scion of Tahitian royalty (not Hinoe) if he did not marry his daughter before the captain returned from the Paumotus; and of Count Polonsky's calling down the black *procureur*, the attorney-general, right in the same tap-room, and telling him he was a "nigger," although they had been friends before.

Tahitian and French and English, but very little of the latter, echoes through the coffee-room. Even I make a feeble struggle to speak the native tongue, and arouse storms of giggles.

The market-place faces the *Mairie*, the city hall, and its center is a fountain beloved of youth. There sit or loll the maidens of Papeete at night, and titter as pass the sighing lads. There wait the automobiles to carry the pleasure bent to Kelly's grove at Fa'a, where the maxixe and the tango rage, the hula-dancers quiver and quaver, and wassail has no bounds.

When the whites are at dinner, the natives meet in the market-place, which is the agora, as the *place du gouvernment* is the forum of the dance and music of these ocean Greeks.

But at this hour it is wreathed with women, scores squat upon their mats on the pave, their goods spread before the eyes of the purchasers.

The sellers of the materials for hats are many. The bamboo fiber, yellowish white, is the choicest, but there are other colors and stuffs. The women venders smoke cigarettes and are always laughing. Old crones, withered and feeble, shake their thin sides at their own and others' jokes.

Already the buyers are coming fast, householders and cooks and bachelors and beaux, tourists and native beauties.

A score of groups are smoking and chatting, flirting and running over their lists. Carriages and carts are tied everywhere, country folk who have come to sell or to buy, or both, and automobiles, too, are ranged beside the Mairie.

Matrons and daughters, many nationals, are assembling. The wife of a new consul, a charming blonde, just from New Jersey, has her basket on her arm. She is a bride, and must make the consul's two thousand dollars a year go far. A priest in a black gown and a young Mormon elder from Utah regard each other coldly. A hundred Chinese cafe-keepers, stewards, and merchants are endeavoring to pierce the exteriors of the foods and estimate their true value. The market is not open yet. It awaits the sound of the gong, rung by the police about half past five. Four or five of these officials are about, all natives in gaudy uniforms, their bicycles at the curb, smoking, and exchanging greetings with friends.

The question of deepest interest to the marketers is the fish. The tables for these are railed off, and, peering through the barriers, the onlookers comment upon the kinds and guess at the prices.

The market-house is a shed over concrete floors, clean, sanitary, and occupied but an hour or two a day. There are three main divisions of the market, meat, fish, and green things. Meat in Tahiti is better uneaten and unsung. It comes on the hoof from New Zealand. Now, if you are an epicure, you may rent a cold-storage chamber in the *glacerie*, and keep your steaks and roasts until tender.

Fish is the chief item to the Tahitian. Give him only fish, and he may murmur at his fate; but deny him fish, and he will hie him to the reef and snare it for himself. All night the torches of the fishermen gleam on the foaming reef, and often I paddle out near the breakers and hear the chants and cries of the men as they thrust their harpoons or draw their nets. So it is the women who sell the fish, while the weary husbands and fathers lie wrapped in dreams of a miraculous draught.

There are three great aquariums in the world, at Honolulu, Naples, and New York. There is no other such fish-market as this of Papeete, for Hawaii's has become Asiaticized, and the kanaka is almost nil in the angling art there. But those same fish that I gazed at in amazement in the tanks of the museums are spread out here on tables for my buying.

Impossible fish they are, pale blue; brilliant yellow; black as charcoal; sloe, with orange stripes; scarlet, spotted, and barred in rainbow tints. The parrot-fish are especially splendid in spangling radiancy, their tails and a spine in their mouths giving them their name.

The impression made upon one's first visit to the Papeete market is overwhelming, the plenitude of nature rejoicing one's heart, and the care of the Great Consciousness for beauty and color, and even for the ludicrous, the merely funny, causing curious groping sensations of wonder at the varied plan of creation.

Sexual selection and suitability to survive are responsible. Those vivid colors, those symmetrical markings, and laughable forms are all part of the *going on* of the world, the adaptation to environment, and the desire for love and admiration in the male and female.

These things from the deep seem hardly fish. They are bits of the sunset, fragments of a mosaic, Futuristic pictures; anything but our sodden, gray, or wateryhued fish of temperate climes. Some are as green as the hills of Erin, others as blue as the sky, as crimson as blood, as yellow as the flag of China. They are cut by nature in many patterns, round, or sectional, like a piece of pie, triangular, almost square; some with a back fin that floats out a foot or two behind.

They are grotesque, alarming, apparently the design of a joker. But tread not on the domain of the scientist, for he will prove to you that each separate queerness is only a trick of nature to fit its owner to the necessities of his habitat. The parrot-fish are screamingly fantastic. There are not even in the warm California or Florida waters the duplicates of these rainbow fish. The Garibaldi perch and the electric fish excite interest at Santa Catalina, but here are a hundred marvels, and if I wish I can see them all as they swim in and out of the coral caverns within the lagoon.

Porcupine fish are a delicacy, squid are esteemed, and even the devilfish is on the tables, hideous, repellent, slimy, horned, and tentacled; not mighty enough to crush out the life of the fisher, as was the horrific creature in Victor Hugo's "Toilers of the Sea," whom his hero fought, yet menacing even when dead. It is a frightful figure in its aspect of hatred and ugliness, but good to eat. See that fat Tahitian thrust his finger into the sides of the octopus to plumb its cooking qualities. It is quickly sold.

There are crabs and crawfish, eels and shrimps, prawns and *varos*, all hung up on strings. There are oysters and *maoao*, alive and dripping. The *maoao* is the turbo, a gastropod, a mysterious inhabitant of a twisted shell, who shuts the door to his home with a brightly-colored operculum, for all the world like half of a cuff-button. One eats him raw or cooked or dried. But he is not so odd as the *varo* one of the most delicious and expensive of Tahitian foods. These sea centipedes, as the English call them in Tahiti, are a species of *ibacus*, and are from six to twelve inches long, and two wide. They have legs or feelers all along their sides, like a pocket comb, a hideous head, and tail, and a generally repulsive appearance. If one did not know they were excellent eating, and most harmless in their habits, one would be tempted to run or take to a tree at sight of them. Their shell is a translucent yellow, with black markings. The female has a red stripe down her back, and red eggs beneath her. She is richer in flavor, and more deadly than the male to one who has a natural diathesis to poisoning by *varos*. Many whites cannot eat them. Some lose appetite at their looks, their likeness to a gigantic thousand-leg. Others find that the *varo* rests uneasy within them, as though each claw or tooth of the comb grasped a vital part of their anatomy. I think *varos* excellent when wrapped in *hotu* leaves, and grilled as a lobster. I take the beastie in my fingers and suck out the meat. Amateurs must keep their eyes shut during this operation.

Catching *varos* is tedious and requires skill. They live in the sand of the beach under two or three feet of water. One has to find their holes by wading and peering. They are small at the top, but roomy below. One cannot see these holes through ruffled water. Once located, grapnels, or spools fitted with a dozen hooks, are lowered into them. A pair inhabits the same den. If the male is at home, he seizes the grapnel, and is raised and captured, and the female follows. But if the female emerges first, it is a sure sign that the male is absent in search of food. I have pondered as to this habit of the *varo*, and have tried to persuade me that the male, being a courteous shrimp,—he is a kind of mantis-shrimp,—combats the intruding hooks first in order to protect his loved one; but the grapnel is baited with fish, and though masculine pride would insist that chivalry urges *varo homme* to defend his domestic shrine, fishers for the tidbit say that he is after the bait, and holds to it so tightly that he sacrifices his life. Nevertheless, the lady embraces the same opportunity to rise, and their deserted tenement is soon filled by the sands.

Trapping *varos* calls for patience and much dexterity. The mere finding of the holes is possible only to natives trained from childhood. Six *varos* make a good meal, with bread and wine, and they are most enjoyable hot—also most indigestible.

"Begin their eating by sucking a cold one," once said a *bon vivant* to me. "Only when accustomed to them should you dare them hot and in numbers."

Flying-fish are sold, many of them delicate in taste and shapely.

One may buy favorite sauces for fish, and some of the women offered them to me. One is *taiaro*, made of the hard meat of the cocoanut, with pounded shrimp, and allowed to ferment slightly. It is put up in bamboo tubes, three inches in diameter, and four or five feet long, tied at the opening with a pandanus-leaf for a seal. It is delicious on raw fish. I have seen a native take his fish by the tail and devour it as one would a banana; but the Tahitians cut up the fish, and, after soaking it in lime-juice, eat it with the *taiaro*. It is as tasty as Blue Points and tabasco.

There are two other epicurean sauces, one made of the *omotu*, the soft cocoanut, which is split, the meat dug out and put in the *hue*, the calabash, mixed with a little salt water, lime-juice, and the juice of the *rea*, the saffron, and allowed to ferment. This is the *mitihue*, a piquant and fetid, *puante* sauce that seasons all Tahitian meals. The calabash is left in the sun, and when the sauce dries up, water is poured on the dry ingredients, a perpetual saucebox.

In the arrangement of vegetables our own hucksters could learn. Every piece is scraped and cleansed. String beans are tied together in bundles like cigars or asparagus, and lettuce of several varieties, romaine and endive, parsnips, carrots, beets, turnips, and even potatoes, sweet and white, are shown in immaculate condition. The tomatoes do not rival ours, but Tahiti being seventeen degrees below the equator, one cannot expect such tropical regions to produce temperate-zone plants to perfection. That they are provided at all is due to the Chinese, those patient, acute Cantonese and Amoyans. The Tahitian has no competence in intensive cultivation or the will to toil. Were it not for the Chinese, white residents in many countries would have to forego vegetables. It is so in Mexico and Hawaii and the Philippines, although Japanese in the first two compete with them.

The main food of the Tahitians is *feis*, as is bread to us, or rice to the Asiatic. It is not so in the Marquesas, eight hundred miles north, where breadfruit is the staff, nor in Hawaii, where fermented *taro* (*poi*) is the chief reliance of the kanaka. The *feis*, gigantic bananas of coarse fiber, which must be cooked, are about a foot in length, and three inches in diameter, and grow in immense, heavy bunches in the mountains, so that obtaining them is great labor. They are wild creatures of heights, and love the spots most difficult of access. Only barefooted men can reach them. These *feis* are a separate species. The market-place is filled with them, and hardly a Tahitian but buys his quota for the day. The *fei*-gatherers are men of giant strength, naked save for the *pareu* about the loins, and often their feet from climbing and holding on to rocks and roots are curiously deformed, the toes spread an inch apart, and sometimes the big toe is opposed to the others, like a thumb. There are besides many kinds of bananas here for eating raw; some are as small as a man's finger, and as sweet as honey.

The *fei*-hunters hang six or seven bunches on a bamboo pole and bring them thus to market. One meets these young Atlases moving along the roads, chaplets of frangipani upon their curling hair, or perhaps a single gardenia or tube-rose behind their ears, singing softly and treading steadily, smiling, and all with a burden that would stagger a white athlete.

The *taro* looks like a war-club, several feet long, three inches thick, and with a fierce knob. It and its tops are in demand. The breadfruit are as big as Dutch cheese, weighing four or five pounds, their green rinds tuberculated like a golf-ball. *Sapadillos*, tamarinds, limes, mangoes, oranges, *acachous*, and a dozen other native fruits are to be had. Cocoanuts and *papayas* are of course, favorites. There are many kinds of cocoanuts. I like best the young nut, which has the meat yet unformed or barely so, and can be eaten with a spoon, and holds about a quart of delicious wine. No matter how hot the day, this wine is always cool. One has only to pierce the top of the green rind, and tilt the hole above one's mouth. If one has alcoholic leanings, the wine of a cocoanut, an ounce of rum, two lumps of sugar, a dash of grenadine, and the mixture were paradise enow.

The *papayas*, which the British call mammee-apple or even mummy-apple or papaw, because of the West Indian name, *mamey*, are much like pumpkins in appearance. They grow on trees, quite like palms, from ten to thirty feet high, the trunk scaly like an alligator's hide, and the leaves pointed. The fruit hangs in a cluster at the crown of the tree, green and yellow, resembling badly shaped melons. The taste is musky sweet and not always agreeable to tyros. The seeds are black and full of pepsin. Boiled when green, the papaya reminds one of vegetable marrow; and cooked when ripe, it makes a pie stuffing not to be despised. I have often hung steaks or birds in the tree, protected by a cage from pests, or wrapped them in papaya-leaves to make them tender. The very atmosphere does this, and the pepsin extracted from the *papaya* by science is much used by druggists instead of animal extracts.

The market closed, the venders who have come in carts drive home, while those Tahitians who are not too old adorn themselves with flowers and seek pleasure. Young and old, they are laughing. Why? I need never ask the reason here, but look to the blue sky, the placid sea within the lagoon, the generous fruitage of nature, the palms and flowers ever present and inviting; the very sign of the gentle souls and merry hearts of these most lovable people. When I am alone with them I do not walk. I dance or skip.

Life is easy. The *fei*, the breadfruit, the cocoanut, the mango, and the *taro* are all about. No plow, no hoe, or rude labor, but for the lifting of one's hand there is food. The fish leap in the brine, and the pig fattens for the oven. Clothes are irksome. A straw hut may be built in an hour or two, and in the grove sounds the soft music of love.

Aue! nom de poisson! within a day the market became a wailing-place. There were no fish. The tables daily covered with them were empty. The happy wives and consorts who had been wont to sell the catch of the men remained in their homes, and the fishers themselves were there or idle on the streets. The districts around the island, which for decades had despatched by the daily diligence, or by special vehicle or boat, the drafts of the village nets, sent not a fin. Never in Tahiti's history except when war raged between clans, or between Tahitians and French, had there been such a fish famine.

And, name of a dog! it was due to a *grève*, a strike. It came upon the Papeete people like a tidal wave out of the sea, or like a cyclone that devastates a Paumotu atoll, but, *entre nous*, it had been brooding for months. Fish had been getting dearer and dearer for a long time, and householders had complained bitterly. They recalled the time when for a franc one could buy enough delicious fish for a family feast. They called the *taata hara*, the native anglers, *cochons*, hogs, and they discussed when they gathered in the clubs, or when ladies met at market, the weakness of the authorities in allowing the extortion. But nothing was done. The extortion continued, and the profanity increased. At the Cercle Bouganville Captain Goeltz and the other retired salts banged the tables and said to me:

"*Sacré redingote!* is it that the *indigènes* pay the governor or give him fish free? Are we French citizens to die of hunger that savages may ride in les Fords?"

They shouted for Doctor Funks, and drank damnation to the régime that let patriots surfer to profit *les canaques*. But, in reality, the governor months ago had secretly begun a plan to help them.

One day the governor, his good lady being gone to visit at Raiatea, had given his cook three francs to buy fish for the *déjeuner* at the palace. When they came on the table, a bare bite for each of the company, the governor had called in the chef.

"*Mais*, I gave you three francs for the fish, *n'est-ce pas?*"

"*Mais, vous don' lai moi t'ree franc, oui, oui,*" answered the Chinese. "*Moi don'lai canaque po po'sson.*"

The governor had led in the chorus of *sácres* and *diables*. All at the table were of the redingote family, all feeding from the national trough at Paris, and they had the courage and power to end the damnable imposition on the slender purses of Papeete citizens. *Sapristi!* this robbery must cease. He must go slow, however. Being an honest and unselfish man, he investigated and initiated legislation so carefully and tardily that the remedy for the evil was applied only four days ago. He had returned to France, so one could not say that he consulted his own purse; but the present governor, an amiable man and a good bridge-player, also liked fish, and they pay no bonanza salaries, the French. The fishermen had known, of course, of the approaching end of their piracy, but, like Tahitians, waited until necessity for action. The official paper in which all laws are published had the ordinance set out in full. Translated, briefly, from the French, it ran like this:

That the Governor of the establishments of France in Oceania, a chevalier of the Legion of Honor [this information is inserted in every degree, announcement and statement the governor makes, and stares at one from a hundred trees], in view of the "article *du decret du* 21 decembre, 1885," etc. [and in view of a dozen other articles of various dates since], considering that fish is the basis of the alimentation of the Tahitians, that in the Papeete public market, fish has been monopolized with the result that its price has been raised steadily, and a situation created injurious to the working people, the cost of living necessitating a constant increase in salaries, orders that after a date fixed, fish be sold by weight and at the following prices per kilo, according to the kind of fish:

30 cents a kilo	25 cents a kilo	20 cents a kilo
1st category	2d category	3d category
Aahi	Auhopu	Ature
Ahuru	Au aavere	Atoti
Anae	Ioio	Aoa-Ropa
Apai	Mahimahi	Faia
Ava	Moi	Fee
Lihi	Nato	Fai
Mu	Nape	Honu
Nanue	Orare	Inaa
Oeo	Paere	Maere
Paaihere	Parai	Maito
Paraha peue	Puhi pape	Marara
Tehu	Tohe veri	Manini
Varo	Taou	Mao

Oura (chevrette)	Uhi	Mana
Paapaa (crabs)	Ume	Ouma
Oura-miti (langouste)	Vau	Oiri
	Roi	Pahoro
	Tuhura	Patia
		Puhu miti
		Pahua
		Tapio

As a kilo is two and a fifth pounds, the *ature* that Joseph caught by the Quai de Commerce, being in the third category, would cost, under the ukase, less than ten cents a pound. Crabs being in the first category—*paapaa*,—would cost about thirteen cents a pound, and the succulent *varo* the same, whereas they were then two francs, or forty cents a pound. We lovers of sea centipedes toasted the brave governor vociferously.

The decrees were nailed to the trees on the Broom Road, in the rue de Rivoli, and in the market-place. The populace were joyous, though some old wholesale buyers like Lovaina questioned the wisdom of the governor's edict and the effect on themselves.

"If they do that," said she, "maybe, by'n'by they fix my meal or lime squash."

Until the date of carrying out the mandate, one picked out a pleasing fish or string of fish, all nicely wrapped in leaves, and one asked, "*A hia?* How much?"

When Lovaina inquired the price, she smiled her sweetest, rubbed the saleslady's back, and uttered some joke that made her sway with laughter, so that price became of no importance. But a sour-faced white or a pompous bureaucrat paid her saving, and Chinese, who kept the restaurants, invoked the curse of barrenness upon the venders.

The day came for the new scheme of fish-selling to go into effect. The mayor, a long-bearded and shrewd druggist, had bought up all the half-way accurate scales in the city, for there had not been a balance in the market. Everything was by strings, bunches, feels, and hefts. The fish counters, polished by the guardian of the *marché*, were now brilliant with the shiny apparatus.

The long-awaited morning found a crowd peeping through the railing half an hour earlier than usual. All would have a fill of delicacies. Lovaina with the Dummy drove down to the Annexe for me. Vava was making queer signs to her which either were unintelligible or which she thought absurd. She waved her long forefinger before him, which meant: "Don't talk foolishness. I am not a fool."

We reached the market-place when only a score or two had gathered.

A thousand devils! there was not a fish on the slabs. The merry wives were absent. The condition was plain.

The Dummy uttered a demoniacal grunt, and shook his head and hands before Lovaina in accusation. She answered him with a movement of her head up and down, which signified acquiescence.

"Dummy know," she said mysteriously. "That Vava he find everything. He like old-time *tahutahu*, sorcerer. He tell me Annexe no fish. He say now no fish till finish those masheen."

She laughed and rubbed my shoulders.

"The fish slip away," she said, "and leave only their scales! *Aue!*"

M. Lontane, the second in command of the gendarmes, was sent scouting, and reported to the governor—not the one who originated the manifesto—that the famine was the result of an organized revolt against the law and order of the land. Fishermen he had questioned, replied simply, "*Aita faito, paru! Aita hoo, paru!*" Which, holy blue! meant, "No scales, fish! No price, fish!"

What to do? One cannot make a horse drink unless one gives him red peppers to eat. Even the Government could not make a fisherman fish for market, as there was a law against enforced labor except as punishment for crime or in emergencies, such as during the existence of martial law, the guarding against a conflagration, or a tidal wave or cyclone. At the Cercle Militaire many of the bureaucrats, and especially the doctor who had treated the cow-boy, were for martial law, anyway. Napoleon knew, said the fierce *médecin*. "A whiff of grapeshot, and the reef would be again gleaming with lights, and the diligences would pour in with loads of fish."

Doctor Cassiou, a very old resident, and not at all fierce, asked his confrere against whom would the grapeshot be directed. Would he gather the fishermen from all over Tahiti, and decimate them, the way the Little Corporal purged mutiny out of his regiments? Lontane was sent out again. In the Cerele Bougainville he took a rum punch before starting on his bicycle, and he swore by his patron saint, Bacchus, that he would solve the problem even if denied the remedy of *force majeure*.

Within three hours of his return from Patutoa, a meeting was called of the council of state, the governor, the doctors, the druggist, a merchant or two, and a lawyer, and before it M. Lontane disclosed that the natives were possessed by a new devil that he feared was a recrudescence of the ancient struggle for independence.

Each fisherman he had examined refused to answer his interrogations, saying only, "I dobbebelly dobbebelly."

The governor scratched his ear, and the mayor wiggled his hands behind, as he had on the wharf after the battle of the limes, coal, and potatoes. The lawyer said it must be an incantation, but that it was not Tahitian, for that language had no "d" in its alphabet. M. Lontane and all his squad were given peremptory orders to unriddle the enigma.

Meanwhile the fishless market continued. It was not entirely fishless, for before the bell rang we would see over the railings a few handfuls of *varos*, crayfish, and shrimps and perhaps a dozen small baskets of oysters. A policeman prevented a riot, but could not stay the rush when the bell rang and the gate was opened. The lovers of shellfish and the servants of the well-to-do snatched madly at the small supply, and paid whatever extravagant price was demanded. The scales were never touched, and any insistence upon the new legal plan and price was laughed at. With these delicacies beyond their means, the natives stormed the two pork butchers, the *Tinitos*. They grabbed the chops and lumps of pig, poking and kneading them, shouting for their weight, and in some instances making off without paying. There was such a howdy-do that extra policemen were summoned to form all into line.

There were no scaly fish, and it came out that the shellfish were caught by women, widows who had no men to obey or please, who had children, or who wanted francs to buy gewgaws or tobacco; and a few unsocial men fishers who did not abide by the common interests of their group.

At Lovaina's we were on a tiresome round of canned salmon, eggs, and beef, and eggs rose to six sous each. In about a fortnight we began to have fish as usual, and Lovaina signed to me that the Dummy procured them in the country. I was very curious, and asked if I might accompany him. She said that he would call for me at the Annexe the next time he went.

I was awakened after midnight in my room—the doors were never locked—by the Dummy leaning over and shaking me. I opened my eyes, and he put his fingers to his lips. I dressed, and went with him in the old surrey. We drove through the night along the Broom Road. Once past the cemetery we were in the country. The cocoanut-trees were gray ghosts against the dark foliage and trunks of the breadfruits and the sugar cane; the reef was a faint gleam of white over the lagoon and a subdued sound of distant waters.

We jogged along, and as we approached Fa'a, I lit a match and looked at my watch. It was nearly two o'clock. The Dummy stopped the horse at Kelly's dance-hall in a palm grove. The building was of bamboo and thatch, with a smooth floor of Oregon pine, and was a former *himene* house. Kelly had rented it from the church authorities. The dancing was over for the night, but a few carts were in the grove, and the lights were bright. We went inside, and found forty or fifty Tahitians, men and women, squatting or sitting on the floor, while on the platform was Kelly himself, with his accordion on the table. He saw me and shouted "*Ia ora na!*" And after a few minutes, while others came, began to speak. What he said was interpreted by a Frenchman, who, to my astonishment, proved to be the editor of one of those anti-government papers printed in San Francisco, that Ivan Stroganoff had shown me.

Kelly addressed the audience, "Fishermen and fellow stiffs." He said that the fish strike was a success, and if they all remained true to one another, they would win, and the scales would be kicked out. The few scabs who sold fish in the market only made sore those unable to buy. He said that he had found out that the law applied only to the market-place, and that a plan would be tried of hawking fish from house to house in Papeete. They would circumvent the governor's proclamation in that way. He praised their fortitude in the struggle, and after the editor had interpreted stiffs by *te tamaiti aroha e*, which means poor children, and scabs by *iore*, which means rats, and had ended with a peroration that brought many cries of "*Maitai*! Good!" Kelly took up his accordion, and began to play the sacred air of "Revive us Again!"

He led the singing of his version:

"Hallelujah! I'm a bum! Hallelujah! Bum again!
Hallelujah! Give us a hand-out! To save us from sin!"

The Tahitians rocked to and fro, threw back their heads, and, their eyes shut as in their religious *himenes*, chorused joyfully:

"Hahrayrooyah! I'm a boom! Hahrayrooyah! Boomagay!
Hahrayrooyah! Hizzandow! To tave ut fruh tin!"

They sang the refrain a dozen times, and then Kelly dismissed the meeting with a request for "three cheers for the I. W. W."

There is no "w" in French or in Tahitian, and the interpreter said, "*Ruperupe* ah-ee dohblevay dohblevay!" And the Tahitians: "Ai dobbebelly dobbebelly!"

Kelly came down from the platform, his freckled face shining and his eyes serious but twinkling. He greeted me as the natives lit cigarettes and filed out.

"I'm runnin' their strike for them," he said. "It 's on the square. The poor fish! They don't make hardly enough to pay for their nets, let alone an honest day's pay, and they're up half the night and takin' chances with the sharks and the devil-fish. They have to pay market dues and all sorts of taxes. They 're good stiffs all right, and every one has a membership card in the I. W. W. applied for."

When we went outside, I saw that the Dummy who had been a witness of the scene in the hall, had a large package of fish in the surrey, and all around there were other packages of them. The men had been selling to those who came to Fa'a for them, the law extending only to the market in Papeete.

The strikers hawked the fish in town the next day, but this was immediately forbidden. Hungry for fish—the Tahitians have one word meaning all that—though the people were, few could drive out to Fa'a to fetch them. Within Papeete fish were mysteriously nailed to the trees at night, and over each was a card with the letters, "I. W. W."

Again a meeting of the council of state was called, and at it M. Lontane revealed the meaning of those cabalistic letters and the leadership of Kelly. He had tracked down the fishermen and found their headquarters at the dance hall.

At the Cercle Bougainville there was an uproar. Merchants drank twice their stint of liquor in their indignation. Syndicalism was invading their shores, and their already limited labor supply would be corrupted.

I could not picture too seriously the wrath of the honest traders at the traitorous conduct of Kelly, "a white man," as told by M. Lontane. I was upbraided because of Kelly being an American with an Irish name. Lying Bill said it was "A bloody Guy Fawkes plot."

M. Lontane took full credit for the discovery of what he termed "A complot that would rival the Dreyfus case."

He struck his chest, and asked me sternly if I knew of M. LeCoq, the great detective, of Emile Gaboriau.

Kelly was arrested in the midst of his dancing soirée at Fa'a. He was put in the calaboose, and when he frankly said that he had come to Tahiti to preach the gospel of I. W. W.-ism and that he believed the fishermen had all the right on their side, he was sentenced as "a foreigner without visible means of support, a vagrant, miscreant, vagabond, and dangerous alien," to a month on the roads, and then to be deported to the United States, whence he had come.

The strike or walk-out was broken. With the cessation of the direction of Kelly and his heartening song, the fishermen gradually went back to their routine, and their women folk to the market. The scales were in operation, but the *himene*, "Hahrayrooyah! I'm a boom! Hahrayrooyah! Boomagay!" was sung from one end of Tahiti to another, and "Ai dobbebelly dobbebelly" was made at the Cercle Bougainville a password to some very old rum said to have belonged to the bishop who wrote the Tahitian dictionary.

Chapter XV

A drive to Papenoo—The chief of Papenoo—A dinner and poker on the beach—Incidents of the game—Breakfast the next morning—The chief tells his story—The journey back—The leper child and her doll—The *Alliance Française*—Bemis and his daughter—The band concert and the fire—The prize-fight—My bowl of velvet.

We had another picnic; this time at Papenoo. Polonsky owned thirty thousand acres of land in the Great Valley of Papenoo, the largest of all the valleys of Tahiti. He had bought it from the Catholic mission, which, following the monastic orders of the church in other countries for a thousand years, had early adopted a policy of acquiring land. But there were too few laborers in Tahiti now. Christianity had not worked the miracle of preserving them from civilization. The priests were glad to sell their extensive holdings at Papenoo, and the energetic Russo-French count said that he would bring Slav families from Europe to populate and develop it. He would plant the vast acreage in cocoanut-trees, vanilla vines, and sugar-cane, and build up a white community in the South Seas. He had noble plans for a novel experiment.

We started from the Cercle Bougainville in the afternoon in carriages pulled by California bronchos. The dour Llewellyn, the handsome Landers, the boastful McHenry, Lying Bill, David, the young American vanilla-shipper, Bemis, an American cocoanut-buyer, the half-castes of the orchestra, and servants, filled three roomy carryalls. The ideal mode of travel in Tahiti in the cool of the day would be a donkey, a slow, patient beast, who might himself take an interest in the scenery, or at least the shrubbery. But the white must ever go at top speed, and we dashed through the streets of Papeete, the accordions playing "Revive us again!" the "Himene Tatou Arearea," and other tunes, and we singing, "Hallelujah! I'm a bum!" and "Faararirari ta oe Tamarii Tahiti! La, li!" One never makes merry privately in the South Seas.

Through Papeete we went along the eastern Broom Road, our train attracting much attention. We stopped at the *glacerie* for ice, and Polonsky insisted that we make a detour to his residence to drink a stirrup-cup of champagne. He donned riding-breeches and took a horse from his well-appointed stable.

Against the road on each side were close hedges of *acalypha*, or false coffee, called in Tahitian *tafeie*, a small tree which grows quickly, and the leaves of which are red or bronze or green, handsome and admirably suited for fencing. Through these hedges and the broad entrances I saw the houses and gardens, the residents and family life of the people. Everywhere was a small prosperity, with gladness; pigs and sheep cropping the grass and herbs, which were a mat of green, rising so fast with the daily showers that only flocks could keep it shorn. On the verandas and on the turf idle men and women were gazing at the sky, talking, humming the newest air, plaiting hats, or napping. No one was reading. There was no book-store in Tahiti. I had not read a line since I came. I had not stepped up to the genial dentist's to see an American journal. After years of the newspaper habit, reading and writing them, it had fallen away in Tahiti as the prickly heat after a week at sea. Of what interest was it that the divorce record was growing longer in New York, that Hinky Dink had been reëlected in Chicago, and that Los Angeles had doubled in population. A dawn on the beach, a swim in the lagoon, the end of the fish strike, were vastly more entertaining.

We passed the gorge of Fautaua, where Fragrance of the Jasmine and I had had a charmed day. The pinnacles of the Diadem were black against the eastern sky. Aorai, the tallest peak in sight, more than a mile high, hid its head in a mass of snowy clouds.

Not far away was the mausoleum of the last king of the Society Islands, Pomaré the Fifth, with whose wide-awake widow, the queen, I had smoked a cigarette a day ago. It was a pyramid of coral, a red funeral-urn on top, and a red P on the façade. Pillars and roof were of the same color, and a chain surrounded it. The tomb was rococo, glaring, typical of the monuments in the South Seas where the aboriginal structures of beauty or interest were destroyed by the missionaries to please their Clapham Seminary god. Pomaré, who had been the victim of French political chicane, enjoyed now but one privilege. If his spirit had senses, it heard the lapping of the waves upon the beach of the lagoon across which his ancestor, the first Pomaré, had come from Moorea to be a king.

We left the Broom Road for Point Venus to see the monument to Captain James Cook, the great mariner of these seas. The only lighthouse on Tahiti is there. On that spot Cook and his astronomers had observed the transit of Venus in 1769, and it was there the first English missionaries landed from the ship *Duff* to convert the pagan Tahitians. Cook has a pillar, with a plate of commemoration, in a grove of *purau*-trees, cocoanuts, pandanus, and the red oleander; Cook who is an immortal, and was loved by a queen here.

We left behind Paintua, Taunoa, Arahim, Arue and Haapape, and came to a shore where no reef checked the waves in a yeasty line a mile or less from the beach. The breakers roared and beat upon a black shore, strangely different from the Tahitian strand that I had seen. For miles a hundred feet of sable rocks, pebbles, some small and others as big as a man's hand, lay between the receded tide and the road, and all along huge islets of somber stone defended themselves as best they could against the attack of the surf. Signs of surrender showed in some, caverns and arches cut by the constant hammer of swell and billow.

Sugar-cane, vanilla, pineapples, coffee, bananas, plantation after plantation, with the country houses of Papeete's merchants, officials, lawyers, and doctors, moved past our vehicle, and, as we increased the distance from the capital, the beautiful native homes appeared.

Simple they were, with no windows or doors, mere shelters, but cool and cheap, with no division of rooms, and no furniture but the sleeping mats and a utensil or two. Natives were seen cooking their simple meal of fish and breadfruit, or only the latter. The fire was in the ground or under a grill of iron on stones. They would not go hungry, for mango-trees lined the road, and bananas, *feis*, and pineapples were to be had for the taking.

We drove through Aapahi and Faaripoo and saw a funeral. In the grounds of the dead man sat two large groups of people, the men and the women separate. They talked of his dying and his property, and his children, while those who liked to do so made him ready for the grave. A hundred yards away, in a school-yard, twoscore men, women, boys, and girls played football. The males were in *pareus*, naked except about the waist, and they kicked the heavy leather sphere with their bare feet.

Pare, Arue, and Mahina districts behind us, we were in Papenoo, a straggling village of a few hundred people along the road, the houses, all but the half-dozen stores of the Chinese, set back a hundred yards, and the domestic animals and carts in the front.

With a flourish we drove into the inclosure of the largest, newest, and most pretentious house, and were greeted by Teriieroo, the Tahitian chief, all native, but speaking French easily and musically. Count Polonsky shook hands with him, as did we all, but when a daughter appeared, neither Polonsky nor we paid her any attention. Yet she was Polonsky's "girl," as they say here, and he kept her in good style in a house near her father's, sending his yellow automobile for her when he wanted her at his villa near Papeete.

The chief's house had four bedrooms, each with an European bed, three-quarter size, and with a mattress two feet high, stuffed with *kapok*, the silky cotton which grows on trees all over Tahiti, These mattresses were beveled, and one must lie in their middle not to slip off. The coverlets were red and blue in stamped patterns.

It was dark when we touched the earth after two hours' driving, and leaving the coachman to care for the horses, we went with the chief, each of us carrying a siphon of seltzer or a bottle of champagne or claret. Our way was through an old and dark cocoanut grove, a bare trail, winding among the trees, and ending at the beach.

Polonsky had had built a pavilion for the revel. Fifty feet away was a kitchen in which the dinner was cooking, its odors adding appetite to that whetted by the several cocktails which Polonsky had mixed when the ice was brought in a wheelbarrow from the wagon.

We sat down in chairs on the turf a foot from the jetty boulders, and watched the inrush of the breakers. A light breeze outside had stirred the water, and the combers were white and high.

"Every sea is really three seas," said McHenry, pipe in hand, as he sipped his Martini. "We fellows who have to risk our cargoes and lives in landing in the Paumotus and Marquesas, study the accursed surf to find out its rules. There are rules, too, and the ninth wave is the one we come in on. That is the last of the third group, the biggest, and the one that will bring your boat near enough to shore to let all hands leap out and run her up away from the undertow."

Lights were placed in the new house. It was elegantly made, of small bamboos up and down, with a floor of matched boards, the roof of cocoanut-leaves, and hung with blossoms of many kinds. The table had been spread, and there was a glitter of silver and glass, with all the accoutrements of fashion. We sat down, eight, the chief making nine, and ate and drank until ten o'clock. The *pièce de résistance* was the sucking pig, with *taro* and *feis*, but roasted in an oven, and not in native style; and there was a delicious young turkey from New Zealand, a ham from Virginia, truffles, a salad of lettuce and tomatoes, and a plum pudding from London. The claret was 1900 and 1904, a vintage obtained by Polonsky in Paris. The champagne, also, was of a year, and frappéd. Tahitian coffee, with brown sugar from the chief's plantation, ended the banquet.

There was no conversation of any interest. The Parisian count was far removed in experience and culture from the others, and probably only the necessity of companionship in revelry and cards brought them together. Europe, and all the earth, was his playground, and doubtless he had lavished a fortune in pleasure in the capitals of the Continent. Llewellyn had an education in the universities of England and Germany, but since young manhood had been in his birthplace, and the others were the rough and ready stuff of business or seafaring.

The table for the gambling was moved to the sward by the shingle, and lamps hung upon bamboos planted at each end. It was balmy, and we sat in our shirts, the bosoms open for the breeze, the count with his gorgeous Japanese god shining upon his ivory breast, and the round glass in his eye. The tattooed skeleton upon his forearm was uncanny in the flickering light, the black shadows of the eyes seeming to open and close as the rays fell upon it.

Landers, though he had drunk with all, was appreciative of every nicety of the game, and won fifteen hundred francs. He alone was cool, watching the faces of the players at every crisis, quick to detect a weakness, to interpret rightly a gesture or counting of losses and gains, remorselessly hammering home his victories, and always suave and generous in action.

Llewellyn would withdraw his attention to listen to the *himene* of the musicians thirty feet away, which consisted mostly of familiar American airs, interpolated with bizarre staves and dissonances. One caught a beloved strain, and then it wandered away queerly as if the musician had forgotten the score and had done his best otherwise. I never heard in Tahiti one air of Europe or America played through as composed, without variation or omission, except the national anthem of France.

"They are happy, those boys," mused Llewellyn. "They get more out of life than we do. Why should we fool with these cards here when we might sing?"

Llewellyn was only a quarter Tahitian, but at times the island blood was the only pulse he felt. One noticed it especially during the *himenes*, when he seemed to wander far from the business in hand. That business being poker, and Landers all attention to the cards and the psychology of his antagonists, every time Llewellyn harked to the *himene* he lost a little, and when he became entangled in a jackpot of size, and drew too many cards on account of his abstraction, he was mulcted of fifty francs and failed of winning the two hundred he might have won.

"Unlucky at cards, lucky in something else," said he, self-consolingly.

"Ye want to drop that other thing when ye're playing cards," McHenry advised as he scooped in the pot. "The cards are all queens to you."

Chief Teriieroo a Teriieroterai sat ten feet removed from the players, but kept his eyes on the money. They played with notes, five francs being the smallest, and the others twenties and hundreds. The chief smiled whenever Count Polonsky drew in a heap of these, and when one fell on the floor, he scrambled under the table to prevent it being blown on the rocks. The Javanese served the drinks, and a crowd of natives watched curiously the shifting vantages from a respectful distance.

It was three o'clock when the scores were settled, and, the chief leading with a lantern, we tramped through the great cocoanut-grove to his residence. Landers and I each took a bed, I being warned to be forehanded by my experience in Moorea, where I slept on the floor. The chief retired, and

Polonsky went off with his arm about his inamorata's waist, she having apparently awaited his return. When Llewellyn and McHenry appeared half an hour later, having emptied a bottle reminiscent to McHenry of his father's liking for Auld Reekie, they were discomfited by the beds being all occupied, the other two having been early claimed by two men who ate and drank and immediately slept.

When I awoke, the sun was up half an hour, and Landers and I went for a bath in the brook. We found a pool famed in the legends of the natives. In the olden days the kings and chiefs would have made it tabu to themselves.

Landers had on a *pareu* only, his two hundred and fifty pounds of bone and muscle a refreshing sight, and his eyes as bright as if he had had the prescribed eight hours. They looked at him, sighingly, the young women of the village, even at this hour busied cooking breadfruit or fish and coffee; and Landers flirted with each one and in Tahitian called out words which made them laugh, and sometimes hide their heads coquettishly.

"I dated them all," he said to me when we were under the water. We threw off our garments at the edge of the pool and plunged in. The water was as soft as milk and as clear as crystal, cool and invigorating. I drank my fill of it as I swam.

Breakfast we had in the chief's house, the remains of the *amuraa rahi* of the night before. The chief drank coffee with us, and when we had gone to sit on the veranda, his eight children and wife took the board. I talked with Teriieroo a Teriieroterai for half an hour in French. He was thirty-eight years old, very engaging, and had several grandchildren.

"*Eh bien*," he said to my question, "I will tell you. I was married first at sixteen years of age and this is my third wife." He pointed over his shoulder to a tow-headed German for all I could see, and who certainly showed no sign of the native except in her dress and manners and avoirdupois.

"My first wife died," continued the *arii*, contemplatively. "I divorced the second, and the third is just now eating the first *déjeuner* in that room. I have eight children, and will have twenty, and I am the chief of the Papenoo district, but this is not the place of my *ancienne famille*. I was appointed here by the French Governor three years ago to administer the district, which needed a strong hand. I like it, and have bought land and built this house. I will stay my days here. There is the *farehau*, the administration building where I meet the people and we have conferences."

He pointed to a wooden cottage near by, with what looked like a dancing-pavilion attached. There the people come to squat upon the floor and relate their grievances. Most of the disputes before minor and major courts were over land and water rights.

It was half past seven o'clock when we inspanned for the trek to Papeete, a balmy, brilliant morning. The banks and cliffs were masses of ferns, the living imposed upon the dead, and hibiscus and gardenias and clumps of bamboo in a dissolving pageant mingled with plots of taro and yams, pineapples and bananas. The majestic bread trees and the spreading mangoes, the latter with their fruit verging from gold to russet, were surflnounted by the soaring cocoanuts, the monarchs of the tropics, whose banners fly from every atoll, and fall only before the most terrible might of the King of Storms.

A cocoanut-palm bears at eight years and when about twenty-five feet high. It rises seventy or eighty feet, and has a hundred curves. It is the wily creature of the winds, but outwits them in all but their worst moods. To the tropical man the cocoa-palm is life and luxury. He drinks the milk and eats the meat, or sells it dried for making soaps and emollients and other things; the oil he lights his house with and rubs upon his body to assuage pain; he builds his houses and wharves of it, and thatches his home with the husks, which also serve for fuel, fiber for lines and dresses and hats, leaves for canoe-sails and the shell of the nut for his goblet. Its roots he fashions into household utensils. The cocoa grows where other edibles perish. It dips its bole in the salt tide, and will not thrive removed from its beloved sea.

To me there is an inexpressible sentiment in the presence of these cocoa-palms. They are the symbol of the simplicity and singleness of the eternal summer of the tropics; the staff and gonfalons of the dominion of the sun. My heart leaps at their sight when long away. They are the dearest result of seed and earth. I drink their wine and esteem dwelling in their sight a rare communion with the best of nature.

They joked Count Polonsky about his girl, and he began to explain.

"I was here a year before I found one that suited me," he said as he rode beside the wagon. "I don't love her, nor she me, but I pay her well, and ask only physical fidelity for my physical safety. Her father is practical and influential, and will help me with my plans for development of the Papenoo valley, which I have bought."

Three tall and robust natives in *pareus* of red and yellow, and carrying long spears, went by, accompanied by a dozen dogs. We stopped them, and they said they were from the Papara district on their way to hunt pig in the Papenoo Mountains for Count Polonsky. The latter remembered he had ordered such a hunt, and explained through Llewellyn that he was their employer.

They faced him, and seldom was greater contrast. Magnificent semi-savages, clothed in only a rag, their powerful muscles responsive to every demand of their minds, and health glowing in their laughing countenances: Polonsky, slight, bent, baldish, arrayed in Paris fashions, a figure from the Bois de Boulogne, his glass screwed in his weak eye, the other myopic, teeth missing, and face pale. But at his command they hunted, for he had that which they craved, the money of civilization, to buy its toys and poisons. Polonsky had a reputation for generous dealing.

A bent native man repairing the road near Faaripoo had his face swathed in bandages. He greeted us with the courteous, "Ia ora na!" but did not lift his head.

"He is a leper," said Llewellyn. "I have seen him for years on this road. He may not be here many more days, because they are segregating the lepers. The Government has built a lazaretto for them up that road."

We saw a group of little houses a short distance removed from the road. They were fenced in and had an institutional look.

"There's hundreds of lepers in Tahiti," remarked McHenry.

"Mac, you're a damned liar," replied Llewellyn. He was an overlord in manner when with natives, but his quarter aboriginal blood caused the least aspersion on them by others to touch him on the raw.

"Well, there's a bloody lot o'them," broke in Lying Bill.

"Eighty only," stated Llewellyn, conclusively. "The Government has taken a census, and they're all to be brought here. Did you hear that Tissot left for Raiatea when he heard of the census? He's a leper and a white man. They seized young Briand yesterday."

I was astonished, because the latter had lived opposite the Tiare Hotel, and I had met him often at the barber's. I had been "next" to him at Marechal's shop a week before.

"He did not know he was a leper until they examined him," Llewellyn went on. "He does not know how he contracted the disease. I don't mind it. I am not afraid. You get used to it. I tell you, the only leper I ever knew that made me cry was a kid. I used to see on the porch of a house on the road to Papara from Papeete a big doll. A little leper girl owned it, and she was ashamed to be seen outside her home, so she put on the veranda the doll she loved best to greet her friends. She made out that the doll was really herself, and she loved to listen when those who might have been playmates talked to the doll and fondled it. She lived for and in the doll, and those who cherished the little girl saw that each Christmas the doll was exchanged secretly for a bigger one, keeping pace with the growth of the child. I have caressed it and sung to it, and guessed that the child was peeping and listening inside. She herself never touched it, for it would be like picking up one's own self. Each

Christmas she saw herself born again, for the old dolls were burned without her knowledge. And all the time her own little body was falling to pieces. Last Christmas she was carried to the door to see the new doll. I bought it for her, and I had in it a speaking-box, to say *'Bonjour!'* I sent to Paris for it. She's dead now, poor little devil, or they'd have shut her up in the lazaretto."

Bemis bought cocoanuts for shipment for food purposes. His firm sold them all over America to fruitdealers for eating raw by children, and shredded and prepared them for confectioners and grocers. He was the only buyer in Tahiti of fresh nuts, as all others purchased them as copra, split and dried, for the oil. Bemis had been here years ago, he said.

"I'm married now," he told me, "but in those days I was a damn fool about the Tahitian girls. I put in six months here before I was married."

He became thoughtful, and asked me to accompany him to the soiree of the Alliance Française, in the Palais cinema-hall. The Alliance was for encouraging the study and use of the French language. A few decades ago Admiral Serre, the governor, had forbidden the teaching of French to girls in the country districts as hurtful to their moral weal. It was feared that they would seek to air their learning in Papeete, and, as said Admiral Serre, be corrupted. A new regime reckoned a knowledge of French a requisite of patriotism.

At the Palais the scene was brilliant. Two large banana-trees were apparently growing at the sides of the stage, and the pillars of the roof were wreathed in palm-leaves. Scores of French flags draped the walls. Pupils of the government schools occupied many seats, and their families, friends, and officials the others. The galleries were filled with native children. Marao, the former queen, and her daughters, the Princesses Boots and Tekau, with a party of English acquaintances, were in front, and the general audience consisted of French and every caste of Tahitian, from half to a sixteenth. The men were in white evening suits, and the women and girls in décolleté gowns, white and colored.

It was eight o'clock when the governor entered on the arm of the president of the Alliance, Dr. Cassiou. He was in a white drill uniform, with deep cuffs of gold bullion, and a blazing row of orders on his breast. The *république* outdoes many monarchies in decorating with these baubles its heroes of politics. The governor, a wholesome-looking diplomat, was the image of the famous host of the Old Poodle Dog restaurant in San Francisco, who himself would have had a hundred ribbons in a just democracy.

The band of native musicians played "The Marseillaise," but nobody stood. With all their embellishments, the French would not incommode themselves at the whim of a baton-wielder, who in America had only to wave his stick in "The Star-Spangled Banner," and any one who did not humor his whim by getting on his feet was beaten by his neighbors, who would not suffer without him.

With the governor were the *inspecteurs colonials*, the bearded napkin-wearers of Lovaina's. They, too, had a line of gay ribbon from nipple to nipple. These three and the *boulevardier*, the gay secretary, sat upon the stage beside a stack of gilded red books. The band played "La Croix d'Honneur," and the good Dr. Cassiou read from a manuscript his annual address in a low voice becoming a ministrant at sick-beds. Another piece by the band, and the books were distributed to the pupils, who went tremulously upon the stage to receive them from the governor's hand. This was a lengthy process, but each child had a *claque*, which communicated enthusiasm to the others of the audience, and there was continuous clapping.

"Les Cadets de Russie" by the band preceded the allocution by the governor. He also spoke *sotto voce*, as if to himself, and as no one heard his words, the fans of native straw and Chinese turkey feathers were plied incessantly. The heat was oppressive. A sigh of relief came with the entr'acte, when all the grown folk flocked to the attached saloon. I joined the queen's group for a few moments, and drank champagne with her and her daughters, and I was called over to have a glass of Perrier Jouet with the governor's party. Most of the natives drank bottled lemonade from the *glacerie* at five sous a bottle. The queen wore a rose in her hair. She was very large, with almost a man's face, shrewd, heavy, determined, and yet lively, and without a shade of pretense. Her walk was singularly majestic, and was often commented upon.

The Princess Tekau was beautiful, quite like a Spanish senorita in color and feature, her ivory skin gleaming against a pale-blue bodice, and her blue-black hair piled high. We talked French or English, with many Tahitian words thrown in, according to the mood or need of the moment. Every one was laughing. After all, Tahiti was very simple, and even officialdom could not import aristocracy or stiffness into a climate where starch melted before one could impress a spectator.

The *inspecteurs* and others of the suite had smiles and quips for humbler girls than princesses. I saw one of the awesome whiskerandos from Paris, haughty and secretive toward the French, lighting the cigarette of a *blanchisseuse* at the Pool of Psyche, his arm about her, and his black bristles nearer than necessary to her ripe mouth. A merchant dining away from home slapped caressingly the hips of the girls who waited upon him, nor concealed his gestures. Hypocrisy had lost her shield in Tahiti, because, except among a few aged persons, and the pastors, she was not a virtue, as in America and England, but a hateful vice.

Back again in the Palais, cooled and made receptive to music by the joyous quarter of an hour in the buffet, we heard Mme. Gautier sing "Le Cid," by Massenet, and the Princess Tekau accompany her effectively on the piano. A solo *de piston*, a violin, a flute, all played by Tahitians, entertained us, and then came the fun. M. X—— was down for a monologue. Who could it be? He bounced on the stage in a Prince-Albert coat and a Derby hat, rollicking, truculent, plainly exhilarated. Why, it was M. Lontane in disguise, the second in command of the police, the hero of the battle of the limes, the coal, and the potatoes. He gave a side-splitting burlesque of the conflict. He acted the drunken stoker, the man who would write to "The Times" when M. Lontane placed his pistol at his stomach, and he made us see the fruit and coal flying. It was all good natured, and his dialogue (monologue) amusing. We saw how we Anglo-Saxons appeared to the French, and learned how the hoarse growl of the British sailor sounded.

The governor was delighted, the *inspecteurs* also. The officials took their cue, the entire audience laughed, and the galleries of children, not understanding at all, but convulsed at the antics of the head policeman, yelled *encore*. The British consul grinned, and the governor turned and winked at him. The *entente cordiale* was cemented again. The second in command, who provoked the sundering of the tie, had reunited it by his comicality. Ire dissolved in glee.

A play followed, in which several of the players were in the audience, and in which my barber, M. Bontet, shone, and moving-pictures followed. The babies were long asleep, and we yawning when we were dismissed at half past twelve.

Bemis, the cocoanut-buyer, sat through the *entr'acte*, not accompanying me to the buffet. He received a shock during the handing out of the premiums and was silent afterward. Bemis was a striking man, because the very regular features of his young face were set off by a mass of white hair. He was placid, without a disturbing intellect, and interested solely in the price and condition of fresh cocoanuts for shipment. I had seen him start when a little girl of distinctive expression was called to the stage to receive her book. She sat with her mother and putative father, and their other children. When I first saw her, I pulled his arm.

"Bemis," I said, "for heaven's sake, look at that girl!"

He looked, and his face tensed, growing ashen white. "She's the image of you, Bemis," I pursued.

"For God's sake, talk low!" he cautioned. "People are rubbering at me now. She is mine, I'm sure. I was here six months a dozen years ago and had an affair with her mother, who sits there. What can I do? I have my own at home in Oakland. I could not tell. I never knew about that girl until a week ago. She doesn't know me. I saw her on the Broom Road, so I came to-night to have a good look at her. I was afraid to come alone. It would do no good for me to tell her. She's taken care of. She's lovely, isn't she? I'd like to take her in my arms once."

We walked to the Annexe.

"I'll tell you," he resumed. "I can't blame myself. I was like any young fellow who comes down here,—I wasn't more than twenty-five,—but I feel like hell. That child's face is almost identical, except for color, with my baby of eight or nine at home. I'm afraid I'll see it at night when I go back."

On the trees, which carry all the public announcements, appeared a notice of a concert by the local band:

Fanfare de Papeete
Le public est informé la Fanfare donnera son
Concert sur la Place du Gouvernement Mardi Soir a 8 heures.
RETRAITE
aux Flambeaux!

All day it rained, but at seven a myriad of stars were in the sky. The Place du Gouvernement is a large lawn between the group of buildings devoted to administrative affairs, with seats for several score, but not for the hundreds who attended the band concert. The notice about the *flambeaux* drew even the few boys and youths who might not have come for the music.

In the center of the lawn was a kiosk, and on the four sides the rue de Rivoli, the garden of the Cercle Militaire, the grounds of the former palace of the Pomarés, now the executive offices, and the pavilion of the Revues.

I went early when the lights were being turned on. Only the sellers of wreaths had arrived, and they seated themselves along the square, their ferns and flowers on the ground beside them. Then came the venders of sweets, ice-cream, and peanuts, and soon the band and the throng.

An *allegro* broke upon the air, and stilled for a moment the chatter. Most of the people stood or strolled in twos or dozens. They bought wreaths and placed them on their bare heads, while the few who wore hats encircled them with the brilliant greens and blossoms. Bevies of handsome girls and women in their prettiest tunics, many wearing Chinese silk shawls of blue or pink, their hair tied with bright ribbons, sat on the benches or grouped about the confectionery-stands. Many carriages and automobiles were parked in the shadows, holding the more reserved citizens—the governor, the royal family, the bishop, the clergy, and dignified matrons of girth.

The bachelors and male coquets of the Tahitians and French, with a sprinkling of all the foreigners in Papeete, the officers and crews of the warship *Zélée* and sailing vessels, smoked and endeavored to segregate *vahines* who appealed to them. The dark *procureur général* from Martinique had an eye for beauty, and the private secretary of the governor was in his most gallant mood, a rakish cloth hat with a feather, a silver-headed stick, a suit of tight-fitting black, and a *tiare* Tahiti over his ear, marking him among the other Lotharios.

The band was led by a tall, impressive native who both beat and hummed the airs to guide the others. A tune ended, the bandsmen hurried to mix with the audience, to smoke and flirt. The shading acacia-trees lining the avenues permitted privacy for embraces, kisses, for making engagements, and for the singing of *chansons* and *himenes* of scandalous import. Better than the Latin, the Tahitian likes direct words and candor in song.

French naval officers and sailors passed and repassed, or sought the obscurity of the mangoes or the acacias. One heard the sibilance of kisses, the laughter, and the banter, the half-serious blows and scoldings of the *vahines* who repelled over-bold sailors. In an hour the sedate and the older took leave; the governor and the *procureur* turned into the Cercle Militaire for whist or écarté and a glass of wine, the carriages withdrew, and the band's airs and manner of playing took on a new freedom and abandon. A polka was begun, and couples danced upon the grass, the ladies in their *peignoirs*, their black hair floating, and their lips chanting, their wreaths and flowers nodding to their motions.

In retired nooks where the lamp-lights did not penetrate ardent ones threw themselves into the postures and agitations of the *upaupa*, the *hula*.

Boys now began to light the flambeaux for the *retraite*. These were large bundles of cocoanut-husks and candlenuts soaked in oil, and they gave a generous flare. Suddenly, we heard the mairie-bell tolling. The band-leader climbed upon the roof of the kiosk, descended, and gave a vigorous beat upon the air for "the Marseillaise," which ends all concerts.

It was quickly over, and seizing the flambeaux, all rushed from the Place du Gouvernement, lighting the way of the *retraite*, now more furious even than planned. The band struck up, "There'll be a Hot Time in the Old Town To-night," the drum and bugle made warlike notes, and down the rue de Rivoli we went madly toward the conflagration sighted by the leader. After the band and the flambeaux-bearers danced the jolly commoners, with here and there a more important pair of legs, an English clerk, a tourist, or an official, all excited by the music, the torches, and the running to the fire. The flambeaux reeled to and fro with the skipping and leaping of their carriers, the multitude sang loudly, and the music became broken as the leader lost control of his men. They came to the house of the hose-cart, and transformed themselves into firemen, laying down their instruments and harnessing themselves to the lines. Away we went again, now at top speed. Other carts with apparatus dashed into the Broom Road from side streets and caught up with us.

The pullers yelled warnings in Tahitian to those who might impede their way or be run over. The stir was tremendous, for fires were rare and greatly feared. The regulations of the possession and storage of combustibles were severe, even a wagon or handcart containing as little as one can of kerosene being compelled to fly a red flag.

After a mile we came to the fire, a Chinese restaurant beside a little creek and in a cocoanut-grove. The roof had fallen in and there were reports that a woman and two children had been killed. Two men with quart cans threw water from the stream on the edge of the blaze.

The little hose-carts, with a small ladder, arrived with éclat, native gendarmes clearing the road, and Frenchmen and natives shouting the danger of death by these formidable engines. They were of no purpose, the water-taps which were conspicuous in the main streets being absent here, and no water under pressure was available. They knew this, of course, but the hose was unreeled, and a dozen people tripped up by its snakelike movements, the while bandsmen and gendarmes roared out manoeuvers. By now a thousand were there. I counted roughly several hundred bicycles and two public automobiles, holding thirty persons each, came from the center of town, the enterprising owners canvassing the coffee-shops and saloons for passengers. These carryalls drew up by the stream within forty feet of the blaze, forcing the pedestrians and cyclists to retreat.

Lovaina appeared, puffing furiously. Vava was roused to a high pitch. He told me by signs how he had seen the fire and given the alarm to the *mairie*, or city hall, the bell of which tolled for an hour.

There was no wind, and the flames rose straight up, scorching the cocoanut-leaves, but unharming other houses within twenty-five feet. The crowd lingered until the last timber had fallen. After seeing that there was small danger to the adjoining buildings, and learning that the loss fell upon Chinese only, that no one had been hurt, and that a can of kerosene had exploded, interest in the conflagration dropped, and friends and acquaintances who had met chatted amiably on other subjects. The proximity of the fire and the marshy condition of the ground made it proper for the ladies with well-turned legs to raise their gowns high, displaying garterless stockings held up by the "native twist" above the calf. Accordions and mouth-organs enlivened the talk, and not until only charred boards remained did we leave.

Besides the occasional concerts of the band, boxing and moving-pictures made up the public night life of Papeete. Attached to the theaters were bars, as at the Palais, and these were the foci of those who hunted distraction, and the trysting-places of the amorous. One found in them or flitting about them all the Tahitian or part Tahitian girls in Papeete who were not kept from them by higher ambition or by a strict family rule. From Moorea, Raiatea, Bora-Bora, and other islands, and from the rural districts of Tahiti, drifted the fairest who pursued pleasure, and to these cafés went the male tourists, the gayer traders, the sailors, and the Tahitian men of city ways, the chauffeurs, clerks, and officials.

Boxing and cinemas were novelties in Tahiti, and though the bars were only adjuncts of the shows, they had become the scenes of a hectic life quite different from former days. The groves, the beach, and the homes were less frequented for merrymaking, the white having brought his own comparatively new customs of men and women drinking together in public houses. And there had crept in on a small scale an exploitation of beauty by those who profited by the receipts at the prize-fights, the cinemas, and the bars. The French or part castes who owned these attractions were copying the cruder methods of the Chinese.

Llewellyn, David, and McHenry were habitués of these resorts, and I not an infrequent visitor. We went together to a prize-fight, which had been well advertised. A small boy with a gong handed me a bill on the rue du Four, which read:

	Casino de Tahiti	
	Ce Soir Vendredi	
Pour le championnat des Etablissements français de l'Oceanie		
Grand Match de Boxe Entre MM.	Great Boxing Match Between MM.	Moto Raa rahi i rotopu ia
Opeta (Raratonga)	&	Teaea (Mataiea)
	10 Rounds	
Moni parahiraa 1re 2f. 50	2me 2f.	3me 1f. 50

The bill said further in French and Tahitian that this was to be the climax of all ring battles in the South Seas between natives, the Christchurch Kid and Cowan, the bridegroom, being *hors concours*.

Every seat was reserved by noon. All day the automobile stages ran into the country districts to bring natives, and from Moorea came boat-loads of spectators. On the streets native youths emulated the combatants, and at every corner boys were at fisticuffs. The Casino de Tahiti was on the rue de Rivoli, a large wooden shed painted in polychromatic tints, and with a gallery open to the air for the band, which played an hour before all events to summon patrons. Groups were in the street by eight o'clock, many having been unable to buy seats, and others there merely to hear the music and to laugh. Many were Chinese, queueless, smartly dressed in conventional white suits and American straw hats. The storekeepers had come in from the country. The men heatedly discussed the merits of the boxers. Opeta of Raratonga was mentioned as the champion of the world—this part of it.

Smoking was not allowed inside, so not until the last moment did the men file in. Hundreds of women were long in their places, some white, many part white, and others Tahitians. They were in their best gowns, flirting, eating fruit and nuts, laughing, and talking. Every girl of the Tiare Hotel was there, and all the guests. I was wedged in between Lovaina and Atupu, and the latter stroked my leg often, as one does a cat or dog, affectionately, but without much thought about it. Lovaina, too, rubbed my back from time to time.

A picture preceded the fight. It was of cow-boys, robbers, and the Wild West, with much shooting. A half-caste explained it, and his wit was considerable, tickling the ears as the scenes tickled the eyes. The natives applauded or execrated the films as the Parisians do at the opera. They encouraged the heroes and cursed the villains. Lovaina was interested, but said:

"Those robber in picshur make all boy bad. The governor he say that maybe he stop that Bill 'Art kind of picshur. Some Tahiti boy steal horse and throw rope on other boy for lassoo."

When the screen was removed, a roped enclosure, a square "ring," was disclosed. The announcer spoke in Tahitian of the signal achievements of the two fighters, of their determination to do their best then and there. The women cheered these declarations. Seated just below me was a red-headed French girl, with perhaps a slight infusion of Polynesian blood, who had a baby in a perambulator. Her strawberry plaits dangled temptingly as she cooed to the baby. She was for Opeta, the foreign competitor.

A white-haired Australian woman, with a strong accent, favored Teaea, and when the Raratonga youth was winning, shouted to Teaea:

"'It 'im 'arder, Ol' Peet! 'E's outa wind! Knock 'is shell hoff!"

The Casino de Tahiti had two galleries, and in the topmost, at a franc, five sous each, sat the little gods, as with us. Others were perched on doors, on projections of cornices, and in every nook.

The fighters were naked except for breech-clouts. They were barefooted. They wore their hair longish, and it appeared like rough, black caps, which now and again fell over their faces and was flung back by a toss of their heads. They were handsome men, framed symmetrically, lithe, and healthy-looking. Their bodies soon shone with the sweat. Their eyes, as soft as velvet to begin, grew fiery as they punished each other. In truth, this punishment was not severe from American prize-ring standards. The islander was unused to blows, and the gloves were of the biggest size, such as those worn by business men in gymnasiums.

Opeta had as seconds American beach-combers; and Teaea, natives. They had all the pugilistic appurtenances of towels, bottles, etcetera, and fanned and rubbed their men between rounds as if they were matched for a fortune.

Teaea had a green ribbon in his loin-cloth. He was taller and heavier than Opeta, but showed his inferiority quickly. They danced about and fiddled for an opening, sparred for wind, and did all the fancy footwork of the fifth-class fighter, but they seldom came together except in clinches. The referee, the Christchurch Kid, was the martyr, for he had to pull them apart every minute. The rounds were of two minutes' duration, and the rests one minute. After seven very tame rounds, the spectators became angered, and in the eighth Teaea went down, and took the count of ten on his hands and feet, warily watching his opponent. In the ninth, Opeta, excited by the demands of the gallery, slugged him in the head. Teaea sought the boards again, and the counting of ten by the referee began.

The Mataiea boxer was on his back, but his glazing eyes stared reproachfully at Opeta. The latter, now clearly the victor, glanced at the red-headed girl, who was dancing on the floor beside her perambulator and waving her congratulations. The house was on its feet yelling wildly to Teaea to rise. Those who had bet on him were calling him a knave and a coward, while Opeta's backers were imploring him to kill Teaea if he stood up. The Raratonga champion became excited, confused and when Teaea, at the call of eight, cautiously turned over and lifted his head, he struck him lightly.

The inhabitants of the country districts vociferated in one voice:

"*Uahani! Uahani!*"

"*Faufau! Faufau!*" cried the gods.

"Foul! Foul! 'E 'it' im, 'hand' e's hon 'is 'ands hand kneeses," exclaimed the Australian woman.

The audience took up the chorus in French, Tahitian, and English. Though Opeta had won them all by his ability and fairness and was plainly the better man, the sentiment was for the rules. The Christchurch Kid thought a moment, and conferred with the announcer, who talked with all the seconds. The spectators were insistent, and though loath to end the show, the Kid held up the gloved hand of the Mataiean.

The announcer declared him the "*champignon*" of Papeete, but naïvely declared that Opeta was still full of fight, and challenged the universe. The Raratonga man was dumfounded at the result of his forgetfulness, and gazed coldly and accusingly at the red plaits. The people, too, now regretted their enthusiasm for the right, which had shortened their program of rounds, and demanded that the battle go on. But the band had left, the lights were dimmed, and gradually the crowd departed.

The Australian waited to shake the hand of her knight, to whom she said:

"I bloomin' well knew you 'd do 'im hup! 'E's got nothin' hin 'is right. 'E's a runaw'y, 'e is."

David and I went into the buffet of the cinema after the fight to hear the arguments over it, and he to collect bets. He had chosen the winner by the toss of a coin. The French Governor of the Paumotus was there, gaily bantering half a dozen girls for whom he bought drinks. We joined him with Miri and Caroline and Maraa and others, the best-known sirens of Papeete. They were handsome, though savage-looking, and they had lost their soft voices. Alcohol and a thousand *upaupahuras* had made them shrill. They smoked endless cigarettes. Some wore shoes and stockings, and some were barefooted. Their dresses were red or blue, with insertions of lace and ribbons, and they were crowned with flowers in token of their mood of gaiety.

David insisted on a bowl of velvet, three quarts of champagne, and three of English porter mixed in a great urn. The champagne bubbled in the heavier porter, and the brew was a dark, brilliant color, soft and smooth. It was delicious, and seemed as safe as cocoanut milk. I drank my share of it in the cinema cafe, and after that was conscious only vaguely of going to the Cocoanut House garden, where Miri and Caroline and Maraa danced nude under the trees by the light of the full moon.

Then came blankness until I awoke several hours after midnight. I was sitting on the curbing of the Pool of Psyche, and some one was holding my hand.

I thought it must be Atupu or Lovaina, and groped for a moment before I could pull my senses together. I looked up, and saw a wreathed and bearded native, and then down and saw his attire, mixed man's and woman's, and knew he was one of the *mahus* who loafed about the queen's grounds. I drew away my hand as from a serpent's jaws, and clasped my head, which rocked in anguish. A horrid chuckle or dismal throaty sound caused me to see the Dummy standing in the gateway, looking contemptuously at me, and witheringly at my companion. I had a second's thought of myself as a son of Laocoön.

The *mahu* got up and hastened away, and Vava put his hand on my shoulder and lifted me as a child to the road. He pointed toward the Annexe, and as I went haltingly with him, he now and again uttered unearthly cackles and bawls as if enjoying a farce I could not see. He, like the mahu, was one of those mishaps of nature assigned to play an absurd and sorry part in the tragicomedy of life in which all must act the rôles assigned by the great author-manager until death puts us out of the cast. In that scene I myself was the buffoon of fate.

Chapter XVI

A journey to Mataiea—I abandon city life—Interesting sights on the route—The Grotto of Maraa—Papara and the Chief Tati—The plantation of Atimaono—My host, the Chevalier Tetuanui.

Life in the country made me laugh at myself for having so long stayed in the capital. The fever of Papeete had long since cooled in my veins. A city man myself, I might have known that all capitals are noxious. Great cities are the wens on the body of civilization. They are aggregations of sick people, who die out in the third generation. Greed builds them. Crowded populations increase property values and buy more manufactured luxuries. The country sends its best to perish in these huddlements. In America, where money interests boom cities and proudly boast their corruption in numbers, half the people are already in these webs in which the spider of commerce eats its victims, but ultimately may perish for lack of food. Brick and steel grow nothing.

I had made excursions from Papeete, but always carrying the poisons of the town with me. At last my playmates deserted me. Lying Bill and McHenry sailed on their schooner for the Paumotu and the Marquesas islands, Landers left for Auckland, and Count Polonsky for a flying visit to America. Llewellyn, though an interesting study, learned in native ways, and with comparisons of Europe and America, was too atrabilious, and, besides, had with his young partner, David, abandoned himself to the night life, the cinema bars, with their hilarious girls and men, the prize-fights, and the dancing on the beach in the starlight. Schlyter, the tailor, an occasional companion, was busied cutting and sewing a hundred uniforms for a warship's crew.

I bethought me of the letter Princess Noanoa Tiare had given me to the chief of Mataiea, and with a bag I departed for that village at daybreak, after *taofe tau* for four sous at Shin Bung Lung's *Fare Tamaaraa*. The diligence was open at the sides and roofed with an awning, and was drawn by two mules, with bells on their collars.

On the stage I paid twenty centimes a kilometre, or six and a half cents a mile. It carried the mail, passengers, and freight. In every district there was a mailbox on the fence of the *chefferie*, the chief's office, and on the trees alongside the road at regular intervals, and the driver took mails from people who hailed him. Arriving at a *chefferie*, the stage halted, the district *mutoi*, or native policeman-postman, appeared leisurely, opened the locked box on the diligence, looked at ease over the contents, took out what he liked, and put back the remainder, with the postings of the *chefferie*.

A glance at the map of Tahiti shows it shaped like a Samoan fan, or, roughly, like a lady's hand mirror. It is really two islands, joined by the mile-wide isthmus of Taravao. The larger island is Poroiunu or Tahiti-nui (big Tahiti), and the smaller Taiarapu, or Tahiti-iti (little Tahiti). Tahiti-nui is almost round; and Tahitiiti, oval. Both are volcanic, distinct in formation. They are united by a sedimentary piece of land long after they were raised from the ocean's bed.

Mataiea is twenty-seven miles from Papeete, and well on toward the isthmus.

Most of our passengers were Chinese, and I realized the Asiaticizing of Tahiti. They were store-keepers, small farmers, or laborers. The Broom Road lay most of the way along the beach, back of the fringe of cocoanut and pandanus-trees, and between the homes and plantations of Tahitians and foreigners. I saw all the fruits of the islands in matchless profusion, intermingled with magnificent ferns, the dazzling bougainvillea, the brilliant flamboyant-tree, and a thousand creepers and plants. Every few minutes the road rushed to the water's-edge, and the glowing main, with its flashing reef, and the shadowy outlines of Moorea, a score of miles away, appeared and fled. Past villages, churches, schools, and villas, the shops of the Chinese merchants, the sheds for drying copra, rows of vanilla-vines, beaches with canoes drawn up and nets drying on sticks, men and women lolling on mats upon the eternal green carpet of the earth, girls waving hands to us, superb men, naked save for *pareus*, with torsos, brown, satiny, and muscled like Greek gladiators, women bathing in streams, their forms glistening, their breasts bare; and constant to the scene, dominating it, the lofty, snakelike cocoanuts and their brothers of less height and greater girth.

At Fa'a a postwoman appeared. Before opening the mail-box she tarried to light a cigarette and to chat with the driver about the new picture at the cinema in Papeete. She commented laughingly on the writers and addressees of the letters, and flirted with a passenger. The former *himene*-house, which had been the dance-hall of Kelly, the leader of the fish-strike, was vacant, but I heard in imagination the strains of his pagan accordion, and the *himene* which will never be forgotten by the Tahitians, "Hallelujah! I'm a bum!" Kelly had gone over the water to the jails of the United States, where life is hard for minstrels who sing such droll songs.

In Punaauia, the next district to Fa'a, was a schoolhouse and on it a sign: $2 \times 2 = 4$.

M. Souvy, a government printer of Tahiti, had given the site out of his humble savings. By the sign, in his blunt way, he struck at education which does not teach the simple necessity of progress—common sense.

"Cela saute aux yeux," he had said.

He was long dead, but his symbol provoked a question from every newcomer, and kept alive his name and philosophy. I never saw it but I thought of an article I had once written that led to the overturning of the educational system of a country. How all guide-posts point to oneself! Near the schoolhouse, a dozen yards from the salt water, was a native house with a straw roof, a mere old shell, untenanted.

M. Edmond Brault, the government employee and musical composer, a passenger on the diligence, had with him his violin, intending to spend the day in company with it in a grove. He remarked the tumbledown condition of the house, and said:

"I have sat under that *toil de chaume*, that straw roof, and talked with and played for a painter who was living there quite apart from the world. He was Monsieur Paul Gauguin, and he had a very *distingué* establishment. The walls of his *atelier* were covered with his canvases, and in front of the house he had a number of sculptures in wood. That was about 1895, I think. I can see the *maitre* now. He wore a *pareu* of red muslin and an undershirt of netting. He said that he adored this corner of the world and would never leave it. He had returned from Paris more than ever convinced that he was not fitted to live in Europe. Yet, *mon ami,* he ran away from here, and went to the savage Marquesas Islands, where he died in a few years. He loved the third *étude* of Chopin, and the *andante* of Beethoven's twenty-third sonata. You know music says things we would be almost afraid to put in words, if we could. If Flaubert might have written 'Madame Bovary' or 'Salambô' in musical notes, he would not have been prosecuted by the censor. We musicians have that advantage."

"In America," I replied, "we have never yet censored musical compositions, and many works are played freely because the censors and the reform societies' detectives cannot understand them. But if our inquisitors take up music, they may yet reach them. For instance, the prelude of 'Tristan and Isolde,' and Strauss' 'Salome.'"

"No," returned the Frenchman, quickly; "music would make them liberals."

A little farther on, in the valley of Punaruu, the amiable violinist and pianist showed me the ruins of defense works thrown up by the French to withstand the attacks of the great chieftain, Oropaa of Punaauia, who with his warriors had here disputed foot by foot the advance of the invaders. These Tahitians were without artillery, mostly without guns of any sort, but they utilized the old strategy of the intertribal wars, and rolled huge rocks down upon the French troops in narrow defiles.

We saw from our seats through the shadows of the gorge of Punaruu two of the horns of Maiao, the Diadem. In the far recesses of those mountains were almost inaccessible caves in which the natives laid their dead, and where one found still their moldering skeletons. M. Brault touched my shoulder.

"Rumor has it that the body of Pomaré the Fifth is there," he said; "that it was taken secretly from the tomb you have seen near Papeete, and carried here at night. There are photographs of those old skeletons taken in that grotto of the *tupapaus*, as the natives call the dead and their ghosts. The natives will not discuss that place."

It was from Punaauia that Teriieroo a Teriierooterai had gone to Papenoo to be chief. This was the seat of his *ancienne famille*. Here he had been a deacon of the church, as he was in Papenoo, because it meant social rank, and was possible insurance against an unknown future. The church edifice was the gathering-place, as once had been the *marae*, the native temple. This was Sunday, and I passed a church every few miles, the Roman Catholic and the Protestant vying. They had matched each other in number since the French admiral had exiled the British missionary-consul, and compelled the queen to erect a papal church for every bethel.

Along the road and in the churchyards the preachers and deacons were in black cloth, sweating as they walked, their faces beatudinized as in America.

Many carried large Bibles, and frowned on the merry, singing crew who went by on foot, in carriages and automobiles. Everywhere, in all countries, the long, black coat and white or black cravat are the uniforms of evangelism. In Tahiti I saw ministers of the gospel, white and brown, appareled like circuit-riders in Missouri; hot, dusty, and their collars wilted, but their souls serene and sure in their mission. They associated God and black, as night and darkness.

The sound of sermons echoed from chapels as we progressed, the voices raised in the same tone one heard in a Methodist camp-meeting in Kansas, and the singing, when in French, having much the same effect, a whining, droning fashion; without spirituality or art.

But why look for a moment at these unfortunates or listen to their dull chants when marvels of nature unfolded at every step! There was never such luxuriant vegetation, never such a riot of color and richness of growth as on every side. The wealth of the bougainvillea's masses of lustrous magenta was matched by the dazzling flamboyant, trees forty feet high, and their foliage a hundred in circumference, a sheen of crimson. Clumps of bamboo as big as a city lot and towering to the sky, with the yellow *allamanda* framing the bungalows, and a tangle of bananas, *lantana*, *tafeie*, cocoas, and a hundred other fruits, flowers and creepers, made the whole journey through a paradise.

Around many cocoanut-palms were bands of tin or zinc ten or twenty feet from the earth. These were to foil the rats or crabs which climb the trees and steal (can a creature steal from nature?) the nuts. Every available piece of thin metal was used for this. The sheets were often flattened kerosene- and gasoline-cans and were drawn taut and smooth. These are impasses for the wily climbers.

"*Ils ne passeront pas*," said the French; "*Aita haere!*" the Tahitians.

The road was good, but narrow, in few places room for two to pass except by turning out, skirting the beach at the water's-edge, crossing causeways over inlets, and in admirable curves clinging to the hillsides, which bathed in the sea. Moving over a small levee we came to the pointe de Maraa, where was the Grotto of Maraa, a gigantic recess worn in the solid wall of rock, a dark mysterious interior, which gave me a momentary surge of my childhood dread and love of caves and secret entrances to pirates' lairs. The diligence halted at the request of M. Brault, and he and I jumped out and ran to the grotto. In it was a lake with black waters, and down the face of the cliff, which rose hundreds of feet straight, dripped a million drops of the waters of the hills, so that the ground about was in puddles. The inside walls and arched ceiling were covered with a solid texture of verdant foliage, wet and fragrant. We found a little canoe fastened to a stone, and adventured on the quiet surface of the pond until at about eighty yards of penetration we came to a blind curtain of stone.

"This grot," said M. Brault, "was for centuries the retreat of those conquered in war, sacred to gods, and a sanctuary never violated, like those cities of refuge among the Hebrews and Greeks. Now it is a picnic rendezvous, very dear to Papeete whites and to tourists. *C'est la vie.*"

Tahitian women passengers were adorning their heads with wreaths of maiden-hair and rare ferns from the cavern. Great lianas hung down the walls, and these they climbed to reach the exquisite draperies of the chamber. The farther we left behind the capital, the more smiling were the faces, the less conventional the actions and gestures of the people.

Papara was at hand, the richest and most famous of all the districts of Tahiti. The village was a few Chinese stores, a Catholic and a Protestant church, a graveyard, and a scattered collection of homes. I bade *au revoir* to my delightful companion, Edmond Brault, having determined to walk the remaining kilometers, and to send on my inconsiderable bag of clothing.

Lovaina had given me a note to the chief of Papara, Tati, whose father was Salmon, an English Jew, and whose sister was Marao, the relict of the late king, and known as the queen. His father was the first white to marry formally a Tahitian noblewoman. Pomaré IV had generously granted permission for the high chiefess of Papara to ally herself with the shrewd descendant of the House of David, and their progeny had included the queen, Tati, and others celebrated in Tahitian life.

Tati welcomed me with the heartiness of the English gentleman and the courtesy of the Tahitian chief. He was a man of large parts himself, limited in his hospitality only by his means, he, like all natives, having thrown away most of his patrimony in his youth. He was the best-known Tahitian next to Prince Hinoe, but much abler than he. He knew the Tahitian history and legends, the interwoven tribal relations, the descents and alliances of the families, better than any one else. Such knowledge was highly esteemed by the natives, for whom chiefly rank still bore significance. The Tatis had been chiefs of Papara for generations, and had entertained Captain Cook.

He lived in a bungalow near the beach, handsome, spreading, and with a mixed European and indigenous arrangement and furnishing that was very attractive. I met his sons and daughters, and had luncheon with them. Tati, of course, spoke English fluently, yet with the soft intonation of the Tahitian. Some of the dishes and knives and forks had belonged to Robert Louis Stevenson, who, said Tati, had given them to him when he was departing from Tahiti. Tati's sister, a widow, was of the party, and together we went to the Protestant churchyard to her husband's tomb. It was imposing and costly, and the inscription read:

In Memory of Dorence Atwater, beloved husband of arii inoore Moetia Salmon. Born at Terryville, Conn., Feb. 3, 1845. Died at San Francisco, Cal., November 28, 1910. As a last tribute to his name there was erected in his native state a monument with this inscription:

This memorial is dedicated to our fellow townsman, Dorence Atwater, for his patriotism in preserving to this nation the names of 13,000 soldiers who died while prisoners at Andersonville, Ga.

He builded better than he knew; some day, perchance, in surprise he may wake to learn:

He builded a monument more enduring than brass.

Tupuataroa.

The name given Atwater when he married Moetia Salmon was Tupuataroa, which means a wise man. Mrs. Atwater was rich and melancholy. She mourned her dead. Atwater had come to Tahiti as American consul, and had piled franc on franc in trade and speculation, with great dignity and success. He had been the leading American of his generation in the South Seas, and had left no children.

Tati said that when the church was dedicated—it was a box-like structure of wood and coral, whitewashed and red-roofed—three thousand Tahitians had feasted in a thatched house erected for the *arearea*. The *himene*-chorus was made up of singers from every district in Tahiti and Moorea. Tati had presided.

"We ate for three days," he related to me. "More than two hundred and fifty swine, fifteen hundred chickens, and enough fish to equal the miraculous draft on the shores of Galilee. We Polynesians were always that way, Gargantuan eaters at times, but able to go fifty miles at top speed on a cocoanut in war."

Tati would have me stay indefinitely his guest, but I had written to Mataiea of my intended arrival there, and though there were insistent cries that I return soon, I said farewell.

Tati himself walked with me to the bridge over the Taharuu River, one of the hundred and fifty streams I crossed in a circuit of Tahiti.

"My ancestor, the old chief Tati," he told me, "cut down the sacred trees of our clan *marae* near by, the *aitos, tamanus*, and *miros*. He had become a Christian, as was fashionable, and at the instigation of the English missionaries destroyed many beautiful and ancient trees, statues, carvings, and buildings. The Tahitians who mourned his iconoclasm had a chant which said that the Taharuu River ran blood when their gods were dishonored."

From the stream the vast domain of the plantation of Atimaono stretched to Mataiea. It had been planted in the sixties, when British demands for cotton, and the blockade and laying waste of the South in the American Civil War caused a thousand such speculations all over the world.

It was for this plantation, the most celebrated in Tahiti, that Chinese were imported, and a thousand had their shanties where now is brush. Those were the times that the Marquesas had their cotton boom, and lapsed, too. Upon a hill of this plantation the English manager, a former cavalry officer, had built himself a palatial mansion, and lived like a feudal lord, the most powerful resident of Tahiti. Travelers from all the world were his guests. Fair ladies danced the night away upon his broad verandas and drank the choicest wines of France. Scandal wove a dozen strange stories of intrigues, of a high official who sold his wife to him, of Arioian orgies, and all the associations of semi-regal rule and accountability to none. Cotton prices declined, the bubble burst in bankruptcy, the miserable death of the aristocrat, and the fury of cheated English investors.

The plantation was now owned by a storekeeper of Tahiti, prosy and disliked, who had fattened by ability to outwit the natives; but the glory had departed, and the place languished, ruins and jungle, the prey of guava and lantana. The neighborhood was known as Ati-Maono, "The Clan of Maon."

The lines between village and country were not rigid, and often the hamlet straggled along the road for much of the district. Every kilometer there was a stone marking the distance from Papeete. One knew the villages more by the Chinese stores than by any other feature.

"You will find the Papara country full of oranges," Fragrance of the Jasmine had said.

The fruit was as sweet and delicious as any I had eaten, and the trees larger than their parents of Sydney, Australia. I strolled along the road eating, speaking all who passed or were in sight within their gardens, and came to Mataiea, where I was to live months and to learn the Tahitian mind and language.

Ariioehau Amerocarao, commonly known as Tetuanui Tavana, or Monsieur le Chef de Mataiea, Tetuanui, and his wife, Haamoura, were the salt of the earth. The chief was a large man, molded on a great frame, and very corpulent, as are most Polynesians of more than thirty years. He was about sixty, strong and sweet by nature, brave and simple. His *vahine* was very stout, half blind from cataracts, but ever busied about her household and her guests. As chief and roadmaster of his district, Tetuanui received a small compensation, but not enough for the wants of his dependents, so a few paying white guests were sent to him by Lovaina. The house was set back from the Broom Road in a clearing of a wood of cocoanuts, breadfruits, *badamiers*, and *vi*-apples. The father of Haamoura had given the land to his daughter, and they had built on it a residence of two high stories, with wide verandas.

The chief and his wife had no children, but had adopted twenty-five. They had brought most of these to manhood and womanhood, and many were married. Perhaps their care, *dots* for the daughters, and estates for the sons, had made the parents poor. One was the blood son of Prince Hinoe, and was now a youth, and worked about the plantation of the chief. His christened name was Ariipaea Temanutuanuu Teariitinorua Tetuanui a Oropaa Pomare. He was a prince and very handsome and gentle, but he gathered the leaves from the volunteer lawn for the horses. There was an atmosphere of affection and happiness about the home I have not sensed more keenly anywhere else.

The Duke of Abruzzi's photograph and one of the Italian war-ship *Liguria*, were on a wall in the drawing-room, with others of notable people whom the chief had entertained. He himself wore the cross of the Legion of Honor, which had been presented to him in Paris when he visited there many years before.

The house was raised ten feet from the earth, and the ground below was neatly covered with black pebbles from the shore. Shaded by the veranda-floors, which formed the ceilings of their open rooms, the family sat on mats, and made hats, sewed, sang, and chatted. They laughed all day. A dozen children played on the sward where horses, ducks, geese, chickens, and turkeys fed and led their life. When rice or corn was thrown to them, the mina-birds flocked to share it. These impudent thieves pounced on the best grains, and though the chickens fought them, they appeared to be afraid only of the ducks. These hated the *minas*, and pursued them angrily. But the *minas* can fly, and, when threatened, lazily lifted themselves a few feet out of reach of the bills, and returned when danger was over.

The chief's plantation extended from the sea to the mountain, altogether about ten acres, which in Tahiti is a good-sized single holding. Cocoanuts, breadfruit, limes, oranges, *badamiers*, mangoes, and other trees made a dense forest, and a hectare or more was planted with vanilla-vines that grew on the false coffee of which hedges were usually made. A hundred yards away a stream meandered toward the sea, and there women of the household sat and washed clothes.

They had no *taro* planted, though there was much about. *Taro*, the staple food of Hawaiians, either simply boiled or fermented as *poi*, was not a decided favorite in Tahiti. The natives thought it tasteless compared with the *fei*, so rich in color and flavor. The *taro* is a lily (*Arum*), and its great bulbs are the edible part, though the tops of small *taro*-plants are delicious, surpassing spinach, and we had them often on our table.

Our customary meals at eleven and at six were of raw oysters, shrimp, crabs, craw-fish, or lobsters; fish of many kinds, chicken, breadfruit, *vi*-apples stewed, bananas, oranges, *feis*, cocoanuts, and sucking pigs. The family ate sitting or squatting on the ground, but I had a table and silver, glass and linen. It is the way of the Tahitian. The big house, well furnished, was not inhabited by the chief's family. It was their monument of success. They slept in one of several houses they had near by, and their elegant dishes were unused except for white guests.

On the beach at the river's mouth the heron sat or stalked solemnly, and the tern flew about the reef. The white *iitae* lived about the cocoanut-trees.

From the broad veranda in front was a view of the sea, and all day and night the breakers beat upon the reef a mile away, now as soft as the summer wind in the lime-trees of Seville, and again loud as winter in the giant pine forests of Michigan. The fleecy surf gleamed and shimmered in the sun as it rolled over the coral dam, and when the sea was strong, there was another sound, the lapping of the waves on the sand a hundred yards from me. A little wharf had been built there by the Government, and a schooner arrived and departed every few days, with people and produce.

I ate alone mostly, at a table on the veranda in front of my chamber, waited on by Tatini, a very lovely and shy maiden of fourteen years. To her I talked Tahitian, as with all the family, in an effort to perfect myself in that tongue.

I was happy that I had pulled up anchor in Papeete, and as contrast is, after all, comparative, I felt like a New-Yorker who finds himself in Arcadia, though I had thought Papeete, on first sight, the garden of Allah. In Mataiea I realized the wonder of the Polynesian people, and found my months with the whites of the city a fit background for study of and ardent delight in the brown islanders I was to know so well.

Chapter XVII

My life in the house of Tetuanui—Whence came the Polynesians—A migration from Malaysia—Their legends of the past—Condition of Tahiti when the white came—The great navigator, Cook—Tetuanui tells of old Tahiti.

Happiness in civilization consists in seeing life other than it really is. At Mataiea the simple truth of existence was joy. In the house of the chief, Tetuanui, I knew a peace of mind and body as novel to me as my surroundings. For the first time since unconcerned childhood I felt my heart leap in my bosom when the dawn awoke me, and was glad merely that I could see the sun rise or the rain fall. All of us have had that feeling on certain mornings; but was it not interwoven with the affairs of the day—a picnic, a rendezvous, our wedding, a first morning of the vacation encampment? In Mataiea it was spontaneous, the harking back to a beneficent mood of nature; the very sense of being stirring the blood in delight, and girding up the loins instantly to pleasurable movement.

I slept without clothing, and in a bound was at the door, with my *pareu* about me. Already the family had begun the leisurely tasks of the day. The fowls were on the sward under the breadfruit and papaya-trees, and the mina-birds were swooping down on the grass near them to profit by their uncovering of food. Those discriminating birds are like the Japanese, seldom pioneering in wild places, but settling on developed lands to gain by the slower industry of other peoples. "Birds that live on cows," the Tahitians call the minas, because where there are enough ruminants each bird selects one, and spends the day upon its back, eating the insects that infest its skin.

The sun at six barely lit the beach and revealed the lagoon, into which a stream from the mountains poured within Tetuanui's confines. I threw off my garment and plunged into a pool under a clump of pandanus-trees. It was cool enough at that hour to give the surface nerves the slight shock I craved, but warmed as I lay in the limpid water and watched the light sweeping past the reef in the swift way of the tropics.

I danced upon the beach and pursued the land crabs to their burrows. I hoped to see one wrench off a leg to prove what I had been told—that if one in its movement to the salt water through the tall grass beyond the sand, touched any filth, it clawed off the polluted leg, and that a crab had been seen thus to deprive itself of all its eight limbs, and after a bath to hobble back to its hole with the aid of its claws, to remain until it had grown a complement of supports. I wondered why it did not content itself with washing instead of mutilation. To the biblical expounder it was an apt illustration of "cutting off an offending member," as recommended in the Book.

At the house the family were preparing their first meal, and I shared it with them—oranges, bananas, coffee, and rolls. The last, with the New Zealand tinned butter, came from the Chinese store. We sat on mats, and we drank from small bowls. The coffee was sweetened with their own brown sugar, and the juice of nearly ripe cocoanuts, grated and pressed, made a delicious substitute for cream. Over the breakfast we talked, Tetuanui and Haamoura answering my questions and taking me along the path of my inquiry into far fields of former customs and ancient lore. They were, as their forefathers, gifted in oral tradition, with retentive memories for their own past and for the facts and legends of the racial history. We who have for thousands of years put in writing our records cannot grasp the fullness of the system by which the old Polynesian chiefs and priests, totally without letters, or even ideographs, except in Easter Island, kept the archives of the tribe and nation by frequent repetition of memorized annals. So we got Homer's Odyssey, and the Song of Solomon.

What Tahiti was like before the white? That was to me a subject of intense interest, now that I was fully aware of the situation after a hundred and fifty years of exploitation, seventy-five years of French domination, and thirty years of colonialism. The nature of the people was little changed. The Tahitian was still naïf, hospitable, gentle, indolent except as to needs, valuing friendship above all things, accepting the evangelism of many warring Christian sects as a tumult among jealous gods and priests, and counting sex manifestations free expressions of affection, and of an appetite not more sacred nor more shameful than hunger or thirst.

A human bronze
Photo from Dr. Theo. P. Cleveland

Early morning at Papenoo

These were the qualities and rules of conduct ascribed to the Tahitians by the first discoverers, especially by those who were not narrowed in judgment by inexperience and religious fanaticism, as were the British and French missionaries of early days, peasants and apprentices who had forsaken the fields and workshops for the higher sphere of devoteeism and freedom from manual labor. These clerics, though often self-sacrificing and yearning for martyrdom, attributed all differences from their standards or preachments to inherent wickedness or diabolism.

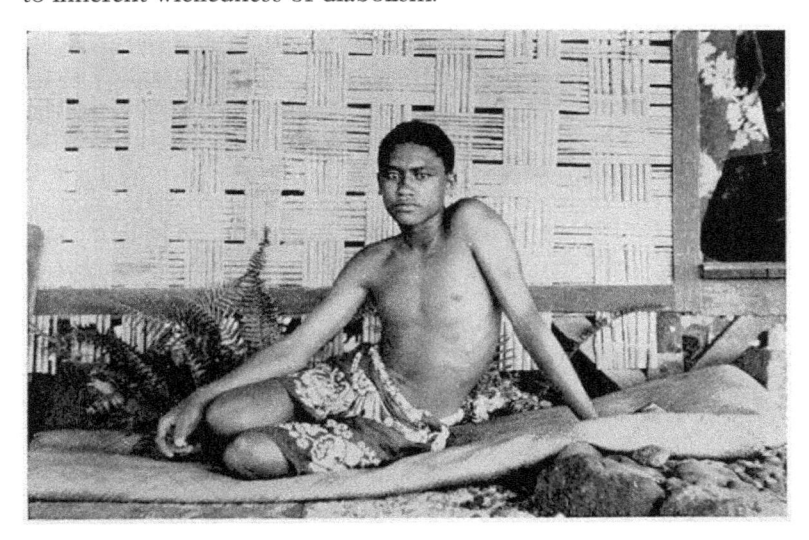

A friend in my house at Tautira

One of the ablest of them had regretted sorrowfully his having to inform the Tahitians that all their ancestors were in hell. Some clerics had made wearing bonnets the test of decency, and all had taught that God hated any open ardor of attraction for the opposite sex. Yet it was almost entirely to them that the far-away student had to turn to learn any of the details of native life undefiled. The mariners had stayed too brief a time to enter into these, and could not speak Tahitian.

I knew that Tahitian life, political and economic, social and religious, had been utterly changed, but I longed for an understanding of what had been; a panorama of it before my eyes. I set out to obtain this by constant interrogations of every one I thought might have even a scrap of enlightenment for me.

On rainy days, when Chief Tetuanui did not oversee the making or repair of roads in his district, and always when we were both at leisure, I sat with him, and the elders of the neighborhood, and queried them, or repeated for correction and comment my notes upon their antiquities—notes founded on reading and my observation.

Whence had come these Polynesians or Maoris who peopled the ocean islands from Hawaii to New Zealand, and from Easter Island to the eastern Fijis? A race set apart by its isolation for thousands of years from all the rest of the world, distinguished in all its habitats— Hawaii, Samoa, the Marquesas, Tonga, the Paumotus, and the Society archipelago, and New

Zealand—by beauty of form, tint and uniformity of color, height, and soft expression—an expression they vainly sought to make terrible by tattooing?

The legends and chants of the race unfolded much of the mystery; its language's relation to others, more. These Tahitians and all their kind were ancient Aryans who in the dim past were in India, and afterward in the Indian archipelago. They were in Sumatra, in Java, in the Philippines long before the Malays. Certainly their blood brothers, changed by millenniums of a different environment, remain in Malaysia, known there as the aborigines (Orang-Benoa), by the majority races. D'Urville said the Harfouras of Celebes were identical physically with the Polynesians. At some unfixed date the first of the Polynesians pushed out in their insecure craft for this sea, driven away by the Malay-Hindu invasion or by interracial feuds.

The pioneer, according to the legend, was Hawaii-uli-kai-oo, Hawaii and the Dotted Sea, a great fisherman and navigator. He sailed toward the Pleiades from his unknown home in the far West, and arrived at eastern islands. So pleased was he with them, that he returned to his western birthplace for his family, and brought them to Polynesia.

Other Polynesians left the Asiatic archipelago about the end of the first century, and went to many islands. Finally they reached the Samoan, Tongan, Marquesan, Paumotuan, and Society groups, and Easter Island and New Zealand. In pushing eastward they skirted Papua, but were unable to stay, because the Papuans, whom the Polynesians had long ago driven out of the Asiatic archipelago, were stronger than the emigrants. They next tried Fiji, and tarried there longest, leaving those powerful imprints on the Papuans in appearance and language that make Fiji the anomaly of Melanesia. But the Fiji-Papuans at last drove them out, and they left with blood in their eyes. When the whites found the Marquesans in the sixteenth century, they were building at Vaitahu great war-canoes to "attack the black people who used bows and arrows." No living Marquesan had ever seen them nor could they have attained Fiji in any strength, yet the historical hate persisted.

The Marquesans of the north said their race came from Hawaii, and those of the south from Vavao. Seventeen places they had stopped at in their great migration eastward, they said.

Pu te metani me Vevau
A anu te tai o Hawa-ii!
Pu atu te metani me Hawa-ii
A anu te ao e Vevau!

Blow winds from Vavao

And cool the sea of Hawaii!
Blow back, winds from Hawaii,
And cool the air of Vavao!

That was the Marquesan legendary chant, the primal command of their God after creation. Vevau and Hawaii were placed in their former abode toward India (Hawaii being undoubtedly Java; and Vevau being Vavao, in Malagasy); but they had brought the names with them, and when they reached the present American territory, of which Honolulu is the capital, they called it Hawaii, as they had an island of the Samoan group, Sawaii. It was in the fifth century they peopled the now American Hawaii, and they remained unknown there until the eleventh, when Marquesans, Tahitians, and Samoans began to pour in on them, and continued to do so for a few generations. Then the present Hawaiians were isolated and forgotten for twenty-one generations until rediscovery by Captain Cook in 1778.

They gave the old names to Polynesia that they knew in Asia, as all over the world emigrants carry their home names, not only Hawaii, or Savaii, for Java, but Moorea, a Javan place, to the island near Tahiti; Bora-Bora from Sumatra to a Society island; Puna of Borneo to places in Tahiti, Kauai, and Hawaii; Ouahou of Borneo to Oahu, on which Honolulu is; and Molokai, from the Moluccas, to another island of Hawaii. One might cite hundreds of examples, all going to prove their far-away origin, as Florida, San Francisco, and Los Angeles, New England, New York, and Albany, indicate theirs.

That there were any inhabitants in the South Sea islands occupied by the Polynesians is improbable but a race of mighty stone-carvers had swept through that ocean, perhaps many thousands of years before, and had left in the Ladrones and in Easter Islands monuments and statues now existing which are a profound mystery to the ethnologist, the archaeologist, and the engineer. If the Polynesians came upon any of the stone builders, they had killed or absorbed them.

The interpretation of the curious ideographs carved on wood in Easter Island by some of the Polynesians there half a century ago would denote there had been intercourse with the people who had made them, and who were not the Polynesians.

Once in Samoa, and finally at home there, after their Fiji disaster, they had gone adventuring, or the canoe drift of unfortunates caught by wind and tide had brought populations to all the other Polynesian islands, and principally to Tahiti. This island in the center of Polynesia, and especially favored by nature, had been a source of growth and distribution of the race, the Paumotus, New Zealand, and probably the Marquesas, and Hawaii having been stocked from it, the language developing furthest in it, and customs, refinements, and leisure reaching their highest pitch in the marvelous culture, savage though it was, which astounded the Europeans. Yet all these people remained curious as to what might be beyond the distance, and a hundred years ago were fitting out exploring expeditions to search for Utupu, a Utopia from which the god Tao introduced the cocoanut-tree. They looked to the westward for the mystic land of their forefathers, as from Ireland to India the happy isles of the west was a myth. The mariners of Erin had long seen the Tir-n'an-Oge just beyond the horizon.

The Tahitians had a legend of the god Maui, that "he brought the earth up from the depths of the ocean, and when mankind suffered from the prolonged absence of the sun and lived mournfully in obscurity, with no ripening fruits, Maui stopped the sun and regulated its course, so as to make day and night equal, as they are in Tahiti."

Does not this hark back to a clime where the inequality of day and night was greater than in the tropics?

Lieutenant Bovis of the French navy, who seventy years ago, after ten years of study in Tahiti, wrote his conclusions, said that after him it would be useless to hunt in the memories of the living for anything of the past, for the old men were dead or dying, and those now in middle age did not even speak or understand the old language in which the records were told. He had, he said, arrived in Tahiti when the real Tahiti, the Tahiti of the true native, the Tahiti unspoiled by European civilization, was only a memory, but by years of labor he had taken from the lips of the venerable their recollections of conditions in their childhood and early manhood, and what their fathers had told them, and by comparison he had been able to write intelligently of former times.

If Bovis found the real Tahiti no longer existent seventy years ago, what must I look for when two generations or three had died since, and swift steamships coursed where only the clipper had sailed? Yet Tahiti was the least spoiled of islands on liner routes, because France being so far from it, and the French such poor business men, they had not exploited the natives except in the way of taxes. The bureaucracy lived on the imposts, but they had not reformed the people by laws and punishments, and made them see the wisdom of acquiescence in a scheme of regular work, as had the British missionary government in Tahiti and the American missionary government in Hawaii, in the name of an avenging and critical Lord. No people believed in the dignity of labor more than the Tahitians, because they refused to do any more than was requisite for health, cleanliness, comfort, and pleasure, and saw no more dignity or greater indignity in helping me on with my boots or bringing me my dinner or massaging my body than in listening to a sermon or catching fish.

They thought absurd and artificial the ideas foisted by politicians, merchants, and lawyers that it was dignified to sit in an office, to sell goods, or to draw up agreements, or undignified to disembowel a pig, make a net, or dig an oven. They saw governors and bankers spend all day chasing a boar or angling for a fish which they did not eat when they possessed it. They thought them queer, and that their own regimen of work and play was more sensible.

"What land is this?" asked Cook, and understanding him, the Tahitians answered, "*Otaiti oia*" or, "This is Tahiti."

Cook put it down as Otaheite, pronounced by him Otahytee. It was Cook's carpenter who was building a house for a chief, a friend of Cook's, and lost all his tools during the visit of the high priest of the god Hiro and his acolytes. Hiro was the first king in their myths, and, until Christianity came, the god of business. When Cook sailed away, the tools were taken to the *marae*, or temple of Hiro, where the priest said he would cause the prized tools to reproduce their kind, like fruit. He planted them in a field near by and watched for results. The lack of any result except rust was an able argument for the Christian missionaries, when they came, to destroy his cult by laughing at the foolishness of his ideas and the weakness of his god.

The discoverers reported that the Tahitians and all other Polynesians were thieves and liars, for the reason that they often seized pieces of iron, tools, and firearms that they saw on the ships or ashore in the houses occupied by the first whites, and then lied about their actions. The whites killed scores for these crimes, one of the initial murders of Cook's crew being the shooting of Chief Kapupuu as he departed in his canoe from their ship with some bits of metal he had taken. Malo, the native historian, who heard the account from eye-witnesses, explained the incident as follows, first mentioning the sighting of Cook's vessels and the wonder of the natives:

One said to another, "What is that great thing with branches?" Others said, "It is a forest that has slid down into the sea," and the gabble and noise was great. Then the chiefs ordered some natives to go in a canoe and observe and examine well that wonderful thing. They went, and when they came to the ship, they saw the iron that was attached to the outside of the ship, and they were greatly rejoiced at the quantity of iron.

Because the iron was known before that time from wood with iron [in or on it] that had formerly drifted ashore, but it was in small quantity, and here was plenty. And they entered on board, and they saw the people with white foreheads, bright eyes, loose garments, corner-shaped heads, and unintelligible speech.

Then they thought that the people [on board] were all women, because their heads were so like the women's heads of that period. They observed the quantity of iron on board of the ship, and they were filled with wonder and delight.

Then they returned and told the chiefs what they had seen, and how great a quantity of iron. On hearing this, one of the warriors of the chief said, "I will go and take forcible possession of this booty, for to plunder is my business and means of living."

The chiefs consented. Then this warrior went on board of the ship and took away some of the iron on board, and he was shot at and was killed. His name was Kapupuu. The canoes [around the ship] fled away and reported that Kapupuu had been killed by a ball from a squirt-gun.

And that same night guns were fired and rockets were thrown up. They [the natives] thought it was a god, and they called his name Lonomakua, and they thought there would be war.

Then the chiefess named Kamakahelei, mother of Kaumualii, said, "Let us not fight against our god; let us please him that he may be favorable to us." Then Kamakahelei gave her own daughter as a woman to Lono. Lelemahoalani was her name; she was older sister of Kaumualii. And Lono [Captain Cook] slept with that woman, and the Kauai women prostituted themselves to the foreigners for iron.

Cook was one of the best of the navigators of the South Seas, a devout churchman, and a believer in the decalogue of Moses. He thought stealing or lying odious before the Lord and men. But the Polynesians did not so think. Most of their possessions were in common, and telling the truth was unimportant. If one asked them about anything they had no interest in, they might tell the truth or might not. If they had interests, these were served by their replies. This is as in diplomacy to-day, when the interests of one's country allows prevarication, and even in Christian ethics both patriotism and self-preservation, as well as hospitality, permit flat falsehood. Our own spies are honest heroes, and the man who would not deceive a man who sought to kill him or burn his house would be considered a fool and not worth saving.

"There is plenty more in the kitchen," we say to guests out of hospitality and pride, though the kitchen is as bare as Mother Hubbard's cupboard. She could not lie to the dog.

Now, to the native who saw all around him on the ship huge masses of the material most precious to him in the world, it was as if an American in

Yucatan saw in a native hut heaps of gold and diamonds not valued by the savage. Suppose the savage left the American alone with the treasure!

But the Tahitians did not murder for blood lust, had no assassination, and virtually no theft. Our own Anglo-Saxon law laid down the maxim, "Caveat emptor!" "Let the buyer beware!" which meant that the truth notwithstanding, the buyer must not let the seller of anything cheat him by failure to state the exact facts or faults, and expect the law to remedy his stupidity.

Chief Tetuanui's word was his bond because he had learned that square-dealing brought him peace of mind, but other natives had found out that to cheat the white man first was the only possible way of keeping even with him. The maxim of the king of Apamama, quoted by Ivan Stroganoff, was pertinent. Hospitality was as sacred to the Tahitians as to the old Irish. It was shameful not to give a guest anything he desired.

"Es su casa, señor!" said the Spaniard, and did not mean it; but the Tahitians literally did mean that the visitor was welcome to all his valuables, and did not reserve his family, as did the don.

The chevalier of the Legion of Honor upon whose mat I sat was emphatic as to the respect of the old Tahitians for their chiefs.

"It was the whole code," said he, "and when the French broke it down they destroyed us. There is Teriieroo a Teriierooterai, whose family were chiefs of Punaauia for generations, shifted to Papenoo. Each governor or admiral made these transfers here, as in the Marquesas and all the islands, with the primary object of lessening native cohesion, of Frenchifying us. They ruined our highest aspirations and our manners."

I had seen something of the same sweeping away of a code and the resultant evils and degradation in Japan. When Bushido imposed itself on all above the herd, they had a sense of honor not surpassed by the people of any nation; but commerce, the destruction of the castes of *samurai*, *heimin*, and *eta*, the plunging of a military people into business and competition with Western cunning, and the lacquer of Christianity which had done little more than Occidentalize to a considerable degree a few thousands, without giving them the practice of the golden rule, or an appreciation of the Sermon on the Mount, had robbed the Japanese of an ancient code of morality and honor, and replaced it with nothing worth while—an insatiable ambition to equal Occidental peoples and to conquer Oriental ones, and a thousand factories which killed women and children.

"We were divided into three distinct castes," said Tetuanui. "The Arii, or princes; Raatira, or small chiefs and simple landed proprietors; and the Manahune, or proletariat. Alliances between Arii and Raatira made an intermediate class—Eietoai. There was also a caste of priests subject to the chief, their power all derived from him, but yet tending to become hereditary by the priests instructing their sons in the ceremonies and by taking care of the temple."

"That's the way the Aaron family got control of the Jewish priesthood," I interpolated. "They gave the people what they wanted, first a golden calf god, and then an ark, and they had charge of both."

The chief frowned. He was a confirmed Bible reader, and the Old Testament was so much like the Tahitian legends that he believed every word of it.

"The Arii," he said, "were sacred and had miraculous strength and powers. The food they touched was for others poison. There was a head in each Arii family to whom the others were subject; he was often an infant, and almost always a young man, for the eldest son of the chief was chief and the father only regent. This custom continued until comparatively recently in most families besides those of the Arii. The Arii were the descendants of the last conquerors of these islands. But their advent must have been ancient, for their power was uncontested, and their rights were so many, their duties so few, and the devotion of the people to them was so great, that only centuries could have established them so firmly. Probably they came after the Raatira. The Raatira were separated by too great a barrier to have assisted in the conquest. No Raatira could become an Arii; no Arii a Raatira. The latter were closer to the commoners, and paid the same respect to the Arii as did the Manahune.

"If an Arii woman wedded a Raatira man, the marriage was said to be with a *taata ino, ino* meaning literally bad, and *taata* man. This term applied to all not Arii, and indicated the contempt of the Arii for all below them. The Arii had many words solely for their own use, and *tapu*, or prohibited, to all others; they had a hundred privileges. The Raatira were probably the power broken by the Arii. The Raatira had conquered the Manahune, and were themselves bested by the Arii, the newest come."

The chief sighed. He was like an old Irish storyteller recounting the departed glories of Erin.

I read to him in French Bovis' opinions that the Raatira, defeated, retained part of their lands, served the new masters, and kept in subjection the people they had themselves beaten. They attached themselves to the Arii of their district, fought for them in their quarrels or wars, and were consulted in assemblies, and allowed to speak to the crowd. I recalled that this was a privilege dearly prized by all Polynesians, the lack of reading and writing having, as in Greece, developed oratory and orators to a remarkable excellence. I was in Hawaii when the offices of the first legislature under the

American flag were campaigned for, after years of repression by the sugar planters' oligarchy, and I had heard the natives speak a score of times, and always with delight and wonder. They valued free speech.

"The Arii were shrewd," said Chief Tetuanui, "and early invented a plan for keeping the Raatira in subjection. If two Raatira disputed possession of land, the one who believed himself defrauded could yield to the king or a member of the royal family the land, to which he usually had no right at all. The Arii thus got possession of more and more land from time to time, and the Raatira were loath to contend among themselves.

"The Manahune owned nothing by law, but they lived on the lands of Arii and Raatira, and were seldom evicted. They had the fruits of their labor with a tithe or so for their masters; they left to their children their accumulations, tentative, but actual, and their service was pleasant; more in the nature of gifts than rent. The Manahune could not rise above his caste except by the rare nomination of the king, but they could become *Teuteu Arii*, or servants of an Arii, and might thus acquire immense importance.

"Like the eunuchs at courts or the mistresses of the noble and rich," I remarked.

The chief shrugged his shoulders.

"The Manahune might become a priest or even join the society of the Arioi," he rejoined. "The government was simple. The will of the prince was supreme, but by custom things ran smoothly, and the prince, or Arii, had seldom to urge his power. There were, of course, instances of extortion, of bursts of anger, of feuds, of jealousies; but most of the time the Raatira saw that the Arii were well served, and were their intermediaries with the commoners. The regular obligations of the inferior classes were to meet at certain times to hand to the chiefs presents, food, clothing or useful instruments, and they sought to exceed one another in generosity. They met to build houses, to repair them, or to construct the rock foundations of houses, according to the importance of the chief, or Arii. They built the canoes, made the nets, and did the fishing. The sea was divided into properties, as was the land. The Arii had the reefs where the fish most abounded.

"War was declared with religious ceremonies. Sacrifices were the basis of these ceremonies, and a human victim the most efficacious. The augurs examined the entrails, the auspices, much as did the pagans of old. Certain priests had certain duties. The *Tahua Oripo*, night runners, reported the movements of the enemy. They were professional war spies, and they acquired a marvelous ability. Sometimes they were able to lead their party so as to surprise the enemy and slaughter them, but usually there were preliminaries to war which warned the other side. A herald was sent in the costume of a great warrior. He was of high birth or famous for his fighting. He delivered himself of his mission ceremoniously, and was never attacked. Every locality had its war-chants, its songs of defiance. Today only a few fragments survive. Wars were waged mostly on account of the ambitions of princes, as to-day in Europe and Asia. But the effort of Christianity to oust paganism in Tahiti brought about many sanguinary conflicts, and plainly God was with the missionaries, who caused the battles. In 1815 the Battle of *Feipi* gave Tahiti to Pomaré the Great, and to the Protestant ministers, who were his backers. Over three hundred were killed. A woman, the queen of the island of Huahine, commanded in the absence of Pomaré.

"Sometimes after a battle the vanquished sent heralds to signify their yielding and to know the wish of the victor; they disbanded their troops, left their arms on the field, and the war was over. Usually the defeated warriors were allowed to return home without more ado after their confession of failure, but when the rage was great, the victors, with furious cries, gave the signal of carnage, and slew all they met. If the prince beaten escaped the first consequences of the rout, he was safe and lost only a portion of his territory, and in some wars only his prestige. He remained respected, and his privileges were about the same as before. The Arii were all of the same tribe, all related, and though they ruled different districts and valleys, and fought one another, they would not degrade one of their own family and rank. Thus power remained in the same families, princes, chiefs, and priests, and only the Raatira and the Manahune, the bourgeoisie and the commoners, really suffered.

"We copied you in Europe," I interposed. "There the kings, kaisers, and czars took care not to lower the dignity of monarchy, and are virtually all related. None of them ever deposed another of long enthroning, and none of them has been killed in a battle in centuries."

"*Aue!*" exclaimed the chief. "Ioba said, 'Wisdom is no longer with the old.' "

"Job talked like a revolutionist," I said. "That would be treason among the diplomats and lawyers of Europe and America. How did women get along in your father's day?"

Tetuanui got up to stretch his huge body. He had been squatting on his haunches for an hour.

"Let Haamoura, my wife, say as to them," he returned laughingly. "She knows all the old ways. I must see if the nets are to be stretched to-day."

Mme. Tetuanui and I had a lengthy confabulation. No Tahitian was better informed than she upon the former status of her sex in Tahiti, and from her I gained a lively summary.

Woman was inferior among the old Tahitians. Man had here as everywhere so ordained, and religion had fixed her position by taboos, as among the Hebrews. She was often merely a servant, yet she maintained a unique sex freedom. Her body was her own, and not her husband's as in the English common law. She prepared the man's food and never sat at meals with him. If she ate at the same time, which was seldom, she sat at a distance, but near enough to hear his commands. It is so to-day when Tahitian men gather for feasting without foreigners, as in the Philippines, Japan, and China, and in many European countries. The *Hausfrau* of the small merchant, laborer, or farmer is a drudge. In Japan the woman remains subject to the hourly whims and wants of her husband, and to his frequent infidelity, though she is true to him.

The Tahiti wife had the care of the canoe, the paddles, and all the fishing and hunting things, and she accompanied her husband often in these pursuits. The husband had to make the fire, prepare the oven, kill the pig or dog or fowl, and do the outside chores; but she had a lesser position than he at all public observances. She could not become a priest or enter the temple, but must remain always at a distance from the *marae*. Yet she could be a queen or a chiefess, and as such was as powerful as a man, making war in person, and often leading her troops valiantly. The Tahitian women were nearly as strong as the men and mentally their full equal. They wound their husbands around their fingers or treated them cruelly in many instances, astonishing the whites by their independence. Only religion, the taboos, held them in any restraint.

If a queen bore a child by an unknown father, the child was as royal as if the descendant of a long line of kings; but if the father was notoriously a commoner, the child remained a prince, though not so high of rank as if his father had been an Arii. If a king had children by a woman beneath his rank, they had no rights from their father, but held a mixed position proportioned to the power of the father. He established their rank by his personal prestige, as the kings of Europe forced their bastards on the courts. Sixty years ago Tamatoa, King of Raiatea of the Society Islands, himself the highest born of all the chiefs of the archipelago, was forced to adopt a child of King Pomaré of Tahiti to succeed him because his own children were by a woman of the people.

The woman thus had an advantage over the man in being able to transmit her rank to her children, a survival of the matriarchate custom once ruling the world. Polygamy was rarely indulged, though not forbidden. A chief here and there might have two or three wives. Women were allowed only one husband, but often avowed lovers were tolerated, if not feared, by the husband. Mr. Banks, president of the Royal Astronomical Society of England, was horrified after he had made love to Queen Oberea of Papara in the absence of her husband to find her attendant was a *cavalière servente*. His Anglican morals were shocked. He had thought himself the only male sinner by her complacence.

Before Christianity was forced on them, the Tahitians married in the same rank, and with considerable right to choice. The tie might be dissolved by the same authority binding it, the chief or head of the clan. Inequality of rank, or near consanguinity, were the only obstacles to marriage. Rank might be overcome, but never the other. It was as in China, where Confucius himself laid down the law: "A man in taking a wife does not choose one of the same surname as himself." And in one of the Chinese commentaries the following reason is given for this law: "When husband and wife are of the same surname, their children do not do well and multiply." The prohibited degrees were more distant than among us. It was a horror of incest that had led to the general custom all over Polynesia of exchanging children for adoption. Only this explanation could reconcile it with the almost superstitious love the Polynesian father and mother have for children. Their feeling surpasses the parental affection prevailing in the remainder of the world, yet adoption is a stronger bond than blood. No child was raised by its own genitors. The Tetuanuis had brought up twenty-five, all freely given them at birth or after weaning. The taboo was strict.

Illegitimate children were as welcome as others. The husband might have been so jealous as to meditate killing his wife; but when her child was born, although he knew it to be a bastard, he gave it the same love and care as his own. There were exceptions, but one might cite on the opposite side innumerable cases where, despite the most open adultery, the husband has taken his wife's offspring for his own. It was well that this was so, for adultery was so habitual that were bastards not made welcome, there would have been much suffering by children, innocent themselves. Here, as in civilization, men love their bastards often more than their legitimate sons and daughters.

This prohibition against keeping one's own must have arisen when there were very few inhabitants in Tahiti, for it is the outcome of a natural guarding against sexual relationship in tribes or communities where all are thrown together intimately, and stringent opposition to such practices needed to prevent promiscuity. One must look, as in the case of taboos, deeper than the surface for the beginning of this custom of trading babies, for that is what it often amounted to—friends exchanging offspring as they might canoes.

It is said that the powerful sentiment among historical nations opposing marriage between brother and sister and other close kindred originated in the desire to make such connections odious, to preserve virtue and decency among those in hourly intimacy. Monarchs and nations long refused to bend to it. The Ptolemies and Pharaohs married incestuously; Cleopatra, her brother. The Ptolemies married their daughters, as did Artaxerxes, who wedded Atossa. The Ballinese married twins of different sex. Abraham married his half-sister by the same father. Moses's father married his aunt. Jacob took to wife two sisters, his own cousins. In Great Russia until this century a father married his son to a young woman, and then claimed her as his concubine. When a son grew up, he followed his father's example, though his wife was old and with many children. The Tamils of southeast India, the Malaialais of the Kollimallais hills, have the same custom. Inbreeding maintains a fineness of breed, but at the cost of its vigor. That inbreeding is harmful is fairly certain. Examples to the contrary are numerous in human and animal life. More than nine hundred residents of Norfolk Island are descendants of the mutineers of the British ship Bounty. They were begat by eight of the mutineers, and intermarried for a century. They show no deterioration from this cause.

Hardly any crime is more loathed than incest, but the abomination grew slowly as man progressed. Such ties have been abhorrent for long in most countries. A belief that incestuous children were weak mentally or physically came much later in the ages. The Polynesians must have remarked that inbreeding accentuated the faults in a strain, making for an accumulation of them. This would be a very far advance in human observation; but the Polynesian, by experience, or knowledge brought from his old Asiatic home, must have held such a theory, and sought in the system of adoption, and in not bringing up consanguineous children together, to ward off such misfortune. This at least is a plausible reason for such an unnatural practice among a people so unquestionably child-lovers.

The Marquesans had no totemism to save them. There were no exogamous taboos. The tribe or clan was the chief unit, not the family. The phratry tie was stronger than that of the father and mother. In the totem scheme of other islands and continental groups all the women of his mother's totem were taboo to a man, though their relationship might be remote. Yet as husband and wife had different totems, and children took their mothers' totems, a man might in rare instances, even with this barrier, wed his own daughter. This has happened in Buka and in North Bougainville.

The plan of adoption in Polynesia is matched to a degree by the fosterage common in Ireland in early days. There children were sent to be reared in the families of fellow-clansmen of wealth. At a year they left their own thresholds, and their fosterage ended only at marriage. Every fostered person was under obligation to provide for the old age of his foster-parents, and the affection arising from this relationship was usually greater and regarded more sacred than that of blood relationship. This is true to-day of the Tahitians.

"But children nowadays are often brought up by their own parents," said Mme. Tetuanui, rising to prepare the *déjeuner*, and I for a swim in the lagoon, "and if adopted, they go from one home to the other as they will. Parents are not as willing as before to let go their children; for whereas my grandmother had fifteen, I have none, and few of us have many. We are made sterile by your civilization. Tetuanui and I were happy and able to persuade the mothers of twenty-five to give their infants to us because we were childless and were chiefs and well-to-do. Our race is passing so fast through the miseries the white has brought us that little ones are as precious as life itself."

Chapter XVIII

The reef and the lagoon—Wonders of marine life—Fishing with spears and nets—Sponges and hermit crabs—Fish of many colors—Ancient canoes of Tahiti—A visit to Vaihiria and legends told there.

About a mile from the beach was the reef, on which the breakers beat clamorously or almost inaudibly, depending on the wind and the faraway surge of the seas. The Passe of Rautirare afforded entrance for small vessels. It was an opening in the wall about the island caused by the Vairahaha, the stream which emptied into the lagoon at our door, and the fresh waters of which had ages ago prevented the coral zoöphytes from building a structure there, as at Papeete and all other passages. Fresh water did not agree with these miraculous architects whose material was their own skeletons.

I went out toward the reef many mornings in a little canoe that Tiura, the eldest son of the chief, loaned me. I carried from the house a paddle and three harpoons of different sizes. The canoe had an outrigger and was very small, so that it moved fast through the usually still lagoon, propelled by the broad-bladed paddle. In the bottom of it might be an inch of water, for occasionally I shipped a tiny wave, but wetness was no bother in this delicious climate; a *pareu* was easily removed if vexatious and a cocoanut-shell was an ample bale.

Low tide was at sunrise, and warmed with my fruit and coffee, and the happy *ia ora na,* Maru! of the family, I paddled to the reef with never-failing expectation of new wonders. The marine life of the Tahiti reef is richer than anywhere in these seas, as the soil of the island is more bountiful.

At that state of the tide the surf barely broke upon the reef, and, almost uncovered, its treasures were exposed for a little while as if especially for me. The reef itself was a marvel of contrivance by the blind animals which had died to raise it. If I had been brought to it hooded, and known nothing of such phenomena, I would have sworn it was an old concrete levee. The top was about fifty feet wide, as level as a floor, pitted with innumerable holes, the hiding-places of millions of living forms which fed on one another, and were continually replenished by the rolling billows. The wall of the reef opposed to the sea was a rough slope from the summit to the bottom, buttressed against the attacks of storms, and defended by *chevaux-de-frise* such as the Americans sank in the Hudson River in 1777. I ventured cautiously over the edge. A student of ancient tactics would have found there all the old defenses in coral—caltrops, and abatis, molded in dark-gray coral, battered and shot-marked. It was a dream of a sunken city wall of old

Syracuse, and conjured up a vision of the hoary Archimedes upon it before the inundation, directing the destruction, by his burning-glass, of the enemy's ships. The side of the reef toward the land was as sheer as an engineer could make it with a plumb-line. The coral animals had as accurate a measure of the vertical as of defense against the ocean.

Over this levee rolled or slid a dozen kinds of shellfish spying out refuges against the breakers and their brother enemies in the troughs and holes of the coral floor. With my small spears I pried out dozens of them, *Mao*, starfish, clams, oysters, furbelowed clams, sea-urchins, and sponges. The *mao* is the turbo, the queer gastropod sold in the market in Papeete. He lives in a beautiful spiral shell, and has attached to him a round piece of polished shell, blue, green, brown, or yellow, which he puts aside when he wishes to feed on the morsels passing his door, and pulls shut when he wants privacy. He fits himself tightly into a hollow in the reef and dozes away the hours behind his shield, but ready to open it instantly at the perception of his favorite food. The *mao* was wedged in the recess so cleverly that it was difficult to extract him by my hand alone. His portal I kept after eating him raw or cooked, to have set in silver as an exquisite souvenir of my visit. These jewels studded the drinking cups from which the Vikings drank "Skoal to the Northland!"

The starfish were magnificent, of many colors, and one with fifteen arms covered with sharp, gray spines, and underneath pale yellow, fleshy feelers with suckers like a sea-anemone. These were as pliant as rubber in the water, but, when long out, as hard as stone. The sea-urchins were of many kinds, some with large spikes, as firm as rock, and others almost as brittle as glass, their needles, half a dozen inches long and sharp, dangerous to step on even with my rubber-soled, canvas shoes. All hues were these urchins, blood-red and heavenly blue, almost black, and as white as snow, the last with a double-star etched upon his shell. Others were round like blow-fish, with their spickles at every angle, menacing in look.

The clams and oysters were small, except the furbelowed clam, whose shell is fluted, and who grows to an immense size in the atolls of the Paumotus. I always ate my fill of these delicacies raw as I walked along the reef, smashing the shells to get at the inmates.

When the tide was approaching high or when it began to ebb I had immortal experiences upon the reef. I went with Tiura or with the chief and a party, and found the waves dashing and foaming upon the natural mole, sweeping over it with the noise of thunder, crashing upon the sloping front, and riding their white steeds over the solid flagging to the lower lagoon. In this smother of water we stood knee-deep, receiving its buffets upon our waists and the spray upon our faces, and watched for the fish that were carried upon its crests. With spears couched, we waited the flying chance to arrest them upon the points, a hazardous game, for often they were powerful creatures, and were hurled against us with threatening impact.

But inspiring as was this sport at sunset or by moonlight, it was even more exciting when we trod the reef with torches of dried reeds or leaves or candlenuts threaded upon the spines of cocoanut-leaves, and lanced the fish that were drawn by the lure of the lights, or which we saw by their glare passing over the reef. The gleam of the torches, the blackness all about, the masterful figures of the Tahitians, the cries of warning, the laughter, the shouts of triumph, and the melancholy *himenes*, the softness and warmth of the water, the uncanny feel of living things about one's feet and body, the imaginative shudder of fear at shark or octopus or other terrible brute of the sea, the singing journey home in the canoes, and the joyous landing and counting of the catch—all these were things never to be forgotten, pictures to be unveiled in drabber scenes or on white nights of sleeplessness.

The sponges were oddities hard to recognize as the tender toilet article. Some were soft and some were full of grit. The grit was their skeletons, for every sponge has a skeleton except three or four very low specimens, and some without personal skeletons import them by attraction and make up a frame from foreign bodies. I examined and admired them, reasoning that I myself, in the debut of living creatures, was close in appearance to one; but my basic interest in them was to sit on them.

Many times I went only to where the coral began, half-way to the reef. This was away from the path of the Vairahaha River, and where the coral souls had manifestly indulged a thousand fancies in contour and color. After the million years of their labor in throwing up the bastion of the reef, with all its architectural niceties, they had found in the repose behind it opportunities for the indulgence of their artistry. They were the sculptors, painters, and gardeners of the lagoon.

I brought with me a lunette, the diver's aid, a four-sided wooden frame fifteen inches each way, with a bottom of glass and no top. I stuck my head in the box and looked through the glass, which I thrust below the surface, thus evading the opaqueness or distortion caused by the ripples. One did not need this invention ordinarily, for the water was as clear as air when undisturbed, and the garden of the sea gods was a brilliant and moving spectacle below my drifting canoe. One must be a child again to see all of it; the magic shapes, the haunting tints, the fairy forms. The gardener who had directed the growth of the aquarium believed in kelpies, undines, and mermaids, and had made for them the superbest playground conceivable even by sprites.

There were trees, bushes, and plants of yellow and white coral, of scarlet corallins, dahlias and roses, cabbages and cauliflowers simulated perfectly, lilies and heaps of precious stones. On flat tables were starfish lazying at full width, strewn shells, and hermit-crabs entering and leaving their captured homes. Mauve and primrose, pink and blue, green and brown, the coral plants nodded in the glittering light that filtered through the translucent brine. They were alive, all these things, as were the sponges, with stomachs and reactions, and impulses to perpetuate their species and to be beautiful. They had no relation to me except as I had to nature, but they were my beginnings, my simple ancestors who had stayed simple and unminded, and I was to count those hours happy when I communed with them.

Taken from their element they died, but left their mold, to harden in the air they could not breathe, and to amaze the less fortunate people who could not see them in their own estate. The seaweeds grew among them, green or brown, more primordial than the corals, with less of organic life, vegetables and not animals, but eager, too, for expression in their motions, their increase in size, and their continuance through posterity. All these were the display of the kindness of the same spirit who rode the thunder, who permitted a million babes to starve, who stirred in men the madness to slay a myriad of their brothers, and who fixed the countless stars in the firmament to guide them in the darkness.

The hermit-crabs drew my minute attention, and I anchored my canoe and with the lunette watched them by the hour. They were as provident and as handy—with claws—as the bee that stores honey. The hermit inhabits the vacant shells of other mollusks, entering one soon after birth, sometimes finding them untenanted, and sometimes killing the rightful occupant, and changing his house as he grows. I had been surprised to see small and large shells moving fast over the reef, and on the beach at the water's-edge; shells as big as my thumbnail and nearly as big as my head. I seized one, and behold! the inmate was walking on ten legs with the shell on his back, like a man carrying a dog-house. I attempted to pull him out of his lodging, and he was so firmly fastened to the interior by hooks on his belly that he held on until he was torn asunder. His abdomen is soft and pulpy and without protecting plates, as have other crabs, and he survived only by his childhood custom of stealing a univalve abode, though he murdered the honest tenant. In one I saw the large pincher of the crab so drawn back as to form a door to the shell as perfect as the original. When he felt growing pains the hermit-crab unhooked himself from his ceiling and migrated in search of a more commodious dwelling.

Interesting as were these habits of the cenobite crustacean, his keeping a policeman or two on guard on his roof, and moving them to his successive domiciles, was more so. These policemen are anemones, and I saw hermit crab-shells with three or four on them, and one even in the mouth of the shell. When the anchorite was ready for a new shell, he left his old one and examined the new ones acutely. Finding one to suit his expected growth, he entered it belly first, and transferred the anemone, by clawing and pulling loose its hold, to the outside of his chosen shell. How skilfully this was done may be judged by the fact that I could not get one free without tearing the cup-like base which fastened it. The anemone assisted in the operation by keeping its tentacles expanded, whereas it withdrew them if any foreign object came near. The stinging cells of the anemone prevent fishes from attacking the hermit, and that is the reason of his care for the parasite. It is the commensalism of the struggle for existence, learned not by the individual crab, but by his race. Some crabs wield an anemone firmly grasped in each claw, the stinging nematocysts of the parasite warding off the devilish octopus, and the anemone having a share of the crab's meals and the pleasure of vicarious transportation. The anemone at the mouth of the shell keeps guard at the weakest spot of the hermit's armor.

These sea-anemones themselves are mysterious evidences of the gradual advance of organisms from the slime to the poem. They are animals, and attach themselves by a muscular base to the rocks or shells, or are as free-swimming as perch. I saw them two feet in diameter, seeming all vegetable, some like chrysanthemums and some resembling embroidered pin-cushions. They were of many colors, and are of the coral family.

In this wonderful sea garden, where lobsters, crabs, sea-urchins, turbos, starfish, and hundreds of other sentient beings lived, I saw a thousand true scaled fish, most of them highly colored, and many so curiously marked, fashioned, and equipped with eccentric members that I was startled into biblical phrases. In the market they were strange enough, dead and on the marble slabs, or in green leaves, but in the lagoon they were a kaleidoscope of complexions and shapes. They were the lovely elves to complement the fantastic shellfish, yellow, striped with violet; bright turquoise, with a gold collar; gold, with broad bands of black terminating in winglike fins; scarlet, with cobalt polka-dots; silver, with a rosy flush; glossy green, dazzling crimson, black velvet, solid red.

They darted and flashed in and out of the caves in the coral, caressed the sea-anemones, idled about the shells, avoided by dexterous twistings and turnings a thousand collisions, and continued ever the primary endeavor, the search for those particular bits of food their appetites craved.

The effect upon me of all this splendor and grace of water life, as I bent over the surface of the lagoon or walked with lunette among the beds of coral, was, after the oft-repeated periods of bewilderment at the gorgeousness and whimsicality of the universe, a deep rejoicing for its prodigality of design and purpose, and a merry sorrow for those who would inflict dogma and orthodoxy on a practical and heterodox world. I leaned on the side of the canoe or on my spears and laughed at the fools of cities, and at myself, who had been a fool among them for most of my life. Just how this train of reasoning ran I cannot say, but it moved inexorably at the contemplation of the sublime radiancy of the vivarium of the Mataiea lagoon. It always appeared a symbol of the cosmic energy which poured the bounty of rain upon the sea as upon the thirsty earth, and which is beyond good and evil as we reckon them.

When I became myself the hunter for fish, and stood upon the hummocks of coral in water up to my waist or neck, lunette in one hand and spears in another, I saw a different aspect of the garden. I, naked among the coral and the plants, must have looked to them like a frightful demon, white and without scales, a horrible devil-fish, my arms and legs glabrous tentacles, and the lunette and spears adding to my hideousness and foul menace. I know that was the impression I made on the rainbow-fish, for they fled within the caves, and only by peeping in through the glass could I see them to drive the spear into them. These slender spears were a dozen feet of light, tough wood, two of them with single iron points two feet long, and a third fitted with ten fine-pointed darning-needles. For small fish I used the latter, and in thrusting into a school was pretty sure to impale one or two.

I tied the rope of pandanus-leaves about my shoulder, and pulled the canoe along with me as a creel, tossing the fish into it as I took them. The first seven were often of different kinds, and I did not despise the yellow and black eels, the lobsters, the *mao*, or the oysters and clams.

I would rest my spears in the canoe, and meander slowly and meditatively over the coral terraces, repeating verses:

We wandered where the dreamy palm
Murmured above the sleepy wave;
And through the waters clear and calm
Looked down into the coral cave
Whose echoes never had been stirred
By breath of man or song of bird.

When sky and wind were propitious, and other signs familiar to the Maori indicated that fish were plentiful in the lagoon, the whole village dragged the net. This belonged to the chief, who for his ownership received a percentage of the catch. The net was a hundred and fifty feet long, and was carried out by a dozen canoes or by half a hundred or more men and women, who let it sink to the bottom when up to their necks in water. They then approached the shore with the net in a half-circle, carrying it over the coral heaps, and artfully driving into it all the fish they encountered. In shallow water others waited with little baskets, and, scooping up the fish from the net, emptied them into larger baskets slung from their waists. These fish were not very big, but when larger ones were netted, marksmen with spears waited in the shallows to kill any that leaped from the seine. If the haul was bigger than the needs of the village, the overplus was sent to the market in Papeete, or kept in huge anchored, floating baskets of wicker. These fishermen had been heart and soul in the *tahatai oneone*, the fish strike, and when we had poor luck, often the best spearsman led the clan in the air taught them by the leader whom they remembered with pride and affection:

Hayrahrooyah! I'm a boom! Hayrahrooyah! Boomagay!

They associated the air and words with the fish, and deep down in their primitive hearts thought it an incantation, such as their tahutahu, the sorcerers of the island, spoke of old.

"Tellee *haapao maitai!* Kelly was a wise man!" they would lament.

Every one used a fine casting-net when fishing alone along the shores. The net was weighted, and was thrown over schools of small fish so dexterously that hundreds were snared in one fling. The tiniest fish were the size of matches. When cooked with a paste, they were as dainty as whitebait served at Greenwich to a London gourmet, and sung by Shakespere. The nets were plaited of the fibers of the hibiscus, banyan, or pandanus-bark, and when a mighty catch was expected, one of small mesh was laid inside a net of stronger and coarser make, to intercept any large fish that might break through the first line of offense. The weights were stones wrapped in cocoanut-fiber, and the floats were of the buoyant hibiscus-wood. In front of the grounds of the *chefferie* there hung on the trees a long line of nets drying in the breeze.

Before a feast, if there were not conditions auspicious for a *tuu i te upea toro*, a dragging of the seine, the village was occupied during the day or the wind was unfavorable, we went out at night after the trades had died down, and in a dozen or twenty canoes we speared them by torchlight. One was at the paddle, and the other at the prow, with uplifted flambeau, searching the waters for the fleeing shadows beneath, and launching the dart at the exact instant of proximity. The congregation of lights, the lapping of the waves, and perhaps the very gathering of humans excited the fish. They leaped and splashed, and unaware of their betrayal of their presence to slayers, informed our eyes and ears of their whereabouts. I could not compete with the Tahitians with the spears, and held a paddle, and that slight occupation gave me time and thought for the scene. The torches threw a lurid glare upon the exaggerated, semi-nude figures of the giant bronzes on the beaks of the pirogues, their arms raised in the poise of the weapon, each outlined against the darkness of the night, glorious avatars yet of their race that had been so mighty and was so soon to pass from the wave.

"Maru," said the chief, when we sat on the mats at late supper after a return from the lagoon, "it is a pity you were not here when the Tahitians had their *'ar'ia* and *pahi*, our large canoes for navigating on the *moana faa aro*, the landless sea. The *'ar'ia* was a double canoe, each seventy feet long, high in the stern, and lashed together, outrigger to outrigger. A stout, broad platform was held firm between the canoes with many lashings of sennit, a strong, but yielding, framework on which was a small house of straw where the crew lived. We had no nails, but we used wooden pegs and thousands of cocoanut-fiber ropes, so that everything, aloft and alow, was taut, but giving in the toss of the sea.

"The *pahi* was eighty feet long, broad in the middle, very carefully and neatly planked over inside, forming a rude bulkhead or inner casing, and had a lofty carved stem rising into one or two posts, terminating in a human form. It was in these vessels that we made the long journeys from island to island, the migrations and the descents upon other Polynesian peoples in war. Both the *'ar'ia* and the *pahi* were propelled by a huge *'i'e*, or mat sail of pandanus-leaves shaped like a leg of a fat hog. In modern times these great canoes were built in Bora-Bora, the island the Hawaiians say they came from, and the name of which means 'Land of the Big House Canoes.' With a good wind we could sail a hundred and twenty miles a day in those vessels. We would attend the *fa'a-Rua*, which we now call the *ha'a-Piti*, the wind that blows both ways, for we waited for the northeast or southwest trade-winds according to the direction we made for."

The chief lifted his glass of wine, and chanted:

"Aue mouna, mouna o Havaii!
Havaii tupu ai te ahi veavea!"

"Hail! mighty mountains, mountains of Havaii!
Havaii where the red, flaming fire shoots up high!"

Brooke had been to Lake Vaihiria, and suggested that I go. The excursion had been long in my mind, for every time an eel was caught or served some one exclaimed, "*Aue!* You should see the eels in Vaihiria. But, be careful!"

The warning referred to the dangers of the climb, but also to a mysterious menace of *tupapaus*, or ghosts. I had seen a canoe with the head of an eel carved in wood, and had heard often a hesitant reference to a legend of metempsychosis, of a human and eel transmigration. The chief, after much persuasion, said that the clans of Mataiea had always believed they were descended directly from eels; that an eel of Lake Vaihiria had been the progenitor of all the people of the valley. A *vahine* of another clan had been overcome by the eel's sorcery, as Mother Eve by the serpent, which doubtless was an eel.

As the eel and the water-snakes are the only serpentine animals in Tahiti, his reasoning was sound. The lake lies high in the mountains, at the very summit of the valley of Mataiea, and overlooks the Great Valley of Papenoo, owned by Count Polonsky, the cultivated Slav-Frenchman.

Tiura, the chief's oldest adopted son, arranged for the journey, and led the four of us who made it. One was an Australian, a doctor of the bush country of Queensland, in his thirties, very tall, and strong, though thin. He was a guest of the chief, and had walked entirely around Tahiti, barefooted, as had Mr. and Mrs. Robert Louis Stevenson, to the consternation of the conservative English residents of Tahiti, who wanted them to live in Papeete and hold teas. Two pleasant native youths went with us to carry our necessities.

One cannot make the trip in the wet season, usually, but we had had a period of quite dry weather, and were nearing the end of the rainy period. The beginning of the Valley of Vaihiria, the next to that of Mataiea, was reached within an hour by the crooked road that leaves the beach. The valley was very fertile, and its picturesqueness a foretaste of the heights. The brook that ran through it murmured that it, too, climbed to the mountains, and would be our music on the way. The ascent was difficult and wearisome. We walked through long grass, over great rocks, and pulled ourselves around huge trees. The birds, so rare near the sea-shore, sang to us, and we saw many nests of fine moss. The scenery was different from that of the Valley of Fautaua, which I had climbed with Fragrance of the Jasmine, more rugged, and less captivating, yet beautiful and inspiring. The enormous blocks of basalt often poised upon a point alarmed us, and Tiura said that many times they had crashed down into the abyss. We saw a score of white cascades. It seemed:

A land of streams. Some like a downward smoke,
Slow-dropping veils of thinnest lawn, did go;
And some through wavering lights and shadows broke,
Rolling a slumbrous sheet of foam below.

We arrived at a plateau after seven hours of hard toil, almost all the time pursuing a rocky path: it was the crown of the mountain and the borders of the lake. Though we had surmounted only thirteen hundred feet of vertically, we had come by such steeps that we could not wait an instant before throwing off our light garments and plunging into the water. The lake occupied an extinct crater, surrounded by four mountains unequally raised up—Tetufera, Urufaa, Purahu, and Terouotupo. It is half a mile long and a third wide, of curious shape, the banks making it appear in the dusk like a babe in swaddling-clothes with its arms outside the band. A great natural reservoir, fed by many subterranean springs, it gives birth to many others at the feet of the mountains, in Mataiea and Papeari.

After a repast, it being already late, we built a house to sleep in away from the dews of the heights, and Tiura recalled that the first Pomaré took his name from a time when he had spent the night here and coughed from the exposure. His followers had spoken of the *po mare*, meaning literally, night cough, and the euphony pleased the king so that he adopted the name and bequeathed it to four successors. All these Polynesians took their names at birth or later from incidents in their own or others' lives, as my own chief's—"Deal Coffin," from a relative being buried in a sailor's chest; "Press Me" because the chief so named had heard these as the last word uttered by a dying grandchild, and Dim Sight because his grandfather had weak eyes.

Taata Mata, the name of a charming Tahitian woman I knew, signifies "Man's Eye," her own large eyes, perhaps, explaining the name, and Mauu, the name borne by a Tahitian man of good family in Papeete, "Moist." In all Polynesia one found picture names for people, as among the American Indians, and as among all nations, though with Europeans the meanings are forgotten. Moses means "Pulled out of the Water," or "Water Baby." Some of our names of people and places have ridiculous import in Tahiti. I remember Lovaina laughed immoderately, and called all the maids to view a line in the Tiare Hotel register in which a man had put himself down from "Omaha."

After we had eaten, we sat smoking in the darkness, I feeling very close to the blue field of stars. In the tropics the mountains, even so low as these, are impressive of a vast harmony of nature and of kinship with the force that rumpled them with its mighty hand. They have always inspired great thoughts. Moses framed in the mountains the ten taboos of Israel, which we hold as sacred as did the chosen people. Jesus made the mountains the seat of his most important acts, and was there transfigured in glory.

We had been pointed out by Tiura a great crack in the precipice, called *Apoo Taria*, the "Hole of the Ears." In the bloody struggles of the ancient tribes here the conquerors cut off the ears of their victims—some say their captives—and threw them in this hole.

"Because of those ears," said Tiura, "all the eels in this lake have very large ears, and it is so because the father of all the Mataiea folk was an eel. We shall see the eels to-morrow, but I must tell you of the chief of the district of Arue, near Papeete, about which M. Tourjee, the American, wrote the *himene*. The chief was married to a strong woman of this district, and in those days there were so many Tahitians that the mountains as well as the valleys were filled with them. He had a pet *puhi*, an eel named Faaraianuu. The eel had his home in a spring in the Arue district. The spring is there to this day."

"*Oia ia!* It is true!" I interjected. "I have seen it."

"One day," went on Tiura, "the chief remarked to his vahine that he was starting up the mountain to see her grandparents. She wanted to go, too, but he said that he would just hurry along, and be back in a day or two. Against her will he went alone. He did come back in a day or two, and to her questions replied that he had had a delightful visit to her *tupuna*. After that he got the *peu*, the habit, of departing for the mountains and remaining for hours daily. The chief's *vahine* became *anoenoe* (curious) to see what was his real reason for making these journeys every day. So she followed him secretly. She came to the mountain, where she saw him stop by an *umu*, a native oven he had evidently built before. He took out a bamboo, the kind in which we cooked small pieces of meat, and she saw him draw out a piece of meat and heard him say '*Maitai!* Good!' as he ate it. She watched him closely, and was anxious to know what meat he had cooked, for he had said nothing about it.

"When he had left, she rushed to the oven, opened the bamboo, and saw on pieces of meat the special tattoomarks of the thighs of her grandmother and grandfather. *Aue!* She was *riri*. She fell to the earth and wept, and then she was angry. She made up her mind to get even with her false *tane*, and to hurt him the worst way possible. She hurried to his spring by their home in Arue, and caught his pet eel, Faaraianuu, who was sunning himself on the surface. She slashed him with her knife of pearl shell, and baked him in an *umu*. She ate his tail at once and put the remainder of the eel in a calabash. Then she left, with the *ipu* in her hand, for Lake Vaihiria."

Tiura halted his tale a minute to point out the constellation of the Scorpion, and to say, "Those stars are Pipiri Ma, the children, who lived at Mataiea long ago. That is a strange story of their leaving their parents' house for the sky!"

"*Aue!* Tiura," said I, "the stars are fixed, but there was the *vahine* with all but the tail of Faaraianuu in her *ipu*, walking toward this very spot. What became of her?"

The son of Tetuanui smiled, and continued:

"On her way she stopped to see the sorcerer, Tahu-Tahu and his *vahine*. They were friends. After a *paraparau*, the usual gossip of women, they asked her what she had in her calabash, and she replied, 'Playthings.' Then they told her her journey would be unsuccessful, but she kept on to this lake and put the remains of the eel in the water, right here where we are. But the eel would not stay in the lake, and though time and again she threw him in, he always came out. Finally she put him back in her *ipu* and returned to the house of Tahu-Tahu. She told her misfortune, and Tahu-Tahu made passes and thrashed about with the sacred *ti*-leaves, and commanded her to put Faaraianuu in the lake again. This she did, and he stayed, but even now, if you put a cocoanut in this lake at this spot, it will come out at the spring in Arue. The eel still has power over that spring."

Tiura spoke in Tahitian and French, and I handed on his narrative.

"The eel in Tahiti, from what I hear, has seen better days," commented the Queensland doctor. "All over the world the primitive people endowed this humble form of animal—the serpentine—with a cunning and supernatural power surpassing that of the four-footed creatures. I think it was because in the cradle of the human family there were so many hurts from the bites of snakes and sea-eels—they couldn't guard against them—that man salved his wounds by crediting his enemy with devilish qualities. That's the probable origin of the garden of Eden myth."

Again Tiura spoke of the Scorpion in the sky, and I knew he desired to talk of Pipiri Ma. The other Tahitians were already under the roof on their backs, upon the soft bed of dried leaves gathered by them for all of us, but the long, lean physician listened with unabated interest. He had run away for a change from the desert-like interior of his vast island, where he treated the ills of a large territory of sheep-herders, and to be on this mountain under such a benignant canopy, and to hear the folk-lore of the most fascinating race on earth, was to him worth foregoing sleep all night.

Tiura assumed a serious pose for the divulgement of secret lore. His language became grandiose, as if he repeated verbatim a rune of his ancestors:

"We Maoris lived at that time in the great peace of our long, quiet years. No outside influence, no evil wind, troubled our dreams. The men and women were *hinuhinu*, of high souls. At the head of the valley, in a grove of breadfruit, lived Taua a Tiaroroa, his *vahine* Rehua, and their two children, whose bodies were as round as the breadfruit, and whose eyes were like the black borders of the pearl-shells of the Conquered atolls. They were named Pipiri and Rehua iti, but were known as Pipiri Ma, the inseparables. One night when the moon, Avae, was at the height of its brilliancy, Taua and Rehua trod the green path to the sea. They lifted their canoe from its couch upon the grass, and with lighted torch of cocoanut-leaves glided toward the center of the lagoon.

"The woman stood motionless at the prow, and from her right hand issued the flames of their torch with a hissing sound—the flames which fell later in smoky clouds along the shore. A multitude of fish of strange form, fascinated by the blinding light, swam curiously about the canoe like butterflies. Taua stopped padpling, and directed his twelve-pronged harpoon toward the biggest fish. With a quick and powerful stroke the heavy harpoon shot like an arrow from his hand and pierced the flashing scales. Soon the baskets of *purau*-fiber were filled, and they took back the canoe to its resting-place, and returned to their house, again treading the emerald trail which shone bright under the flooding moon. On the red-hot stones of the *umu* the fish grew golden, and sent forth a sweet odor which exceeded in deliciousness even the smell of *monoi*, the ointment of the oil of the cocoanut and crushed blossoms. Pipiri Ma rolled upon their soft mats, and their eyes opened with thoughts of a bountiful meal. They awaited with hearts of joy the moment when their mother would come to take them to the cook-house, the *fare umu*.

"The parents did not come to them. The minutes passed slowly in the silence, counted by beats of their hearts. Yet their mother was not far away. They heard the noise of the dried *purau*-leaves as they were placed on the grass. They distinguished the sound of the breadfruit as they rolled dully upon the large leaves, and then the silvery sound of cups filled with *pape miti* and the *miti noanoa* from which a pleasant aroma arose. They heard also the freeing of the cocoanuts from their hairy covering to release their limpid nectar. On their mats the children became restless and began to cry. Their eyes filled with bitter tears, and their throats choked with painful sobs.

" 'All is ready,' said Rehua, gladly, to her husband, 'but before we eat, go and wake our little ones so dear to us.'

"Taua was afraid to break the sweet sleep of the babies. He hesitated and said:

" 'No, do not let us wake them. They sleep so soundly now.'

"Pipiri Ma heard these touching words of their father. Why was he afraid to wake them to-night when always they ate the fish with their parents—the fish just from the sea and golden from the *umu*? Had the love of their father been so soon lost to them, as under the foul breath of a demon that may have wandered about their home?

"Taua eats and enjoys his meal, but Rehua is distracted. A cloud gathers on her brow, and her eyes, full of sadness, are always toward the house where the children are sleeping. The meal finished, she, with her husband, hurry to the mats on which the children slept, but the little ones had heard the noise of their feet upon the dewy leaves.

" '*Haere atu!* Let us go!' said the brother to the sister. The door is closed, and with his slender arms he parts the light bamboo palings which surround the house, and both flee through the opening.

"A long time they wandered. They followed the reaches of the valley. They dipped their bruised feet in the amorous river that sang as it crept toward the ocean. They broke through the twisted brush which was shadowed by the giant leaves, and while they so hurried they heard often the words of their parents, which the echoes of the valley brought to their ears:

" 'Come back! Come back to us, Pipiri Ma! Ma! *Haere mai, haere mai*, Pipiri Ma!'

"And they called back from the depths of their bosoms, 'No, no; we will never come back. The torchlight fishing will again yield the children nothing.'

"They hid themselves on the highest mountains which caress the sky with their misty locks. They climbed with great difficulty the lower hills from which they looked down on the houses as small as a sailing canoe on the horizon. They came upon a dark cave where the *tupapaus* made their terrible noises, and in this cavern dwelt a *tahu*, a sorcerer. They were afraid, but the sorcerer was kind, and when he awoke, spoke so softly to them they thought they heard the sough of the *hupe*, the wind of the night, out of the valley below them.

"When he spoke, the spirit with whom the *tahu* was familiar let down a cloud and from it fell a fringe of varied hues. Pipiri Ma seized the threads that looked the most seducing, threads of gold and rose, and upon these they climbed to the skies. Their parents who saw them as they ascended, begged them, 'Pipiri Ma, come back! Oh, come back to us!' but the babes were already high in the heavens, higher than Orohena, the loftiest mountain, and their voices came almost from under the sun: 'No, we will never return. The fishing with the torches might be bad again. It might not be good for the children.'

"Taua and Rehua went back to their hut in tears. Whenever the torchlight fishing was bountiful, and the fish were glowing on the hot stones of the *umu*, Rehua lifted sorrowful eyes toward the skies, and vainly supplicated, 'Pipiri Ma, return to us!' and Taua answered, shaking his head with a doleful and unbelieving nod, 'Alas! it is over. Pipiri Ma will not come back, for one day the torchlight fishing was bad for the children.' "

Tiura finished with a finger pointing to Antares, of the Scorpion constellation.

"That," he concluded, "is the cloud which was itself transformed."

The doctor shook out his pipe as we entered the flimsy hut.

"Sounds like it was written by a child who wanted a continuous supply of sweets, but these people are so crazy on children that their legends point a moral to parents and never to the kiddies. They reverse 'Honor thy father and mother.'"

In the morning the Valley of Vaihiria unrolled under the rays of the sun like a spreading green carpet, and the sea in the distance, a mirror, sent back the darts of the beams. After breakfast we built a raft of banana-trunks, which we tied with lianas, and on it we floated about to observe the big-eared eels. Except by the shore the natives warned us against swimming for fear of these monsters, but we were not disturbed. We looked into the dismal pit, Apo Taria, and tumbled rocks down it.

"It has no bottom," said Tiura. "We have sounded it with our longest ropes."

The sun was now climbing high, and we began the descent, moving at a fast pace, leaping, slipping and sliding, with the use of the rope, and arriving at the *Chefferie* a little after noon.

The long draft of a cocoanut, a full quart of delicious, cooling refreshment, and we were ready for the oysters and the fish and *taro*.

Chapter XIX

The Arioi, minstrels of the tropics—Lovaina tells of the infanticide—Theories of depopulation—Methods of the Arioi—Destroyed by missionaries.

Lovaina came out to Mataiea with the news and gossip of the capital. A wretched tragedy had shocked the community. Pepe, the woman of Tuatini, had buried her new-born infant alive in the garden of the house opposite the Tiare Hotel. Lovaina was full of the horror of it, but with a just appreciation of the crime as a happening worth telling. The *chefferie* was filled with *aues*.

"*Aue!*" cried Haamoura, the chief's wife.

"*Aue!*" said the chief, and Rupert Brooke, with whom I had been swimming.

"*Aue!*" exclaimed O'Laughlin Considine, the Irish poet of New Zealand, stout, bearded, crowned with a chaplet of sweet gardenias, and quoting verses in Maori, Gaelic, and English.

There were laments in Tahitian by all about, sorrow that the mother had so little loved her babe, that she had not brought it to Mataiea, where Tetuanui and Haamoura or any of us would have adopted it. And Lovaina said, in English for Considine, whom she had brought to Mataiea, and for Brooke:

"She had five children by that Tuatini. He is custom-officer at Makatea, phosphate island, near T'ytee. He been gone one year, an' she get very fat, but she don' say one thing. Then she get letter speakin' he come back nex' week. One ol' T'ytee woman she work for her to keep all chil'ren clean, an' eat, an' she notice two day ago one mornin' she more thin. She ask her, 'Where that babee?' She say the *varua*, a bad devil, take it. The ol' woman remember she hear little cry in night, an' when a girl live my hotel tell her she saw Pepe diggin' in garden, she talk and talk, an' by 'n' by police come, an' fin' babee under rose-bush. It dead, but Cassiou, he say, been breathe when bury, because have air in lung. Then gendarme take hol' Pepe, and she tell right out she 'fraid for her husban', an' when babee born she go in night an' dig hole an' plant her babee under rosebush. Now, maybe white people say that Pepe jus' like all T'ytee woman."

Lovaina wore a wine-colored *peignoir*, and in her red-brown hair many strands of the diaphanous *reva-reva*, delicate and beautiful, a beloved ornament taken from the young palm-leaf. O'Laughlin Considine and Brooke were much concerned for the unhappy mother, and asked how she was.

"She cut off her hair," answered Lovaina, "like I do when my l'i'l boy was killed in cyclone nineteen huner' six. It never grow good after like before." Her hair was quite two feet long and very luxuriant, and like all Tahitian hair, simply in two plaits.

Brooke expressed his curiosity over what Lovaina had said, "jus' like all T'ytee woman."

"Was that a custom of Tahiti mothers, to bury their babes alive at birth?" he asked.

Lovaina blushed.

"Better you ask Tetuanui 'bout them Arioi," she replied confusedly.

The chief pleaded that he could not explain such a complicated matter in French, and if he did, M. Considine would not understand that language. But with the question raised, the conversation continued about infanticide and depopulation. The chief quoted the death-sentence upon his race pronounced by the Tahitian prophets centuries ago:

"E tupu te fau, et toro te farero, e mou te taata!"

"The hibiscus shall grow, the coral spread, and man shall cease!"

"There were, according to Captain Cook, sixty or seventy thousand Tahitians on this island when the whites came," continued the chief, sadly. "That number may have been too great, for perhaps Tooti calculated the population of the whole island by the crowd that always followed him, but there were several score thousand. Now I can count the thousands on the fingers of one hand."

We talked of the sweeping away of the people of the Marquesas Islands and of all the Polynesians. The Hawaiians are only twenty-two thousand. When the *haole* set foot on shore there, he counted four hundred thousand.

Time was when so great was the congestion in these islands, as in the Marquesas and Hawaii, that the priests and chiefs instituted devices for checking it. Infanticide seemed the easiest way to prevent hurtful increase. Stringent rules were made against large families. On some islands couples were limited to two children or only one, and all others born were killed immediately. Race suicide had here its simplest form. The Polynesian race must have grown to very great numbers on every island they settled from Samoa to Hawaii, and perhaps these numbers induced migrations. They doubtless grew to threatening swarms before they began checking the increase. Thomas Carver, professor of political economy at Harvard, says:

Even if the wants of the individual never expanded at all, it is quite obvious that an indefinite increase in the number of individuals in any locality would, sooner or later, result in scarcity and bring them into conflict with nature, and, therefore, into conflict with one another. That human populations are physiologically capable of indefinite increase, if time be allotted, is admitted, and must be admitted by any one who has given the slightest attention to the subject. Among the non-economizing animals and plants, it is not the limits of their procreative power but the limits of subsistence which determine their numbers. Neither is it lack of procreative power which limits numbers in the case of man, the economic animal. With him also it is a question of subsistence, but of subsistence according to some standard. Being gifted with economic foresight he will not multiply beyond the point where he can maintain that standard which he considers decent. But—and this is especially to be noted—so powerful are his procreative and domestic instincts that he will multiply up to the point where it is difficult to maintain whatever standard he has.

Instinct early taught society everywhere protection against the irksome condition of too many people and too little food. The old were killed or deserted in wanderings or migrations, and infanticide and abortion practised, as they are commonly in Africa to-day. Six-sevenths of India have for ages practised female infanticide, yet India increases two millions annually, and famine stalks year in and year out. Fifteen million Chinese are doomed to die of starvation in 1921, according to official statements.

Able-bodied adults in their prime bear the burdens of society everywhere. The elders and their children are a burden on them, especially in primitive society, where capital is not amassed, and food must be procured by some labor, either of the chase, fishing, or gathering fruits and herbs. Only advance in economic power has arrested infanticide. The Greeks thought it proper; the Romans, too. The early Teutons exposed babes. The Chinese have always done so.

Procreation, if not a dominant passion, would probably have ceased long ago, and the race perished. Individual and even national "race suicide" in France and New England indicated the possibilities of this tendency. The teachings of asceticism which had such power among Christians until the sixteenth century are again heard under a different guise in at least one of the modern cults most successful in the United States. Neo-Malthusianism is found exemplified in the two-child families of the nobles of France and Germany and the rich of New England. Parents want to do more for children, and so have fewer, and think proper contraception and even killing the foetus in its early stages. Modern medicine has aided this. Many women in many countries for ages have practised abortion in order not to spoil their bodies by child-bearing. To-day the demands of fashion and of social pleasures have caused large families to be considered even vulgar among the extremists in the mode. Organizations incited by the new feminism send heralds of contraception schemes on lecture tours to instruct the proletariat, and brave women to go to prison for giving the prescription. The well-to-do have always been cognizant of it.

The Tahitians have ever been adoring of little ones, and if their annals are stained by the blood of innumerable innocents murdered at birth, let it be remembered that it was a law, and not a choice of parents—a law induced by the sternest demands of social economy. Religion or the domination of priests commanded it. They obeyed, as Abraham did when he began to whet his knife for his son Isaac. To-day in Europe conditions prescribe conduct. Morality fades before race demands. Polygamy or promiscuity looms a possibility, and may yet have state and church sanction, as in Turkey.

In Tahiti, from time immemorial, as native annals went, there was a wondrous set of men and women called Arioi who killed all their children, and whose ways and pleasures recall the phallic worshipers of ancient Asian days. Forgotten now, with accounts radically differing as to its composition, its aims, and even its morals, a hundred romances and fables woven about its personnel, and many curious hazards upon its beginnings and secret purposes, the Arioi society constitutes a singular mystery, still of intense interest to the student of the cabalistic, though buried with these South Sea Greeks a century ago.

The Arioi, in its time of divertisement, was a lodge of strolling players, musicians, poets, dancers, wrestlers, pantomimists, and clowns, the merry men and women of the Pacific tropics. They were the leaders in the worship of the gods, the makers and masters of the taboo, and when war or other necessity called them from pleasure or religion, the leaders in action and battle.

The ending of the celebrated order came about through the work of English Christian missionaries and the commercialized conditions accompanying the introduction among the Tahitians of European standards, inventions, customs, and prohibitions. The institution was of great age, without written chronicles, and, like all Polynesian history, obscured by the superstitions bred of oral descent.

"The Arioi have been in Tahiti as long as the Tahitians," said the old men to the first whites.

Of all the marvels of the South Seas unfolded by their discovery to Europeans, and their scrutiny by adventurers and scientists, none seems so striking and so provocative of curiosity as the finding in Tahiti of a sect thoroughly communistic in character, with many elements of refinement and genius, which obliterated the taboos against women, and though nominally for the worship of the generative powers of nature, mixed murder and minstrelsy in its rites and observance. For what wrote red the records of this society in the journals of the discoverers, missionaries, and early European dwellers in Tahiti, was the Arioi primary plank of membership—that no member should permit his or her child to live after birth. As at one time the Arioi society embraced a fifth of the population, and had unbounded influence and power, this stern rule of infanticide had to do with the depopulation of the island, or, rather, the prevention of overpopulation. Yet while the Arioi had existed as far back as their legends ran, Captain Cook, as said Tetuanui, estimated the Tahitians to number seventy thousand in 1769. The chronicles say that the bizarre order was rooted out a hundred years ago. There are barely five thousand living of this exquisite race, which the white had found without disease, happy, and radiantly healthy. Evidently the Arioi had merely preserved a supportable maximum of numbers, and it remained for civilization to doom the entire people.

The Arioi fathers and mothers strangled their children or buried them immediately after birth, for it was infamous to have them, and their existence in an Arioi family would have created as much consternation as in a Tibetan nunnery.

Infanticide in Tahiti and the surrounding islands was not confined to the Arioi. The first three children of all couples were usually destroyed, and twins were both killed. In the largest families more than two or three children were seldom spared, and as they were a prolific race, their not nursing the sacrificed innocents made for more frequent births. Four, six, or even ten children would be killed by one couple during their married life. Ellis, an English missionary, says that not fewer than two-thirds of all born were destroyed. This was the ordinary habit of the Tahitians. The Arioi spared not one.

Ellis wrote ninety years ago. He helped to disrupt the society. The confessions of scores of its former members were poured into his burning ears. In his unique book of his life in Tahiti, he described their dramas, pantomimes, and dances, their religious rituals and the extraordinary flights to which their merriment and ecstasy went. Says Ellis:

These, though the general amusements of the Ariois, were not the only purposes for which they were assembled. They included:

"All monstrous, all prodigious things."

And these were abominable, unutterable; in some of their meetings, they appear to have placed invention on the rack to discover the worst pollutions of which it was possible for man to be guilty, and to have striven to outdo each other in the most revolting practices. The mysteries of iniquity, and acts of more than bestial degradation, to which they were at times addicted, must remain in the darkness in which even they felt it sometimes expedient to conceal them. I will not do violence to my sensibilities or offend those of my readers, by details of conduct, which the mind cannot contemplate without pollution and pain.

In these pastimes, in their accompanying abominations, and the often-repeated practices of the most unrelenting, murderous cruelty, these wandering Ariois passed their lives, esteemed by the people as a superior order of beings, closely allied to the gods, and deriving from them direct sanction, not only for their abominations, but even for their heartless murders. Free from care or labor, they roved from island to island, supported by the chiefs and priests; and were often feasted with provisions plundered from the industrious husbandman, whose gardens were spoiled by the hands of lawless violence, to provide their entertainments, while his own family were not infrequently deprived thereby for a time, of the means of subsistence. Such was their life of luxurious and licentious indolence and crime.

Yet each Arioi had his own wife, also a member of the society. Improper conduct toward an Arioi's wife by an Arioi was punished often by death. To a woman such membership meant a singular freedom from the *tabus*, prohibitions, that had forbidden her eating with men, tasting pig, and other delicacies. She became the equal and companion of these most interesting of her race, and talent in herself received due honor. She sacrificed her children for a career, as is done to-day less bloodily.

Believers in the immortality of the soul, the Arioi imagined a heaven suited to their own wishes. They called it *Rohutu noa-noa*, or Fragrant Paradise. In it all were in the first flush of virility, and enjoyed the good things promised the faithful by Mohammed. The road to this abode of houris and roasted pig was not to be trod in sackcloth or in ashes, but in wreaths and with gaily colored bodies. To the sound of drums and of flutes they were to dance and sing for the honor of their merry god, Oro, and after a lifetime of joy and license, of denial of nothing, unless it hurt their order, they were to die to an eternity of celestial riot.

As old as the gods was the society of the Arioi, said the Tahitians. Oro, the chief god, took a human wife, and descended on a rainbow to her home. He spent his nights with her, and every morning returned to the heavens. Two of his younger brothers searched for him, and lacking wedding presents, one transformed himself into a pig and a bunch of red feathers. The other presented these, and though they remained with the wedded pair, the brother took back his own form. Oro, to reward them, made them gods and Arioi. Ever after a pig and red feathers were offerings to the idol of Oro by the Arioi. The brothers formed the society and named the charter members of it in different islands, and by these names those holding their offices were known until they were abolished.

When called together by their chief, the members of the order made a round of visits throughout the archipelago, in as many as seventy great canoes, carrying with them their costumes and musical instruments and their servants. They were usually welcomed enthusiastically at their landing, and pigs, fruits, and *kava* prepared for their delectation. They were gorgeous-looking performers in their pantomimes, for besides tattooing, which marked their rank, they were decorated with charcoal and the scarlet dye *mati*, and wore girdles of yellow *ti*-leaves, or vests of ripe, golden plantain-leaves. Their heads were wreathed in the yellow and red leaves of the *hutu*, and perhaps behind an ear they wore a flower of brilliant hue.

They had seven ranks, like the chairs of a secret order in Europe or in the United States nowadays. The first, the highest, was the *Avae parai*, painted leg. The Arioi of this class was tattooed solidly from the knees down. The second, Otiore, had both arms tattooed; the third, Harotea, both sides of the body; the fourth, Hua, marked shoulders; the fifth, Atoro, a small stripe on the left side; the sixth, Ohemara, a small circle around each ankle, and the seventh, Poo, were uninked. They were the neophytes, and had to do the heavy work of the order, though servants, not members, termed *fauaunau*, were part of the corps. These were sworn not to have any offspring.

The Arioi kept the records of the Tahitian nation. In their plays they reënacted all the chief events in the history of the race, and as there was no written account, these dramas were, with the legends and stories they recited, the perpetuation of their archives and chronicles. They were apt in travesty and satire. They ridiculed the priests and current events, and by their wit made half the people love them and half fear them. A manager directed all their performances. They aimed at perfect rhythm in their chants and dances, and grace and often sheer fun in their pantomimes. Some were wrestlers, but boxing they left for others. As with the Marquesans to-day, they had a fugleman, or leader, in all songs, who introduced the subject in a prologue, and occasionally gave the cue to a change.

No man could reach high rank with them except by histrionic ability and a strict compliance with their rules. Exceptions to the first requirement might be found in the great chiefs. A candidate came before the lodge in gala fashion, painted, wreathed, and laughing. Leaping into their circle, he joined madly in the rout, and thus made known his desire for admittance. If worthy, he became a servant, and only after proving by a long novitiate his qualities was he given the lowest rank. Then he received the name by which he would be known in the society. He swore to kill his children, if he had any, and crooking his left arm, he struck it with his right hand, and repeated the oath:

"The mountain above, the sacred mountain; the floor beneath Tamapua, projecting point of the sea; Manunu, of majestic forehead; Teariitarai, the splendor in the sky; I am of the mountain *huruhuru*." He spoke his Arioi name, and snatched the covering of the chief woman present.

Occasionally there might be persons or districts that felt themselves unwilling or too poor to entertain the Arioi. These had many devices to overcome such obstacles. They would surround a child and pretend to raise him to kingly rank, and then demand from his parents suitable presents for such a distinction.

At death there were rites for the Arioi apart from those for others. They paid the priest of Romotane, who kept the key of their paradise, to admit the decedent to Rohutu noa-noa in the *reva* or clouds above the mountain of Temehani *unauna*, in the island of Raiatea. The ordinary people could seldom afford the fees demanded by the priest, and had to be satisfied with a denial of this Mussulman Eden reserved for the festive and devil-may-care Arioi, as ordinary people perforce abstain from intoxicants in America while the rich drink their fill. The historian Lecky says:

It was a favorite doctrine of the Christian Fathers that concupiscence, or the sensual passion, was the "original sin" of human nature; and it must be owned that the progress of knowledge, which is usually extremely opposed to the ascetic theory of life, concurs with the theological view, in showing the natural force of this appetite to be far greater than the well-being of man requires. The writings of Malthus have proved, what the Greek moralists appear in a considerable degree to have seen, that its normal and temperate exercise would produce, if universal, the utmost calamities to the world, and that, while nature seems, in the most unequivocal manner, to urge the human race to early marriages, the first condition of an advancing civilization is to restrain or diminish them.

Conceive the state of Tahiti, where, as through all Polynesia, the girls have their fling at promiscuity from puberty to the late teens or early twenties, when an immense and increasing population compelled the thinking men to devise a remedy for the starvation which in times of drought or comparative failure of the *feis* or breadfruit or a scarcity of fish menaced the nation! That the cruel remedy of infanticide was chosen may be laid to ignorance of foeticidal methods, and the indisposition of the languorous women to suffer pain or to risk their own lives or health.

Lecky says that however much moralists may enforce the obligation of extra-matrimonial purity, this obligation has never been even approximately regarded. One could hardly expect from the heathen Tahitians moral restraint. Malthus, a Christian clergyman, did not until the second edition of his book add that to vice and misery as checks of nature to an increase of humans faster than the means of subsistence. Nor have most Christian or civilized nations made such a check effectual.

The ever-dominant and only inherent impulse in all living beings, including man, is the will to remain alive—the will, that is, to attain power over those forces which make life difficult or impossible.

All schemes of morality are nothing more than efforts to put into permanent codes the expedients found useful by some given race in the course of its successful endeavors to remain alive.

Did not Zarathustra so philosophize, and is not the national trend in Europe exalting his theory? With the difference that nationalism takes the place of individualism in the scheme of survival and a better place in the sun is the legend on the banners.

Unable to find enemies to keep their numbers down, exempt from the epidemics and endemics of Europe and Asia, unacquainted with the contraceptives known until recently only by our rich, but now preached by organized societies to the humblest, the Tahitian, Marquesan, and Hawaiian came to consider the blotting out of lives just begun worthy deeds.

"The only good Indian is a dead Indian," was our own cynical Western maxim when life and opportunity to lay by for the future meant ceaseless struggle with the dispossessed.

We, in situations of dire necessity, eat our own fellows. We have done it at sea and on land. We eat their flesh when shipwreck or isolation urges survival. We let children die by the myriad for lack of proper care and sustenance, and kill them in factories and tenements to gain luxuries for ourselves. One justification for slavery was that it gave leisure for culture to the slave-owners, and that Southern chivalry and the charm of Southern womanhood outweighed the fettered black bodies and souls in the scale of achievement.

The Tahitian did the best he could, and the Arioi set the example in a total observance not to be demanded or expected of the mass. It is related that if the child cried before destruction, it was spared, for they had not the heart to kill it. If Arioi, the parents must have given it away or otherwise avoided the opprobrium.

Another explanation of the bloody oath of the Arioi might be found in an effort of the princes of Tahiti to prevent in this manner the excessive growth of the Arii, or noble caste. The Arioi society was founded by princes and led by them, but that they sought to break down the power of the nobles is evidenced by their admitting virtually all castes to it, thus making it a privileged democracy, in which birthrights had not the sway they had outside it, but in which the chap who could fight and dance, sing, and tell good stories might climb from lowly position to honor and popularity, and in which a clever woman could make her mark.

The early missionaries who had to combat the influence of the Arioi may have exaggerated its baseness. In their unsophisticated minds, unprepared by reading or experience for comparisons, most of them sailing directly from English divinity schools or small bucolic pastorates, the devout preachers thought Sabbatarianism of as much consequence as morals, and vastly more important than health or earthly happiness. They believed in diabolical possession, and were prone to magnify the wickedness of the heathen, as one does hard tasks. When Christianity had power in Tahiti, the bored natives were sometimes scourged into church, and fines and imprisonment for lack of devotion were imposed by the native courts. Often self-sacrificing, the missionaries felt it was for the natives' eternal walfare, and that souls might be saved even by compulsion. The Arioi society melted under a changed control and Christian precepts.

Livingstone in the wilds of primeval Africa, making few converts, but giving his life to noble effort, meditated often upon the success of the missionaries in the South Seas—a success perhaps magnified by the society which financed and cheered the restless men whom it sent to Tahiti. Livingstone in his darker moments, consoling himself with the accounts of these achievements in the missionary annals, doubted his own efficacy against the deep depravity and heathenism of his black flock. The fact unknown to him was that the missionaries in Polynesia preached and prayed, doctored and taught, ten years before they made a single convert. It was not until they bagged the king that a pawn was taken by the whites from the adversaries' stubborn game. The genius of these strugglers against an apparent impregnable seat of wickedness was patience, "the passion of great hearts."

But conquering once politically, the missionaries found their task all but too easy to suit militant Christians. As the converted drunkard and burglar at a slum pentecost pour out their stories of weakness and crime, so these Arioi, glorying in their being washed white as snow, recited to hymning congregations confessions that made the offenses of the Marquis de Sade or Jack the Ripper fade into peccadilloes.

Christian says:

Their Hevas or dramatic entertainments, pageants and tableaus, of varying degrees of grossness, similar to the more elaborate and polished products of the early Javanese and Peruvian drama ... one cannot help fancying must be all pieces out of the same puzzle ... I have with some pains discovered the origin of the name "Arioi." It throws a lurid light on the character of some of the Asiatic explorers who must have visited this part of the Eastern Pacific prior to the Europeans. In Maori the word Karioi means debauched, profligate, good-for-nothing. In Raratonga [an island near Tahiti] the adjective appears as Kariei. These are probably slightly worn down forms of the Persian Khara-bati, which has precisely the same significance as the foregoing. One is forced to the conclusion that the Arabian Nights stories of the voyages of Sindbad the Sailor were founded on a bed-rock of solid fact, and that Persian and Arab merchants, pirates and slave-traders, must have penetrated into these far-off waters, and brought their vile, effeminate luxury and shameful customs with them from Asia, of which transplanted iniquity, the parent soil half-forgotten, this word, like several others connected with revelry and vice, like a text in scarlet lettering, survives to this day.

The first Jesuit missionaries to the Caroline Islands found there an organization with privileges and somewhat the same objects as the Arioi, which was called Uritoi. As "t" is a letter often omitted or altered in these island tongues, it is not hard by leaving it out to find a likeness in the names Arioi and Urioi. The Carolines and Tahiti are thousands of miles apart, and not inhabited by the same race.

Ellis was a missionary incapable by education, experience, and temperament of appreciation of the artistic life of the Arioi. He would have chased the faun into seclusion until he could clothe him in English trousers, and would have rendered the Venus of Milo into bits. Despite an honest love for mankind and considerable discernment, he saw nothing in the Arioi but a logical and diabolical condition of paganism. Artistry he did not rank high, nor, to find a reason for the Arioi, did he go back of Satan's ceaseless seeking whom he may devour.

Bovis, a Frenchman, world traveled, having seen perhaps the frescos of Pompeii, and familiar with the histories of old Egypt, India, Greece, Persia, and Rome, knew that Sodom and Gomorrah had their replicas in all times, and that often such conduct as that of the Arioi was associated among ancient or primitive peoples with artistic and interesting manifestations.

He searched the memories of the old men and women for other things than abominations, and gave the Arioi a good name for possession of many excellent qualities and for a rare development of histrionic ability. But more than being mere mimes and dancers, the Arioi were the warriors, the knights of that day and place, the men-at-arms, the chosen companions of the king and chiefs, and in general the bravest and most cultivated of the Tahitians. They were an extended round-table for pleasure in peace and for counsel and deeds of derring-do in war. The society was a nursery of chivalry, a company which recruited, but did not reproduce themselves. They had a solid basis, and lasted long because the society kept out of politics.

The members never forgot the duty due their chiefs. They accompanied them in their enterprises, and they killed their fellow-members in the enemy's camp, as Masons fought Masons in the American Civil War and in the wars of Europe. In peace they were epicures. They consorted together only for pleasure and comfort in their reunions. The Arioi made their order no stepping-stone to power or office, but in it swam in sensuous luxury, each giving his talents to please his fellows and to add luster to his society.

To the English missionaries who converted the Tahitians to the Christian faith the Arioi adherent was the chief barrier, the fiercest opponent, and, when won over, the most enthusiastic neophyte. In that is found the secret of the society's strength. It embraced all the imaginative, active, ambitious Tahitians, to whom it gave opportunities to display varied talents, to form close friendships, to rise in rank, to meet on evener terms those more aristocratic in degree, and, above all, to change the monotony of their existence by eating, drinking, and being merry in company, and all at the expense of the other fellow. But—and the more you study the Polynesian, the subtler are his strange laws and taboos—the main provision in the Arioi constitution was undoubtedly conceived in the desire to prevent overpopulation.

Pepe, the woman of Tuatini, had returned to the ways of the Arioi because her husband had adopted the white convention of jealousy and monogamy. Only Tahitians like Tetuanui now knew anything about the order, and so many generations had they been taught shame of it that the very name was unspoken, as that of the mistletoe god was among the Druids after St. Patrick had accomplished his mission in Ireland.

Chapter XX

Rupert Brooke and I discuss Tahiti—We go to a wedding feast—How the cloth was spread—What we ate and drank—A Gargantuan feeder—Songs and dances of passion—The royal feast at Tetuanui's—I leave for Vairao—Butscher and the Lermontoffs.

At Mataiea weeks passed without incident other than those of the peaceful, pleasant round of walking, swimming, fishing, thinking, and refreshing slumber. My mind dismissed the cares of the mainland, and the interests thrust upon me there—business, convention, the happenings throughout the world. I achieved to a degree the state in which body and spirit were pliant instruments for the simple needs and indulgences of my being, and my mind, relieved of the cark of custom in advanced communities, considered, and clarified as never before, the values of life. It was as if one who had been confined indoors for years at a task supervised by critical guardians was moved to a beautiful garden with only laughing children for playmates and a kindly nature alone for contemplation and guide.

Brooke, who was busied an hour or two a day at poems and letters, and was physically active most of the time, spoke of this with me. There were few whites in Tahiti outside Papeete except in the suburbs. The French in the time of Louis le Debonnaire and of all that period thought nature unbeautiful. The nation has ever been afraid of it, but let natural thoughts be freely spoken and written, and natural acts be less censured than elsewhere. Even in late years their conception of nature has been that of the painter Corot, delicate, tender, and sad; not free and primitive. They had possessed Tahiti scores of years, and yet one hardly saw a Frenchman, and never a Frenchwoman, in the districts. The French seldom ever ventured in the sea or the stream or to the reef. Other Europeans and Americans found those interesting, at least, a little. Brooke and I swam every day off the wharf of the *chefferie*. The water was four or five fathoms deep, dazzling in the vibrance of the Southern sun, and Brooke, a brilliant blond, gleamed in the violet radiancy like a dream figure of ivory. We dived into schools of the vari-colored fish, which we could see a dozen feet below, and tried to seize them in our hands, and we spent hours floating and playing in the lagoon, or lying on our backs in the sun. We laughed at his native name, Pupure, which means fair, and at the titles given Tahiti by visitors: the New Cytherea by Bougainville, a russet Ireland by McBirney, my fellow voyager on the *Noa-Noa* and Aph-Rhodesia by a South-African who had fought the Boers and loved the Tahitian girls and who now idled with us. Brooke, as we paddled over the dimpled lagoon, quoted the Greek for an apt description, the innumerable laughter of the waves. Brooke had been in Samoa, and was about to leave for England after several months in Tahiti. He wrote home that he had found the most ideal place in the world to work and live in. On the wide veranda he composed three poems of merit, "The Great Lover," "Tiare Tahiti," and "Retrospect." He could understand the Polynesian, and he loved the race, and hated the necessity of a near departure. Their communism in work he praised daily, their singing at their tasks, and their wearing of flowers. We had in common admiration of those qualities and a fervor for the sun. For his Greek I gave him St. Francis's canticle, which begins:

Chapter

Laudate sie, mi signore, cum tuote le tue creature,
Spetialmente messer lo frate sole.

Praised be my Lord, with all his creatures, and especially our brother the Sun, our sister the Moon, our brother the Wind, our sister Water, who is very serviceable unto us and humble and chaste and clean; our brother Fire, our mother Earth, and last of all for our sister Death.

We remarked that while we plunged into the sea bare, Tahitians never went completely nude, and they were more modest in hiding their nakedness than any white people we had ever met. They could not accede to the custom of Americans and Englishmen of public school education when bathing among males of stripping to the buff and standing about without self-consciousness. The chief had said that in former times men retained their *pareus* except when they went fishing, at which time they wore a little red cap. He did not know whether this was a ceremonial to propitiate the god of fishes or to ward off evil spirits in scales. Man originated on the seashore, and many of the most primitive habits of humans, as well as their bodily differences from the apes, came from their early life there. Man pushed back from the salt water slowly.

The official affairs of the *chefferie*, beyond the repair of roads and bridges, were few. Crime among Tahitians being almost unknown, the chief's duties as magistrate were negligible, and the family uttered many *aues* when I related to them the conditions of our countries, with murders, assaults, burglaries and rapine as daily news. The French law required a civil ritual for marriage, and Tetuanui tied the legal knots in his district. I was at the *chefferie* when a union was performed. The bride and groom were of the middle class of prosperous landholders. They arrived in an automobile wonderfully adorned with flowers, with great bouquets of roses and ferns on the lamps. They were accompanied by cars and carriages filled with their families and friends. The bride was in a white-lace dress from Paris, with veil and orange-blossoms, and the groom in a heavy black frock-coat over white drill trousers with lemon-colored, tight shoes; both looking very ill at ease and hot. The father of the groom must have us to the church and to the wedding feast, so Brooke and I rode in a cart, I on the mother's lap, and the poet on the knees of the father. The jollity of the *arearea* was already apparent, and the father vainly whipped his horse to outspeed the automobile. All the vehicles raced along the road and into the yard of the Protestant church of Mataiea at top gait.

It was the season of assemblage of the *manu patia*, the wasps brought from abroad, and quite ten thousand were clustered on the church ceiling, while thousands more patrolled the air just over our heads, courting and quarreling, buzzing and alighting on our heads and necks. The preacher in a knee-length Prince Albert of black wool, opened so that I saw he had nothing but an undershirt beneath, recited the ceremony and addressed the couple. He took a ring from his trousers-pocket, unwrapping and opening its box. A bridesmaid in a rose-colored satin gown had taken off the bride's glove, and the pastor put the ring upon her finger. A number of young men acted as aids and witnesses, and all who stood were pounced upon by the wasps. They betrayed no evidence of nervousness, but at the installation of the ring, the groom, with a desperate motion, tore off his stiff collar and bared his robust neck. He did not replace it that day. The bride's mother wept upon my shoulder throughout the quarter of an hour. Not a trace was indicated of the old wedding customs of the Tahitians, as Christianity had effaced them rigorously, and though the Tahitians had had plenty of ceremonies for all public acts, as had the Greeks and Romans, many had been forgotten under the scourge of orthodoxy before any white wrote freely of the island. They are lost to record with the old language.

After the rite, all made a dash for their equipages, and raced for the bride's home, where, as customary, the *fête champêtre* was given. Again on mama's lap, and Brooke on papa's, both ample, we hurried, the *bon père* not averse to taking a wheel off the bridal party's motor-car. With cries of delight we drove into a great cocoanut-grove, and a thousand feet back from the Broom Road emerged into a sunlit, but shady, clearing. *Huro!* the banquet was already being spread. From different parts of the plantation men came bearing huge platters of roasted pig, chicken, *taro*, breadfruit, and *feis*, with bamboo tubes of the *taiaro* sauce like the reeds of a great pipe-organ. Caldrons of shrimp, crabs, prawns, and lobsters bubbled, and monstrous heaps of tiny oysters were being opened. Fresh fruit was in rich hoards: bananas, oranges, custard-apples, *papayas*, pomegranates, mangoes, and guavas.

A magnificent bower a hundred feet long, broad and high, had been erected of bamboo and gigantic leaves. It was similar to a temple builded by the ardent worshipers of Dionysus to celebrate the vine-god's feast. The roof of green thatch was supported on a score of the slender pillars of the *ohe*, the golden bamboo, and there were neither sides nor doors. The pillars were wreathed with ferns and orchids from the forest near by, and on the sward between them were spread a series of yellow mats woven in the Paumotu atolls. They carpeted the green floor of the temple, and upon them, in the center, the graceful leaves of the cocoanut stretched to mark the division of the vis-à-vis.

From these long leaves rose graduated alabaster columns, the inner stalks of the banana-plants, and on them were fastened flowers and ornaments, fanciful creations of the hands of Tahitian women, fashioned of brilliant leaves and of bamboo-fiber and the glossy white arrowroot-fiber. From the top of each column floated the silken film of the snowy *reva-reva*, the exquisite component of the interior of young cocoa-palm-leaves, a gossamer substance the extraction of which is as difficult as the blowing of glass goblets. *Varos*, marvelously spiced, prawns, and crayfish, garlanded the bases of these sylvan shafts, all highly decorative, and within reach of their admirers.

The stiff hand of the white which had garbed the wedding party in the ungraceful clothing of the European mode had failed to pose the natural attitude of the Tahitian toward good cheer.

A pile of breadfruit-leaves were laid before each feaster's space in lieu of plates, and four half-cocoanut-shells, containing drinking water, cocoanut-milk, grated ripe cocoanut, and sea-water. The last two were to be mixed to sauce the dishes, and the empty one filled with fresh water for a finger-bowl.

The bride and groom sat at the head of the leafy board, their intimates about them, and the pastor, who had joined them, stood a few moments with bowed head and closed eyes to invoke the blessing of God upon the revel, as did the *orero*, the pagan priest of Tahiti a few generations ago. The pastor and I, with the owner of the Atimaona plantation and a Mr. Davey, had had an appetizer a moment before.

We all sat on the mats according to bodily habit, the lithe natives on their heels, the grosser ones and we whites with legs crossed, and with the minister's raising of his head we fell to, with ease of position, and no artificial instruments to embarrass our hands. We transferred each to his own breadfruit-leaves what he desired from the stores in the center, meat and vegetables and fruit, and seasoned it as we pleased. New leaves brought by boys and girls constantly replaced used ones, and the shells of salt and fresh water were refilled.

Barrels of white and red wine had been decanted into bottles, and with American and German beer stood in phalanges beside the milky banana columns, and from these all replenished their polished beakers of the dark nuts.

The oysters, of a flavor equaling any of America or Europe, were minute and of a greenish-copper hue, and we removed them with our tongues, draining the ambrosial juice with each morsel, and ate twenty or thirty each. The fish was steeped in lime-juice, not cooked, and flavored with the cocoanut sauce and wild chillies. The crayfish were curried with the curry plant of the mountains, the shrimp were eaten raw or boiled, and the goldfish were baked.

The sucking pig and fowl had been baked in a native *umu*, or oven, on hot stones, and the *taro* and yams steamed with them. *Taro* tops were served with cocoanut cream. One was not compelled by any absurd etiquette to choose these dishes in any sequence. My left-hand neighbor was indifferent in choice, and ate everything nearest to him first, and without order, taking *feis* or bananas or a goldfish, dozens of shrimps, a few prawns, a crayfish, and several *varos*, but informing me, with a caress of his rounded stomach, that he was saving most of his hunger for the chicken, pig, and *poi*. He was a Tahitian of middle age, with a beaming face, and happy that I spoke his tongue. When the pig and *poi* were set before us, he devoured large quantities of them. The *poi* was in calabashes, and was made of ripe breadfruit pounded until dough with a stone pestle in a wooden trough, then baked in leaves in the ground, and, when cooked, mixed with water and beaten and stirred until a mass of the consistency of a glutinous custard. He and I shared a calabash, and his adroitness contrasted with my inexperience in taking the *poi* to our mouths. He dipped his forefinger into the *poi*, and withdrew it covered with the paste, twirled it three times and gave it a fillip, which left no remnant to dangle when the index was neatly cleaned between his lips. Custom was to lave the finger in the fresh-water shell before resuming relations with the *poi*.

My handsome neighbor ate four times as much as I, and I was hungry. His appetite was not unusual among these South Sea giants. I noticed that he ate more than three pounds of pig and a quart of *poi* after all his previous devastation of shellfish, *feis*, chicken, and *taro*, besides two fish as big as both my hands. My right-hand neighbor was Mr. Davey, an urbane and unreserved American, who informed me in a breath that he was a dentist, a graduate of Harvard University, seventy-two years old, and had been in Tahiti forty-two years. He called his granddaughter of eighteen to meet me, and she brought her infant. Only he of his tribe could speak English, but she talked gaily in French.

He practised his profession, he said, but with some difficulty, as the eminent Acting-Consul Williams had by law a monopoly of dentistry in the French possessions in the South Seas. The monopoly had been certified to by the courts after a controversy between them, but his Honor Willi did not enforce the prohibition except as to Papeete, and besides was very rich, and had more patients than he could possibly attend.

At the lower end of the mats the bachelors sat,—there were only three whites at the feast,—and merriment had its home there. After the first onslaught, the vintages of Bordeaux and of the Rhineland, and the brews of Munich and Milwaukee shared attention with the viands. The head of the mats had a sedate atmosphere, because of the several preachers there, and those Tahitians ambitious to shine in a diaconal way talked seriously of the problems of the church, of future *himenes*, and the waywardness of those who "knew not the fear of Ietu-Kirito." Their indications of grief at the hardness of the heathens' hearts grew more lively as they sipped the wine, thinking perhaps of that day when the Master and the disciples did the same at another wedding feast.

Soon their voices were drowned by the low notes of an accordion and the chanting by the bachelors of an ancient love-song of Tahiti. Miri and Caroline and Maraa, being of Mataiea, had returned for this *arearea*, and were seated with the young men. The Tahitians are charitable in their regard of very open peccadilloes, especially those animated by passion or a desire for amusement, thinking probably that were stones to be thrown only by the guiltless, there would be none to lift one; certainly no white in Tahiti. The dithyramb of a bacchanal sounded, and the outlaw dentist was reminded of his former intimate friend, King Pomaré the Fifth.

"I was a bosom chum of the king," he said confidentially as he poured me a shell of Burgundy. "He was much maligned. He drank too much for his health, but so do almost all kings, from what I've read and seen. Lord! what a man he was! He'd sit around all night while the *hula* boomed, applauding this or that dancer, and seeing that the booze circulated. He was a fish, that's a fact. He never had enough, and he could stow away a cask. Good-hearted! When he would go to the districts he always sent word when he had laid out his course, and after a few days in each place he would go on with his crowd. He paid for everything except, of course, gifts of fruit and fish. Every night there would be a big time, dancing and drinking. Jiminy! But times were different then. Look at me! I've lived freely all my life, and I am over forty years here, but you wouldn't know I was past seventy. It's the climate and not worrying or being worried about clothes or sin."

The bride had long since left the table, removed her shoes, and put on a Mother Hubbard gown. She and her mother I saw having a bite together in private comfort.

There were many speeches by Tahitians, most of them long, and some referring to the happy couple and their progeny in the quaint way of the medieval French in the chamber scenes after marriage, as related in story and drama. The pastors depressed their mouths, the deacons filled theirs with food to stifle their laughter, and the groom was the subject of flattering raillery. The women did not sit down, because mostly occupied in the service; but the hetairæ, Miri, Caroline, and Maraa, entertained the bachelors without criticism or competition. The Tahitian women had no jealousy of these wantons, or, at least, no condemnation of them. They have always had the place in Polynesia that certain ancient nations gave them, half admired and half tolerated. They had official note once a year when the most skilful of them received the government *cachet* for excellence in dances before the governor and his cabinet celebrating the fall of the Bastile. They became quite as well known in their country by their performance on those festal days as our greatest dancers or actresses.

When the mats became deserted, and the pastors had taken their carts for their homes, a little elated but still quoting holy writ, the nymphs and a dozen other girls of seething mirth took possession of the temple with a score of young men, and sang their love-songs and set the words to gesture and somatic harmony. Brooke and I lay and mused as we listened and gazed. When a youth crowned with ferns began to play a series of flageolets with his nose, the poet put his foot on mine.

"We are on Mount Parnassus," he whispered. "The women in faun skins will enter in a moment, swinging the thyrsus and beating the cymbals. Pan peeps from behind that palm. Those are his pipes, as sure as Linus went to the dogs."

I met others of the royal family than the former queen, Marao, and her daughters, the Princesses Tekau and Boots, at an *amuraa maa* given at the mansion of Tetuanui. The preparations occupied several days, and we all assisted in the hunt for the oysters, shrimp, crabs, *mao*, and fish, going by twos and threes to the lagoon, the reef, the stream, and the hills for their rarest titbits. The pigs and fowl were out of the earth by the day of the feast, and Haamoura and Tatini set the table, a real one on legs. The veranda was elegantly decorated with palms, but the table was below stairs in the cooler, darker, unwalled rooms, on the black pebbles brought from a far-away beach. The pillars of the house were hung with banana-leaves and ferns, but the atmosphere was not vividly gay because of the high estate and age of Tetuanui and his visitors.

The company arrived in automobiles, conspicuous among them Hinoe Pomaré, the big hobbledehoy son of Prince Hinoe, and, next to his father, heir to the throne. With him was his sister, Tetuanui, who was departing for Raratonga, and her husband. He was a brother of Cowan, the prize-fighter, and in their honor was the luncheon. Introduced to all by the chief of

Mataiea, I was asked to sit with them. The group was extraordinarily interesting, for besides the prince's heir and his sister, Chief Tetuanui, and his brother-in-law Charlie Ling, was Paraita, son of a German schooner captain, who was adopted by Pomaré V, and Tinau, another adopted son of the late king, who owned, and ran for hire, a motor-car. There were other men, but among the women, all of whom sat below the humblest man, myself, was the Princesse de Joinville of Moorea, mother of Prince Hinoe, and grandmother of the youth at the head of the table, and of the boy, Ariipae, who attended to the chief's garden.

This grandmother, known as Vahinetua Roriarii, was one of the very last survivors among the notable figures of the kingdom. She had a cigarette in the corner of her sunken mouth, but she tossed it away when she and Haamoura, the chief's wife, kissed each other on both cheeks in the French way. The Princesse de Joinville was tottering, but with something in her face, a disdain, a trace of power, that attracted me before I knew her rank or history. Her once raven hair was streaked with gray, she trembled, and her step was feeble; but all her weaknesses and blemishes impressed me as the disfigurement by age and abrasion of a beautiful and noble statue. She was more savage-looking than any modern Tahitian woman, more aboriginal, and yet more subtle. I once contemplated in the jungle of Johore an old tigress just trapped, but marked and wounded by the pit and the blows of her captors. She looked at me coolly, but with a glint in her eye that meant, I thought, contempt for all that had occurred since her last hour of freedom.

In the curious network of lines all over the worn face of the princess there were suggestions of the sensual lure that had made her the mistress of the court; a gentle but pitiful droop to the mouth that I had noticed persisting in the roués and sirens of Asia after senility had struck away all charm. The princess refused a third glass of wine at the table, but smoked incessantly, and listened absent-mindedly to the music and the songs. Her thoughts may have been of those mad nights of orgy which Davey, the dentist, and Brault, the composer, had described. Her cigarettes were of native tobacco wrapped in pandanus leaf, as the South American wraps his in corn husk. They were short; merely a few puffs.

Afa, the *tane* of the lovely Evoa of the Annexe, brought to the luncheon Annabelle Lee, the buxom wife of Lovaina's negro chauffeur. She was a quadroon, a belle of dark Kentucky, with more than a touch of the tar-brush in her skin and hair, and her gaudy clothes and friendly manner had won the Tahitians completely. She was receiving much attention wherever she went in Tahiti, for she had the fashion and language and manners of the whites, as they knew them, and yet was plainly of the colored races. The chauffeur himself, a self-respecting negro, had sat at table with Lovaina many times. There was in Tahiti no color-line. In America a man with a drop of colored blood in his veins is classed as a colored man; in Cuba a drop of white blood makes him a white man. The whites honor their own pigment in all South America, but in the United States count the negro blood as more important. In Tahiti all were color-blind.

The *amuraa maa* was over in a few hours. There were no speeches, but much laughter, and much singing of the *himene* written by the king, "*E maururu a vau!*"

The tune was an old English hymn, but those were all the words of the song, and they meant, "I am so happy!" They were verses worthy of monarchy anywhere, and equaled the favorite of great political gatherings in America, "We're here because we're here!"

"When I was made chief of Mataiea," said Tetuanui, reminiscently to me as we sang, "I went, as was the custom, to Papeete to drink with the king. He had just fallen down a stairway while drunk, and injured himself severely, so that our official drinking was limited. He hated stairs, anyhow, but his trouble was that he mixed his drinks. That is suicidal. He would empty into a very large punch-bowl champagne, beer, absinthe, claret, whisky and any other *boissons*, and drink the compound from a goblet. He could hold gallons. He was dead in two weeks after I had my chiefly toasts with him. His body was like an old calabash in which you have kept liquor for a quarter of a century. We had no alcohol until the whites brought it." Tetuanui ended with a line of Brault's song about Pomaré: "*Puisqu'il est mort ... N'en parlons plus!*"

Mataiea was the farthest point on Tahiti from Papeete I had reached, and wishing to see more of the island, I set out on foot with Tatini, my handmaid. We bade good-bye to Tetuanui and Haamoura and all the family after the dawn breakfast. Mama Tetuanui cried a few moments from the pangs of separation, and the chief wrung my hand sorrowfully, though I was to be back in a few days.

From the reef at Mataiea I had glimpsed the south-west of Tahiti, the lower edge of the handle of the fan-shaped double isle, mountainous and abrupt in form, and called commonly the *presqu'ile de Taiarapu*. The chief said that at the isthmus of Taravao, the junction of the fan and handle, there was the Maison des Varos, a famous roadhouse, kept by M. Butscher, where one might have the best food in Tahiti if one notified the host in advance.

"One must wake him up," said Tetuanui. "He is asleep most of the time."

I wrote him a letter, and on the day appointed, Tatini and I, barefooted, started. We went through Tetuanui's breadfruit-grove, and there, as wherever were choice growths, I stopped to examine and admire. No other tree except the cocoa equals the *maori* in usefulness and beauty. The cocoa will grow almost in the sea and in any soil, but the breadfruit demands humus and a slight attention. The cocoas flourish on hundreds of atolls where man never sees them, but the *maoris* ask a clearing of the jungle about their feet. The timber of the breadfruit is excellent for canoes and for lumber, and its leaves, thick and glossy, and eighteen inches long by a foot broad, are of account for many purposes, including thatch and plates. There are half a hundred varieties, and each tree furnishes three or four crops a year, hundreds of fruits as big and round as plum-puddings, green or yellow on the tree, pitted regularly like a golf-ball, in lozenge-shaped patterns. The bark of the young branches was used for making a tough *tapa*, native cloth, and resin furnishes a glue for calking watercraft. The tree bears in the second or third year, is hardy, but yields its life to a fungus, for which there is no remedy except, according to the natives, a lovely lily that grows in the forest. Transplanted, at the roots of the maori, the lily heals its disease and drives away the parasite. The missionaries cited this as a parable of Christianity, which would save from damnation the convert no matter how fungusy he was with sin. In tribal wars the enemy laid a sea-slug at the heart of the maori, and, its foe unseen, the tree perished from the corruption of the hideous trepang.

Papeari, the next district west of Mataiea, was well watered, as its name signified, and we passed cows and sheep and horses grazing under the trees or in pastures of lush grass. Swamps had been ditched and drained, and there was evidence of unusual energy in agriculture. The country gained in tropical aspect as we approached the narrow strip of land which is the nexus of Tahiti-nui and Tahiti-iti, of the blade and the handle of the fan. Tahitian mythology does not agree with geology, any more than does the catechism; for though the scientists aver that these separate isles were not united until ages after their formation, a legend ran that at one time the union was complete, but that a sea-god conceived a hatred for the inhabitants of the Presqu'ile of Taiarapu, the fearless clans of the Teva-i-tai and the Te-Ahupo.

One very dark night when the moon was in the ocean cavern of this evil *Atua*, he began his horrid labors to sever the tie. He smote the rocks from the foundations, and the people heard in terror throughout the night the thunders of his blows. He had almost achieved his task when the goodly sun-god appeared over the mountains far in advance of his usual time, and blinded the Titan so that he sought safety beneath the ocean. Tatini showed me the fearful signs of the demon's fury. Monstrous masses of rock were in the sea, and the isthmus was reduced to a mere mile of width, an extensive bay filling the demolished area. The deep inlet of Port Phaëton swept in there like the Gulf of Corinth in Greece. All this peninsula of Taiarapu was ceded to Captain Cook. He called it Tiaraboo in his journal, but he never took possession of his principality, realizing that the cession was in the fashion of the Spaniard who says, "All I have is yours," but would think you unmannerly to carry away anything of value.

Port Phaëton is famed in the annals of the early French conquerors, for in it they anchored their warships, and the Paris chauvinists dreamed of a navy-yard and a large settlement there. On the plateau of Taravao, a hilltop raised fifty feet, is an old fort of the French, a solid construction against the stubborn Tahitians whom they insisted, with cannon and musket, must receive Christianity through the French clergy of the Order of the Sacred Heart of Jesus instead of through English dissenters. From the plateau we could see the immense extent of the forests, which rose almost from the water to the tops of the mountains.

A dozen magnificent kinds of trees were all about us. The earth wore a verdant coat of grass, ferns, and vines, so profuse and bright that by contrast a remembrance of the barren parts of America crossed my mind, with the fulsome praise of them by the pious thieves of that region who sell them. It would be impossible and cruel, I reflected, to convey to those extravagants in adjectives the richness of herbage and the brilliancy of scene about the isthmus. The vegetation was ampler than anywhere else in Tahiti.

The *tamanu-*, the *hotu-*, and the *mape*-trees were in abundance. The *tamanu* yields *tacamac*, a yellow, resinous substance with a strong odor and a bitter, aromatic taste, that is used as incense and in ointments. The Tahitians call the *tamanu* the healing-tree. It grows just above high water on any kind of shore, embowering, with dark foliage, and peculiarly easeful in midday on the hot sands. I have had a *tamanu*-leaf soaked in fresh water laid upon my eye inflamed by too long a vigil in the sun on the reef. The small gray ball within its round green fruit affords a greenish oil that is a liniment of wizardry for bruises, stiffness, rheumatism, and fevers. In every house was a gourd stored with it.

The *mape*, the Tahitian chestnut, grew farther from the water, a powerful, commanding figure, with flowers of sublimated sweetness, and with it the *tiairi*, or *tutui*-tree, covered with blossoms, like white lilac, and bearing nuts with oily kernels. It is the candlenut-tree, which has furnished lights for Tahitians since they wandered to these latitudes. The nuts are baked to make brittle their shell, and the kernels of walnut size easily extracted and pierced. Strung on the midrib of a palm-leaf, the combination makes wax and wick, and has lighted many a council and many a dance in Polynesia.

The *pandanus* likes the coral sand, and is in appearance a tree out of a dream. It grows twenty feet high and stands on aërial roots resembling inclined stilts. The leaves are in tufts at the tips of the branches, set like a screw, twisting around the stem in graceful curves, and marking the stem with a spiral pattern from the root upward. The leaves are edged with spines. The wood is close, hard, and hollow, and full of oil. From the pandanus are made posts five or six inches through. The leaves, four or five feet long, are torn into strips for making hats, thatch, mats, and canoe sails. They are steeped in seawater, and beaten with a mallet to remove the green outer skin, the residue being white, silken fiber. This is dyed to weave hats and belts. The aërial roots are crushed to make a tougher fiber for ropes, baskets, and mats. The fruit is something like a coarse pineapple, and the blossoms are very fragrant. The ripe fruit is crimson, and strings like beads into favorite necklaces. The fruit separates into cones, and one chews the inner end like licorice, while, when dried, the kernels can be ground into a brown, sweet flour for cakes, a wholesome, nourishing food, but esteemed only in more barren islands, where fish and cocoanuts are the principal diet. From the fruit is distilled a fiery liquor that the early whalers taught the line islanders to drink.

At the isthmus was the only crossing of the belt or, Broom Road, about Tahiti. One had to choose the left or the right, and we wound to the right to reach the *Maison des Varos*. To the left we could have gone to Tautira, famous as the last stand of the god Oro against the cross, and still under the chieftaincy of Ori-a-Ori, with whom R.L.S. and his family lived several months.

The road was a fairy-tale brightly illuminated by plantation, jungle, and garden, by reef and eyot. The sea lapped gently on sand as white as the fleecy clouds. Carts of Chinese and Tahitians passed, carrying their owners and produce. The Chinese said, "*Yulanna!*" for "*Ia ora na!*" and the natives called to us to eat with them in their near-by homes. But we walked on, saying, "*Ua maururu!*" "Much obliged!"

M. Butscher had a good-sized, rambling house, with verandas for dining, and bedrooms for sleep. We found him on his largest table, lying flat on his back, and contemplating, in the eternal and perplexing way of the Polynesians. The Daibutsu, the great Buddha of Kamakura, had no more peaceful, meditative aspect than had the Taravao taverner. He was long and meager, as dry as a cocoanut from the copra oven, as if all the juices of his body and soul had been expressed in his years of cooking the sea-centipedes for which he was celebrated. Tatini addressed him slowly: "*Bocshair, ia ora na!*"

He sat up stiffly, and regarded us with indifference. He was cast for an old and withered Mephistopheles, his lines all downward, his few teeth fangs, and his smile a threatening leer, as if he thought of a joke he could not tell to decent visitors, but which almost choked him to withhold. His clothes were rags, and his naked feet like the flippers of seals. He opened his mouth, yawned, and said, "*Iiii*," a word which means, "I slept with my eyes open."

He settled back upon the table, and became immersed again in reverie. On the floor by the kitchen was a Tahitian woman with a baby and a pandanus-basket of *varos*. They squirmed and wriggled, contorted and crackled like giant thousand-legs, and almost excited in me a repulsion.

The *vahiné* laughed at me.

"I fished for them with a dozen grapnels," she said. "It was good fishing to-day. I put a piece of fish on each group of hooks. You know those holes are very small at the top and under two or three feet of water. Not many know how to find them. I set a grapnel in each hole, and then returned to the first to pull out the *varo*. I have more than twenty here."

Butscher rose, and sluggishly began to prepare the breakfast. He wrapped the *varos* in *hotu*-leaves, and put them in the *umu* to steam on the red-hot stones, and began to open oysters and fry fish in brown butter, as Tatini and I hastened to the beach for a bath. The sea was studded with coral growth, and sponges by the thousand, and we sat on these soft cushions under the surface, and watched the little fishes' antics, and chatted. Tatini had gathered half a dozen *nono*, a fruit that has a smooth skin and no stone, and she threw them at me.

"Do you know about the *nono*?" she asked merrily. "It was in our courtship. When a crowd of young men were gathered to bathe in the pools or to lie on the banks under the shade of the trees, suddenly a missile struck one of them on the shoulder. The others began to shout at him and to sing, for it was a sign that a *vahiné* had chosen him. He jumped to his feet and ran in the direction of the hidden thrower, and she ran, too, but no farther than away from the eyes of the others."

"Tatini," I said, "the *nono* was the Tahitian arrow of a little fat god we have called Cupid."

"*Aue!*" she replied. "It was not always *oaoa* for him, because it might be an old woman, or some one he did not like, but who loved him. The Arii, the aristocratic ladies, no matter how old, threw *nono* at the youngest and handsomest youth, and they had to pursue them, because of good manners. You know, Maru, that an illegitimate child is called to-day *taoranono*, and *taora* means to throw."

"When I was in Hawaii," I told her, "the old natives used to talk of a game there which, under King Kalakaua, their next to last sovereign, was played at night in Iolani palace or in the garden, but a ball of twine took the place of the *nono*, and all stood about, men and women, in a circle, to speed and receive the token of passion. The missionaries severely condemned the game."

At the *Maison des varos* I breakfasted alone, for Tatini was too shy to break the taboo that separated the sexes at meals. Butscher waited on me, bringing one plate of ambrosia after another—oysters, shrimp, *varos*, and fish. I warmed his frigid blood with a cup or two of Pol Roger, 1905, a bottle of which he dragged from a cave.

"I am born in Papenoo," he volunteered, "fifty-three years ago. My father came from Alsace seventy-five years ago, when Tahiti had not many white people. I am a tinsmith, but I gave up that business many years ago to keep this *maison*. I was a catechist in the Catholic church here nine years, teaching the ignorant. I gave it up; it didn't pay. I got nothing out of it. I worked about the church, read the prayers, and led the service when the priest was not there, and I never made a penny. Everything for me was the future life. *Vous savez, monsieur, toute à l'avenir! Sacré!* what a fool I was! *Mais*, one day when I was lying on that table as you found me, I was *iiii*, and I dreamed that there was no hell and that I was a fool. I turned over a new leaf that moment. Now I never go near the church, and the future can take care of itself. That's my son-in-law going by in the cart. He's the richest young man in Taravao. Ah, *oui*! he'll spend a hundred francs here with me in a week for drinks. That's their baby."

Butscher's leathern, yellow visage contracted in an appalling grin.

"They have been married long?" I remarked politely.

"*Mais*, they are not married yet," replied the father-in-law. "There is no hurry."

Leaving Tatini to her own pleasures, I rented a horse and cart of Mephistopheles and drove into the district of Vairao. From the outset I realized the iniquitous character of the Atua who had tried to destroy or set adrift the people of the *presqu'île* of Taiarapu, for they were handsomer and, if possible, more hospitable than those of Tahiti-nui. The road was closer to the water of the lagoon, and the reef and coral banks were nearer. I allowed the horse to go his own gait, and we jogged slowly, stopping to browse and to consider the landscape. The beach was covered with seeds and pods, the square-shaped seeds of the *Barringtonia* in their outer case of fiber, *tutui-nuts*, cocoanuts, flowers and bits of wood, and objects that would cause a naturalist to weep for lack of time. Our beaches of the temperate zones are wastes compared with these, for not only were the sands strewn with a vast débris of forest and jungle, but animal life abounded. The hermits toddled about, carrying their stolen shells, some as small as watch charms, and the land-crabs fed on the *purau* and hibiscus-leaves. They are the scavengers of the shore, eating everything, and thus acting as conservators of health, as do the lank pigs of the Philippines. They were in myriads, rushing about seemingly without purpose, and diving into their holes beneath the palm-roots. Their legs, unshelled, are as excellent food as the crabs of the Atlantic. In the water a foot or two away moved exquisite creatures, darting fish, and sailing craft—Portuguese men-of-war, and other almost intangible shapes of pearly hue.

The village of Vaieri is opposite the pass of Tapuaeraha. Far from the capital, and from the distractions of tourists and bureaucracy, this tiny group of homes along the beach was less touched by the altering hand of the white than Mataica, its setting and atmosphere affectingly unspoiled. There was a mildness, a reticence, a privacy surrounding the commune that bespoke a gentle people, living to themselves. It was almost at the end of the belt road, which virtually terminated at Puforatiai. Gigantic precipices, high cliffs, and rugged mountains forbade travel, and from a boat only could one see the extreme southern end of Tahiti-nui Marearea, Great Tahiti the Golden, as it was called by its once proud race.

Vaieri was environed by all the plants of this clime. They ran along the road and embosomed the houses. Guavas and oranges were tangled with bananas, roses, reeds, *papayas*, and wild coffee. The blue *duranta* and the white oleander, the cool gray-green hibiscus with lemon-colored blossoms, the yellow *allamanda*, the trumpet lily, acacias, lilac *ipomaea*, tree ferns, and huge bird's-nest ferns mingled with white convolvulus, and over all lifted groves of cocoas and the symmetrical breadfruit.

In this surrounding was a wooden house, built partly over the water, so that a seaward veranda extended into the lagoon, high on posts, and commanded a view of the sea and the mountain. I saw on this veranda a more arresting figure of a white man than I had before come upon in Tahiti. His body, clothed only in a *pareu*, was very brown, but his light beard and blue eyes proved his Nordic strain. He was of medium size, powerful, with muscles rounded, but evident, under his satin skin, and with large hands and feet. He was reading a book, and as I ambled by, he raised his head and looked at me with a serious smile.

I checked the horse, and tied him to a candlenut-tree. I felt that I had arrived at the end of my journey.

I spent the remainder of the day and the night there. The man and his wife were as stars on a black night, as music to a blind bard. His name was Nicolai Lermontoff, born in Moscow, and his wife was an American, Alaska her place of birth, and of residence most of her life. They were each about forty years old, and of extraordinary ease of manner and felicity of expression.

"*Muy simpatica*," had said the old Gipsy at the Generalife in Granada when I had spoken *bolee* with him. Lermontoff shook hands with me. His was as hard as leather, calloused as a sailor's or a miner's, and so contradicted his balanced head, intellectual face, and general air of knowledge and world experience that I said:

"You have the horniest palm in Tahiti."

"I am a planter," he replied. "We have been here a few years, and after buying the ground I had to clear it, because it had been permitted to go to bush. There were a few hundred cocoanut-trees, but nothing else worth while. I began at the highest point and worked to the sea."

I drew from him that he had bought eighteen acres of land for twelve hundred dollars, and had spent most of a year in preparing it for vanilla, cocoanuts, a few breadfruit, a small area of coffee and *taro*, and a vegetable patch.

"We have very little money," he explained, "and live largely on catches in the sea and stream, and fruit and vegetables, with a dozen chickens for eggs. I pull at the net with the village. Actually, we figure that fifteen dollars a month covers our expenditures. This house cost five hundred and eight dollars, but, of course, I did a lot of work on it. The chief items for us are books, reviews, and postage."

Three walls of the house were covered with books, and the fourth stopped at the floor to make the wide veranda over the lagoon.

Mrs. Lermontoff had on the *peignoir* of the natives, and was barefooted within the house, but wore sandals outside. She sat before a sewing-machine.

"I am making a gown or two for a neighbor who is sick," she said. "I do not give many hours to sewing. I like better the piano."

She knew all the Russian composers well, had studied at a conservatory in the German capital, and she also played Grieg for me with much feeling and a strong, yet delicate, touch. For dinner we had a broiled fish, which I myself cooked on stones outside the house, and *tuparo*, mountain *feis* steamed and mashed into a golden pulp, with cocoanut cream. With these we ate boiled green *papaya*, which tasted like vegetable marrow; and for dessert sweet oranges with grated fresh cocoanut, and for drink, the wine of the nut.

After the food we sat and looked at the reef, the purple sea, and the stars, and talked. These two were weary of life in the big countries of the world, and would rest in Tahiti. If they made enough money, they would like to go to America and work for the revolution they hoped for. They did not believe in bringing it about by violence, but by acting on the Christ principle, as they interpreted it. Yet they were not religionists.

"Of course one is not sure of the aims and end of life," said Lermontoff. "I have no greater certainty than the kaisers and czars or your great men,

Morgan and Rockefeller; but, at least, theirs are not worth while for the race of man. I hold that man is the greatest product of life so far, and not government or trade. That the whirling spheres are made for man I disbelieve, but on this planet, and in our ken, he is the object we most prize, and rightfully. Therefore to build him in health and character, in talent and happiness, is all of existence. The life after death we are not sure of, but beauty is on earth, and to know it and worship it in nature, and in man and his thoughts and deeds are our ends. The individual man gains only by sacrifice for his fellows. He must give freely all he has. This is his only way out of the shadow that may be inherent in our growth, but in any event has been made certain by machinery and business control of world ethics."

They were believers in the doctrines of Leo Tolstoi, and especially in non-resistance, and the possessing little or no property to encumber their free souls. In the village they had become the guides of the Tahitians in the devious path of enforced civilization.

Mrs. Lermontoff, in lamenting the Tahitian's degradation, physical and spiritual, said that she was reminded always of the Innuit, the Eskimo, among whom she and her husband had passed several years.

"They are the most ethical, the most moral, the most communal people I know of," she commented. "They have a quality of soul higher than that of any other race, a quality reached by their slow development and constant struggle. I imagine they went through a terrible ordeal in the more temperate zones farther south before they consented to be pushed into the frozen lands of Canada, and then, following the caribou in the summer, to mush to the Arctic sea. There, while they had to change their habits, clothing and food, to learn to live on the seal and the bear and the caribou in the midst of ice and snow, they were spared for thousands of years the diseases and complexes of civilization, and reached a culture which is more worth while than ours."

I was skeptical, but she quoted several eminent anthropologists to support her statement that the Eskimo were better developed mentally than other people, and that in simplicity of life, honesty, generosity, provision for the young and the old, in absence of brutality, murder and wars, they had a higher system of philosophy than ours, which admits hells, prisons, asylums, poor houses, bagnios, famines and wars, and fails even in the recurrent periods of hard times to provide for those stricken by their lash.

"But," said Lermontoff, "the Innuit, too, is corrupting under the influence of trade, of alcohol, and the savage lust of the white adventurer. He attained through many centuries, perhaps thousands of years, of separation from other peoples, and without any of the softening teachings of Christianity, a

Jesus-like code and practice, which the custodians of Christianity have utterly failed to impress on the millions of their normal adherents."

I looked out upon the reef where the waves gleamed faintly, upon the scintillating nearer waters of the lagoon, and upon us, barefooted, and clothed but for decency, and I had to jolt my brain to do justice to the furred and booted Eskimo in his igloo of ice. The difference in surroundings was so opposite that I could barely picture his atmosphere climatological and moral. I led the conversation back to their situation in Vaieri.

He had planted his vanilla-vines on coffee-bushes, the vanilla being an orchid, a parasite, that creeps over the upstanding plants, coffee, or the vermillion-tree. Lermontoff said that it was a precarious crop, a world luxury, the price of which fluctuated alarmingly. Yet it was the most profitable in Tahiti, which produced half of all the vanilla-beans in the world.

This man and woman made a deep impression upon me. They had seen cities everywhere, had had position and fashion, and were, for their advanced kind, at peace.

"We have no nerves here," said Mrs. Lermontoff. "Our neighbors are all fishermen, and we are friends. We drink no wine, we want no tobacco. We have health and nature; books and music supply our interests. Life is placid, even sweet."

When I bade them good-by it was with regret. They had found a refuge, and they had love, and yet they wanted to aid in the revolution they believed in. I restrained myself from pointing out that Tolstoi, at the last, forsook even his family to seek solitude and die.

Chapter XXI

A heathen temple—The great Marae of Oberea—I visit it with Rupert Brooke and Chief Tetuanui—The Tahitian religion of old—The wisdom of folly.

Reading one day from Captain Cook's Voyages about a heathen temple not far from Mataiea which Cook had visited, I suggested to Brooke that we go to it. None of the Tetuanui younger folk had seen it, but Haamoura directed us to return toward Papara as far as the thirty-ninth kilometer-stone, and to strike from that point towards the beach. Cook had had a sincere friendship, if not a sweeter sentiment, for Oberea, the high chiefess of the clan of Tevas at Papara, and whom at first he thought queen of Tahiti. He described her as "forty years of age, her figure large and tall, her skin white, and her eyes with great expression." That handsome lady had led him a merry chase, her complacent husband, Oamo, abetting her in the manner of Polynesia, where women must have their fling. The temple Cook and his officers inspected was the tribal church of the noble pair. The Voyages say:

The morai consisted of an enormous pile of stone work, raised in the form of a pyramid with a flight of steps on each side, and was nearly two hundred and seventy feet long, about one-third as wide, and between forty and fifty feet high. As the Indians were totally destitute of iron utensils to shape their stones, as well as mortar to cement them when they had made them fit for use, a structure of such height and magnitude must have been a work of infinite labor and fatigue. In the center of the summit was the representation of a bird, carved in wood; close to this was the figure of a fish which was in stone. This pyramid made part of one side of a wide court or square, the sides of which were nearly equal; the whole was walled in, and paved with flat stones.

When we reached the thirty-ninth kilometer-stone we met my host, Tetuanui, in his one-horse vehicle, inspecting the road. He agreed, though a little reluctantly, to take us to the *marae* (pronounced mah-rye). We turned down a road across a private, neglected property, and for almost a mile urged the horse through brambles and brush that had overgrown the way. We were going toward the sea along a promontory, "the point" upon which Cook's mariners saw the *etoa*-trees a century and a half ago, about the time that Americans were seeking separation from England, before Napoleon had risen to power, and when gentlemen drank three bottles of port after dinner and took their places under the table.

"Tooti was in love with Oberea," said the chief. "She was *hinaaro puai.*"

The expression is difficult to translate, but Sappho and Cleopatra expressed it in their lives; perhaps ardent in love would be a mild synonym.

At last, after hard struggles, we reached Point Mahaiatea, the "point" of Cook, on the bay of Popoti, which swept from it to the beginning of the valley of Taharuu. The reef was very close to the shore, and the sea had encroached upon the land, covering a considerable area of the site of the *marae*. The waves had torn away the coral blocks, and they lay in confusion in the water. The beach, too, was paved with coral fragments, the débris of the temple. Though devastated thus by time, by the waves, and by the hands of house-, bridge-, and road-builders, by lime-makers, and iconoclastic vandals, the *marae* yet had majesty and an air of mystery. It was not nearly of the original height, hardly a third of it, and was covered with twisted and gnarled *toa*, or ironwood, trees like banians, the *etoa* of Cook, and by very tall and broad pandanus, by masses of *lantana* and other flowering growths. Tetuanui, Brooke, and I stumbled through these, and walked about the uneven top, once the floor of the temple.

"Every man in Tahiti brought one stone, and the *marae* was builded," said Tetuanui. "We were many then."

He had not been there in fifty years.

We crawled down the other side, a broken incline, and to the beach. Land-crabs scrambled for their holes, the sole inhabitants of the spot once given to chants and prayers, burials, and the sacrifice of humans to the never-satisfied gods. There was an acrid humor in the name of the bay on which we looked, Popoti meaning cockroach. That malodorous insect would be on this shore when the last Tahitian was dead. It existed hundreds of millions of years before man, and had not changed. It was one of the oldest forms of present life, better fitted to survive than the breed of Plato, Shakespere, or Washington. Its insect kind was the most dangerous enemy man had: the only form of life he had not conquered, and would be crooning cradle-songs when humanity, perhaps through its agency, or perhaps through the sun growing cold, had passed from the earth. Not impossibly, insects would render extinct all other beings, and then the cockroach could proclaim that creation had its apotheosis in it.

The *marae* was the cathedral of the Tahitians. About it focused all the ceremonies of the worship of divinity, of consecration of priests and warriors to their gods and their chiefs. The oldest *marae* was that of Opoa, on the island of Raiatea, the source of the religion of these groups. It was built by Hiro, the first king of Raiatea, who, deified after death, became the god of thieves. The Papara *marae* was made of coral, but the quarried mountain rock was laid at the foundation, and these ponderous, uneven stones being patched with coral, in time the blocks had become tightly cemented together. A lime-kiln was along the land side of this *marae* of Oberea, and for years had furnished the cement, plaster, and whitewash of the district.

In the rear of the *marae* was the ossary where the bones of the victims were thrown. In Manila I had viewed immense heaps of these discarded skeletons of humans dragged from niches in a wall and flung indiscriminately on the ground by the monks, who owned the Paco cemetery, because the rent for the niches was past due. Tetuanui said that in his grandfather's day there was a bad odor about the ossary, as there was in Paco until the American Government abolished the iniquity.

The altar itself was called *Fatarau*. Here were laid the offerings of fruit and meat, but human victims were not exposed on it. Their bodies were thrown into the ossary after the ceremony was completed. The altar was always bare except at these times, and none ascended it but priests, ecstatics, and the man who carried the god. Only he and the high priest might touch this idol. The demoniacs were usually in collusion with the priests, willy-nilly.

The idol was the king's or prince's god. Each had his own. A royal idol was wrapped in precious cloths and adorned with feathers, made usually of ironwood, and was about six feet long. They diminished in size with the importance of the owner, and among the commoners might be put in a pocket or a piece of bamboo, like the pocket saints one buys in Rome. Besides, every chief and little chief had his own *marae*, which might be very small indeed, as family shrines. Of great religious events the royal *maraes* were the scenes, and the high priests were attached to these. The personnel of the *marae* was:

The king, chief, or master of the temple; all ceremonies were for his benefit. The high priest and his assistants, the latter ordinary priests. The high priests served only the *maraes* of the first rank. The *orero*, who were preachers or poets; the *oripou*, or night runners; the guardian porters of the idol. The sorcerers or demoniacs.

Thus there were six ranks in the service of the temple. The high priest was supreme under the king, and decided when a human sacrifice was demanded by the gods. He was a kind of cardinal or bishop, and his jurisdiction extended over the *maraes* in the territory of his master. The priests' functions were like those of the high priest except that they were subordinate, and they could not replace him in certain ceremonies. The *orero* was the living book of the religion, the holy chants of tradition, of ancestry, and of state. He must recite without hesitation these various records before the *marae* in the middle of an immense crowd. The *orero* cultivated their memories marvelously. They were usually sons of *oreros* or priests, and trained by years of study to retain volumes, as actors do parts. The *oripou* or *haerepo* were youths, neophytes, intended for the priesthood, and assisted the ordinary priests; but their special duties were singular and interesting. They were the couriers of the night, the spies of their districts upon neighboring clans. In war-time their work was arduous and most important, and their calling very honorable. Kings' sons sometimes were *oripou*. The idol-carriers were tabu. Their persons might not be touched nor their food.

The sorcerers, ecstatics, and demoniacs were not regularly organized into a caste. When a man fancied himself possessed by a god, he became a recognized saint. He was tabu. He ascended to the altar and danced or gyrated as he pleased. The old missionaries, who believed these sorcerers inhabited by devils, record incredible deeds by them. Often the spirit forsook them, and they became common clay, but when primed with the deity's power, they would ascend vertical rocks of great height by touching the smooth surface with tiny idols which they held in their hands, and without any contact by their feet. These demoniacs recall the oracles of ancient nations, and especially Simon Magus, the precursor of innumerable fathers of new religions, who by the power of the "Christian God" fell to a horrible death when he tried to fly before the Roman emperor on the wings of the devil.

Before a day of sacrifice a victim was selected by the high priest. The victim had no knowledge of his approaching end. He must not be informed, and though his father and mother and family were told in advance, they never warned their unfortunate loved one. No hand was lifted to avert his fate, for he was tabu to the gods. Though no excuse could be offered for the slaying of their own clansman except the direful hold of religion, which in Tahiti, as in Europe not so long ago, put Protestant and Catholic on the pyre in the name of Christ, yet so soft-hearted were these people that they could not disturb the peace of mind of the offering, and until the moment when he was struck down from behind he was as unconcerned as any one. They never tortured as the English and French tortured Joan of Arc, and as the police of America torture thousands of Americans every day.

I looked long at this ruined pagan tabernacle, this arc of the covenant for Oberea and Oamo, and for Tetuanui's fathers. The chief said that his grandfather had seen it in its palmy period. Oberea was an ancestress of my host of Papara, Tati Salmon, who had the table-ware of Stevenson, and who was of the clan of Teva, as she.

Wrecked, battered by the surf, torn to pieces by pickaxes, undermined by the sea, and overgrown by the rank foliage of the tropics, the *marae* preserved for me and for Brooke, too, a solemnity and reminiscent grandeur that brought a vision of the beauty and might of the passionate Oberea, who had commanded it to be built. Though different in environment as the sea from the desert, and in size and aspect, materials and history, I was transported from this Tahitian temple to the pyramids on the sands of Egypt. Forty centuries later I could trace the same aspiration for community with deity and for immortality of monument which had sweated a hundred thousand men for twenty years to rear the lofty pile of Gizeh. In Borobodo, in the jungle of Java, I had seen, as near Cairo, the proudest trophy, temple, and tomb of king and priest humbled in the dust by the changing soul of man in his fight to throw off the shackles of the past.

This *marae* had not been a place of cannibalism, as the Paepae Tapu of the Marquesas Islands. The Tahitians had no record of ever having eaten humans. They replied to the first whites who asked them if they ate people:

"Do you?"

Yet when a human sacrifice was made, the presiding chief was offered the left eye of the victim, and at least feigned to eat it. Was this a remnant of a forgotten cannibalistic habit, or a protest of the Tahitians and Hawaiians against the custom as not being Polynesian, but a concession to a fashion adopted in fighting the Fijian anthropopogi?

The people of Huahine, an island near Tahiti, had a supreme god named Tané, who might be touched only by one human being, a man selected for that purpose. He was the sole bachelor on the island, being forbidden to marry. Whenever the priests wanted Tané moved to a shrine, this chap, *te amo atua* (the god-bearer) had to pack him on his back. The idol was a heavy block of wood, and when his bearer wearied, it had to appear that the god wanted to rest, for a god-bearer could not be tired. The missionaries burned Tané with glee, after a battle between the Christian converts and the heathen reactionaries. The progressives won, and convinced the enemy that Tané was a wretched puppet of the priests, so that they dragged the god from his lofty house, and kicked him on to his funeral pyre. "There was great rejoicing in heaven that day," says a pious English commentator.

The Polynesians had very fixed ideas upon the origin of the universe and of man. In Hawaii, Taaroa made man out of red earth, *araea*, and breathed into his nostrils. He made woman from man's bones, and called her *ivi* (pronounced eve-y). At the hill of Kauwiki, on the eastern point of the island of Maui, Hawaii, the heaven was so near the earth that it could be reached by the thrust of a strong spear, and is to-day called *lani haahaa*.

The Marquesans said that in the beginning there was no light, life, or sound in the world; that a boundless night, *Po*, enveloped everything, over which *Tanaoa*, (Darkness), and *Mutu-hei*, (Silence), ruled supreme. Then the god of light separated from *Tanaoa*, fought him, drove him away, and confined him to night. Then the god *Ono*, (Sound), was evolved from *Atea*, (Light), and banished Silence. From all this struggle was born the Dawn, (Atanua). *Atea* married the Dawn, and they created earth, animals, man.

In most of Polynesia there are legends of a universal flood from which few escaped. In Fiji it was said that two races were entirely wiped out, one of women, and the other of men and women with tails. A little bird sat on the top of the uncovered land and wailed the destruction. The Marquesans built a great canoe like a house, with openings for air and light, but tight against the rain. The ark was stored with provisions, and the animals of the earth were driven in two by two, fastened in couples. Then the family of four men and four women entered the ark, sacrificed a turtle to God, and retired to rest amidst the terrific din of the confined animals. The storm burst, and the waters covered the entire land. The storm ceased and a black bird was sent over the sea of Hawaii. It returned to the ark, and a wind set in from the north. Another bird was loosed, and alighted on the sea-shore. It was recalled, and a third bird brought back twigs. The ark soon grounded, and the four men and four women released the beasts, and went ashore. These repopulated the earth.

The Samoans believed that the earth was once covered with water and the sky alone was inhabited, until God sent his only begotten daughter in the form of a *kuri*, or snipe, to look for dry land. She found a spot, and brought down to it earth, and a creeping plant, which grew and decomposed into worms, and, lo! the worms turned into men and women.

In Hawaii Nuu was saved from a similar flood, and with him his three sons and their families. Ten generations later Kanehoalani was commanded by God to introduce circumcision. He went to a far-off country, had a son by a slave woman and one by his wife. He was then commanded, this descendant of Nuu in the tenth generation, to go up on a mountain and perform a sacrifice. He sought a mountain, but none appeared suitable; so he communed with God, who told him to travel to the east, and he would find a precipice. He departed with his son and a servant. The Hawaiians still call the mountains back of Koolau, near Honolulu, after the name of the three, and when the missionaries gave them the Jewish sacred books, were delighted to point out that long before Christ came to earth they had believed as above, and that Abraham was the tenth from Noah, that Abraham practised circumcision, and was father of Isaac and the illegitimate Ishmael, and that their descendant of Nuu, as Abraham, became the father of twelve children, and the founder of the Polynesian race, as Abraham had of the Jews.

One might detect some relation to the Hebraic scriptures in the legends of the Maoris of New Zealand and Tonga that the older son of the first man killed his brother, and that in Fiji one still is shown the site where a vast tower was built because the Fijians wanted to peer into the moon to discover if it was inhabited. A lofty mound was erected, and the building of timber upon it. It was already in the sky when the fastenings broke, and the workmen were precipitated over every part of Fiji.

The sun stood still for Hiaka when she attempted to recover the body of Lohiau, her sister Pele's lover. There was not daylight enough to climb the mountain Kalalau and bring down the body from a cave, so she prayed, and the sun set much later than usual. Aukelenui-a Iku, the next to the youngest of twelve children, was hated by his brothers because he was his father's favorite, and they threw him into a pit to die. His next eldest brother rescued him, and he became a traveler, and found the water of life, with which he restored his brother who had been drowned years before. The Chaldeans had a similar legend. Ninkigal, goddess of the regions of the dead, ordered Simtar, her attendant, to restore life to Ishtar with the "waters of life."

Naula-a-Maihea of Oahu, not far from Honolulu, was upset from his canoe while paddling to Kauai, and was swallowed by a whale, which kindly threw him up on the beach of Wailua.

Kana-loa and Kane-Apua, prophets, walked about the world, causing water to flow from rocks, as did Moses, and in the ancient litany, recited by priest and congregation, the responses of "*Hooia, e oia!*" meant "It is true!" as does Amen, the response of Christian litanies to-day. The custom of using holy water prevailed all over Polynesia.

"The ocean which surrounds the earth was made salt by God so it should not stink," said the legend, "and to keep it salt is the special work of God."

To celebrate God's act, the priests of Polynesia blessed waters for purification, for prayer, and for public and private ceremonies, and to exorcise demons and drive away diseases, as the priests of America and Europe do. Holy water was called *ka wai kapu a Kane*, and from the baptizing of the new-born child to the sprinkling of the dying its sacred uses were many. To-day the older people use these pagan ablutions to alleviate pain and cure maladies. The old Greeks used salt water for the same purposes, and had holy-water fonts at the temple gates, as do the Catholic churches to-day.

Levy and Woronick believed, or pridefully affected to believe, that at a remote period a band of Israelites, perhaps one of the lost tribes carried away by the Assyrians, peopled these islands; or settled in Malaysia before the Polynesian exodus from there, and gave them their lore. Père Rambaud of the Catholic mission at Papeete considered it more probable that Spaniards, reaching Hawaii from wrecked Spanish galleons voyaging between Mexico and Manila, brought the holy doctrines. His explanation, however, often advanced, fell utterly before the fact that the Polynesians had no knowledge of Jesus or any man or god like him, and knew nothing of original sin; but, more convincing, all Polynesia had these legends, and there had been no communication with the Maoris of New Zealand and with Fiji after the Spanish entered the Philippines. It is to me quite certain that the Polynesians brought with them from Malaysia or India or from farther toward Europe those traditions of the beginnings of mankind which grew up hundreds of thousands of years ago, and were dispersed with each group setting out for adventure or driven from the birthplace of thinking humans.

Taaroa, whose name was spelt differently in separated archipelagos, was the father of the Tahitian cosmogony. His wife was Hina, the earth, and his son, Oro, was ruler of the world. Tané, the Huahine god, was a brother of Oro, and his equal, but there were islands which disputed this equality, and shed blood to disprove it, as the sects of Christianity have since the peaceful Jesus died by the demands of the priests of his nation.

Haui was the Tahitian Hercules. Of course he, too, bade the sun to stay a while unmoving, and it did. Joshua, the son of Nun, whose astronomical exploit at Gibeon brought him immortal fame, was a glorious warrior; but Haui's unwritten achievements, as chanted by the *orero* at the *marae* where Tetuanui, Brooke, and I stood, would have forced the successor of Moses to have withdrawn his book from circulation, as too dull.

The Polynesian creator put on earth hogs, dogs, and reptiles. There were many kinds of dogs in their mythology, including the "large dog with sharp teeth," and the "royal dog of God." Among reptiles was Moo, a terrible dragon living in caverns above and beneath the sea, who was dreaded above all dangers. He was to them the monster that guarded the Hesperides garden, and the beast that St. George slew; but as the common lizard was the largest reptile in Polynesia, this, too, was an heirloom from another land. In the old Havaii—probably Java—they must have known those fierce crocodiles that I have seen drag down a horse drinking in the river at Palawan, and noted swimming in the open sea between Siassi and Borneo.

The chief and Brooke and I sat in the shade of the *etoa*-trees, and conversed about these ancient stories. Fixed in the mind of the race by the repetition of ages, they are the most difficult of all errors to erase, and the professors of this wisdom stamp it upon the heart and brain of the child in almost indelible colors, and make it tabu, sacrilege, or treason to deny its verity. Half a century ago repairs became necessary to Mohammed's tomb at Medina, and masons were asked to volunteer to make them, and submit to beheading immediately after. There was no lack of desirous martyrs. One descended into the mausoleum, finished the task, and, reaching the air again, knelt, turned his face toward Mecca, and bent his head for the ax. The Mussulman keepers of the tomb justified their act, as, the forbidding telling the truth about religion and government, about war and business, is justified. Their words were:

"We picture those places to ourselves in a certain manner, and for the preservation of our holy religion, and the safety of society, there must not be any one who can say they are otherwise."

It was noon when Brooke and I—Tetuanui having gone to instruct his gang—plunged into the sea in front of the *chefferie*, and laughed in the joy of the sweet hour. He had written lines of beauty that interpreted our humor:

Tau here, Mamua,
Crown the hair, and come away!
Hear the calling of the moon,
And the whispering scents that stray
About the idle warm lagoon.
Hasten, hand in human hand,
Down the dark, the flowered way,
Along the whiteness of the sand,
And in the water's soft caress
Wash the mind of foolishness,
Mamua, until the day.
Spend the glittering moonlight there,
Pursuing down the soundless deep
Limbs that gleam and shadowy hair;
Or floating lazy, half-asleep.
Dive and double and follow after,
Snare in flowers, and kiss, and call,
With lips that fade, and human laughter
And faces individual!
Well this side of Paradise! ...
There's little comfort in the wise.

Chapter XXII

I start for Tautira—A dangerous adventure in a canoe—I go by land to Tautira—I meet Choti and the Greek God—I take up my home where Stevenson lived.

Seeing the way the Lermontoffs lived, caused me to resolve that during the remainder of my stay in Tahiti I would go even farther from Papeete than Mataiea. They suggested Tautira, a village they had never visited, but which was at the very end of the habitable part of the Presqu'île of Taiarapu. My easiest route to Tautira was by crossing the isthmus of Taravao, to the other side of the peninsula, as nowhere in Tahiti except at Lake Vaihiria were there even passable trails across the lofty spine of the island. I was for sending back the cart and horse to Taravao and taking a canoe to Tautira. A council of the elders of Vaieri opposed me, but yielded to my persistence by advising me at least to ride as far as possible in the cart along the western road, and to find, nearer to Tautira, in Maora, or farther on, in Puforatoai, a canoe and canoeists for the risky attempt.

Tatini, who had lagged behind at Butscher's, appeared as I harnessed the horse. She had accompanied the Tinito storekeeper of Taravao to Vaieri, and would not permit me to go on alone. She climbed into the vehicle, and we wended a winding road, and forded several streams until we came to Puforatoai, having gone through Hatiti and Maora. There was a pass in the reef admitting to a questionable shelter, Port Beaumanoir, used by the French when little gunboats threatened to bombard villages to force the rule of Paris.

Puforatoai was a handful of houses, hardly a village. My advent was of importance, and its few people gathered about us. They voiced their amazement when Tatini announced our wish to find a navigator and vessel to Tautira. They all said it was impossible, that the coast to Pari, with the submerged reef of Faratara, was too rough now for any but a large power boat, and the wind would be baffling and threatening. But as fear of the sea was unknown to them, they expressed a will to make the attempt. We launched a large canoe, and two sturdy natives, relations of Tatini, took the paddles. They had made the journey more than once, but not at this season.

We got into difficulties from the start. The shores were very different from those of Mataiea, Papeari, and Vairao, the three districts I had come through from the house of Tetuanui. The alluvial strip of land which in them stretched from a quarter of a mile to a mile from the lagoon to the slopes of the hills, here was cramped to the barest strip. The huts of the indigenes, few and far apart outside of Puforatoai, seemed to be set in terraces cut at the foot of the mountains which rose almost straight from the streak of golden sand to the skies. In every shade of green, as run by the overhead sun upon the altering facets of precipice and shelf, of *fei* and cocoa, candlenut and *purau*, giant ferns and convolvulus, tier upon tier, was a riot of richest vegetation. But everywhere in the lagoon were bristling and hiding dangers from hummocks of coral and sunken banks.

Our canoe was twenty feet long, and with a very strong outrigger, but though all four of us paddled, Teta, the chief man of Puforatoai, in the stern, steering, the *vaa* labored heavily. Tatini was adept in canoeing, and with a quartet of *hoë* we would have ordinarily sent the *vaa* spinning through the water; but we were nearing the southernmost extremity of the Presqu'île, and the wind and current from the northeast swept about the broken coast in a confusion of puffs and blasts, choppy waves and roaring breakers, and made our progress slow and hazardous. The breeze caught up the foam and formed sheets of vapor which whipped our faces and blinded us, while an occasional roller broke on our prow, and soon gave Tatini continuous work in bailing with a handled scoop.

Opposite the pass of Tutataroa our greatest peril came. The ocean swept through this narrow channel like a mill-race. The first swell tossed us up ten feet, and we rode on it fifty before Teta could disengage us from its clasp, and, without capsizing, divert our course westward instead of toward the parlous shore. One such jeopardy succeeded another. We were in a quarter of an hour directly under black and frowning heights from which a score of cascades and rills leaped into the air, their masses of water, carried by the gusts, falling upon us in showers and clouds, aiding the flying scud in shielding the distance ahead from our view.

"*Aita e ravea*," shouted Teta to me. "It is impossible to go on."

We were all as wet as if in the sea, our faces and bodies stung by the spindrift, and we were barely able to glimpse a dark and heaving panorama of surf, rock, and bluff in the mists that now and again were penetrated by the hot sun.

"Maitai! Hohoi!" I replied above the clangor, and raised my paddle.

Carefully and in a wide circle the *vaa* crept around to head back toward our port, and it was after sunset before we were in Teta's house in Puforatoai. The villagers met us with torches and incredulous *aues* and we walked up the road singing the song of the "Ai Dobbebelly Dobbebelly," which was known wherever a fisher for market dwelt in all Tahiti. The farther from Papeete and more and more as time passed, the words lost resemblance to English, and became mere native sounds without any exact meaning, but with a never-forgotten sentiment of rebellion against government and of gild alliance.

"Give us a hand-out!" had changed from "*hizzandow*" in Papeete, to "*Hitia o te ra!*" which meant that the sun was rising. Within a year or two the entire text would doubtless merge into Tahitian with only the martial air of "Revive us again!" and the dimming memory of the fish-strike to recall its origin. I had known a native who, whenever he approached me, sang in a faltering tone, "Feery feery!"

I asked him after many weeks what he meant, and he said that that was a *himene*, which a young American had sung at his potations in his village in the Marquesas Islands. I had him repeat "Feery feery!" dozens of times, and finally snatched at an old glee which ran through my mind: "Shoo Fly, don't bother me!" and when I sang it,

"I feel, I feel, I feel,
I feel like a morning star!"

he struck his thigh, and said, "*Ea*! That is the very thing!" And to be fair to all races, one has only to listen to an American assemblage singing "The Starspangled Banner" to learn that after the first few lines most patriots decline into "ah-ah-la-la-ha-la-ah-la-la."

Before our supper of fish and *fei*, Teta, who was a deacon in the Protestant church, but of superior knowledge of his own tongue and legends, asked a blessing of God, and afterward recited for me the Tahitian chant of creation, the source of which was in the very beginnings of his race, perhaps even previous to the migration from Malaysia. He intoned it, solemnly, as might have an ancient prophet in Israel, as we sat in the starlit night, with the profound notes of the reef in unison with his deep cadence:

He abides—Taaroa by name—
In the immensity of space.
There was no earth, there was no heaven,
There was no sea, there was no mankind.
Taaroa calls on high;
He changes himself fully.
Taaroa is the root;
The rocks (or foundation);
Taaroa is the sands;
Taaroa stretches out the branches (is wide-spreading).
Taaroa is the light;
Taaroa is within;

Taaroa is, ———
Taaroa is below;
Taaroa is enduring;
Taaroa is wise;
He created the land of Hawaii;
Hawaii great and sacred,
As a crust (or shell) for Taaroa.
The earth is dancing (moving).
O foundations, O rocks,
Oh sands! here, here.
Brought hither, pressed together the earth;
Press, press again!
They do not ———
Stretch out the seven heavens; let ignorance cease.
Create the heavens, let darkness cease.
Let anxiety cease within;
Let immobility cease;
Let the period of messengers cease;
It is the time of the speaker.
Fill up the foundation,
Fill up the rocks,
Fill up the sands.
The heavens are inclosing.
And hung up are the heavens
In the depths.
Finished he the world of Hawaii.
E pau fenua no Hawaii.

The cart at my request had been driven back to Taravao; so in the morning Tatini and I walked back to the isthmus. We drank coffee at five, and at three we had covered the twelve miles in the sauntering gait of the Tahitian girl, stopping to make wreaths, and to bathe in several streams. Butscher was on his table in his after-breakfast lethargy, and I regretted disturbing his *iiii* to ask him to serve us. Again Tatini refused to sit at table with me. Evidently, she feared the scowls of Butscher, who had none of the white's ideas of the equality of females with males at the board. Butscher added many francs to my bill by pouring me another bottle of Pol Roger, 1905, which after several days of cocoanut juice took on added delight. I made up my mind to tarry with Butscher a day, while Tatini returned to the Tetuanui mansion by diligence, and despatched my bags to me by the same carrier. I sent with her my love to the Tetuanui clan, and some delicacies from the Maison des Varos for the half-blind Haamoura. The diligence did not run farther than Taravao, and the next day, with my impedimenta in the cart, and with a boy to drive it, I turned my back on the road to Papeete, and began the jog trot to the famous, but hardly ever visited, district of Tautira.

I counted it the third stage in my pilgrimage in Tahiti. The first had been in and about the capital, mingling mostly with white men, and living in a public inn; the second at Mataiea had taken me far from those rookeries, and had introduced me to the real Tahitians, to their language, their customs, and their hearts; but still I had been a guest, and a cared-for and guarded white among aborigines. Now I wanted to cut off entirely from the main road, to sequester myself in a faraway spot, and to live as close to the native as was possible for me. My time was drawing near for departure. I must see all of the Etablissements Français de l'Oceanie, the blazing Paumotu atolls, and the savage Marquesas, and I must make the most of the several months yet remaining for me in Tahiti.

The highway along the eastern portion of the Presqu'île was much like that between Taravao and Puforatoai, tortuous, constricted, and often forced to hang upon a shelf carved out of the precipice which hemmed it. The route hugged the sea, but at every turn I saw inland the laughing, green valleys, deserted of inhabitants, climbing slowly between massive walls of rock to which clung great tree ferns, with magnificent vert parasols, enormous clumps of *feis*, with huge, emerald or yellow upstanding bunches of fruit; candlenut- and ironwood-trees. Uncounted, delicious odors filled the air, distilled from the wild flowers, the vanilla, orchids, and the forests of oranges, which, though not of Tahiti, were already venerable in their many decades of residence. Not a single path struck off from the belt road, except that as we came toward the centers of Afaahiti and Pueu districts the inevitable store or two of the Chinese appeared, the *cheferie*, a church or two, and the roofs of the Tahitians. These were always near the beach, set back a few hundred feet from the road in rare instances, but mostly only a few steps from it. The Tahitian never lived in hamlets, as the Marquesan and the Samoan, but each family dwelt in its wood of cocoanuts and breadfruit, or a few families clustered their inhabitants for intimacy and mutual aid. The whites, missionaries, conquerors, and traders found this system not conducive to their ends. Churches demand for prosperity a flock about the ministrant, business wants customers close to the store, and government is more powerful where it can harangue and proclaim, parade before and spy upon its subjects. Individualistic and segregated domestic circles give rise to tax evasions, feuds, and moonshining, plots and the growth of strong men. The city is the corral where humans mill like cattle in a panic, are more easily ridden down *en masse*, and become habitual buyers of unnecessary things.

The French, after their bold seizure of the island in the name of liberty for the earnest friars, and sealing their brave conquest in the blood of the obstinate Polynesian who had hated to learn a new liturgy and to unlearn his old Protestant songs, feared that the dispersion of the people upon their little plantations, to which they were greatly attached, would make their Frenchifying a long task. So, about sixty years ago, a governor, who, ten thousand miles from his superiors, with an exchange of letters taking many months, was an autocrat, decided that all the people of the same region must be huddled in a village. His name was Gaultier de la Richerie. His office was snatched from him by another politician before he could carry out his plan, and only one village exemplified it. In all the districts I had passed through from Papeete, while in each was the knot of *chefferie*, churches, stores, and perhaps a house or two, the other residences stretched along the entire length of the political divisions, from six to eight miles.

I was approaching the exception, Tautira, which, though farthest of all from the palace of the governor, had been chosen for the first experiment, and which had adapted its life to the paternal will of M. de la Richerie, now long since laid in the bosom of Père Lachaise.

The estimable troubadour, Brault, had advised me of the history of Tautira. It was seldom visited by white tourists, as even the post brought by the diligence ended at Taravao, and letters for farther on were carried afoot by the *mutoi*, or postman-policeman of the adjoining district, who handed on to his contiguous confrère those for more distant confines. But for centuries Tautira was known as a focus of the wise, of priests, sorcerers, and doctors, and, said the knowing Brault, especially of the dancers, and those who, he explained, under the banner of Venus.

Ont vu maintes batailles
Et reçu nombre d'entailles
Depuis les pieds jusqu'au front.

The little boy and I chatted as the horse ambled at will, occasionally urged to a trot by a shaking of the reins. The country as we progressed became far more beautiful than that behind. A new wildness, not fierce and rugged as between Vaiere and Puforatoai, but gentler and more inviting, preluded the exquisite setting of the village. We had to ford a stream three or four feet deep, the Vaitapiha, and the struggle through it was a rare pleasure, the child on the back of the animal, and I with the reins and a *purau* twig directing and commanding in vain. We had to leap into the water and remove a boulder or two that stymied the wheels. When we had pulled through to the opposite shore, I was reduced to a dry *pareu*, and in it alone, barefooted, I reached the rustic paradise, the loveliness of which was to content me more than any spot except the strangely fascinating valley of Atuona in the sad isle of Hiva-Oa.

In a delta formed by the Vaitapiha the settlement lay among tents of verdure. For a mile it sprawled around a small point of land which thrust out into the sea, and which was guarded by the most wonderful of walls, a reef of madrepore, as solid as granite and sixty feet wide. The road was arched by splendid trees of many kinds, and facing it, every several hundred feet, was a home. Many of these were cottages in modern style, but a dozen or so were the true Tahitian *faré*, of bamboo and thatch. All were covered with flowering vines, and surrounded by many fruiting trees.

"*Tautira nei!*" announced my coachman. "Tautira is here!"

He pulled up the horse. I had not given any thought to my lodging, and I jumped out and looked around. The brook curved about a mango grove, and under its high trees was a new native house, a replica of the commodious dwellings of old days. I walked into the grove, and was admiring the careful, but charming, arrangements of ferns and orchids, which, though brought from the forests, had been fitted into the scene to simulate a natural environment. All of a sudden a something I could not see hurled itself from a limb upon my head, and two affrighting paws seized my right ear and my hair, grown long at Mataiea, and tried to tear them out by the roots, while at the same time many fierce teeth closed, though without much effect, on my tough and weathered shoulder. In horror at the attack, I covered yards in two bounds, and my assailant was torn from its hold upon me.

I then turned and saw that it was a monkey tied to a rope fastened to the limb of the tree. He stood upright on the ground, his jaws agape, and a look of devilish glee upon his uncannily manlike face. At the same moment a white man ran from the house and called in English:

"You damned little scoundrel! How often have I whipped you for that same trick! I would better have left you in the slums in San Francisco."

And then apologetically to me:

"I ought to kill him for that. He's a devil, that monkey. He has bitten all the children around here, has killed all my chickens, and raised more hell in this village than the whole population put together. I swear, I believe he just enjoys being mean. Come in and have a snifter after that greeting! Did he hurt you?"

My would-be host was himself a very striking somebody. He wore only a *pareu*, as I, of scarlet muslin, with the William Morris design, but he had wound his about so that it was a mere ornamental triangle upon his tall, powerful, statuesque body. His chest and back had a growth of red-gold hair, which, with his bronzed skin, his red-gold beard, dark curls over a high forehead, handsome nose, and blue eyes, made him all of the same color scheme. He was without doubt as near to a Greek deity in life, a Dionysus, as one could imagine. He had two flaming hibiscus blossoms over his ears, and he looked in his late twenties. Accustomed as I was to semi-nudity and to white men's return to nature, I had never seen a man who so well fitted into the landscape as the owner of the ape. He was the faun to the curling locks and the pointed ears, with not a trace of the satyr; all youth and grace and radiance.

He walked on before me to the *faré*, and, opening the door, bade me welcome. The house differed from the aboriginal in a wooden floor and three walls of wire screen above four feet of wainscot. The roof was lofty, of plaited pandanus-leaves, with large spaces under the eaves for the circulation of air; but the immediate suggestion was of an aviary, a cage thirty feet square. Attached to this room was a lean-to kitchen, and near by, hidden behind the cage, was another native house for sleeping. The aviary was the living- and dining-quarters, protected from all insect pests, and an arbor covered with vines led to the water.

Many canvases were about, on an easel an unfinished group of three Tahitian boys, and a case of books against the one solid wall.

Half a dozen Tahitian youths were lolling outside in the shade, and one, at the request of the host, led up the horse and the boy who guarded it. The child skirted the circumference of the monkey's swing, and then, a few feet away, squatted to regard the animal with intense surprise and interest.

"Uritaata," he said; "I never saw one before, but I have read in my schoolbook that they have those dogmen in French colonies."

Uri means dog and *taata* man, and the compound name was that which sprang to the lips of the Tahitians on seeing a monkey, just as they called the horse *puaa horo fenua*, the pig that runs on the earth, and the goat, *horo niho*, the pig with horns. The pig and the dog were the only land mammals they knew before the white arrived. The race-track near Papeete was *puaa horo fenua faa titi auraa*. If a pig could talk, he would say that man was a wickeder and stronger pig. Jehovah has whiskers like a Rabbi. The Rabbis made him like themselves. Man has no other ideal.

The Tahitian youth addressed the Greek god as T'yonni, which was an effort to say John, and I adopted it instanter, as he did my own Maru. T'yonni said that Uritaata was the bane of his existence at Tautira. After building his *faré* he had been called to America, and had danced in Chinatown the night before his steamship departed for his return to Papeete. He remembered obscurely drinking grappo with a deep-sea sailor, and had awakened in his berth, the vessel already at sea, and Uritaata asleep at his feet. Many Tahitians, he said, had never seen such a fabulous brute, and T'yonni had stirred in them a mood of dissatisfaction by telling that their forefathers had descended from similar beings.

"How about Atamu and Eva?" they had asked the pastors.

Those conservatists had replied emphatically that Adam and Eve, the first man and woman, were created by God, which agreed thoroughly with the Tahitian legends, and after that T'yonni's generosity was ranked higher than his knowledge. He laughed over the stories as we sat at breakfast with my coachman in the kitchen. T'yonni said that the deacon of the Protestant church expressed a belief that the Paumotuans or even the French might have followed the Darwinian course of descent, but that Tahitians could not swallow a doctrine that linked them in relationship with Uritaata. The Tongans, Polynesians like themselves, had a tradition that God made the Tongan first, then the pig, and lastly the white man.

"He quoted the Tongan with compassion for me," said T'yonni. "And now about a place where you can live. Choti, a painter, whose pictures you see around here, lives with the school-teacher up the road, and he might find you a place. He's an American, as I am, and I suppose you, too."

I raised my glass to our native land, and finding that the boy of Taravao had eaten his fill of *fei* and fish, I said *ariana* to T'yonni, and drove to Choti's. The painter was on the veranda of a cottage, finishing the late breakfast. He received me with enthusiasm. Tall, very spare, and his skin pale despite his wearing only a *pareu* and never a hat, Choti's black eyes shone under long, black hair, and over a Montmartre whisker that covered his boyish face from his chiseled nose.

"Hello!" he said. "Come and have *déjeuner?*"

The manner of both T'yonni and Choti, while hospitable, and their glances at my bags, showed a probable wonderment of my intentions.

Was I an average tourist or loafer come to put an unknown quantity in their smoothly working problem of a pleasant life in this Eden? The artist must have looked me over for indications of familiarity with brush and palette.

I replied to Choti that I had breakfasted with T'yonni, and he smiled at my knowledge of his friend's Tautira name.

"How about getting an apartment or a suite of rooms?" I inquired.

Choti sucked the last particle of *poi* from his forefinger, dipped it into a shell of water, shook hands, and against my pleadings, accompanied me to the house of Ori-a-Ori, the chief of the district. The chief, an excessively tall man, quite six and a half feet and big all over, but not fat, like many natives, was very dark and slightly grizzled. He had a singular solemnity of address, a benignity and detachment which were the externals of a thoughtful, simple, generous nature, no longer interested deeply in trifles. His house was toward the farther end of the main street, and set upon a spacious lawn a hundred feet from the street, which, by the same token, was also a lawn, for there was no sign of the unadorned earth. So little wheeled traffic was there that bare feet walked on a matting of grass and plants as soft as seaweed on the beach. The street was bordered with cocoanuts and pandanus, and the chief's dwelling had about it breadfruit, *papayas*, and cocoanuts. The grounds were divided from neighbors' parks by hedges of tiare Tahiti, gardenias, roses, and red and white oleanders. I drew in their perfume as Ori-a-Ori said, "*Ia ora na!*" and took and held my hand a moment, while his grave eyes studied my face in all kindliness.

Choti put him the question of my habitation, and he instantly offered me either a room in his own house or a small, native building on the opposite side of the road and nearer the beach. We walked over, and found it unoccupied. It was a bird-cage, all one room, with a thatch of pandanus and a floor of dried grass covered with mats. The walls were of split bamboo, like reeds, and the sun and air penetrated it through and through; but hanging mats were arranged, one as a door, and others to keep out the rain. It was exactly suited for sleeping and lounging purposes, and the chief said that I could cook in a convenient hut. I brought in my belongings, which included bedding, and in half an hour was enough at home to dismiss the coachman and his equipage, and to lie down, as was my wont during the heat of the day. I put my bed in the doorway, and before I fell into my first sleep at Tautira, filled my eyes with the blue of the shimmering lagoon and the hoary line of the reef. I sank into dreams, with the slumbrous roar upon the coral barrier like the thunder of a sea god's rolling drum.

Chapter XXIII

My life at Tautira—The way I cook my food—Ancient Tahitian sports—Swimming and fishing—A night hunt for shrimp and eels.

T'yonni and Choti were the only aliens except myself in all Tautira, nor did others come during my stay. The steamships, spending only twenty-four hours in Papeete port every four or five weeks, sent no trippers, and the bureaucrats, traders, and sojourners in Papeete apparently were not aware of the enchantment at our end of the island. T'yonni had found Tautira only after four or five voyages to Tahiti, and Choti had first come as his guest. T'yonni had no art but that of living, while Choti had studied in Paris, and was bent on finding in these scenes something strong and uncommon in painting, as Gauguin, now dead, had found. They lived separately, T'yonni studying the language and the people,—he had been a master at a boys' school in the East,—and the artist painting many hours a day. But we three joined with the villagers in pleasure, and in pulling at the nets in the lagoon.

The routine of my day was to awake about six o'clock and see the sun swinging slowly up out of the sea and hesitating a moment on the level of the horizon, the foliage brightened with his beams. I sprang from my bed, washed my hands and face, and hastened to the *faré umu*, the kitchen in a grove of pandanus trees, a few steps away. There from a pile of cocoanut husks and bits of jetsam I selected fuel, which I placed between a group of coral rocks on which were several iron bars. I lit the fire, and put into a pot three tablespoonfuls of finely ground coffee and two cups of fresh water. The pot was a percolator, and beside it I placed a frying-pan, and in it sliced bananas and a lump of tinned butter from New Zealand. Leaving these inanimate things to react under the dissolving effect of the blaze, I ran to the beach, where I watched the sunrise. There recurred to me the mornings and evenings in the Orient when I had seen the Parsees, the fire-worshippers of India, offer their devotions, standing or kneeling on their rugs on the seashore. I, too, raised my hands in silent admiration of the mother of all life. Then I observed about me the hurry and scurry of the dwellers on the sands and in the water. Small hermit-crabs in shells many sizes too big for them toddled about, land-crabs rushed frantically and awkwardly for their holes, and Portuguese men-of-war sailed by the coast, luffing to avoid casting up on the beach. A brief period of observation, and I dashed back to the *faré umu*, and trimmed the fire. When cooked, I brought my food to my house, where I had a low table like a Japanese zen, and with rolls from the Chinese store I made my first meal, adding oranges, papayas and pineapple.

From the doorway, for all I encompassed in my view, I might have been the sole human on this island. I could look to the reef and far across the lagoon to Hitiaa or down the beach, but from that spot no other house was in sight. If I went around the house, I was almost on the Broadway of Tautira, the home of Ori-a-Ori before me, and a coral church close to it, with other buildings and groves toward the mango copse of T'yonni. On the bushes huge nets were drying, and canoes were drawn up into the *purau* and pandanus clumps. As the day advanced, the artless incidents of the settlement aroused my interest. I saw about me scenes and affairs which had caused a famous poet after a week or two in this very lieu to write:

Here found I all I had forecast:
The long roll of the sapphire sea
That keeps the land's virginity;
The stalwart giants of the wood
Laden with toys and flowers and food;
The precious forest pouring out
To compass the whole town about;
The town itself with streets of lawn,
Loved of the moon, blessed by the dawn,
Where the brown children all the day
Keep up a ceaseless noise of play,
Play in the sun, play in the rain,
Nor ever quarrel or complain;
And late at night in the woods of fruit,
Hark! do you hear the passing flute?

The school-house was near to the master's home where Choti lived, and often I heard the children learning by singsong, the way I myself had been taught the arithmetical tables. The teacher was Alfred, a Tahitian, who, being a scholar, must have a French name, and wear clothes and shoes when in his classes, but who very sensibly sat with Choti upon his veranda in only his *pareu*. Much of the time the pupils played in the grounds, hopscotch and wrestling on stilts being favorite games. Alfred regretted that the ancient Tahitian games which his grandfather played were out of style. Among these was a variation of golf, with curved sticks, and a ball made of strips of native cloth; and foot-ball with a ball of banana-leaves tightly rolled. Grown-ups in those Tahitian times were experts in all these sports, women excelling at foot-ball, with thirty on each side, and captains, backs, and guards, or similar participants, and with hard struggles for the ball, which, as the games were played on the beach, often had to be fought for in the sea. The spectators, thousands, did not view the contest from seats, but literally followed it as it surged up and down within the space of a mile.

Wrestling was the most notable amusement, and boxing was fashionable for women, some of whom were skilled in fistic combats. The wrestlers, as their Greek prototypes, first invoked the favor of the gods, and offered sacrifices when victorious. The palestra was on a lawn by the sea, and in formal contests district champions met those of other districts, and islands competed for supremacy with other islands. The *maona* wore a breech-clout and a coat of cocoanut oil freshly laid on, but not sand, as in the Olympiads. When one was thrown, the victor's friends shouted in triumph and sang and danced about him to the music of tom-toms, while the backers of the loser met the demonstrations with ridicule. This was much like the organized yelling on our gridirons; and when the wrestling began again there was instant silence. It was all good-humored, as was the boxing.

Spear-throwing and stone-slinging at targets were both fun and preparation for war, for in the battles the slingers took the van. The stones were here, as in the Marquesas, as big as hens' eggs, and rounded by the action of the streams in which they were found. Braided cocoanut-fiber formed the sling, or flax was used, and looped about the wrist the sling was flung down the back, whirled about the head, and the missile shot with deadly force and accuracy.

Archery was associated with religion in Tahiti, as in Japan, between which countries there are many strange similarities of custom. The costumes of the bowmen and their weapons were housed in the temple, and kept by devotees, and were removed and returned with ceremonies. The bows, less than six feet, the arrows, half that long, were never used in war or for striking a mark, but merely for distance shooting, and the experts were credited with reaching a thousand feet.

Tatini had pointed out to me, when we walked the peninsula of Taravao, a projecting rock, marked with deep-worn grooves, from which the Tahitians once flew very large kites. These were tied to the rocks, and the ropes of cocoanut sennit in the course of hundreds of years had worn the stones away. Often when the wind was favorable, they intrusted themselves to their kites, and slipping the ropes, flew to the opposite side of the bay, forerunners in the air of a certain Lyonnais of 1783, and contemporaneous with the Siamese who centuries ago indulged their levitative dreams by leaping with parachutes.

Alfred had registered all these obsolete things in his memory, while most Tahitians had no detailed knowledge of them, being crammed with the lore of theology, of saints, of automobiles, and moving pictures, and prize-fights for money. Matatini Afaraauia, son of Faaruia, of chiefly descent, a boy of seven, and of a guileless, bewitching disposition, made me his intimate friend, and through his sharp eyes I discovered phenomena that might have escaped my untutored mind. He lifted a stone, and beneath it was a spider larger than a tarantula. It was tabu to Tahitians, harmless, and a voracious eater of insects. Spiders are larger in these tropics than elsewhere, and here, too, the male was smaller than the female. Being seized and slain and devoured by his lady love even in the very transports of husbandly affection, it had been bitten in on his subconscious sensibilities that diminutiveness was life-saving, and natural selection had made him inferior in size to his cannibal mate. He had a very shrinking attitude in her presence, as Socrates must have affected about Xantippe.

At eleven o'clock of the forenoon I, with Matatini and Raiere, a youth of twenty, strolled down the grassy street to the garden of Alfred, where Choti might be painting under the trees, and if a halloo did not bring him bounding to us, we went on to T'yonni's, where he would surely be, either under the mango trees or in the salon. Choti had many canvases completed, some six feet long, and he also did excellent silver-point heads of the villagers. Tahitians were indifferent models, as they were not much interested in pictures, not seeing objects, as we do, and found posing irksome. Only Choti's friendship for them, his bonhomie, and many merry jokes in their tongue could keep them still for his purposes.

T'yonni's house was half a mile from my own. A quarter of a mile farther, and the same distance from the junction of lagoon and river, we had our swimming-place. On an acre or two of grass and moss, removed from any habitation, grew a score of lofty cocoas, and under these we threw off our *pareus* or trousers and shirts. The bank of the stream was a fathom from the water which was brackish at high tide and sweet at low. With a short run and a curving leap we plunged into the flowing water. It was refreshing at the hottest hour. The Tahitians seldom dived head first, as we did, but jumped feet foremost, and the women in a sitting posture, which made a great splash, but prevented their gowns from rising. As I remarked before, we three Americans bathed stark when with men, but the modest Tahitian men never for a moment uncovered themselves, but wore their *pareus*. Captain Cook said that in their houses he had not seen a single instance of immodesty, though families slept in one room. Choti avowed that he had to make love to his girl models to induce them to pose in the altogether, for money would not make them adopt the garb of Venus.

The Tahitians did not enter the sea for pleasure. The rivers and brooks were their bathing- and resting-places. They attributed sicknesses to the too frequent touch of salt water. They had not the habitute of swimming within the lagoons, as at Hawaii; it was not with them an exercise or luxury, but a part of their every-day activities in fishing and canoeing. A farmer after his day's work does not run foot-races. Yet in gatherings these people often vied for supremacy in every sort of sea sport, and beforetime, in bays free of coral, developed an astonishing skill in surf-riding on boards, in canoes, and without artificial support. Such skill was ranked on a par with or perhaps the same as proficiency in the pastimes of war, as did the Greeks, who addressed Diagoras, after he and his two sons had been crowned in the arena: "Die, for thou hast nothing short of divinity to desire." These ambitions had been ended in Tahiti by the frowns of the missionaries, to whom athletics were a species of diabolical possession, unworthy souls destined for hell or heaven, with but a brief span to avert their birthright of damnation in sackcloth and ashes.

We entered the river regularly at eleven and four, but Choti, T'yonni, and I also swam in the lagoon at the mouth of the river, and never suffered bad consequences unless we cut or scraped ourselves on coral. About noon I prepared my *déjeuner à la fourchette*, and had a wide choice of shrimp, eels, fish, taro, chicken, breadfruit, yams, and all the other fruits. The solicitude of the homesick missionaries had added to those indigenous, oranges, limes, shaddocks, citrons, tamarinds, guavas, custard apples, peaches, figs, grapes, pineapples, watermelons, pumpkins, cucumbers and cabbages. They had grown these foreign flora many years before they made sprout a single shoot of Christianity.

I invented a stove from a five-gallon oil tin. With a can-opener I cut a strip out on opposite sides ten inches from the bottom, and laid two iron bars across, and under them, inside the receptacle, built a fire. Upon this I cooked my coffee in the percolator, while upon the earth and hot stones other delicious dishes boiled, stewed, and fried. If I baked, I used the native oven in the ground, with earth and leaves inclosing.

I passed hours on the reef with Raiere and Matatini or in canoes, drawing the nets and catching shrimp and eels. In the lagoon we usually secured a plentiful draft of fish, brilliant creatures of silver and crimson, as they leaped from the sea into the nets, and were later tumbled into canoes or on the beach. The *orare, aturi,* and *paaihere* were like the gleaming mesh purses worn by the women of our cities, but the *ihi* was as red as the beard of the Greek god T'yonni. These fish we kept in tubs of sea water, alive and even moderately happy until cooked.

Saturday's parties went far into the woods to gather a choice kind of *fei*, and the oranges and limes of the foot-hills. Raiere, Matatini, and another boy, Tahitua, hunted the shrimp and eel. After our suppers, about seven or eight o'clock, when it was quite dark, we equipped ourselves for the chase, each with a torch and two or three lances, all but Tahitua, who carried a bag.

We followed the *grand chemin*, as Alfred called it, along the lagoon and past the clump of trees in which lived Uritaata, whom we saw sleeping peacefully a dozen feet from the earth in the branches of a mango. He lay on his back, with his arms above his little head, and one foot grasping a leaf, and did not arouse to notice our passing. The Tahitians gave him wide avoidance, with a mutter of exorcism. We descended the bank, and entered the stream at a point just below the last hut of the village.

Raiere cast a glow upon the water with his torch, and we saw the shrimp resting upon the bottom or leaping into the air in foot-wide bounds. He poised his smallest lance and thrust it with a very quick, but exact, motion, so that almost every time he impaled a shrimp upon its prongs. The *oura* was instantly withdrawn, and Tahitua received it in his bag. All but he then began in earnest the quest of the *bonnes bouches*. We separated a hundred feet or so, and treading slowly the pebbled or bouldered and often slippery floor of the river, keeping to the shallow places, we lighted the rippling waters with our torches, and sought to spear the agile and fearful prey. The *oura* lances were five feet long, not thicker than a fat finger, and fitted with three slender prongs of iron—nails filed upon the basalt rock. One saw the faintest glimpse of a shrimp on the bottom, or a red shadow as the animal darted past, and only the swiftest coordination of mind and body won the prize. Whereas Raiere and even Matatini secured most of those they struck at, I made many laughable failures. I missed the still body through the deceptive shadows of the water, or failed to strike home because of the lightning-like movements of the alarmed shrimp.

The sport was fascinating. The water was as warm as fresh milk, transparent, and with here a gentle and there a rapid current. A million stars glittered in a sky that was very near, and the trees and vegetation were in mysterious shadows. Only when our torches lit the darkness did we perceive the actual forms of the cocoanuts, mango- and *purau*-trees which bordered the banks and climbed the hills into the distance. The *puraus* often seemed like banians, stretching far over the water in strange and ghostlike shapes, with twisting branches and gnarled trunks that in the obscurity gave a startling suggestion of the fetish growths of the ancients. I felt a faint touch of fear as I groped through the stream, now and again falling into a deep hole or stumbling over a stone or buried branch, and I looked often to reassure myself that Raiere's gigantic figure loomed in the farther gloom. There was no danger save in me; the scene was peaceful, but for our own disturbance of the night and the river, and not even a breeze fluttered the dark leaves of the trees. The mountain rose steeply at our backs, and constellations appeared to rest upon its shadowy crest.

At last we came to a place where a tiny natural dam caused the stream to break in glints of white on a crooked line of rocks, and pausing there, Raiere suddenly bent over. He called peremptorily to Tahitua to bring him the big lance, which the little boy carried along with the bag.

"Puhi! Haere mai!" he said in a low, but urgent, voice.

Tahitua flew through the ripples, and we all hurried to see the new adventure.

"Puhi! Puhi!" again said Raiere, and pointed to the rocks. We cautiously stepped that way, and saw, apparently asleep at the foot of the stones, a tangle of huge eels. Their black and gray slate-colored bodies lay inert in folds, as if they had gathered for a night's good slumber, and not until Raiere, with unerring aim thrust the great spear, with its half-dozen points of iron, into one of them, did the others scatter in a mad swim for safety. The mere transfixing of the eel did not always mean his securing, but another of us must put a lance in the contorting curves and with quick and dexterous motion lift him to the bank where his struggles might be ended with knife or rock. The release of him for a second might permit him to wriggle to the river and escape.

With the finding of the first eel, began an hour's search for his fellows. We had struck their haunt, but they did not yield us half a dozen of their kind without diligent, though pleasant, work. We splashed to places when one sang out that an eel was in sight, and pursued them in their divagations through the river, trusting to drive them into eddies or under the fringe of plants hanging from the banks where we hunted them out.

In a couple of hours we found ourselves with a full creel of eels and *oura*, and I a trifle dismayed at facing the march home. Raiere relieved Tahitua of the burden, and a song shortened the way. I gave them the ditty of the New-Zealand Maori, who metaphorically toasted his enemy:

O, the saltiness of my mouth
In drinking the liquid brains of Nuku
Whence welled up his wrath!
His ears which heard the deliberations!
Mine enemy shall go headlong
Into the stomach of Hinewai!
My teeth shall devour Kaukau!
The three hundred and forty of my enemy
Shall be huddled in a heap in my trough;
Te Hika and his multitudes
Shall boil in my pot!
The whole tribe shall be
My sweet morsel to finish with! E!

Chapter XXIV

In the days of Captain Cook—The first Spanish missionaries—Difficulties of converting the heathens—Wars over Christianity—Ori-a-Ori, the chief, friend of Stevenson—We read the Bible together—The church and the himene.

Captain Cook barely escaped shipwreck here. The Bay of Tautira is marked on the French map, "Mouillage de Cook," the anchorage of Cook. That indomitable mariner risked his vessels in many dangerous roadsteads to explore and to procure fresh supplies for his crews. When he had exhausted the surplus of pigs, cocoanuts, fowls, and green stuff at one port, he sailed for another. Scurvy, the relentless familiar of the sailor on the deep sea, made no peril or labor too severe. At night Cook's ships approached Oati-piha, or Ohetepeha, Bay, as his log-writers termed this lagoon, from the Vaitapiha River, flowing into it, and the dawn found them in a calm a mile and a half from the reef.

They put down boats and tried to tow off their ships, but the tide set them in more and more toward the rocks. For many hours they despaired of saving the vessels, though they used "warping-machines," anchors, and kedges. From my cook-house I saw where they had struggled for their lives with breaker, current, and chartless bottom. A light breeze off the land saved them, and in another day they returned to "obtain cocoanuts, plantains, bananas, apples, yams and other roots, which were exchanged for nails and beads." From the very pool into which I dived Cook's hearties filled their casks with fresh water, after shooting "two muskets and a great gun along the shore to intimidate the Indians who were obstinate."

Cook, on his third voyage to Tahiti, found here a large wooden cross on which was inscribed in Latin:

Christ conquered
Charles the Third Emperor
1774

It was plain that Spaniards had erected the cross, for Charles III was King of Spain. These English tars hated the dons, with whom they had but recently been embattled. When they were convinced that a Spanish ship had been at Tautira twice since they had departed, and that the builders of the cross had earned the respect and affection of the natives, the Britons, in their old way of fair and assertive dealing, left the cross standing after carving on the reverse in good Latin as a claim of prediscovery:

George III King
1767, 1769, 1773, 1774, 1777.

Two Spanish priests, they learned, had lived in the village between the arrival and return of the Spanish ships from Peru. They left no imprint of their Catholic religion except the cross and a memory of kindness; and why they resigned their mission to Tahiti is not known. The British missionaries did not come until 1797, on the *Duff*. They planted gardens and worked diligently and prayed. They had vast patience, and confidence in their all-powerful and avenging God, and a rapt devotion to his son, who forgave the sins of those who adopted His faith. Their ideals were as fixed as the stars, and their courage superior to the daily discouragements of their lives and continuous hardships of separation from home. But they could not break the strength of the superstitions of the pagans. A dozen years these English ecclesiastics delved in their gardens, built their houses, and begged Jehovah and Jesus to give them victory. Five years they mourned without message or aid from England. Their clothes were in tatters, and as covering their whole bodies with European garments from feet to scalp, except face and hands, was a rigid prescription of their own morals' and an example to the almost nude Tahitians, they suffered keenly from shame. When, after half a decade, a brig arrived, its supplies were found ruined by salt water and mold. The poor clerics, in an earthly paradise, but hostile atmosphere, with little to report to an unheeding England save the depths of the untilled field of heathenry and depravity, might not have been blamed if they, too, had given up their mission. The fruits of twelve years of gardening and horticulture were destroyed in a day by ravaging parties. The fact that their lives were spared and their persons not attacked, except in a rare instance of an individual piece of villainy, is proof of the mild dispositions of the infidels. The Tahitians worshiped their gods with a superstitious awe not exceeded anywhere, and the outlandish white men proclaimed openly that these gods were dirty lumps of wood and stone and fiber, and to be despised in comparison with the Christian Gods, Father and Son, which they implored them under pain of eternal punishment to adopt. Imagine the fate of strangers who settled in New England or Spain a hundred and twenty years ago and who announced daily year in and year out that all the ancestors of the people there were in hell, that their God and their angels, saints, priests, and images were demons, or doing the work of demons, and that only by acknowledging their belief in a deity unheard-of before, by having water sprinkled on their heads, and ceasing the customs and thoughts taught as most moral and divine by their own revered priests, could they escape eternal misery as a consequence of a mistake made by a man and a woman named Atamu and Ivi six thousand years earlier! In Spain at that date the king whose name had been coupled with Christ's on the cross near my house at Tautira was expelling the Jesuits from his kingdom, and the Holy Office recorded its thirtieth thousand human being burned at the stake in that country in the name of Jesus Christ.

The incredulous Tahitians tolerated the queer white men who wore long, black coats and who had learned their language, and who, except as to religion, spoke gently to them, healed their wounds, patted their children on the head, and taught them how to use iron and wood in unknown fashions. They saw that these men drank intoxicants in great moderation, lived in amity, and did not advantage themselves in trade or with the native women, as did all the other white men. And they wondered.

But they were convinced of the truth of their own religion. Their chiefs and priests replied:

"If your first man and woman took the lizard's word and ate fruit from the tabu tree, they should have been punished, and if their children killed the son of your God, they should have been punished; but why worry us about it? We have not killed you, and our first man and woman respected all tabu trees."

They disdained the cruel message that their forefathers were in the perpetually burning *umu*, the oven, as did that Frisian king, Radbod, who with one leg in the baptismal font, bethought him to ask where were his dead progenitors, and was answered by the militant bishop, Wolfran, "In hell, with all unbelievers."

"Then will I rather feast with them in the halls of Woden than dwell with your little, starveling Christians in heaven" said the pagan, and withdrew his sanctified limb to walk to an unblessed grave in proud pantheism.

Otu, the son of King Pomaré, had a revelation that the god Oro wished to be removed to Tautira from Atehuru. The chiefs of that district protested, and Otu's followers seized the idol, and went to sea with him. They landed as soon as it was safe, and mollified the god by a sacrifice; and having no victim, they killed one of Pomaré's servants. The island then divided into hateful camps, and Moorea joined the fray. The mission sided with the king, and the crews of two English vessels fortified the mission, and with their modern weapons helped the royal party to whip the other faction. Wars followed, the mission was again invaded, the houses burned, and the missionaries, not desiring martyrdom, fled to Australia, thousands of miles away. But two remained, and kept at their preaching, and finally the genius of the Clapham clerics triumphed. Pomaré ate the tabu turtle of the temple, and a Christian nucleus was formed, headed by the sovereign. For years a bloody warfare over Christianity distracted the islands, comparable in intensity of feeling to that between Catholics and Huguenots in France. The Christian converts were slaughtered by the hundreds, and the pagans drove all the survivors to Moorea. After a season the conquerors grew lonesome, and invited them to return and abjure their false god, Ietu Kirito, whom they had defeated, and who by the Christians' own statement had been hanged on a tree by the Ati-Iuda, the tribe of Jews. Pomaré and eight hundred men landed from Moorea, and with the missionaries began a song service on the beach, and "Come, let us join our friends above," and "Blow ye the trumpets, blow!" echoed from the hills.

Couriers carried all over Tahiti word of the outrage to the gods, and the incensed heathens rose in immense numbers and attacked the hymners. Fortunately, says the missionary chronicle, the Christians had their arms with them, and after prayers and exhortations by the clergy, Pomaré led his cohorts, men and women; and by the grace of God and the whites, with a few muskets, they smote the devil-worshipers hip and thigh, and chased them to the distant valleys.

Pomaré, directed by the now militant missionaries, sent a body of gunmen to Tautira to capture the god Oro, whose principal temple was very near where stood my kitchen. The iconoclasts, with the zeal of neophytes, destroyed every vestige of the magnificent *marae*, and, unwinding the many coverings of Oro, carried to the king the huge log which had been the national god for ages. The king first used it in his cook-house as a shelf, and finally for firewood.

From then on the cross hecame the symhol of the new religion, and those who had been most faithful to the old were the strongest disciples. Until the French expelled the missionary-consul of England, Pritchard, the missionaries virtually governed Tahiti; but with the conflict of sects and the growing claims of trade, piety languished, until now church-going was become a social pastime, and of small influence upon the conduct of the Tahitians. The pastors were no longer of the type of the pioneers, and with the fast decrease of the race, the Tahitians were left largely to their own devices. Half a dozen religions supported ministers from America and Europe in Papeete; but there was no longer a fire of proselytizing, as all were nominally Christians. In Tautira everybody went to the Protestant or the Catholic church, the latter having a fifth as many attendants as the former. A reason for this may have been that there was no French priest resident at Tautira, and no Tahitian priests, whereas Tahitian preachers abound. Also the chiefs were Protestants, and their influence notable.

Ori-a-Ori, though busied in his official duties, and by nature a silent man, assumed of me a care, and in time gave me a friendship beyond my possible return to him. I sent to Papeete for a variety of edibles from the stores of the New-Zealand and German merchants, and spread a gay table, to which I often invited Choti and T'yonni, who were my hosts as frequently. Ori-a-Ori every evening sat with me, and numbers of times we read the Bible, I, first, reciting the verse in French, and he following in Tahitian. His greatest liking was for the chapters in which the Saviour's life on the seaside with the fishermen was described, but the beatitudes brought out to the fullest his deep, melancholy voice, as by the light of the lamp upon the low table the chief intoned the thrilling gospel of humility and unselfishness.

Never before had I appreciated so well the divine character of Jesus or conjectured so clearly the scenes of his teaching upon the shores of the Lake of Galilee. Excepting the tropical plants and the eternal accent of the reef, the old Tahitian and I might have been in Palestine with Peter and the sons of Zebedee and the disciples. They were people of slender worldly knowledge, the carpenter's son knew nothing of history, and ate with his fingers, as did Ori-a-Ori; but their open eyes, unclouded by sophistication and complex interests, looked at the universe and saw God. They lived mostly under the open sky in touch with nature, dependent on its manifestations immediately about them for their sustenance, and with its gifts and curses for their concerns and symbols.

Occidentals, who seldom muse, to whom contemplation is waste of time, do not enjoy the oneness with nature shared by these Polynesians with the sacred Commoner whose beatitudes were to bring anarchy upon the Roman world, and destroy the effects of the philosophies of the ablest minds of Greece. The fishermen of Samaria were gay and somber by turn, as were the Tahitians, doing little work, but much thinking, and innocent and ignorant of the perplexing problems and offensive indecencies of striving and luxury. The air and light nurtured them, and they confidently leaned upon the hand of God to guide and preserve.

Thoreau's "Cry of the Human" echoed in the dark as the chief and I chanted the idealistic desires of the friend of man:

We talk of civilizing the Indian, but that is not the name for his improvement. By the wary independence and aloofness of his dim forest life he preserves his intercourse with his native gods and is admitted from time to time to a rare and peculiar society with nature. He has glances of starry recognition to which our salons are strangers. The steady illumination of his genius, dim only because distant, is like the faint but satisfying light of the stars compared with the dazzling and shortlived blaze of candles.

One evening when we had walked down to the beach to gaze at the heavens and to speculate on the inhabitants of the planets, we sat on our haunches, our feet lapped by the warm tide, and for the first time I drew our conversation to a man who in a brief friendship had won the deep affection of this noble islander.

"Ori-a-Ori," I began, "in America, in the city where I lived, my house was near a small *aua*, a park in which was a *tii*, a monument, to a great writer, a teller of tales on paper. On a tall block of stone is a ship of gold, with the sails spread; so she seems to be sailing over the ocean. The friends of the teller of tales built this in in his honor after he died. Now that writer was once here in Tautira—"

Ori-a-Ori leaned toward me, and in a voice laden with memories, a voice that harked back over a quarter of a century, said slowly and meditatively, but with surety:

"Rui? Is the ship the *Tatto*?"

I had awakened in his mind recollections, doubtless often stirred, but very vague, perhaps, almost mythical to him, after so long a time in which nothing like the same experience had come to him. Yet that they were dear to him was evident. They were concerned with his vigorous manhood, though he was a youthful grandfather when the *Casco* brought Robert Louis Stevenson to Tahiti to live in the house of Ori. I reminded him of their exchanging names in blood brothership, so that Stevenson was Teriitera, and Ori was Rui. Rui was his pronunciation of Louis, as all his family in Tautira called the Scotch author. Ori-a-Ori had known them all, his mother, his wife, and his loved stepson, Lloyd Osborne. Nine weeks they had stayed in his house, which the Princess Moë, Pomaré's sister-in-law, had asked Ori to vacate for the visitors before he knew them, but which he was glad he had done when they became friends. Ori and his family had retained only one room for their intimate effects, and had slept in a native house on the site of my own. On the wild lawn across the road, before his home, Rui had given his generous feast, costing him eighty dollars at a time when he was most uncertain of funds, and gaining him the reputation of the richest man known to the Tautirans, the owner of the Silver Ship, as the *Casco* was called by the Paumotuans, and by Stevenson afterward. There were four or five Tahitians I knew here who remembered the *amuraa maa* of the sick man, who had his own schooner, his *pahi tira piti*; but only Ori retained the deep, though misty, impression made by a meeting of hearts in warmest kinship.

"Rui gave me knives and forks and dishes from the schooner to remember him by," said the chief, abstractedly. "Tati, my relation, has them. I have not those presents Rui handed me. Tati said that I ate with my fingers, and that he was the head of the Teva clan; so I gave them to him. Many *papaa* visit

Tati at Papara. He is rich. *Aue!* I have not the presents Rui put down on my table."

I said over for him what Rui had written:

I love the Polynesian; this civilization of ours is a dingy, ungentlemanly business; it drops out too much of man, and too much of that the very beauty of the poor beast ... if you could live, the only white folk, in a Polynesian village, and drink that warm, light *vin du pays* of human affection, and enjoy that simple dignity of all about you....

Paiere, the adopted son of Ori, who was a boy when the *Casco* was at Tautira, claimed a vivid remembrance of many incidents. He especially had been impressed by the numbers of corks that flew in the house and on the green; and when I invited him to a bottle of champagne, he made hissing sounds and a plop to indicate that Rui had a penchant for that kind of wine.

"I used to fetch him oranges and mangoes, and climb for drinking nuts, of which Rui was fond," said Paiere.

Paiere was a deacon or functionary of the Protestant church, as was Ori-a-Ori, and I went with the entire family to the Sunday evening service. For weeks preparations and rehearsals for a *himene nui*, a mammoth song service, had been agitating the village. Under my trees the children gathered of late afternoons and imitated the grown-up folk in their melodies. From the verandas and from the church at night issued the peculiar strain of the *himene*, somehow bringing to me, lying on my mat under the stars, a sense of fitness to the prospect—the clear heavens, the purple lagoon, the wind in the groves, and the low rumble of the surf.

On the Sunday of the *himene nui*, I met the French priest as he tied his horse by the door of the Catholic church. He was in a dark cassock or gown, his long, black beard and a flat, half-melon shaped hat giving him a distinctive appearance in the simple settlement. He was old, and weary from his hot ride, but courteous as world-wide travelers are, and at his request I dropped in on his service before the other. He sat by the middle door, and the twenty or thirty of the congregation on the floor at one end. They sang a *himene*, and he followed and corrected them from a book, so that their method was formal. Congregational singing not being customary in Catholic churches, it was probable that in Tahiti they had had to meet the competition of the Protestants, who from their beginnings in Polynesia had made a master stroke by developing this form of worship in extraordinary consonance with the native mind.

The Protestant temple held a hundred and fifty people. It was a plain hall, with doors opposite each other in the middle, and at one end a slightly raised platform on which sat the pastor and half a dozen deacons. The pastor was delivering his sermon as I entered, he and all his entourage in black Prince-Albert coats. He had a white shirt and collar and tie, but others masked a *pareu* under the wool, and were barelegged. All wore solemn faces of a jury bringing in a death-verdict. Paiere nodded to a volunteer janitor, who insisted upon my occupying a chair he brought.

Every one else was on the floor on mats, in two squares or separate divisions. Babies lay at their mothers' extended feet, and others ran about the room in silence. The pastor's sermon was about Ioba and his *tefa pua*, which he scraped with *poa*, the shells of the beach. He pictured the man of patience as if in Tautira, with his three faithless friends, Elifazi, Bilidadi, and Tofari, urging him to deny God and to sin; and the speaker struck the railing with his fist when he enumerated the possessions taken from Ioba by God, but returned a hundredfold. After he had finished, wiping the sweat from his brow with a colored kerchief, the *himene* began.

The only advance we have made since the Greeks is, in music. Possibly in painting we have better mediums; but in philosophy, poetry, sculpture, decency, beauty, we have not risen. We cure diseases more skilfully, but we have more; in health we are crippled by our cities and our customs. Our violins and pianos, our orchestras, and symphonies, are our great achievements; but in these South Seas, where they do not count, the people had evolved a mass utterance of canticles more thrilling and, more enjoyable than the oratorios of Europe. In these *himenes* one may see transfigured for moments the soul of the Polynesian ascending above the dust of the west, which smothers his articulation.

A woman in the center of a row suddenly struck a high note, beginning a few words from a hymn, or an improvisation. She sang through a phrase, and then others joined in, singly or in pairs or in tens, without any apparent rule except close harmony. These voices burst in from any point, a perfect glee chorus, some high, some low, some singing words, and others merely humming resonantly, a deep, booming bass. The surf beating on the reef, the wind in the cocoanut-trees, entered into the volume of sound, and were mingled in the *emmeleia*, a resulting magnificence of accord that reminded me curiously of a great pipe-organ.

The *himene* was the offspring of the original efforts of the Polynesians to adapt the songs of the sailormen, the national airs of the adventurers of many countries, the rollicking obscenities and drinking doggerel of the navies, and the religious hymns drilled into their ears by the missionaries, English and French. Now the words and the meanings were inextricably confused. A leader might begin with, "I am washed in the blood of the Lamb," or, "The Son of Man goes forth to war, a golden crown to gain; His blood-red banner streams afar—who follows in his train?" But those striking in might prefer such a phrase as, "The old white pig ran into the sea," or, "Johnny Brown, I love your daughter," or something not possible to write down. It was mostly in the old Tahitian language, almost forgotten, and thus unknown to the foreign preachers. Sex and religion were as mingled here as in America.

The airs were as wild as they were melodious; here a rippling torrent of *ra, ra, ra-ra-ra*, and *la, la, la-la-la* breaking in on the sustained verses of the leaders; falsetto notes, high and strident, savage and shrilling, piercing the thrumming diapason of the men; long, droning tones like bagpipes, bubbling sounds like water flowing; and all in perfect time. The clear, fascinating false soprano of the woman leader had a cadence of ecstasy, and I marked her under a lamp. Her head was thrown back, her eyes were closed, and her features set as in a trance. Her throat and mouth moved, and her nostrils quivered, her countenance glorified by her visions which had transported her to the bosom of Abraham.

The atmosphere rang as with the chimes of a cathedral, the echoes—there were none in reality—returning from roof and tree, and I had the feeling of the air being made up of voices, and of whirling in this magic ether. The woman I observed would seem about to stop, her voice falling away almost to no sound, and the prolonged drone of the chorus dying out, when, as if she had come to life again, she sang out at the top of her lungs, and the ranks again took up their tones. I could almost trace the imposition of the religious strain upon the savage, the Christian upon the heathen, like the negro spirituals of Georgia, and I sat back in my chair, and forgot the scene in the thoughts induced by the *himene*.

The souls of the Tahitians were not much changed by all their outward transformation. Superficial, indeed, are the accomplishments of missionaries, merchants, and masters among these Maoris. The old guard dies, but never surrenders; the boast of Napoleon's soldiers might be paraphrased by the voice of the Maori spirit. Our philosophy, our catechisms, and our rules have not uprooted the convictions and thought methods of centuries. Bewildered by our ambitions, fashions, and inventions, they emulate us feebly, but in their heart of hearts think us mad. Old chiefs and chiefesses I have had confess to me that they were stunned by the novelties, commands, and demands of the *papaa* (foreigner), but that their confusion was not liking or belief. In his youth, in the midst of these bustling whites, the Tahitian imitates them and feels sometimes humiliated that he is not one of them. But in sober middle age all these new desires begin to leave him, and he becomes a Maori again. The older he grows, the less attractive seem the white man's ways and ambitions, though pride, habit, and perhaps an acquired fear of the hell painted by priests and preachers from the distant lands keep him church-going. Gods may differ, but devils never.

Choti and T'yonni and I spent an hour at my house before they walked home to bed, and Choti read as a soporific, with a few bottles of Munich beer, the "Sermon to the Fishes" of St. Antonius. As he read, we heard the joyous stridence of an accordion in a *hula* harmony. The *upaupahura* was beginning in the grove where Uritaata lived. The austere St. Antonius had lectured long to the eels on the folly of wiggling, to the pikes on the immorality of stealing, and to the crabs and turtles on the danger of sloth. But:

"The sermon now ended,
Each turned and descended;
The pikes went on stealing,
The eels went on eeling;
Much edified were they,
But preferred the old way.

"The crabs are back-sliders,
The stock-fish thick-siders,
The carps are sharp-set,
All the sermon forget;
Much delighted were they,
But preferred the old way."

Chapter XXV

I meet a sorcerer—Power over fire—The mystery of the fiery furnace—The scene in the forest—Walking over the white hot stones—Origin of the rite.

Walking to the neighboring district of Pueu with Raiere to see the beauties of the shore, we met a cart coming toward Tautira, and one of the two natives in it attracted my interest. He was very tall and broad and proud of carriage, old, but still unbroken in form or feature, and with a look of unconformity that marked him for a rebel. Against what? I wondered. Walt Whitman had that look, and so had Lincoln; and Thomas Paine, who more than any Englishman aided the American Revolution. Mysticism was in this man's eyes, which did not gaze at the things about him, but were blinds to a secret soul.

Raiere exchanged a few words with the driver of the cart, and as they continued on toward Tautira, he said to me in a very serious voice:

"He is a *tahua*, a sorcerer, who will enact the *Umuti*, the walking over the fiery oven. He is from Raiatea and very noted. Ten years ago, Papa Ita of Raiatea was here, but there has been no Umuti since."

"What brings him here now?" I asked. "Who pays him?"

Raiere answered quickly:

"*Aue*! he does not ask for money, but he must live, and we all will give a little. It is good to see the *Umuti* again."

"But, Raiere, my friend," I protested, "you are a Christian, and only a day ago ate the breadfruit at the communion service. Fire-walking is *etené*; it is a heathen rite."

"*Aita!*" replied the youth. "No, it is in the Bible, and was taught by Te Atua, the great God. The three boys in Babulonia were saved from death by Atua teaching them the way of the Umuti."

"Where will the Umuti be?" I inquired. "I must see it."

"By the old *tii* up the Aataroa valley, on Saturday night."

That was five days off, and it could not come soon enough for me. I was eager for this strangest, most inexplicable survival of ancient magic, the apparent only failure of the natural law that fire will burn human flesh. I had seen it in Hawaii and in other countries, and had not reached any satisfying explanation of its seeming reversal of all other experience. I knew that fire-walking as a part of the racial or national worship of a god of fire, had existed and persisted in many far separated parts of the world.

Babylon, Egypt, India, Malaysia, North America, Japan, and scattered Maoris from Hawaii to New Zealand all had religious ceremonies in which the gaining and showing of power over fire was a miracle seen and believed in by priests and laity. Modern saints and quasi-scientists had claims to similar achievements. Dr. Dozous said he saw Bernadette, the seeress of Lourdes, hold her hands in a flame for fifteen minutes without pain or mark, he timing the incident exactly by his watch. Daniel Dunglas Home, the famous Scottish spiritist, was certified by Sir William Crookes and Andrew Lang to handle red-hot coals in his hands, and could convey to others the same immunity. Lang tells of a friend of his, a clergyman, whose hand was badly blistered by a coal Home put in his palm, Home attributing the accident to the churchman's unbelieving state of mind. Crookes, the distinguished physicist, took into his laboratory handkerchiefs in which Home had wrapped live coals, and found them "unburned, unscorched, and not prepared to resist fire."

The scene of the Umuti was an hour's walk up the glen of Aataroa, which began at our swimming-place. On Thursday Choti, T'yonni, and I accompanied Raiere to the place of the *tii*, where the preparations for the sorcery were beginning. We went through a continuous forest of many kinds of trees, a vast, climbing coppice, in which all the riches of the Tahitian earth were mingled with growths from abroad. Oranges and lemons, which had sprung decades before from seeds strewn carelessly, had become giant trees of their kinds; and the lianas and parasites, guava, *lantana*, and a hundred species of ferns and orchids, with myriad mosses, covered every foot of soil, or stretched upon the trunks and limbs, so that exquisite tapestries garlanded the trees and hung like green and gold draperies between them. *Mapé*-trees prevailed, immense, weirdly shaped, often appalling in their curious buttresses, their limbs writhing as if in torture, suggestive of the old fetishism that had endowed them with spirits which suffered and spoke. Utterly uninhabited or forsaken, there was a bare trail through this wood, which, led by Raiere, we followed, wading the Aataroa River twice, and I arriving with my mind deeply impressed by the esoteric suggestiveness of the scene.

On a level spot, under five ponderous *mapé*-trees, eight or ten men of Tautira and of Pueu and Afaahiti were completing the oven. They had dug a pit twenty-five feet long, eighteen wide, and five deep, with straight sides. It had been done with exactitude at the direction of the *tahua*, who was staying alone in a hut near by. The earth from the pit formed a rampart about it, but was leveled to not more than a foot's height. At the bottom of the *umu* had been laid fagots of *purau-* and guava-wood, and on them huge trunks of the tropical chestnut, the mapé. On the trunks were laid basaltic rocks, or lumps of lava, boulders, and the stones about, as big as a man's head. The oven was completed for the lighting.

To the north stood a giant phallus of stone, buried in the earth, but protruding six feet, and inclined toward the north. It was a foot in diameter, and was carved *au naturel* as the Maori *lingam* and *yoni* throughout Polynesia, and in India, where doubtless the cult originated. Before the break-down of their culture, this stone had been sprinkled with water, or anointed with cocoanut-oil, and covered with a black cloth, as in Hawaii. The Greeks called their similar god, Priapus, the Black-Cloaked.

A trench had been made on the west side of the pit from which to ignite the fuel, a torch lit by fire struck from wood by friction. I did not see the lighting, which occurred Friday morning, thirty-six hours before the ceremony. The ordinance was set for eight o'clock. I swam in the river at five on Saturday, and lay down in my bird cage to be thoroughly rested for the night. It was not easy to fall asleep. There was a thicket of pandanus near my house, the many legs of the curious trees set in the sand of the upper beach, and these trees were favorite resort of the *mina* birds, which were as familiar with me as children of a family, and in many cases impudent beyond belief. They were the size of crows, and had bronzed wings, lined with white; but their most conspicuous color was a flaring yellow, which dyed their feet and their beaks and encircled their bold eyes like canary-colored rims of spectacles. Their usual voice was a hoarse croak that a raven might disavow, but they also emitted a disturbing rattle and a whistle, according to their moods. They were thieves, as I have said, but one was more audacious than the others. He would come into my open house at daybreak, and perch on my body, and awaken me pecking at imaginary ticks. He picked up a small compass by its chain and flew away with it.

This particular wretch had learned to speak a little, and would say, "Ia ora na oe!" sharply, but with a decided grackle accent. Despite the irritating cacophony of the *mina*, I must have slept more than an hour; for when I was suddenly awakened, the sun was almost lost behind the hills. The talking *mina* was dancing on my bare stomach and calling out his human vocabulary.

I sprang up, my tormentor uttering a raucous screech as I tossed him away. While I hastily cooked my supper, the colors of the hiding sun spread over the sky in entrancing variety. I could not see the west, but to the northeast were rifts of blood-red clouds edged with gold over a lake of pearly hue, and to the right of it a bank of smoke. Against this was a single cocoa on the edge of the promontory, a banner my eye always sought as the day ended. Rising a hundred feet or more, the curving staff upheld a dozen dark fronds, which nodded in the evening breeze.

There was the slightest chill in the air, unusual there, so that I put on shirt and trousers of thin silk and tennis shoes for my walk, and with a lantern set out for the *tii*. Along the road were my neighbors, the whole village streaming toward the goblin wood. Mahine and Maraa, two girls of my acquaintance, unmarried and the merriest in Tautira, joined me. They adorned me with a wreath of ferns and luminous, flower-shaped fungus from the trees, living plants, the *taria iore*, or rat's-ear, which shone like haloes above our faces. The girls wore pink gowns, which they pulled to their waists as we forded the streams. Mahine had a mouth-organ on which she played. We sang and danced, and the tossing torches stirred the shadows of the black wold, and brought out in shifting glimpses the ominous shapes of the monstrous trees. With all our gaiety, I had only to utter a loud "*Aue!*" and the natives rushed together for protection against the unseen; not of the physical, but of the dark abode of Po. In this lonely wilderness they thought that *tupapaus*, the ghosts of the departed, must have their assembly, and deep in their hearts was a deadly fear of these revenants.

When we approached the *umu*, I felt the heat fifty feet away. The pit was a mass of glowing stones, and half a dozen men whom I knew were spreading them as evenly as possible, turning them with long poles. Each, as it was moved, disclosed its lower surface crimson red and turning white. The flames leaped up from the wood between the stones.

About the oven, forty feet away, the people of the villages who had gathered, stood or squatted, and solemnly awaited the ritual. The *tahua*, Tufetufetu, was still in a tiny hut that had been erected for him, and at prayer. A deacon of the church went to him, and informed him that the *umu* was ready, and he came slowly toward us. He wore a white *pareu* of the ancient tapa, and a white *tiputa*, a poncho of the same beaten-bark fabrics. His head was crowned with *ti*-leaves, and in his hand he had a wand of the same. He was in the dim light a vision of the necromancer of medieval books.

He halted three steps from the fiery furnace, and chanted in Tahitian:

O spirits who put fire in the oven, slack the fire!
O worm of black earth,
O worm of bright earth, fresh water, sea water, heat of the oven, red of the oven, support the feet of the walkers, and fan away the fire!
O Cold Beings, let us pass over the middle of the oven!
O Great Woman, who puts the fire in the heavens, hold still the leaf that fans the fire!
Let thy children go on the oven for a little while!
Mother of the first footstep!
Mother of the second footstep!

Mother of the third footstep!
Mother of the fourth footstep!
Mother of the fifth footstep!
Mother of the sixth footstep!
Mother of the seventh footstep!
Mother of the eighth footstep!
Mother of the ninth footstep!
Mother of the tenth footstep!
O Great Woman, who puts the fire in the heavens, all is hidden!

Then, his body erect, his eyes toward the stars, augustly, and without hesitation or choice of footprints, the *tahu* walked upon the *umu*. His body was naked except for the *tapa*, which extended from his shoulders to his knees. The heat radiated from the stones, and sitting on the ground I saw the quivering of the beams just above the oven.

Tufetufetu traversed the entire length of the *umu* with no single flinching of his muscles or flutter of his eyelids to betray pain or fear. He raised his wand when he reached the end, and, turning slowly, retraced his steps.

The spectators, who had held their breaths, heaved deep sighs, but no word was spoken as the *tahua* signed all to follow him in another journey over the white-hot rocks. All but a few, their number obscured in the darkness, ranged themselves in a line behind him, and with masses of *ti*-leaves in their hands, and some with girdles hastily made, barefooted they marched over the path he took again. When the cortège had passed once, the priest said, "*Fariu!* Return!" and, their eyes fixed on vacancy, six times the throng were led by him forward and back over the *umu*. A woman who looked down and stumbled, left the ranks, and cried out that her leg was burned. She had an injury that was weeks in curing.

At a sign from Tufetufetu, the people left the proximity of the pit, and while he retired to his hut, several men threw split trunks of banana-trees on the stones. A dense column of white smoke arose, and its acrid odor closed my eyes for a moment. When I opened them, my friends of our village were placing the prepared carcasses of pigs on the banana-trunks, with yams, *ti*-roots and *taro*. All these were covered with hibiscus and breadfruit leaves and the earth of the rampart, which was heaped on to retain the heat, and steam the meat and vegetables.

I examined the feet and legs of Raiere and the two girls I had come with, and even the delicate hairs of their calves had not been singed by their fiery promenade.

Meanwhile all disposed themselves at ease. The solemnity of the *Umuti* fell from them. Accordions, mouth-organs, and jews'-harps began to play, and fragments of chants and *himenes* to sound. Laughter and banter filled the forest as they squatted or lay down to wait for the feast. I did not stay. The *Umuti* had put me out of humor for fun and food. I lit my flambeau and plodded through the *mapé*-wood in a brown study, in my ears the fading strains of the *arearea*, and in my brain a feeling of oneness with the eerie presences of the silent wilderness. I was with Meshack, Shadrach, and Abednego in their glorious trial in Nebuchadnezzar's barbaric court. I was among the tepees of the Red Indians of North America when they leaped unscathed through the roaring blaze of the sacred fire, and trod the burning stones and embers in their dances before the Great Spirit.

The *Umuti* was not all new to me. Long ago, when I lived in Hawaii, Papa Ita had come there from Tahiti. His *umu* was in the devastated area of Chinatown, a district of Honolulu destroyed by a conflagration purposely begun to erase two blocks of houses in which bubonic plague recurred, and which, unchecked, caused a loss of millions of dollars.

The pit was elliptical, nine feet deep, and about twenty-four feet long. Wood was piled in it, and rocks from the dismantled Kaumakapili church. The fire burned until the stones became red and then white, and they, too, were turned with long poles to make the heat even. I inspected the heating process several times. At the hour advertised in the American and native papers, in an enclosure built for the occasion, with seats about the pit, the mystery was enacted. The setting was superb, the flaming furnace of heathenism in the shadow of the lonely ruin of the Christian edifice. Papa Ita appeared garbed in white *tapa*, with a wonderful head-dress of the sacred *ti*-leaves and a belt of the same. The spectators were of all nations, including many Hawaiians. The deposed queen, Liliuokalani, was a most interested witness.

Papa Ita looked neither to the right nor left, but striking the ground thrice with a wand of *ti*, he raised his voice in invocation and walked upon the stones. He reached the other end, paused and returned. Several times he did this and when photographers rushed to make a picture, he posed calmly in the center of the pit, and then, with all the air of a priest who has celebrated a rite of approved merit, he retired with dignity. As he departed from the inclosure, the natives crowded about him, fearfully, as viewed the Israelites the safety of Daniel emerging from the lions' den. Did I not see the former queen lift the hem of his *tapa* and bow over it? It was night, the lights sputtered, and I was awed by the success of the incantation. A minute after Papa Ita had gone, I threw a newspaper upon the path he had trod, and it withered into ashes. The heat seared my face. The doctors, five or six of them, Americans and English, resident in Honolulu, shrugged their shoulders. They had examined Papa Ita's feet before the ceremony and afterward. The flesh was not burned, but, well—What? I confess I do not know. A thermometer held over the *umu* of Papa Ita at a height of six feet registered 282 degrees Fahrenheit.

There could be no negation of the extreme heat of the oven of Tufetufetu. I had tested it for myself. No precaution was taken by the walkers. I knew most of them intimately. There was no fraud, no ointment or oil or other application to the feet, and all had not the same thickness of sole. At Raratonga, near Tahiti, the British resident, Colonel Gudgeon, and three other Englishmen had followed the *tahua* as my neighbors had here. The official said that though his feet were tender, his own sensations were of light electric shocks at the moment and afterward. Dr. William Craig, who disobeyed the *tahua* and looked behind, was badly burned, and was an invalid for a long time, though Dr. George Craig and Mr. Goodwin met with no harm. The resident half an hour after his passage tossed a branch on the stones, and it caught fire. In Fiji, Lady Thurston with a long stick laid her handkerchief on the shoulder of one of the walkers, and when withdrawn in a few seconds it was scorched through. A cloth thrown on the stones was burned before the last man had gone by.

What was the secret of the miracle I had witnessed? How was it that in all the Orient, and formerly in America, this power over fire was known and practised, and that it was interwoven with the strongest and oldest emotions of the races? That from the Chaldea of millenniums ago to the Tautira of to-day, the ceremonial was virtually the same? Our own boys and girls who in the fall leaped over the bonfire of burning leaves were unpremeditatedly imitating in a playful manner and with risk what their forefathers had done religiously.

In Raiatea, the chief Tetuanui informed me, the membership of the Protestant church of Uturoa walked on the *umu*, and embarrassed the missionaries, who had taught them, as the Tautirans were taught, that the *Umuti* was a pagan sacrament.

In some islands it was called *vilavilairevo*, and in Fiji the oven was *lovu*. According to legend, the people of Sawau, Fiji, were drawn together to hear their history chanted by the *orero*, when he demanded presents from all. Each, in the brave way of Viti, tried to outdo the other in generosity, and Tui N'Kualita promised an eel that he had seen at Na Moliwai. Dredre, the *orero*, said he was satisfied, and began his tale. It was midnight when he finished. He looked for his present at an early hour next morning.

Tui N'Kualita had gone to Na Moliwai to hunt for the eel, and there, as he sank his arms in the eel's hole, he found it a piece of *tapa* that he knew to be the dress of a child. Tui N'Kualita shouted:

"Ah! Ah! this must be the cave of children. But that doesn't matter to me. Child, god, or new kind of man, I'll make you my gift."

He kept on angling with his hand in the hole, and caught hold of a man's hand. The man leaped back and broke his grasp, and cried:

"Tui N'Kualita, spare my life and I will be your wargod. My name is Tui Namoliwai."

Tui N'Kualita answered him:

"I am of a valiant people, and I vanquish all my enemies. I have no need of you."

The man in the eel's hole called out to him again:

"Let me be your god of property."

"No," said Tui N'Kualita; "the tapa I got from the god Kadavu is good enough."

"Well, then, let me be your god of navigation."

"I'm a farmer. Breadfruit is enough for me."

"Let me be your god of love, and you will enjoy all the women of Bega."

"No, I've got enough women. I'm not a big chief. I'll tell you: you be my gift to the *orero*."

"Very well; and let me have another word. When you have a lot of *ti* at Sawau, we will go to cook it, and will appear safe and sound."

Next morning Tui N'Kualita built a big oven. Tui Namoliwai appeared and signed to him to follow.

"Maybe you are fooling me, and will kill me," said Tui N'Kualita.

"What? Am I going to give you death in exchange for my life? Come!"

Tui N'Kualita obeyed, and walked on the *lovu*. The stones were cool under his feet. He told Tui Namoliwai then that he was free to go, and the latter promised him that he and his descendants should always march upon the *lovu* with impunity.

When I returned to my bird cage at Tautira, I sat down and considered at length all these facts and fancies. I believed in an all inclusive nature; that the Will or Rule of God which made a star hundreds of millions of times larger than the planet I had my body on, that took care of billions of suns, worlds, planets, comets, and the beings upon them, was not concerned in tricks of spiritism or materializations at the whim of mediums or *tahuas*. But I had in my travels in many countries seen inscrutable facts, and to me this was one.

Nobody knew what was the cause of the inaction of the fire in the *lovu* or *umu*. It was not a secret held by anybody, or a deception.

One might believe that the stones arrive at a condition of heat which the experienced sorcerers know to be harmless. One might conceive that the emotion of the walkers produces a perspiration sufficient to prevent injury during the brief time of exposure; or that the sweat and oily secretions of the skin aided by dust picked up during the journey on the oven was a shield; or that the walkers were hypnotized by the *tahua*, or exalted by their daring experiment, so that they did not feel the heat. Even this theory might not account for the failure to find the faintest burn or scorch upon those who fulfilled the injunction of the sorcerers.

The people of Tautira, from Ori-a-Ori to Matatini, had the fullest confidence that Tufetufetu had shown them a miracle, and that it was not evil; but to the American and European missionaries the *Umuti* was deviltry, the magic of Simon Magus and his successors, This was shown clearly in the statement of Deacon Taumihau of Raiatea, which I give in Tahitian and English:

E parau teie te umu a Tupua.

Teie te huru a taua ohipa ra.

Tapuhia te vahie e toru etaeta i te aano. E fatahia taua umu ra i te mahana matamua e faautahia i te ofai inia iho i taua umu ra, eiaha ra te ofai no pia iho i te marae, no te mea te marae ra te faaea raa no te varua ino oia te arii no te po.

E i te po matamua no taua umu ra e haere te mau tahua ora no te ao nei oia Tupua e te mau pipi i Pihaiho i taua umu r ae hio te mau varua taata no te po e haere ratou inia iho taavari ai; ia ore i puai te auahi.

E ei taua po ra, e haere ai hoe taata e hio i te rau Ti, ia i te oia i te rau Ti i te hauti raa mai te hauti ie te matai rahi ra, te o reira te raoere Ti e ofati mai, e tau mau rauti ra te afai hia i te mahana e haere ai te taata na roto i taua umu ra e i te hora maha i te popoi na e tutui hia'i taua umu ra.

Ia ama taua umu ra, e ia puai roa te ama raa ei reira te tahua parau.

Atu ai i te taata pihei te umu, ia oti taua umu ra i te pihei, haere aturaa tupua i te hiti o te umu a parau tana a haere ai i reira.

Teie tana parau: E na taata e tia i te hiti ote umu nei, pirae uri e pirae tea. E tu'u atu i te nu'u Atua ia haere i te umu.

Ei reira Tupua parau ai: E te pape e a haere! E te miti e a haere!

Tairi hia'tura te rauti i te hiti o te umu raparau faahou, atura te tahua. Te Vahine tahura'i e po'ia te tu'u raa ia o te avae iroto i te umu, ei reira toa te mau taata i hinaaro i te haere na roto i te umu ra e haere. Ai na muri iho eiaha ra te hoe taata e fariu imuri; te taata hopea ra e tuo i te tahua e fariu; na fariu ia, mai te mea e tuo te taata i ropu e fariu, tau roa te taata i ropu e fariu, pau roa te taata i te auahi; na reira toa ia haere no te aano o te umu.

Te i te huru o taua ohipa ra, e ohipa tiaporo te tumu ia i taua ohipa a Tupua ra.

E vahine varua ino teie tona ioa o te Vahine tahura'i. O pirae uri, o pirae tea, i ore ratou ia parau hia.

Aita e faufaa i taua ohipa ra. Eiaha Roa'tu orua a rave i taua ohipa ra i te fenua Papa'a na e ama te taata i te anahi, no te mea e ere i te ohipa mau, e ohipa varua ino no te po te reira te huru o taua ohipa a Tupua ra.

Tereira te mau havi rii i roa'a mai ia'u no tau a ohipa ra. Tirara.

Taumihau tane.

This is the word of the oven of Tupua.

This is the way he did that thing. He cut three fathoms of wood. The oven was three fathoms long and three wide. Heap up the wood the first day, and carry by sea the stones for the oven.

Do not take the stones of the marae, for the marae receives the evil spirits, the spirit of the god of the night.

The first night of the ceremony, the sorcerers of Raiatea, Tupua and his kind, march around the oven. They seek the spirits of the men of the night, and they go about the oven, but they do not light the fire.

That same night one goes to find the sacred leaves of the ti. He takes the leaves that float in the wind; those called raoere ti, and which are used as medicine. He gathers the leaves and carries them to the oven.

The fire is lighted at four of the morning. When the fire is burning brightly, and the oven is very hot, the sorcerer gives his assistants charge of the fire, and instructs them as to their duties.

When the flames are down, Tupua approached the oven, and before walking upon it, he pronounced the following prayer.

"O men about the oven! Piraeuri and Piraetea! Let us join the army of the gods in the furnace!"

Then, said Tupua:

"O water, go in the fire! O sea water, go in the fire!"

Waving the ti leaves on the border of the oven, Tupua said:

"O Woman who puts the fire in the heaven and in the clouds, permit us to go on foot over the oven!"

Then those who wish to, pass onto the oven, one after another. If but one falls all will be burned. The last must watch the sorcerer, to return when he makes the sign.

That is the way this deed, the deed of the devil, is done by Tupua.

The woman called Vahine tahura'i is an evil spirit.

Concerning Piraeuri and Piritea, Tupua would better not have spoken, as it was a useless prayer.

Do not introduce the sorcery in the land of the whites!

Do not carry there this custom of lighting the oven!

It is the work of an evil spirit of the night; this act of Tupua.

For that reason I have said little of him in my story. I have spoken.

—Taumihau, The Man.

Chapter XXVI

Farewell to Tautira—My good-bye feast—Back at the Tiare—A talk with Lovaina—The Cercle Bougainville—Death of David—My visit to the cemetery—Off for the Marquesas.

The smell of the burning wood of the *Umuti* was hardly out of my nostrils before my day of leaving Tautira came. I had long wanted to visit the Marquesas Islands, and the first communication I had from Papeete in nearly three months was from the owners of the schooner *Fetia Taiao*, notifying me that that vessel, commanded by Captain William Pincher, would sail for the archipelago in a few days, "crew and weather willing." I was eager for the adventure, to voyage to the valley of *Typee*, where Herman Melville had lived with *Fayaway* and *Kori-Kori*, where Captain Porter had erected the American flag a century before, and where cannibalism and tattooing had reached their most artistic development. But to sever the tie with Tautira was saddening. Mataiea and the tribe of Tetuanui had won my affections, but at Tautira I had become a Tahitian. I had lived in every way as if bred in the island, and had fallen so in love with the people and the mode of life, the peace and simplicity of the place, that only the already formed resolution to visit all the seas about stirred me to depart.

The village united to say good-by to me at a feast which was spread in the greenwood of the Greek god along the shore of the lagoon. T'yonni and Choti, the student and the painter, were foremost in the preparations of the *amuraa ma*, and many houses supplied the extensive, soft mats which were put on the sward for the table, while the ladies laid the cloth of banana leaves down their center, and adorned it with flowers.

Ori-a-Ori sat at the head and I beside him. His venerable countenance bore a smile of delight in being in such jovial company, and he answered the quips and drank the toasts as if a youth. I was leaving early in the afternoon, and the banquet was begun before midday. We had hardly reached the dessert when the accordions burst into the allegro airs of the adapted songs of America and Europe. Between them speeches of friendship were addressed to me by the chief and others, and I sorrowfully replied. Choti gave the keynote to our mutual regrets at my leaving by quoting the letter in Tahitian written by Ori-a-Ori to Rui at Honolulu long ago:

I make you to know my great affection. At the hour when you left us, I was filled with tears; my wife, Rui Telime, also, and all of my household. When you embarked I felt a great sorrow. It is for this that I went up on the road, and you looked from that ship, and I looked at you on the ship with great grief until you had raised the anchor and hoisted the sails. When the ship started I ran along the beach to see you still; and when you were on the open sea I cried out to you, "Farewell, Louis"; and when I was coming back to my house I seemed to hear your voice crying, "Rui, farewell." Afterwards I watched the ship as long as I could until the night fell; and when it was dark I said to myself, "If I had wings I should fly to the ship to meet you, and to sleep amongst you, so that I might be able to come back to shore and to tell to Rui Telime, 'I have slept upon the ship of Teriitera.' " After that we passed that night in the impatience of grief. Towards eight o'clock I seemed to hear your voice, "Teriitera—Rui—here is the hour for *putter* and *tiro* (cheese and syrup)." I did not sleep that night, thinking continually of you, my very dear friend, until the morning; being then still awake, I went to see Tapina Tutu on her bed, and alas, she was not there. Afterwards I looked into your rooms; they did not please me as they used to do. I did not hear your voice saying, "Hail, Rui"; I thought then that you had gone, and that you had left me. Rising up, I went to the beach to see your ship, and I could not see it. I wept, then, until the night, telling myself continually, "Teriitera returns into his own country and leaves his dear Rui in grief, so that I suffer for him, and weep for him." I will not forget you in my memory. Here is the thought: I desire to meet you again. It is my dear Teriitera makes the only riches I desire in this world. It is your eyes that I desire to see again. It must be that your body and my body shall eat together at one table: there is what would make my heart content. But now we are separated. May God be with you all. May His word and His mercy go with you, so that you may be well and we also, according to the words of Paul.

The chief listened throughout the message with his eyes empty of us, conjuring a vision of the Rui who so far back had won his heart; and when Choti had concluded, Ori-a-Ori lifted his glass, and said, "Rui e Maru!" coupling me in his affection with the dim figure of his sweet guest of the late eighties.

The last toast was to my return.

"You have eaten the *fei* in Tahiti *nei*, and you will come back," they chanted.

Raiere drove me in his cart to Taravao, where I had arranged for an automobile to meet me. At Mataiea I was clasped to the bosom of Haamoura, and spent a few minutes with the Chevalier Tetuanui. They could not understand us cold-blooded whites, who go long distances from loved ones. My contemplated journey to the Marquesas Islands was to them a foolish and dangerous labor for no good reason.

The trip to Papeete from Mataiea by motor-car took only an hour and a half, and I was in another world, on the camphorwood chest at the Tiare hotel, by five o'clock.

"*Mais*, Brien, you long time go district!" exclaimed Lovaina. "What you do so long no see you? I think may be you love one country *vahine!*"

She rubbed my back, and said that Lying Bill, who had been at the Tiare for luncheon, hoped to sail in two days. McHenry was to go with us as a passenger on the schooner. Everybody knew everybody's business. Lovaina suddenly bethought herself of a richer morsel of gossip. She struck her forehead.

"My God! how long you been? You not meet that rich uncle of David from America? You not hear about that turribil thing?"

She was on the point of beginning her narrative when the telephone rang, and she was called away. I knew I would catch the before-dinner groups at the Cercle Bougainville, and walked there, waving my hand or speaking to a dozen acquaintances on the route. I climbed the steep stairs, and at the first table saw Fung Wah, a Chinese immigrant importer and pearl merchant, with Lying Bill, McHenry, Hallman, and Landers, the latter only recently back from Auckland. I was immediately aware of the sad contrast with Tautira. The club-room looked mean and tawdry after so many weeks among the cocoas and breadfruits; the floor, tables, and chairs ugly compared with the grass, the *puraus*, the roses, and the gardenias, the endearing environment of that lovely village. The white men before me had as hard, unsympathetic faces as the Asiatic, who was reputed to deal in opium as well as men and women and jewels.

Yet their welcoming shout of fellowship was pleasant, despite a note of derision for my staying so long away from the fleshpots of Papeete. Pincher and McHenry were themselves lately arrived, but evidently had learned of my absence from Lovaina.

"What did you do? Buy a vanilla plantation?" asked McHenry.

"Vanilla, hell!" said Hallman, whose harp had one string, "he's been having his pick of country produce."

Lying Bill said:

"Well, you'd better pack your chest for the northern islands to-morrow if you're goin' with the *Fetia Taiao*. We'll be off for Atuona and Hallman's tribe of cannibals nex' mornin'."

I sat down and quaffed a Doctor Funk, and then inquired idly:

"Where's David?"

"David!" said Hallman. "For God's sake! don't dig into any graves!"

"'E's a proper ghoul, 'e is," Lying Bill said sarcastically. "'E thinks you're a mejum!"

They all stared at me as if I were crazy, and I felt myself in an atmosphere of mystery, in which I had broached a distasteful subject. I wondered what it could be, but determined to know at all hazards, reckoning on no fine feelings to hurt.

"What is the secret?" I asked. "I've been away a few months, and haven't heard the news. Has David run off with Miri or Caroline?"

Was this what Lovaina was bursting with?

They all remained quiet, until McHenry, with an oath, blurted out:

"What the hell's the good of all this bloody silence? He's been away and don't know." Then turning to me, he slapped me on the shoulder and bawled:

"We'll have a drink on you, O'Brien! David blew his brains out on Llewellyn's doorstep just after we left for the Marquesas. Joseph, bring one all around!"

As if at his word Llewellyn came up the stairs. His countenance was blacker than usual, his eyes more than half closed under their clouds of brows. His shoulders drooped, and he thumped his stick on the floor of the club as he came toward us. I felt certain that he detected something in the air—a sudden cessation of talk or a strained attitude on our part. He drooped heavily into a chair, and banged his stick on his chair-leg.

"Joseph," he called, "give me a Doctor Funk. Quick! No, make it straight absinthe."

Our own drinks were coming by now, and as the steward stirred about, Llewellyn for the first time saw me.

"Hello! Where did you come from? I thought you had gone back to the States."

"I've been past the isthmus," I replied, "and I haven't seen a soul or heard a word in that time. What's this terrible thing about young David?"

Llewellyn's arm jerked convulsively toward his body and knocked his glass from the table.

"Joseph, for God's sake, bring me a drink! Bring me a double absinthe!"

Joseph fetched the drink hurriedly, and stopped to pick up the broken glass.

"*Mon dieu!*" snapped Llewellyn, "you can do that afterward. Clear out!"

Then he turned to me, and his eyes contracted into mere black gleams as he asked:

"Are you like all these others? By God! I was passing the opium den here a few minutes ago, and I heard Hip Sing say something like that: What have I to do with David? Was I responsible for his death? Any man can come to your front door and kill himself. He was a friend of mine. I didn't see much of him before he died; I was busy with the vanilla."

Llewellyn swept us with an inclusive glance.

"Now you fellows have got to stop bringing up this David matter when I come in here, or I'll quit this club."

Hallman answered him, spitefully:

"For Heaven's sake, Llewellyn, I never heard a living soul mention David before, except at first, when there was so much curiosity. You're bughouse."

Fung Wah sat there, his small, astute eyes, in a saffron face, fixed alternately upon the speakers, with an appraising grimace but half-veiled. And as he sipped his grenadine syrup and soda water, he admired his three-inch thumbnail, the token of his rise from the estate of a half-naked coolie in Quan-tung to equality with these Taipans, the whites of Tahiti. He may or may not have known what rumors there were, but wanting the good-will of all influential residents in his widening scheme for money-making, he tried to soften the asperities of the interchange:

"Wa'ss mallah, Mis' Le'llyn?" he asked. "Ev'ybody fliend fo' you. Nobody makee tlouble fo' you 'bout Davie. My think 'm dlinkee too muchee, too muchee *vahine*, maybe play cart, losee too muchee flanc. He thlinkee mo' bettah finish."

The words of Fung Wah were poison in the ears of Llewellyn. He leaned forward and, raising his forefinger, pointed it at the Chinese.

"*Aue!* You hold your damned yellow mouth!" he said huskily. "I'll get out of the islands if you people keep up this any longer. I'm sick of it all. That old liar Morton has made my good name black in Tahiti. Everybody knows the Llewellyns. God damn him! I ought to have killed him when he threatened me in the Tiare!"

He took my untouched glass of Dr. Funk, and gulped the mixture, nervously. Then he stood up unsteadily.

"I don't get any sleep," he said, as if to himself, wearily. "I'm going to my shop and lie down."

He moved heavily down the stairs, and we breathed relief.

"Too muchee Pernoud!" Fung Wah commented.

"No, Fung Wah, you've sized 'im wrong," answered Lying Bill. "'E's seein' things. 'E's put enough absint' down his throat, but 'he's proper used to that. Let's take the matter up, an' consider it like ol' Raoul, the lawyer, did when Murray killed the gendarme at Areu. David's a young kid, an' wild, an' without any good home like you an 'me 've got, an' runnin' round the Barbary Coast in Frisco, with those bloody vampires there. 'Is uncle, Morton, is afraid 'e'll get the 'abit, and wants to sen' 'im pretty far. Well, 'e remembers 'e was in Tahiti forty years before, an' 'e been dealin' in a way in vanilla with ol' Llewellyn's 'ouse 'ere. So 'e makes arrangements to put ten thousan' dollars in with our friend that 's jus' gone out, and buy the kid a interest in the business. Down comes David, and Llewellyn takes a shine to 'im, an' soon they're thick as thieves. I see it all between voyages. It's the cinema, the prize-fight, the *upaupa*, the women, an' the bloody booze, day an' night. The vanilla business goes to hell or to Fung Wah or some other Chink. David blows in all 'is bleedin' capital, 'e busts in 'is 'ealth, an' may be, 'e's afraid o' somepin' worse. 'E gets a bloody funk, an' goes to Llewellyn's desk an' gets the gun. Then 'e writes a letter to 'is uncle in Frisco, an' goin' out on the step, 'e blows out 'is brains. I'm on the schooner, so I can't get any blame."

Captain Pincher lit his pipe, and the glasses were refilled.

McHenry attempted to pick up the thread of the tragedy, and began:

"Me, too, I'm with Bill drivin' the *Fetia* for Nuka-Hiva when David croaks himself. I drank as much as he did ashore, and I 'm no slouch with the *vahines*; but I can hold my booze, I can."

Lying Bill, with his drink down, and his pipe smoking, resumed, with no attention to McHenry, and a withering glance at Fung Wah, who was bored and walked over to the wall to glance at the barometer.

"Well, there's David dead on the doorstep,—'e probably shot 'imself about midnight,—and Llewellyn comes rollin' in a couple o' hours later, an' stumbles over 'is bloody corpse. 'E's tired, but 'e gets a lantern, an' sees the kid there, like a bleedin' wreck on the reef. It fair knocks 'im out, an' 'e sits down on the same step, an' when the kanaka comes in the mornin' to sweep up, 'e fin's the two o' them."

Landers broke in:

"Blow me! I'd 'a' hated to been that poor kanaka! But Doctor Cassiou, the coroner, said it was suicide all right. Llewellyn's in the clear."

"Of course, 'e 's in the clear, an' proper right," said Pincher, irritatedly. "But when the letter's mailed to ol' Morton in Frisco, 'e comes down on the nex' steamer, an' carries a gun to kill Llewellyn, an' tells everybody 'at Llewellyn dragged his nephew to 'ell, an' M'seer Lontane takes 'is gun away when Llewellyn meets 'im in Lovaina's porch, an' 'e pulls the gun, an' the Dummy stops 'im, and Llewellyn grabs a knife off the table. Why, there's some reason for 'im comin' in 'ere like a bloody queer un an' abusin' us."

"Hell! that's all over!" said Hallman. "I'll tell you, Llewellyn's always been sour. That's what that dam' German university highfalutin' education does for you. It takes the guts out of you. I know. I never had any of it. I'm a business man, by God! and I'm not crammed full of Dago and other rot. All the Davids in the world could croak on my doorstep, and if the police couldn't get me for it, I'd worry. I—"

"Belay there!" Lying Bill shouted at Hallman. "You don't know Llewellyn like I do. How about the *tupapau*, the bloody ghosts? You forget that Llewellyn's a quarter Kanaka, an' born 'ere. All that German university stuff ain't no good against the *tupapau*. Suppose you were part Kanaka, an' the kid 'ad done what 'e did? I've seen some things myself in these waters. That's what's eatin' Llewellyn, an', believe me, it's goin' to kill 'im if he don't bloody well drink 'imself dead, first. I've seen too many Kanakas go that way when the *tahua* got the *tupapau* after them. Llewellyn remembers what Lovaina said ol' man Morton hollered when M'seer Lontane took the gun away from him at the Tiare. 'All right!' hollered the uncle. 'All right! I'll leave it to God!' The ol' boy loved that kid. 'E told Lovaina 'at 'is whole bloody family was drowned when the *Rio Janeiro* went down off Mile Rock in Frisco bay. The kid was 'is sister's only child, an' 'is uncle left a thousand francs with the American consul for a proper tombstone on 'is grave in the cemetery. The ol' gent worshipped that kid."

Our session was over, the dinner hour having come; but Hallman had his final say:

"If Llewellyn 's got the *tupapau* horrors, for God's sake! let him stay away from the club. It's got so I hate to see him come in here, looking like a death's head. He spoils my drink. I'd rather be in the Marquesas with old Hemeury François, who is dyin' by inches of the spell Mohuto 's put on him. They're alike, these Kanakas; they're afraid of God and the devil, their own and the dam' missionary outfit, too. They've got them coming and going. No wonder they're getting so scarce you can't get any work done."

The next day was all preparation. I would be gone several months, the usual time for the voyage of a trading schooner to the Marquesas and return to Papeete. I had no bother about clothes, as I was to be in the same climate, and in less formal circles even than in Tahiti. But I desired to carry with me a type-writer, and mine was out of order. There was no tinker of skill in Papeete, and I had about given up hope of repairs, when Lovaina said:

"May be that eye doctor do you. He married one of those girl whose father before ran away with that English ship and Tahiti girls to Pitcairn Island, and get los' there till all chil'ren grow up big. He has little house on rue de Petit Pologne."

I found on that street in a cottage an American vendor of spectacles, who by some chance of propinquity had married a descendant of a mutineer of the *Bounty*. I surrendered my machine to him while I talked with his wife, whose ancestors, one English, the other Tahitian, had sailed away from here generations ago, after the crew had possessed themselves of the British warship *Bounty*, and cast their officers adrift at sea. She was a resident of Norfolk Island, and I wished I had time to hear the full story of her life. But before we had come to more than platitudes, the eye doctor had repaired the type-writer, and called his wife to other duties.

We had a going-away dinner at the Tiare hotel, Landers, Polonsky, McHenry, Hallman, Schlyter, the tailor, and Lieutenant L'Hermier des Plantes, a French army surgeon who was sailing on the *Fetia Taiao* to the Marquesas to be acting governor there. Lovaina would not join us, but after we had eaten an excellent dinner, she came in while we drank her health. Llewellyn had been asked, but did not appear, and McHenry said he was "very low" at five o'clock when he passed him on the rue de Rivoli. Lying Bill preferred to spend his last evening ashore with his native wife, or else wished to avoid the chance of a headache on the morrow.

We drank our last toasts at midnight, and I was averse to arising when called at six by Atupu for the early breakfast and the last disposition of my affairs. By nine o'clock I had put my baggage on board the schooner, Lovaina taking me in her carriage, driven by the Dummy. Vava was excited and puzzled by my return from the country, and my sudden departure for the sea. While Lovaina stayed in the garden of the Annexe, gathering a garland of roses for my hat, the Dummy endeavored to narrate to me the tragedy of David. His own part in preventing Morton from shooting, Vava showed in vivid pantomime with a fervor that would have made a moving-picture actor's fame; and when he indicated Morton's abandonment of revenge, though the Dummy could have no knowledge of his words, he gestured with a dignity that conveyed all the meaning of Lying Bill's relation of the incident. In the expression and motion of the dramatic mute the aged uncle had the sublimity of *Lear*. For Vava, in a mask and an attitude, by some cryptic understanding encompassed the resignation and appeal to Deity.

Lovaina had left me on the deck of the *Fetia Taiao*, as Captain Pincher said that it would be an hour or two before he sailed. His crew was having a few extra *upaupas* in the Cocoanut House. I sat on the rail with Vava's dumb-show uppermost in my mind, and a strong desire came to me to see the grave of David, and the tombstone erected by his frenzied kinsman. I strolled up the Broom road to the Annexe, and past Madame Fanny's restaurant to the garden of the Banque de l'Indo-Chine, and continued westward to the cemetery.

It was a lonely spot, that acre of God in these South Seas, for the resting-place of one who had been so alive as that young American. The hours of our last wassail, the bowl of velvet, and my waking by the Pool of Psyche with the *mahu* and the Dummy beside me, were painted on my brain.

"There, but for the grace of God, goes John Wesley," said the exhorter when he saw a murderer on the way to the gallows.

Some such dismal thought assailed me as the lofty exotic cypress in the center of the Golgotha met my eye; the tree of the dead over all the world. I halted to view the expanse of mausoleums and foliage. The rich had built small houses or pagodas to roof their loved from the torrential rains, and, from my distance, only these buildings and the trees could be seen; but as I was about to cross the road to enter the gate, a figure approached. I drew back, for, of all men, it was Llewellyn. He seemed to walk an accustomed course, observing none of the surroundings, and with his head down, and his stick touching the ground like the staff of a blind man. He turned in the entrance and moved up the winding path until he came to a grave. There he stood a few seconds irresolutely, and then stooped beside the white stone. He leaned over, and appeared to read the inscription. Instantly he turned, and started almost to run, but halted after a few paces, and returned to the stone. I saw him put his hand to his forehead, cover his eyes, and then he took off his hat and dropped upon his knees, and bent nearly to the rounded earth. When he stood up again, he kept the hat in his left hand, and, his cane tapping hard upon the soil, came through the gate, and passed me, unseeing. There was a look of terror on his face that affected me deeply.

I crossed the road behind him, and walked swiftly to the grave. My time was short. There I perceived that the tombstone had just been raised, for the tools of the cemetery keeper were near by. On a plain, white slab of marble was the name, Morton David, and the date; and below these, an inscription:

Vengeance Is Mine
I Will Repay.

This was what had frozen that look upon the face of Llewellyn. The *tupaupa* that should haunt him was this inscription. The old uncle who had loved the dead man had well left it to God.

I hurried away and back to the schooner. Lovaina was sitting in her shabby surrey under the flamboyants, the Dummy at the horse's head. Lying Bill was giving orders for raising his bow anchor, and the loosening of the shore lines. McHenry and Lieutenant L'Hermier des Plantes shouted to me to come aboard. Lovaina hugged me to her capacious bosom, the Dummy stroked my back a moment, and I was off for the cannibal isles.

IONEI OE!

A letter from Fragrance of the Jasmine, to Frederick O'Brien, at Sausalito, California:

"Ia ora na oe! Maru:

"Great sorrow has come to Tahiti. The people die by thousands from a devil sickness, the *grippe*, or influenza. It came from your country as we were rejoicing for the peace in France. The *Navua* brought it, and for weeks we have died. Tati is dead. Tetuanui is dead. They cannot lay the corpses in the graves, they fall so fast. There are no people to help. The dogs and pigs have eaten them as they slept their last sleep in their gardens. Now the corpses are burning in great trenches, and drunken white sailors with scared faces burn them, and drive the dead wagons crosswise in the streets. The burning of our loved ones is affrighting, and the old people who are not dead are in terrible fear of the flames. It is like the savages of the Marquesas in olden times.

"Your dear friend Lovaina was the first to die of the *hotahota*, as some call this sickness. Lovaina had a bad cough. The man who looks after the engines of the *Navua* went to see her, and she kissed him on the cheek. Then the good doctor of Papeete who visits the ships was called to see her. Maru, could that doctor have brought the *hotahota* to Lovaina? She was dead in a little while.

"Lovaina had good fortune all her life, for, being the first one to die, she was buried as we have always buried our people. All of Tahiti that was not ill walked with her coffin. Oh, Maru, I wept for Lovaina. Vava, whom you whites call the Dummy, is dead, too. When Lovaina was taken to the cemetery, Vava drove her old chaise with her children in it; and then, Maru, he was seen again only by a Tahitian who had gone to bathe in the lagoon because the fever was burning him. You know how Vava always took the old horse of Lovaina at sunset to swim in front of the Annexe. This man who was ill said that he saw Vava ride the horse into the sea, and straight out toward the reef. Vava signed farewell to the man with the fever. The man stayed in the lagoon to cool his body until the sun was below Moorea, and your friend, the Dummy, did not return. Maru, we loved dear Lovaina, but to Vava she was mother and God.

"It is strange, Maru, the way of things in the world. The lepers who are confined towards Arue were forgotten, and as nobody went near them, the *hotahota* passed them by.

"I cannot write more. O Maru, come back to aid us. It is a long time since those happy days when we walked in the Valley of Fautaua.

"Ia ora na i te Atua!

"NOANOA TIARE."

Milton Keynes UK
Ingram Content Group UK Ltd.
UKHW010845010724
444982UK00005B/378